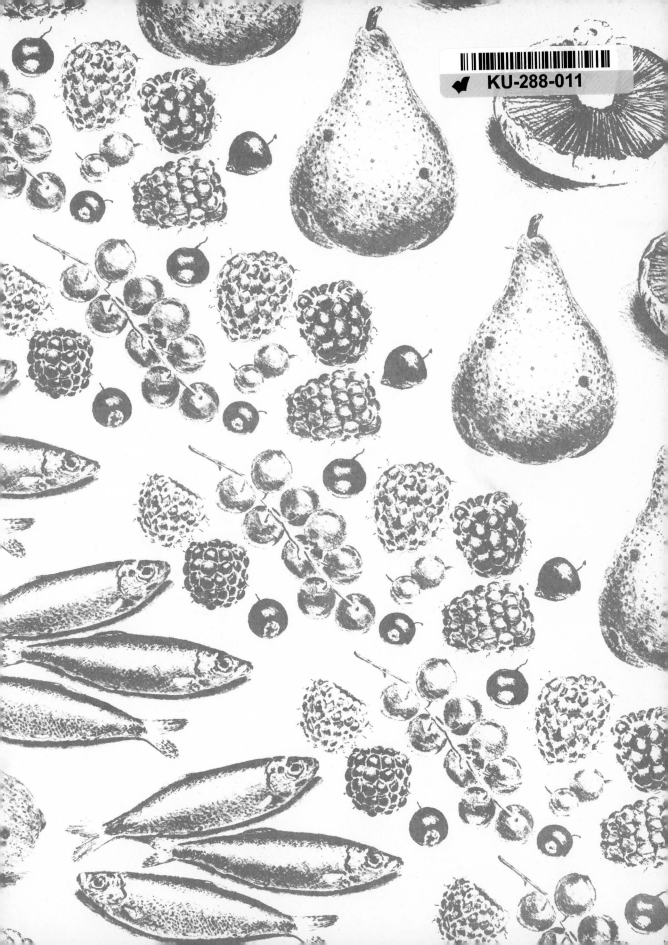

KU-288-011

A COOK'S TOUR
OF
BRITAIN

The WI and Michael Smith
Illustrations by Anne Ormerod

Willow Books, Collins
Grafton Street, London
1984

Willow Books
William Collins & Co Ltd
London   Glasgow   Sydney   Auckland
Toronto   Johannesburg

The WI and Michael Smith
A cook's tour of Britain
1. Cookery, British
I. Title
641.5941   TX717

ISBN 0 00 218050 2

First published 1984
Copyright © in text WI Books Ltd and Michael Smith 1984
Copyright © in illustrations Anne Ormerod 1984

Made by Lennard Books Mackerye End,
Harpenden Herts AL5 5DR

Editor Michael Leitch
Research Sue Jacquemier
Designed by David Pocknell's Company Ltd
Production Reynolds Clark Associates Ltd
Printed and bound in Spain by TONSA, San Sebastian

CONVERSION TABLES

The conversions used in the recipes are based on standard
tables. However, in some recipes it may have been
necessary to modify the basic conversion factors. Please
decide in advance whether to use imperial or metric
measures and then use only those quantities specified in
the recipe concerned. Do not mix metric and imperial
measures in one recipe. All spoon measures are level
unless stated otherwise, and all egg sizes are 1 or 2.

AMERICAN EQUIVALENTS

Butter, margarine	8 oz	225 g	1 cup
Shredded suet	4 oz	110 g	1 cup
Flour	4 oz	110 g	1 cup
Currants	5 oz	150 g	1 cup
Sugar	7 oz	200 g	1 cup
Syrup	$11\frac{1}{2}$ oz	325 g	1 cup

An American pint is 16 fl oz compared with the imperial
pint of 20 fl oz. A standard American cup measure is
considered to hold 8 fl oz.

Contents

The recipes in this book were chosen by Michael Smith
from a collection made by members of the Women's
Institute. He has added introductory comments where this
was felt useful, and a sprinkling of his own recipes to
round out the coverage. The general intention has been to
leave the basic recipes unaltered in order to preserve their
regional character.

Introduction

If you were to ask any foreigner (or Britisher for that matter) what they thought was the most typical and popular English dish, ninety-nine per cent of them would answer 'Roast Beef and Yorkshire Pudding' – and they would be *almost* right. I say 'almost' because the roast beef of Olde England comes quite a way down the chronological scale in the history of food in this country. Their probable second choice, forgetting for a minute Apple Pie, would, or ought to be, Bacon and Eggs. For that's where it all started.

A brisk run-down of the origins of our eating habits might well start in the eleventh century. At that time the population of this country numbered roughly 1.1 million, of whom 150,000 lived in London and the South-East. It was very much a case of the haves and have-nots. On one side were the King and his barons, lords and gentry, on the other the peasants, although the peasants of that time were not so badly off as today's materialistically-minded sociologists would have us believe. There was no middle class.

Almost every peasant household had a cow, a couple of pigs and a clutter of hens in the backyard. The cow yielded milk for drinking and for making curds and whey – the curds very quickly rising in texture from a softish pap cheese to the hard, more stable cheese not dissimilar from the Cheddar or Cheshire we know today. The pigs yielded the fat bacon and ham which kept out the cold, and the hens provided eggs and the occasional welcome change of diet. In the summer there would be whatever green vegetables they chose to grow. In winter, roots would be the staple. Wheaten bread was popular in the southern half of the country, while in the North, Scotland, Wales and Ireland they used the oats which grew more easily in their colder climate and hillier terrain. Herbs, too, were used in plenty; people, remember, particularly in the urban districts, ate their food much less fresh than we do today, and the flavour of herbs could sweeten the rather 'ripe' taste of much of it. Wild flowers, too, were used, and other 'free' foods such as nettles, sorrel and samphire, nuts, brambles, hips and other wild stuff.

The average peasant and yeoman farmer ate two meals a day. The first would consist of a bowl of pottage or gruel and a piece of meat, or fish if there was a local river or lake or they lived near the sea. This would be accompanied by bread and cheese and washed down with ale. The later meal would be a simpler affair of bread, cheese and ale with the occasional added luxury of a wild rabbit, hare or bird poached from the lord's land. Several families might share the cost of nourishing the pig whose body at killing time would then be divided among these families. There was also honeycomb and some butter and cider for the brighter and wiser farmworker.

At the top end of the scale King William I and his barons were eating well from the hands of cooks trained at the Norman courts. Later, at the court of Richard II, the nobility reaped the benefit of goodies brought back from the Crusades in the form of spices, fruits, figs, almonds and dates. The general increase in the variety of foods is borne out by the earliest written record of food in this land – *The Forme of Cury,* a fourteenth-century manuscript compiled by the cooks of Richard II.

The fork, which was to have a considerable influence on our table, did not arrive in this country until much later, when Thomas Coryat introduced it at court in the 1500s. Until then a pointed knife, aided by the fingers or a piece of bread, was the implement which conveyed food to the mouth. A spoon was used for the rich spicy stews and mortrews (soups) which were growing increasingly popular in the larger and wealthier households. Cooks realized also, as their experience grew, that an animal's stomach could be used to contain tasty morsels, and so the first of our savoury puddings was born, soon to be followed by the haggis and the sausage.

Fruits, both cooked and preserved, were quickly adopted – though there was a time when it was thought that fruit was bad for the health. *Crustades* became custards, and coffyns (a flour and water structure designed to contain meats and poultry, fish and game) grew more and more refined until eventually they turned into the pies we know today.

'Subtelties', sweetmeats and flavoured creams, joined the festive board as refinements became the order of the day, and there is early evidence of Yule Cake made with honey, spices, ginger, saffron, fruits and flour. Eaten on Twelfth Night, it was the forerunner of our present-day Christmas Cake.

Gingerbreads were very common in the Middle Ages, and were often sold at local fairs and gatherings. Mention of these partly commercial, partly social occasions might seem to suggest a constant interchange of ideas and fashions. However, the lines of communication were slow and difficult, and it took a long time for changes in social habits to work their way through the country. Today, with the advent of the telephone, radio and television, such changes happen all over Britain almost simultaneously, and even changes of attitude may only require a year or two to happen in less accessible parts, but in years gone by the habits of people living in points north of Watford really did take years to change.

In 1534 Henry VIII made himself supreme leader of the English Church. The Dissolution of the Monasteries which followed meant a decisive break, not only with Rome but with the rest of Europe, whose influence upon us had been so important. From the new view of religion came the first signs of a downward or backward trend. The Puritans, who took over Parliament, would have no feastings; no Christmas or Easter celebrations; wines and spices were banned or at least discouraged. All sensual pleasures were not only frowned upon but were considered sinful and therefore punishable. Was flavour to be lost for ever? Not totally, for in 1660 Charles II, the new monarch, brought from his exile in France the pleasures of French food and the first taste in this country of *champagne!* It was not the champagne we know now, for it did not at that time contain the bubbles it was later to acquire when the legendary Dom Pérignon discovered how to trap them in the bottle; what's more, it could even have been red! (I always believe it was this early champagne, made in the village of Sille, that was used to make the now re-popularized delicacy known as syllabub, or sillebub – a 'bub' being a type of wine drink.)

Charles's brother James II was to perpetuate the new life of luxury at the Court of St James, though little of this influence filtered through to the shires.

Later, William and Mary added their Dutch influence with such innovations as biscuits and waffles. So now there was a confusion of styles in our kitchens, with no outstanding advocate of things English, though many books were being written by ladies and their housekeepers. Some of these declared that the French style should be eschewed as too fanciful, others admitted that it was acceptable, if not desirable, in their household.

In the provincial areas a trip to the local fair was often an excuse to partake of the luxuries available at the food stalls: gingerbreads, jumbals (jumbles), fairings, and so on. Cookshops had also started to open, for the benefit of folk without ovens or other adequate means of preparing the more elaborate meats, pottages and pies; they also were responsible for bringing fish to a wider public.

In the seventeenth century there was also a more extensive use of fruits, vegetables, herbs and flowers in those great houses not ruled by the Puritans – and there were some. The well-to-do spent a great deal not only on their houses, clothes and furniture, but also on their gardens and hothouses. One great diarist of that time, John Evelyn, gives a deal of evidence of the elaboration of the salad in his book *Acetaria,* where he lists no fewer than twenty ingredients for a 'Grand Sallatt', the dressing for which should contain oil, orange juice, spices and honey. Even the vinegars were aromatized with rosemary, lavender and other scents (but with garlic only for 'the Northern Rustics', as he indiscreetly put it).

The eighteenth century was an age of elegance when England was at its golden best. This period brought better agriculture, better meat and fresher fish and poultry. It was now that the roast began to gain stature and reputation in *every* household, not just in the palaces. As the quality of our meat increased it became a social necessity to serve vast roasts – barons of beef, loins of pork, saddles of lamb and haunches of venison. The cooking was simple, though the helpings were generous. It was a necessary manifestation of wealth for the gentry to be *seen* to be able to afford the best, and this attitude prevailed right up to the Second World War. The potato gained in popularity towards the end of the eighteenth century, though only in Ireland, the North, Wales and Scotland. Southerners still preferred 'a pillow of rice' or noodles or 'macraws' (a type of macaroni), which they felt to be more 'subtle' – to use their word for 'nice things'. As the price of sugar came down, so it began to eclipse honey as a regular sweetener. Also in the eighteenth century tea began to overtake coffee and chocolate (and gin!) as a beverage, and was imported in greater quantities from the colonies together with cereals and other goods.

While England, or Britain, was enjoying this period of great wealth, the division between North and South was getting more marked. The North, in spite of the new network of canals, was still remote from the capital. The climate and soil were considered poorer, and the higher, often undulating terrain made agricultural development more difficult without mechanization. There was also a deal of political unrest, and early signs of the Industrial Revolution to come. The *real* poor came out of this revolution, and the cheaply-grown potato was to do a valuable job in eking out the modest amount of meat that the new working classes could (barely) afford. The oats grown in the Northern districts were now being put to good use in oat cakes, porridge and other cheap gruels that warmed the bellies of the needy. It was also found that other cereals, such as sago, rice, millet and – yes – vermicelli, once used in savoury dishes, could be used in sweet ones, and so the first batches of our milk puddings were born. Often these were simple puddings with a grating of nutmeg, but in better-off households they were richer affairs with candied fruits, spices, eggs and liquor to enrich them. It is worth noting that in our own economy-conscious times we have reverted to the simpler versions, though even these are in decline.

For the mass of the population this basic diet endured almost to the present day. Roasts, boiled and fried meats and fish, pickled and collared meats, pies, puddings, eggs, milk, and bread and cheese are as familiar today as they have been through the centuries.

In the later part of the nineteenth century the wealthy Victorians, and in turn the Edwardians, took on the French cooks who chose exile in Britain during and after the Franco-Prussian War. Their influence in the grand hotels of London – and elsewhere – was considerable, but only among the moneyed classes. Many of these French chefs returned to their own country when it was safe to do so, leaving us largely untrained. It certainly was not fashionable for a lady of standing to go into her kitchens; the cook came to her in the drawing-room for instructions. 'Milady's' knowledge of kitchen craft or technique was, not surprisingly, nil.

Then came the two disastrous World Wars with a massive slump in between. Rationing was severe, though fair, in the Second World War, preventing any form of indulgent cooking and instilling into us a great sense of guilt – which remains with us to this day – and a feeling that rich food was, if not indecent or immoral, certainly unpatriotic. Talk about food was limited to boasting of some new-found economy or short-cut – something else which is still with us, alas!

The Second World War, though we were the victors, left us much the poorer. Rationing continued until the early 1950s, so our forays to foreign parts, as we started to travel again, whetted our appetites for 'foreign' dishes which to our deprived and jaded palates were exciting – or so they seemed then. It is little wonder, therefore, that many of the native dishes in this book may seem foreign to many of you, because you may never have tasted a lot of them, even if you have heard of them. But I feel that you, like me, would like to see some evidence of what things were like in our regions in the days of yore. Now is the time to restore a proper respect for the British table and pride in our kitchens.

Michael Smith
London, 1984

General

Why, you may rightly ask, is it necessary to have a General Section in a book on regional cookery? The answer is simple: if we don't have this section, much of what is truly British will be lost by the wayside because there is no natural slot in which to fit this or that particular dish which is popular and with us now.

Another problem is that much of what we find attractive and toothsome today cannot be traced back to any one part of the country, or, if it can be, then you will find it rearing its head but two short counties away under a different name. The ubiquitous fruit cake is only one example, though perhaps the most important. Does it have cherries in it, as in one part of the country? Or almonds on the top, as in another? Does it perhaps have candied peel in the recipe? Or spices? Or liquor?

We would, of course, lose all our delicious potted foods (with the exception of Morecambe Bay's Potted Shrimps) if we didn't provide a home for them. And what would happen to the many soups, much loved by Britishers, and which have appeared at almost every repast since time began? Mulligatawny, Kidney, a delicious Chicken Broth with pearl barley, or a rich brown Oxtail Soup much loved by Queen Victoria judging by its frequent appearances on the menu at Windsor.

The gentry in the grand houses – and I think particularly of that earlier Duchess of Bedford who invented the habit – gave us afternoon tea and all that that implies: delicate sandwiches, fancy cakes, fondants and éclairs, which in spite of their foreign-sounding names are as much a British institution as scones and crumpets. Moreover, I tremble to think of what would happen to those other 'national' dishes eaten by every family from childhood onwards, and which, I expect, make their weekly appearance to this day. Of course, I speak of Shepherd's Pie, Fish Pie, Kedgeree, Macaroni Cheese, and Beef-and-Ham Mould. Life would be unthinkable without them, but where did they come from? Was there really a bright-witted shepherd rustling up a potato

topping for his stew while rounding up his flock in the hills of Cumbria or the Yorkshire Dales, or in Wales or on the South Downs? Likewise, were local fishermen skinning, sousing and bottling their fish on quaysides so as not to waste their catch? I doubt it! I think this cuddlesome range of dishes actually started off as economies and – for once – we actually decided to improve them until we arrived at the ultimate recipes in the ensuing pages.

At the richer, pudding end of the national menu so many of our more delicious confections are of a universal character, and it is in this area, together with cake, bread, jam and chutney-making that we excel most.

What party would be complete without a luscious trifle or a surfeit of syllabubs and fruity jellies? Rich English cream thickened with egg yolks and perfumed with rosewater is the base of that most elegant of desserts, the Burn't Cream. Even the French have the honesty to call a real custard *Crème Anglaise!*

English cream is the best in the world, and is there to be used liberally in such affairs as Sherry Trifle, Caramel Cream, and in all the exquisite fools and flummeries that are now so popular again, despite their widening effect on our waistlines. But we do all need a treat every so often. Can you imagine a berry-packed Summer Pudding without a goodly dollop of double cream?

So now you must be realizing why this General Section is here. It is somewhere to put, for instance, the steamed puddings of yesteryear which today show the rich rewards of an improving hand on their mixtures: Vanilla Sponge with Melba Sauce (*and* cream!), Ginger Pudding, crisp-topped Queen of Puddings, a deep, silky Baked Custard Pie (one of our oldest recipes with no regional home), or a delicious treacle tart. Need I go on?

Legend has it that in 1799 the Neapolitan Admiral Francesco Caraccioli said: 'There are in England sixty different religious sects, but only one sauce.' How wrong he was! What of a creamy, buttery Bread Sauce with Christmas Turkey, or a Golden Apple Sauce made with flavourful Cox's Pippins as a complement to slices from a crispy-skinned roast duck? And a well-made Horseradish Sauce with double cream is unsurpassable with our traditional roast ribs of beef, as is Caper or Onion Sauce with lamb or mutton. Cheese Sauce, Rum Sauce or Rum Butter, Chocolate Sauce, Cumberland Sauce – Admiral Caraccioli ought to be reincarnated and made to rewrite his words!

Whilst our reputation as scoffers of the plastic sliced loaf is hard to live down, it cannot be denied that in the field of bakery the British housewife can hold her own with any foreign counterpart. Her bread tin might well contain Wholemeal and Malt Bread, Scones and Tea Cakes, and her biscuit tin throughout the year might well have held fifteen to twenty different varieties stored between layered sheets of waxed paper. Yet another tin will have held Slices and Flapjacks, Crunches and Macaroons.

That is why this section is here: to bring into our Cook's Tour all those orphans that have flourished over the years, and done so from a countrywide scattering of gastronomic seeds.

Soups

Chicken Broth
Serves 6

1 chicken carcase
2 pt (1.2 l) water
1 oz (25 g) pearl barley or rice
1 onion, peeled and chopped
1 celery stalk, chopped
6 peppercorns
salt
1 blade mace
chopped parsley

Remove any chicken trimmings and flesh from the carcase and cut into small pieces. Break up the carcase and put into a large saucepan with the water, barley or rice, onion, celery, peppercorns, salt and mace. Bring to the boil, reduce heat and simmer for 2 hours. Strain, put in a clean saucepan, add the small pieces of chicken and re-heat. Add a little chopped parsley and serve.

Mulligatawny Soup
Serves 5-6

A highly spiced soup, discovered by our colonial forbears in the East Indies and brought home in the nineteenth century.

1 onion, peeled and sliced
1 oz (25 g) bacon or ham
2 oz (50 g) butter or margarine
1 turnip, peeled and diced
1-2 carrots, peeled and diced
1 small apple, peeled, cored and diced
2 tsp curry powder
$\frac{1}{2}$ tsp curry paste
1 tbsp plain flour
2 pt (1.2 l) beef stock or stock cubes
salt and pepper
1 tsp lemon juice

Fry the onion and bacon in melted butter until lightly browned. Add the turnip, carrot and apple and continue for a few minutes. Stir in the curry powder and paste and the flour. Add the stock, bring to the boil, cover and simmer for about 45 minutes. Either strain and return to a clean pan or liquidize or puree the mixture for a thicker soup. Re-heat, adjust seasonings, add lemon juice and serve.

Kidney Soup
Serves 4-6

1 lb (450 g) ox kidney
salt and pepper
3 tbsp plain flour
1 oz (25 g) butter
2 medium onions, peeled and chopped
1 large carrot, peeled and chopped
1 small turnip, peeled and chopped (optional)
2 pt (1.2 l) beef stock or water

Cut the kidney away from the core and chop into small pieces. Season half the flour and toss the kidney in it. Melt the butter in a saucepan and fry the pieces of kidney gently in it until lightly browned. Add the prepared vegetables, toss lightly and then add the stock. Bring slowly to the boil, remove any scum that rises, season well and simmer as gently as possible for about $1\frac{1}{2}$ hours or until the kidney is tender and the liquid reduced. Blend the rest of the flour into a smooth paste with a little water, add some of the soup and mix them well together before returning to the pan. Simmer for a further 15 minutes, then adjust the seasoning and serve.

Tomato Soup
Serves 2

1 oz (25 g) margarine
1 small carrot, peeled and diced
2 celery stalks, diced
1 onion, peeled and chopped
1 lb (450 g) tomatoes, quartered
1 bouquet garni sachet
salt and pepper
1 tsp sugar
2 cloves
1 pt (575 ml) boiling stock or water
1 oz (25 g) plain flour
2 tbsp cold milk
chopped parsley to garnish

Melt the margarine in a saucepan and fry the carrot, celery and onion until softened. Add the tomatoes, bouquet garni, salt, pepper, sugar, cloves and water or stock and bring to the boil. Cover the pan and simmer for 20 minutes or until all the vegetables are tender. Sieve the soup and return it to a clean pan. Blend the flour with the milk and add to the soup. Bring back to the boil, stirring, and simmer for 15 minutes, stirring frequently. Adjust seasonings and serve sprinkled with parsley.

Oxtail Soup
Serves 6

We are so brainwashed by the tinned and pre-packed varieties of this soup that the original subtle flavour is probably unknown to most of us.

First stage
1 whole oxtail
2 oz (50 g) plain wholemeal flour
4 oz (110 g) butter
4 pt (2.25 l) water
Second stage
2 large carrots
1 head celery
4 oz (110 g) turnip
1 tsp thyme
2 bay leaves
6 cloves
2 tsp Barbados sugar
2 oz (50 g) tomato puree
4 fl oz (110 ml) Madeira or Marsala
3 tbsp oil for frying
salt and freshly ground pepper
croûtons of brown bread (see page 20) and grated orange rind (optional) to garnish

Begin the first stage by getting your butcher to cut the oxtail into small joints, or chop it yourself, through the obvious sections, with a cleaver. Cut off any surplus fat, rinse in cold water and pat dry with a clean towel. Roll each piece in the flour. Melt the butter in a heavy-bottomed frying pan and fry the pieces a few at a time until they are a good brown colour. This will take patience; do not fry them all together or they will not acquire a colour. Cover with water and simmer for 2 hours, skimming when necessary. Meanwhile proceed with the second stage.

Clean, peel and dice all the vegetables. Heat the oil in a second pan until it smokes, add the diced vegetables and fry them until they are evenly browned, stirring to ensure the even colouring and so that they don't burn. Add the tomato puree and reduce the heat *immediately*, for puree burns at a very low temperaure. Add the sugar and seasonings. When the oxtail has simmered for 2 hours, add to it the vegetable mixture and continue cooking gently for 1 hour. Take out the pieces of oxtail, cool, then strip off the lean meat. Cut this into small dice and reserve for the finished soup. Strain the rest of the soup; let it stand to see if any fat rises to the surface, and if it does, skim well. Reheat the soup and add the Madeira or Marsala, check the seasonings, add the diced oxtail and serve with croûtons of brown bread. The grated rind of an orange added before serving is a complement to this soup.

Fish

Kedgeree
Serves 3-4

Like Mulligatawny Soup, this goes back to the days of the Raj and at one time was made with curry powder. The name comes from the Hindi khicari.

12 oz (350 g) smoked haddock or cod fillet
1 tsp salt
saffron powder (optional)
6 oz (175 g) long-grain rice
4 oz (110 g) butter or margarine
4 hard-boiled eggs, chopped
2–3 tbsp cream
freshly chopped parsley

Poach the fish in a little water until it flakes easily. Remove the fish from the pan with a slotted spoon and set aside. Add more water to the pan with the salt and a pinch of saffron, if used, and bring to the boil. Sprinkle in the rice and cook until it is just tender. Drain the rice, rinse and drain again. Meanwhile, flake the fish, removing all skin and large bones. Melt the fat in another saucepan and add the fish, rice, eggs, and another pinch of saffron if liked. Heat through gently, stirring well, add the cream and serve hot, sprinkled with chopped parsley.

Fish Pie
Serves 4

All pies make the main ingredient go further, and Fish Pie has been a staple of fishing communities for many a century.

1 oz (25 g) butter
1 oz (25 g) plain flour
½ pt (275 ml) milk
12 oz (350 g) cooked white fish
8 oz (225 g) mashed potatoes
salt and pepper
2 eggs, separated

Make a sauce with butter, flour and milk. Bring to the boil in a saucepan over a gentle heat. When thickened, gradually add the cooked fish and mashed potatoes. Add salt and pepper to taste, then the beaten egg yolks and heat until all are slightly cooked. Then add the stiffly beaten egg whites and pour into a pie-dish. Bake at 375°F (190°C) Reg 5 for 20–30 minutes.

Finnan Haddock with Parsley Sauce

This gets one away from the piece of smoked haddock afloat in a pint of milk. The fish retains its delicious flavour, and this recipe combines it successfully with a version of one of England's most popular sauces.

3 lb (1.4 kg) smoked haddock

2 pt (1.2 l) cold water

squeeze of lemon

1 sprig parsley

salt and freshly ground white pepper

Parsley Sauce

½ pt (275 ml) fish stock

3 oz (75 g) butter

1 oz (25 g) plain flour

½ pt (275 ml) single cream

a little lemon juice

pinch caster sugar

salt and freshly ground white pepper

2 heaped tbsp freshly and very finely chopped parsley

Wash the fish; cut into serving pieces. Lightly oil the bottom of a shallow pan and put in the pieces of fish; cover with the water, season lightly, add parsley and lemon juice, then cover with a circle of oiled paper to fit the surface. Put a lid on the pan and poach slowly (rapid boiling breaks up the flesh) until the fish is just cooked – about 15 minutes. Remove the fish, taking out any bones and skin; arrange in a warm serving dish, cover with a damp cloth or wetted paper and a lid, and put to keep warm. Reduce the cooking liquor down to ½ pt (275 ml) by boiling rapidly. Melt the butter in a small pan, stir in the flour, strain the fish stock on to this and whisk the sauce until it is smooth. Add the cream and cook for 5 minutes over a very low heat, stirring all the time. Check the seasoning – there will probably be enough salt. Add a little lemon juice and a pinch of sugar. Stir in the abundance of parsley (I sometimes add a few chopped chives), pour over the waiting fish and serve immediately. This rich, bright green parsley sauce is a worthy addition to any repertoire. The same technique can be used for any fish which you want to serve in this way. It is always well to keep a little stock back, just in case the flour you are using is 'stronger' than usual and you wish to thin the sauce down a little.

Smoked Haddock, Bacon and Mushroom Fishcakes

Serves 4

4 rashers bacon

butter

2 oz (50 g) onion, finely chopped

4 oz (110 g) mushrooms, finely chopped

12 oz (350 g) flaked, cooked smoked haddock (weighed after skinning and boning)

1 small (2-3 servings) sachet instant potato, reconstituted

salt and pepper

¼ tsp ground nutmeg

2 eggs, beaten separately

plain flour

fresh white breadcrumbs

Dice the bacon, fry until crisp, remove from pan with a draining spoon. Add a knob of butter to the pan. Fry onion in the pan fats until golden brown and soft. Fry the mushrooms for a minute or so. Mix the mushrooms, onion and bacon with the flaked fish and reconstituted potato. Season lightly (take care with the salt as the smoked haddock may be salty enough). Add nutmeg. Bind with 1 beaten egg. Leave to chill and firm up. On a floured worktop, press out into a flat shape 1 in (2.5 cm) thick. Cut into 3 in (7.5 cm) rounds with a plain scone cutter. Coat each round in flour, beaten egg and breadcrumbs. Fry in hot fat or oil until golden brown, allowing 2–3 minutes on each side. Makes approx 8 cakes.

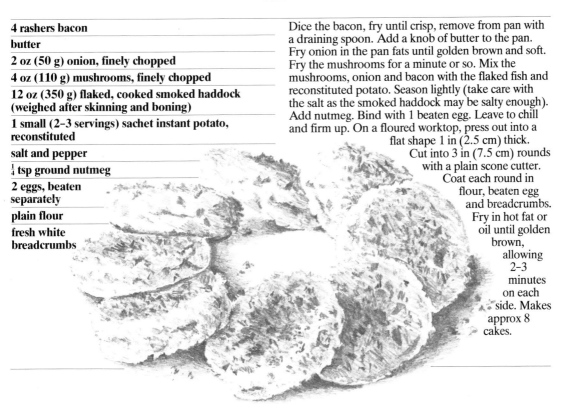

Meat

Steak and Kidney Pudding
Serves 4-5

*This is a true British classic, cooked with or without oysters and served in its pudding basin
surrounded by a freshly starched white napkin.*

Filling

2 lb (900 g) rump steak (or best stewing steak)
8 oz (225 g) veal kidneys
1 heaped tbsp plain flour
salt and freshly ground black pepper
butter for frying
1 large onion
8 oz (225 g) button mushrooms
$\frac{1}{2}$ pt (275 ml) red wine
$\frac{1}{2}$ pt (275 ml) beef stock
1 bay leaf
about 24 oysters (optional)
suet crust pastry to line and cover a 3 pt (1.8 l) basin (see page 253)

Crust 1

8 oz (225 g) self-raising flour
1 tsp baking powder
4 oz (110 g) suet
salt and freshly ground white pepper
pinch of powdered mace, powdered rosemary or powdered bay leaf
cold water to mix

or

Crust 2

8 oz (225 g) self-raising flour
3 oz (75 g) suet
2 oz (50 g) grated cold hard butter
1 tsp lemon rind
salt and freshly ground white pepper
lemon juice and water to mix

First make the filling as follows: trim the meat of all fat and skin, cut the kidneys in half and remove fat, veins, etc. Cut the meat into 1 in (2.5 cm) cubes and slice the kidneys. Mix the flour, salt and pepper in a polythene bag and toss the meats in this until they are completely coated. Melt about 2 oz (50 g) of butter in a heavy-bottomed pan. Fry the onion until golden brown and put this into an ovenproof casserole. Fry the meat until it is brown on all sides. Transfer the meat to the casserole. Add a little more butter to the pan, add the mushrooms and toss. Add these to the meat. Shake any leftover flour from the bag into the casserole and stir in well. Cover with the wine and stock, season with salt and pepper and add the bay leaf. Cook in the oven at 350°F (180°C) Reg 4 for 1-1½ hours, or until the meat is just tender. Check the seasoning and remove bay leaf. Allow the mixture to cool. (If you like oysters in your pudding, these should be added when the mixture is quite cool.) Sieve the flour, salt and pepper. Lightly toss in the suet and/or grated butter, stir loosely with a fork or 'rain' the dry ingredients through the fingers until they are thoroughly mixed. Make a well in the centre and add enough water to make a soft, pliable dough. Gather the ingredients together, kneading as little as possible, until the dough is a workable mass. Have your pan ready with boiling water before you put the pudding in to cook. Dredge a baking board with flour, and cut the dough into 2 pieces. Roll out the first piece as thinly as possible; cut this in half for ease of lining the buttered basin. Fill the lined basin with cold steak mixture up to within ½ in (1 cm) of the rim. Roll the second piece of dough into a round, wet the edges of the lining pastry, and fit the top on. Cover with buttered foil, leaving room for it to rise. Make sure the foil is tightly fitted round the rim so that steam or water cannot enter. Steam for 1½-1¾ hours. Let the water be at least two-thirds up the sides of the basin and keep the water boiling gently. Top up when necessary with boiling water.

Shepherd's Pie

Serves 6

According to legend, Shepherd's Pie has to be made with lamb; if beef is used, it's Cottage Pie. Ideally it should be made with fresh meat but usually the main ingredient is leftover roast. Numerous regional variations include a sprinkling of grated cheese over the topping of potatoes, and pickle mixed with the mince.

1 lb (450 g) minced beef	Heat the oil and fry the onion and meat until brown. If using leftover beef do not fry this. Stir in the flour and stock. Add the parsley, marjoram and salt and pepper to taste. Blend in the Worcestershire sauce and leftover beef. Put this mixture in an ovenproof dish, pipe mashed potato over the top and riffle the surface with a fork. Bake in the oven at 350°F (180°C) Reg 4 for about 45 minutes or until the top is golden brown.
1 tbsp oil	
1 small finely chopped onion	
$\frac{3}{4}$ oz (20 g) plain flour	
$\frac{1}{4}$ pt (150 ml) brown stock	
1 tsp chopped parsley	
pinch marjoram	
salt and pepper	
1 tsp Worcestershire sauce	
1 lb (450 g) mashed potatoes	

Brawn

Serves 8

$\frac{1}{2}$ pig's head	Clean head and leave in brine or dry salt for 4–7 days together with beef, if used, trotters and tail. Wash and cover with cold water and bring to boil. Drain and cover with fresh water, add onion and seasonings and boil for 3–5 hours until tender (pressure cooker cuts down the time). Remove meat from bones and dice. Reduce 2 pt (1.2 l) liquid to 1 pt (575 ml) and mix with meat, enough to moisten mixture well. Taste for seasoning and add more pepper and salt if necessary. Place in damp moulds and leave to set. A boiled fowl, skimmed and with the meat cut up, may be used instead of beef. Sometimes the pig's tongue is cooked and skinned and placed in the centre of a large mould and the other meat packed around it.
8 oz (225 g) shin beef (optional)	
1 pig's tail	
2 pig's trotters	
1 onion	
bunch mixed herbs	
20 peppercorns	
2 blades mace	
$\frac{1}{2}$ tsp ground ginger	
salt and pepper	

Faggots

Makes 10

At one time any group of ingredients bundled or wrapped together was called a faggot. These are traditionally eaten on Boxing Day and served with peas.

1 lb (450 g) pig's fry, ie 12 oz (350 g) liver and 4 oz (110 g) heart	Mince the pig's fry and onions. Mix together with the breadcrumbs, seasoning, spices and herbs. Shape into 10 balls. Cut the caul into squares and wrap each meat ball in a square. Place the meat balls in a greased roasting tin and cook at 350°F (180°C) Reg 4 for 30–45 minutes.
8 oz (225 g) onions, peeled	
3 oz (75 g) fresh breadcrumbs	
$2\frac{1}{2}$ tsp salt	
$\frac{1}{2}$ tsp black pepper	
$\frac{1}{2}$ tsp ground allspice	
1 tsp ground ginger	
$\frac{1}{2}$ tsp dried sage	
1 pig's caul soaked in tepid water	

Braised Brisket of Beef

Serves 6

An established favourite, the brisket is a cheap cut of English meat and this is a tasty way to cook it.

2 tbsp olive oil or meat dripping

3 lb (1.4 kg) rolled brisket

1 onion, peeled and roughly chopped

2 tomatoes, peeled and chopped

1 tbsp tomato puree

salt and freshly ground black pepper

2 tbsp white wine

Heat the oil or dripping in a large heavy frying pan. Add the meat and brown quickly on all sides. Place the meat and onion on a large piece of tin foil. Top with the tomatoes mixed with the tomato puree. Season with salt and freshly ground black pepper, seal into a neatly-wrapped parcel and place in a roasting tin. Cook the meat at 450°F (230°C) Reg 8 for 2 hours. Unwrap the meat and keep it warm. Strain off the juices and combine them in a saucepan with the white wine. Heat through, adjust seasoning if necessary and remove any fat from the surface. Serve the meat with green vegetables and creamy potatoes. This joint is also good served cold.

Roast Duckling

Serves 3

There are numerous ways to stuff a duckling, with sage and onion or milder things such as gooseberries, apples and red wine, or a delicious combination of sorrel, spinach and gooseberries aptly called 'green sauce'. However, I prefer not to stuff ducklings at all but like to serve them straight from the oven, all crisp-skinned and well-roasted, but not dried out!

1 duckling, ideally not more than 4–5 lb (1.8–2.2 kg)

Savoury Butter

2 oz (50 g) butter

1 tsp salt

$\frac{1}{2}$ tsp black pepper

$\frac{1}{2}$ crushed clove garlic

Flavourings

2 tsp grated orange rind, or

2 tsp grated lemon rind, or

2 tsp lemon-thyme, or

2 tsp fresh chopped sage, or

$\frac{1}{2}$ tsp powdered rosemary, or

$\frac{1}{2}$ tsp grated nutmeg, or

2 tbsp brandy

Clip off the wing tips up to the first joint. Scrape away any yellow scaling around the drumsticks. Cut away any excess fat at the rear-end of the bird. Make the butter into a paste with the salt, black pepper and garlic. Add to this any *one* of the flavourings listed here. Rub a little of this paste well into the breast skin of the bird and spread the rest inside the cavity. Stand the bird on a rack in a roasting tin and roast at 400°F (200°C) Reg 6 for 30 minutes. Lower the temperature one mark and finish roasting. The bird is cooked once the juices no longer run pink when it is pierced with a roasting fork under the leg and held up to let the juice run out. If you prefer your duckling to be somewhat pink, then test its cooked condition by gently pulling the leg away from the body; if the meat between the legs looks very bloody and the leg won't 'give' very easily, then it requires more roasting, but if the leg 'gives' nicely and the meat looks a pale pink and is still juicy, but not bloody, then all is well. The leg of a well-roast duck will be crisp and come away immediately any pressure is applied.

Beef, Ham and Lemon Mould
Makes 12–14 slices

The distinguished ancestor of spam, this is best cooked in straight-sided jars. A non-stick loaf tin may be used, though this makes the slices somewhat broad and rather defeats the object of the exercise.

1 lb (450 g) rump steak (or best stewing steak)	Mince the two meats, combine with the parsley, lemon rind, juice and breadcrumbs. Combine with beaten egg. Season well. Fill into buttered jars or moulds. Cover with foil. Steam for 2 hours then cool before refrigerating.
1 lb (450 g) green gammon including fat, but with rind removed	
1 heaped tbsp freshly chopped parsley (or other green herbs)	
1 lemon, shredded rind and juice	
4 oz (110 g) white breadcrumbs	
2 whole eggs, beaten	
salt and milled pepper	

Potted Hare
Serves 10

1 lb (450 g) thinly cut streaky bacon	Cut the rind off the bacon and 'stretch' the rashers with the back of a knife so that they do not shrink. Line a greased ovenproof casserole or tureen with the bacon, leaving enough to overlap across the top of the filled pot. Remove all the meat from the hare and pork, taking off any skin and tissue. Cut all but the leg meat into $\frac{1}{2}$ in (1 cm) cubes and put to marinate in the rum and wine overnight.
1 large brown hare, prepared	
2 lb (900 g) loin of pork	
4 fl oz (125 ml) Jamaica rum	
9 fl oz (250 ml) red wine	
1 lb (450 g) extra pork fat from the back	
2 cloves garlic, crushed	Mince the remaining meats and fat together with the garlic and livers through the fine blade of a mincer, adding any leftover pieces of bacon. Mix this forcemeat with the egg, seasonings and spices and add the liquor from the marinade. Mix in the cubes of meat and use to fill the lined pot. Fold over the bacon to cover filling. Cover with a lid or foil and stand the pot in a meat tin half-filled with hot water. Cook at 350°F (180°C) Reg 4 for $1\frac{1}{2}$–2 hours or until the juices are quite clear. Half an hour before the estimated end of cooking, remove the cover so that the top browns. Leave to cool and then chill. To preserve its attractive appearance, cover with aspic jelly and chill again.
6 large chicken livers (plus a few grouse livers if you can get any)	
1 egg	
salt and freshly ground black pepper	
1 tsp powdered ginger	
1 tsp thyme	
aspic jelly to cover	

Jugged Hare
Serves 6

1 hare	Skin, paunch and wash the hare in a little warm water and rub with salt. Cut away legs and head first, then take off the carcase and cut up the back into squares. Cut up the beef in square pieces and place in the bottom of the jar, then the hare, a bag of sweet herbs, pepper and salt, onions with cloves and the butter, melted. Place the jar in a pan of water with a lid or bladder or brown paper tied over it. Let the water be up to the neck of the jar. Boil for 10 hours. Next day add a good pint (660 ml) of melted butter and the port wine. Warm it up in the oven altogether.
2 lb (900 g) stewing beef	
1 muslin bag sweet herbs (marjoram, thyme, etc)	
butter	
salt and pepper	
1 or 2 onions stuck with cloves	
$\frac{1}{4}$ pt (150 ml) port wine	

Potted Venison

2 lb (900 g) venison	Place venison, butter, wine and seasoning into a casserole with a close-fitting lid and cook at 350°F (180°C) Reg 4 for 2 hours or until tender. Remove venison and mince finely. Make into a paste with a little of the gravy. Season to taste. Press into small pots and cover with clarified butter.
4 oz (110 g) butter	
½ bottle port or red wine	
salt and pepper	
clarified butter (see page 251)	

Potted Meat (Beef)

Until recently, shin of beef was a cheap food. Potted meat was considered a delicacy and was served with thin bread and butter when visitors came to tea. Nowadays it makes a nutritious, moist and flavoursome sandwich filling, or it can be used as a starter.

8 oz (225 g) shin of beef	Cut up meat roughly. Put all ingredients except butter into basin with watertight lid. Steam for 3 hours (or pressure-cook for 20–30 minutes). Remove peppercorns and mace, and pass meat twice or three times through mincer or liquidize until smooth. Add liquid from cooking, and adjust seasoning. Put into small pots, and cover with clarified butter.
12 peppercorns	
1 blade mace	
¼ pt (150 ml) water or red wine	
pepper and salt to taste	
clarified butter (see page 251)	

Christmas Turkey

Serves 12

There is no reason not to eat roast turkey at any other time of year, but it is one of our national quirks that we resist doing so. Fear of feasting too much or too often may have something to do with it, though our Christmas exercises are as nothing compared with the prodigious celebrating that went on until the Puritans took a hand.

12–14 lb (5–6 kg) turkey	Stuff the bird at both ends – a firm carving stuffing at the neck, a softer 'looser' stuffing inside (don't over-fill in this area). Put the sliced vegetables in the roasting tin as a base on which to sit the turkey. Rub the bird all over with the butter and season well. Cover the breasts with the bacon. Fit a double thickness of foil just over the breast. Put the bird into a preheated oven and cook for 1½ hours at 400°F (200°C) Reg 6, then reduce the temperature to 350°F (180°C) Reg 4 for a further 1½ hours. Baste the bird every 45 minutes, removing the foil and replacing it each time. Remove the foil and bacon during the last half-hour of the roasting time.
1 large onion, peeled and sliced	
2 carrots, peeled and sliced	
12 oz (350 g) salted butter	
milled pepper	
8 oz (225 g) fat bacon	
your chosen stuffing(s)	

Salads

Solomongundy (Sallid Magundi)

Serves 4–5

Never has a dish had so many various ways of having its name spelt! This answer to France's Salade Niçoise is well enough known as a joke because of its extraordinary name. Perhaps Saladmagundi or even Salmagundi gives a better clue to the nature of this truly excellent salad which, once tried, will never again be allowed to sink into oblivion. Solomongundy has been with us since Tudor times, but for reasons which no-one can explain it has been ignored for decades.

1 cold chicken, either pot-roast or boiled
1 lettuce
12 button onions
1 × 8 oz (225 g) packet whole frozen beans
4 oz (110 g) grapes, black or green
4 eggs, hard-boiled
1 large cup oil and vinegar dressing
lemon juice and rind
1 tbsp mixed chopped herbs
1 × 2 oz (50 g) tin anchovy fillets
2 oz (50 g) almonds, flaked
2 oz (50 g) raisins, stoned

Skin the chicken and carve the breasts and legs into thin slices. Wash and shred the lettuce and arrange on a large flat platter. Skin and boil the onions leaving them somewhat crisp. Plunge the beans into boiling salted water for 5 minutes, rinse under running cold water until they are cold and drain well on a clean cloth as beans 'hold' water. Skin and de-pip the grapes. Shell and quarter the hard-boiled eggs. Season the dressing well, adding lemon juice and rind and herbs to taste. Arrange all the salad items in attractive groups on the bed of lettuce. Pour over the dressing and when ready to serve the salad, toss everything together.

Tudor Salads

Salads were once a joyous reminder of spring, a time to stop eating salted and dried foods and make up delicious green and healthy salads. As John Evelyn, the seventeenth-century writer, showed us in his Acetaria *on 'sallats' we have lost so much not only in the use of varied ingredients but also in the use of different herbs and dressings. Here then are six different salads for you to try out. Quantities and combinations I leave entirely to your artistic and creative mood. Whether you serve them as a starter, a side dish or a main course is entirely up to the individual. I simply suggest different acidulating agents, aromatics, bases, spices, sweeteners and oils.*

1 Striplets of cold roast beef, ox tongue and sliced onions dressed with oil, vinegar and freshly grated horseradish.

2 Slices of pear dressed with crushed hazelnuts in a light cream cheese dressing and topped with plenty of chopped chives.

3 Shredded red cabbage with grapefruit segments dressed with oil, red wine vinegar, orange zest and a little brown sugar.

4 Peeled and de-seeded cucumber with sliced raw mushrooms dressed with lemon, honey, chopped dill-weed and oil.

5 Young spinach leaves with striplets of crisply fried bacon, tiny fried bread croûtons and a light French dressing mixed with a tablespoon of thick cream.

6 Cooked rice, diced banana, cubes of cheddar cheese dressed with mayonnaise, orange rind and a hint of curry powder.

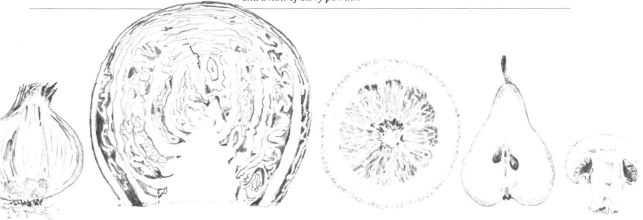

Savouries

Macaroni Cheese

Serves 4

The word probably comes from the Greek makaria, *meaning barley-broth, and macaroni itself came to us via medieval Italy. In eighteenth-century England a dandy might be called a 'macaroni' because of his thin shape; he and his lady – just to complicate matters – might also have eaten macaroons, which in those days consisted of a paste or* pasta *of almonds and egg whites.*

8 oz (225 g) macaroni or bucatini	Cook the macaroni in boiling salted water until *al dente* (almost tender). Drain, rinse and drain again. Put the cooked pasta into a well-buttered gratin or ovenproof dish. Pour over the sauce and sprinkle with all the Parmesan Cheese. Bake at 400°F (200°C) Reg 6 until brown and bubbling, which will take about 20 minutes.
salt	
1 pt (575 ml) cheese sauce (see page 22)	
1½ oz (40 g) freshly grated Parmesan Cheese	

Rissoles

Serves 4

Traditionally a way of using up cold meat, the word deriving from the French rissoler, *to fry. Made from fresh meat, rissoles can be quite exceptionally tasty.*

8 oz (225 g) cooked cold meat	Remove all skin and gristle from the meat and either chop finely or put it through the mincer, then weigh it. Melt the fat in a saucepan, add the chopped onion and cook for a few minutes. Add the flour and stir until slightly brown. Pour in the stock and continue stirring until the mixture begins to draw away from the sides of the saucepan. Add the meat, seasonings, nutmeg and parsley, and mix well together. Add the potato, if used. Turn the mixture on to a plate, smooth it over with a knife and leave to cool. When cold it will be firm and easy to shape. Divide into about 12 even-sized pieces. Shape each piece into a ball with a little flour. Dip the rissoles in egg then coat in breadcrumbs and fry in hot fat until golden brown. Drain well and serve hot on a warmed dish. The rissoles can be coated with flour instead of egg and breadcrumbs if liked.
1 oz (25 g) butter or margarine	
1 tbsp chopped onion	
1 oz (25 g) plain flour	
½ pt (275 ml) stock (use a stock cube)	
salt and pepper	
pinch nutmeg	
1 tsp chopped parsley	
a little mashed potato (optional)	
1 egg, beaten	
breadcrumbs	
fat for frying	

Butter-fried Croûtons

Cut out the appropriate bread shapes, ie hearts, squares, circles, oblongs. It is difficult to give an exact amount of butter, but a thin film should first be melted in a heavy-bottomed frying pan. Add the croûtons and allow them to soak up what they will, adding more butter as necessary. Fry the croûtons over a very low heat, turning them frequently so that they brown evenly on both sides and are crisp right through. If you fry them too quickly, you may well end up with soggy middles. Drain on kitchen paper and leave to cool. If a residue of butter builds up in the pan, drain it to get rid of any burnt crumbs before frying the next batch; this is purely for cosmetic reasons. Croûtons freeze very well, and are ideal not only for serving with game, but as a base for cocktail savouries or a topping for soups. I often dredge the croûtons with a little mace for added interest.

Devils on Horseback
Makes 6

*A bacon savoury featuring the 'devilish' prune and thus making a gastronomic rival to
Angels on Horseback, in which the bacon is wrapped round an oyster.*

6 stewed prunes
6 split almonds
olive oil
cayenne pepper
3 rashers streaky bacon
6 rounds toast or fried bread

Stone the prunes, brown the almonds in a little olive oil and dust with cayenne pepper. Stuff the prunes with the almonds. Cut the rashers in half and wrap a piece of bacon around each prune. Put a skewer through prunes and bacon and grill until brown on both sides. Serve each prune on a small round of toast or fried bread.

Harvest Sausage Rolls
Makes 10-14

One of the great Victorian imports, this sine qua non *of the snack counter has its origins in the French* Brioche de Saucisson *which our wealthy ancestors noticed and approved while staying at their villas in the South of France.*

8 oz (225 g) wholemeal pastry (see page 252)
1 egg (size 5 or 6)
½ tsp dried sage
8 oz (225 g) pork sausagemeat
1 oz (25 g) bran

Roll out half the pastry in a strip about 11 × 4 in (28 × 10 cm). Do the same with the other half. Leave the strips to relax. Beat the eggs and mix half into the sausagemeat with the sage. Wash and dry your hands and dust in wholemeal flour. Mould the sausagemeat into 2 rolls. Put one on each of the strips of pastry. Brush beaten egg along one edge of each and fold over. Press the edges firmly together. Brush each roll with beaten egg and sprinkle with bran. Cut diagonally to make individual sausage rolls. Put on a baking sheet and bake at 400°F (200°C) Reg 6 for 20-30 minutes. Cool on a wire rack. Eat hot or cold. Home-made mustard makes these special sausage rolls even more delicious.

Toad in the Hole
Serves 4

A splendid economy dish: one sausage goes a very great deal further when wrapped generously in batter!

1 lb (450 g) pork sausages
knob of cooking fat
4 oz (110 g) plain flour
1 egg
milk

Place the sausages, pricked, in an ovenproof dish. Add a knob of fat and cook them at 425°F (220°C) Reg 7. Make the batter with the flour, eggs and milk. When the sausages are beginning to cook and the fat is really hot, pour the batter over the sausages and return the dish to the oven for 20-30 minutes.

Forcemeat Balls

From the French farcir, *to stuff, these were literally something added to a meat dish, either by stuffing or arranging beside it.*

2 oz (15 g) fresh breadcrumbs
½ oz (15 g) suet or margarine
2 tsp chopped parsley
1 tsp chopped thyme or herbs as desired
1 small egg
½ tsp grated lemon rind
salt and pepper
1 small onion, grated (optional)

Mix together breadcrumbs, suet or margarine, lemon rind and seasonings. Beat egg and add sufficient to bind the ingredients together. Form into balls of 1 in (2.5 cm) diameter. Use as needed for stuffing or forcemeat balls. These can be added to a casserole, or cooked around a joint or fried in fat or oil and browned.

Sauces

Hollandaise Sauce

1 tbsp wine vinegar

1 tbsp water

6 peppercorns

2 egg yolks

pinch salt

4 oz (110 g) butter

1 tbsp lemon juice

Heat the vinegar, water and peppercorns in a small saucepan and reduce by half. Cream the egg yolks in a small basin, add the salt and stir in the strained vinegar. Divide the butter into 4 pieces. Place the basin over a saucepan containing warm water and heat gently, stirring all the time. Do not let the water boil. (A double boiler may be used instead.) Add a quarter of the butter and whisk well until the butter has melted and the mixture thickens. Continue adding the quarters of butter in the same way. By this time the sauce will be rich and creamy. Add the lemon juice, strain and serve.

Mayonnaise

2 egg yolks

$\frac{1}{2}$ tsp salt

$\frac{1}{2}$ tsp pepper

$\frac{1}{2}$ tsp mustard

a few drops lemon juice

$\frac{1}{2}$ pt (275 ml) oil

2–3 tbsp wine vinegar

Place the egg yolks, salt, pepper, mustard and lemon juice in a bowl and beat well with a wooden spoon to thicken the yolks. Add 2 tbsp of the oil, a drop or two at a time, beating well. Add 1 tsp of the vinegar and beat well. Add more oil, beating continuously. As the mixture thickens, the oil may be added more quickly. Add a little more vinegar from time to time, to taste. A little cream or a tablespoon of boiling water added to the mayonnaise helps to lighten it.

French Dressing

2–3 tbsp olive oil

1 tbsp tarragon vinegar (or part tarragon, part malt)

1 tsp caster sugar

$\frac{1}{2}$ tsp salt

pinch pepper

$\frac{1}{4}$ tsp mustard

1 rounded tsp onion, finely chopped (optional)

Put all the ingredients in a wide-mouthed bottle with a good-fitting screw cap and shake vigorously.

Rich Béchamel Sauce

Makes 1 pt (575 ml)

$\frac{1}{2}$ pt (275 ml) milk

$\frac{1}{2}$ pt (275 ml) single cream

1 small onion, peeled and quartered

1 bay leaf

1 small sprig thyme

2 oz (50 g) lean green gammon (optional)

2 oz (50 g) butter

1 oz (25 g) plain flour

salt and freshly milled *white* pepper

Infuse the mixture of milk and cream by slowly bringing to the boil with the onion, bay leaf, thyme and gammon, then leave to stand for 30 minutes away from the heat. In the top of a double boiler melt the butter, stir in the flour and cook for 10 minutes, with the water underneath at the boil. Bring the milk mixture back to boiling point and strain most of it gradually over the butter roux, whisking steadily. Season with salt and pepper to taste and let the sauce cook for about 20 minutes, whisking from time to time, and finally adding the remaining milk mixture. If the sauce is too thick – it should be the consistency of pouring cream – add a little extra milk. For a coating sauce, increase the flour to 2 oz (50 g). The sauce may be made in an ordinary saucepan but cook gently and stir continuously.

Cheese Sauce

To 1 pt (575 ml) Béchamel Sauce (see above) add:

For a milder sauce

2 oz (50 g) Gouda or Gruyère Cheese, grated

2 oz (50 g) Edam Cheese, grated

$\frac{1}{4}$ tsp ground or grated nutmeg

1 tsp mild French mustard

For a sharper sauce

2 oz (50 g) Cheshire Cheese, grated

2 oz (50 g) mature Cheddar Cheese, grated

or

4 oz (110 g) mature Cheddar Cheese, grated

1 tsp made English mustard

For an Italian cheese sauce

4 oz (110 g) freshly grated Parmesan Cheese

or

2 oz (50 g) freshly grated Parmesan Cheese

2 oz (50 g) freshly grated Provolone Cheese

Horseradish Sauce

¼ pt (150 ml) double cream

1 oz (25 g) grated horseradish

salt and pepper

pinch dry mustard

1–2 tsp vinegar

1 tsp caster sugar

Whisk the cream until thick but not stiff. Fold in the horseradish then season to taste with salt, pepper, mustard, vinegar and sugar.

Mint Sauce

1 large handful mint leaves, washed

2 tsp caster sugar

1 tbsp boiling water

1–2 tbsp vinegar

Place the mint leaves and sugar on a board and chop finely. Put into a sauce-boat, add the boiling water and stir to dissolve the sugar. Add the vinegar. Leave to stand for at least 1 hour before using.

Basic White Sauce

Makes ½ pt (275 ml)

1 oz (25 g) butter

1 oz (25 g) plain flour

¼ pt (150 ml) hot stock (suitable for the main dish)

¼ pt (150 ml) hot milk

pinch grated nutmeg

salt and pepper

Heat the stock and the milk. Melt the butter in a saucepan and stir in the flour. Cook for 1–2 minutes, stirring all the time. Remove from the heat and add the hot milk and stock. Stir well and return to the heat. Bring to the boil, still stirring, and simmer until the sauce thickens.

Sweet White Sauce

Makes ½ pt (275 ml)

1 oz (25 g) butter

1 oz (25 g) plain flour

½ pt (275 ml) milk

1 tbsp sugar

Heat the milk. Melt the butter in a saucepan and stir in the flour. Cook for 1–2 minutes, stirring all the time. Remove from the heat and add the hot milk and sugar. Stir well and return to the heat. Bring to the boil, still stirring, and simmer till the sauce thickens.

Custard Sauce

Makes 1½ pt (850 ml)

1 pt (575 ml) milk (or half milk and half cream)

1 vanilla pod (or 1 tsp vanilla essence)

1½–2 oz (40–50 g) caster sugar

1 tsp cornflour

4 eggs

Bring the milk to the boil, together with the vanilla pod. Mix the sugar with the cornflour, add the eggs gradually and beat the mixture well until smooth. Remove the vanilla pod from the saucepan and pour the boiling milk on to the egg mixture, stirring all the time. Rinse out the pan, leaving a film of cold water in the bottom. Return the custard to the pan and stir it continuously with a wooden spoon over a low heat until it is thick. Plunge the bottom of the pan into a basin of cold water to remove any residual heat which might curdle the custard. Leave to cool. Alternatively, cook the custard in the top of a double saucepan or boil over a saucepan of simmering water – this lessens the risk of curdling.

Melba Sauce

8 oz (225 g) raspberries or a 15 oz (450 g) can

4 tbsp redcurrant jelly

3 oz (75 g) sugar

2 tsp arrowroot or cornflour

1 tbsp cold water

Puree the raspberries by rubbing through a sieve. Place the redcurrant jelly and sugar in a saucepan, heat jelly then bring to the boil. Remove from the heat, add the raspberry puree. Blend the arrowroot or cornflour with the cold water, stir in a little of the raspberry mixture. Return the mixture to the pan, bring to the boil, stirring until it thickens and clears. Cool for serving.

Buttery Chocolate Sauce

4 oz (110 g) plain chocolate

1½ oz (40 g) caster sugar

¼ pt (150 ml) boiling water

2 oz (50 g) unsalted butter, cut into small cubes

squeeze lemon juice

Break the chocolate into pieces and put into a bowl arranged over a pan of boiling water. Add the hot water and caster sugar. Stir until a creamy consistency is reached. Remove from the heat. Just before serving, whisk in the bits of butter, add one or two drops of lemon juice, whisk this in and pour the sauce into a warm sauce-boat.

Bread and Butter Pudding

Serves 6

Here is a famous economy dish that also figures often on menus for children, and is also known as Nursery Pudding.

1 pt (575 ml) milk
2–3 oz (50–75 g) sugar (according to taste)
2 oz (50 g) butter
4 eggs, well beaten
8 slices bread and butter
3 oz (75 g) currants
2 oz (50 g) sultanas
½ tsp ground cinnamon
1 oz (25 g) demerara sugar

Put the milk into a saucepan with the sugar and butter, bring to the boil and pour gradually on to the beaten eggs, whisking until it is well blended. Butter a fairly deep square or oblong dish. Put a layer of bread and butter slices into the dish, cut to fit and sprinkle with currants and sultanas and cinnamon. Continue with alternate layers of bread, fruit and spice finishing with bread. Strain the hot milk and egg mixture into the dish. Cover the dish and leave for 1 hour before cooking. Remove cover and sprinkle the top with demerara sugar. Bake at 375°F (190°C) Reg 5 for 45 minutes until the top is golden brown and crisp and the custard set.

Queen of Puddings

Serves 4

¾ pt (425 ml) milk
½ oz (15 g) butter
1 tsp vanilla essence
grated rind of 1 lemon
½ oz (15 g) sugar
3 oz (75 g) fresh breadcrumbs
2 egg yolks
3 tbsp warm jam
Meringue
2 egg whites
3 oz (75 g) caster sugar

Heat the milk and butter, add the essence, lemon rind and sugar. Pour over the breadcrumbs and soak for 20–30 minutes until swollen. Add the egg yolks, pour into a 1½ pt (850 ml) pie-dish and bake at 325°F (160°C) Reg 3 for about 25 minutes or until lightly set. Spread thinly with warm jam. For the meringue, whisk the egg whites until stiff then gradually whisk in the sugar. Spread the meringue on top of the pudding and return to the oven and bake at 250°F (120°C) Reg ½ until the meringue is firm to the touch and lightly coloured – 30 minutes.

If liked, ¼ oz (15 g) cocoa powder can be added to the above ingredients, dissolved in the milk, but omit the lemon rind. Or 1 oz (25 g) desiccated coconut can be added to the breadcrumbs and allowed to soak in the liquid.

Treacle Tart

Serves 3

4 oz (110 g) shortcrust pastry (see page 252)
4 tbsp golden syrup
1 egg, beaten
2 oz (50 g) breadcrumbs
nutmeg

Roll out the pastry and use to line a pie-plate. Mix the syrup and egg together. Put the the breadcrumbs in the pastry case and pour the syrup mixture over. Sprinkle with grated nutmeg and cook at 375°F (190°C) Reg 5 for 25–30 minutes until pastry is cooked and filling is set. Serve hot or cold.

Ginger Pudding
Serves 4–6

*Ginger is perhaps the spice we most constantly use, in puddings, cakes, biscuits, drinks, etc.
Here it makes a sturdy pudding, often helped on its way by a syrup sauce.*

8 oz (225 g) self-raising flour

4 oz (110 g) shredded suet

2 tsp ground ginger

2 oz (50 g) mixed peel

3 fl oz (75 ml) golden syrup

3 fl oz (75 ml) milk

1 tsp bicarbonate of soda

Sift the flour into a bowl and mix in the suet, ginger and peel. Add the syrup and milk and bicarbonate of soda blended together, and mix well. Turn into a well-greased 2 pt (1.2 l) pudding basin. Cover with greased paper and foil and cook in a saucepan with boiling water coming halfway up the sides of the basin for 2–2$\frac{1}{2}$ hours.

Caramel Cream with Rum-Baked Pears

Caramel

3 oz (75 g) caster sugar

a little water

$\frac{1}{4}$ tsp cream of tartar

Custard

2 oz (50 g) caster sugar

5 eggs

$\frac{1}{2}$ pt (275 ml) milk

$\frac{1}{2}$ pt (275 ml) single cream

vanilla pod or $\frac{1}{2}$ tsp vanilla essence

Garnish

2 oz (50 g) unsalted butter

6 pear halves

3 oz (75 g) sugar

large glass Jamaica rum (optional)

Make the caramel first, to coat a 1$\frac{1}{2}$ pt (850 ml) mould. Put the sugar in a pan with a little water and the cream of tartar. Bring to the boil, stirring until the sugar is dissolved evenly. Leave the sugar to caramelize slowly: it should be darker than golden syrup. Have a sink of cold water ready to plunge the bottom of the pan into as soon as you think it is a good caramel. Pour into the mould and swirl around until the mould is completely coated. To make the custard, preheat the oven to 325°F (160°C) Reg 3. Have a bain-marie of hot water at the ready (a roasting tin half-filled with hot water will do). Cream the sugar and eggs. Infuse the milk, cream and vanilla, slowly letting it come to the boil. Pour it over the egg mixture, stirring well. Strain the custard into the waiting caramel-lined mould. Place this in the bain-marie and bake in the oven for about 45 minutes, or until the custard is set. While the caramel cream is cooking prepare the garnish. Melt the butter and fry the pear halves until brown. Remove them from the pan, add the sugar and cook until dissolved. Add the rum – having lowered the heat in case the alcohol ignites – and simmer this syrup until thick and viscous. Pour over the waiting pear halves and put to chill. When the caramel cream is cooked, leave to cool, then chill. Unmould the cream, and arrange the pear halves round the edges of the dish. Serve the extra 'sauce' separately, or pour round the dish all at one time. Extra whipped cream can be served if liked.

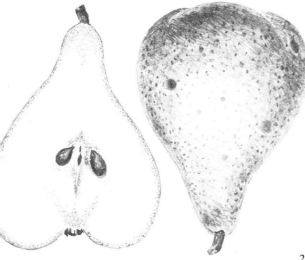

Apple Charlotte

Serves 6

A dish devised for Queen Charlotte, wife of King George III, by her French cooks.

10 dessert apples

4 (110 g) unsalted butter

grated zest of 1 lemon

strained juice of 1 lemon

2 oz (50 g) caster sugar (or more to taste)

3 tbsp sieved apricot jam

slices white bread to line a tin Charlotte mould

butter and caster sugar for mould

melted butter

Use a mixture of apples for a Charlotte. Peel, core and chop them into smallish pieces. Melt the butter in a largish pan, add the apples and, over a low heat, with no extra water, cook them until they are soft, stirring from time to time. Add lemon juice, zest and sugar, and continue cooking until the juices have almost evaporated. The pulp or puree should be thick and firm. Stir in the jam and set aside. Well butter the tin mould and dredge with caster sugar. Line with bread cut lengthways into pieces $1\frac{1}{2}$ in (4 cm) wide (no crusts). Trim to the right height for the mould. Cut rounded segments to fit the base, and larger segments to cover the top. Brush or dip all the pieces in melted unsalted butter. Arrange, overlapping, round the inside of the mould, buttered surface to the mould. Fill with the apple mixture, pressing it well in and giving the mould a firm bang on the table top to settle things in and release any air locks. Cover with the larger bread segments which should also be buttered and sugared, pressing these firmly on top, and cover with a circle of waxed paper or foil. Stand the mould on an oven tray and bake at 400°F (200°C) Reg 6 for 35–40 minutes. Remove from the oven and, using the bowl of a spoon, press or pack the top down (the apples will have shrunk somewhat). Run a palette knife around the sides, place a flat serving dish over the top and turn out. Serve with hot Melba Sauce (see page 23) and/or chilled pouring cream.

Vanilla Sponge Pudding

Serves 4–5

2 eggs

unsalted butter

vanilla sugar or sugar and 2 tbsp vanilla essence

self-raising flour

2 tsp cold water

Weigh the eggs and use the same amount of butter, sugar and flour, ie if the eggs weigh 4 oz (110 g) use 4 oz (110 g) butter, 4 oz (110 g) sugar and 4 oz (110 g) flour. Have the butter at room temperature, add the sugar and beat until every granule of sugar has disappeared. Add 1 tsp of the flour and beat in well. Beat the eggs with the cold water and gradually beat them into the creamed butter and sugar. Now deftly and thoroughly fold in the rest of the flour. Spoon into a buttered pudding basin and cover with a circle of buttered foil that is big enough to give room for the pudding to rise. Make sure the foil is well sealed round the brim of the basin so that no steam can get in and make the top of the pudding wet. Have the steamer ready on the stove so that it is good and hot, ready to give the mixture its initial 'push into space'! Steam for $1\frac{1}{2}$–$1\frac{3}{4}$ hours. Remember to top up the steamer with boiling water. When serving, carefully remove the foil, run a knife around the sides of the basin and invert on a warm serving dish.

Christmas Pudding

*First a frumenty made with hulled wheat and milk, then with beef or mutton broth thickened
with oatmeal and flavoured with eggs, currants, dried plums, mace and ginger, the traditional
Christmas Pudding continued to evolve until the late seventeenth century, by which time the
meat broth had been dropped and the semi-liquid porridge had become a firm plum pudding,
boiled in a cloth.*

1 lb (450 g) white breadcrumbs
1 tsp ground ginger
1 tsp mixed spice
2 tsp salt
8 oz (225 g) suet, shredded or finely chopped
8 oz (225 g) brown sugar
4 oz (110 g) mixed peel, chopped
4 oz (110 g) currants
4 oz (110 g) sultanas
1 lb (450 g) seedless raisins
3 oz (75 g) carrots, grated
3 tbsp brandy
2 tbsp milk
4 oz (110 g) golden syrup

Mix the breadcrumbs, spices, suet, sugar, dried fruits
and carrots together in a large bowl. Blend the
brandy, milk and syrup and stir thoroughly into the
dry ingredients. Let the mixture stand for at least
1 hour, then put it in a greased pudding basin, cover
with greaseproof paper and cloth or foil and steam.
Christmas Puddings may be steamed in various-sized
basins: for a 1 pt (500 ml) pudding allow 5 hours, for
1½ pt (750 ml) 7 hours and 2 pt (1 l) 9 hours. When
cooked, remove from steamer and allow to cool.
Cover with fresh paper and store in a cool place.
Puddings will keep for 12–18 months and improve
and mature during this time. On the day of serving
renew the covering and steam the pudding as follows:
1 pt (500 ml) for 2 hours, 1½–2 pt (750 ml–1 l) for
3 hours. Turn out on to a hot dish, decorate with holly
and flame with warmed brandy, serve with brandy or
rum butter (see page 251) or a sweet white sauce
(see page 23) flavoured with rum.

Rich Baked Custard Pie

¾ pt (425 ml) single cream
1 tsp cornflour
2 oz (50 g) caster sugar
6 eggs
vanilla pod or a few drops of essence
8 oz (225 g) shortcrust pastry (see page 252)

Roll the pastry out on a floured board to the required
size for an 8 in (20 cm) flan ring. Place the ring on a
buttered baking sheet and line it with the pastry,
decorating the edges to your fancy. Fit a second lining
of foil (shiny side to the pastry) and put the pastry in a
cool place to rest for half an hour. Bake the pastry
case at 350°F (180°C) Reg 4 until it is almost cooked.
Take it out of the oven, remove the foil and leave the
case on one side until you have made the filling. Mix
together the cornflour and the sugar; add the eggs one
at a time, beating until all the sugar has dissolved.
Add the vanilla pod to the cream, bring the cream to
the boil and pour on to the egg mixture, whisking all
the time. Remove the pod. Fill the flan case and bake
in the middle of the oven at 275°F (140°C) Reg 1 until
the custard is set. This will take about 30–45 minutes.
Let the flan cool somewhat before removing the ring.
The custard pie can be served warm or cold.

Egg Custard

This is the basic egg custard recipe, and as such the foundation of many superb desserts.

1 pt (575 ml) milk	Heat the milk to just below boiling with the sugar and the vanilla pod. Discard the vanilla pod and then pour the milk slowly on the egg yolks, beating all the time. Return to a gentle heat and, stirring continuously, cook until the custard coats the back of a spoon. Turn into a bowl and cool, with a piece of damp greaseproof paper touching the surface of the custard to prevent a skin forming.
1 oz (25 g) caster sugar	
1 vanilla pod	
4 egg yolks, beaten	

Note:
This is sometimes known as a 'boiled' custard, which it most certainly must not be,
or it will curdle. The addition of 1 tsp cornflour or custard powder at the mixing
stage will help the inexperienced cook to prevent any risk of curdling the custard.

Summer Pudding

Serves 4–5

*One of our most delicious puddings, which is at its best when made during that short spell
when red and black berry fruits are in season (raspberries, redcurrants, blackcurrants, etc).
The best bread to use is a two-day-old Jewish 'egg loaf'.*

white bread to line a 2 pt (1.2 l) basin

1½ lb (700 g) raspberries or other soft fruit

1½ lb (700 g) redcurrants or other soft fruit

4 fl oz (110 ml) gin, vodka or Kirsch

8 oz (225 g) caster sugar

Cut the bread into long slices, take off the crusts and cut into broadish wedge shapes. Put a circle of wax paper in the bottom of a mould or basin. Cut a circle of bread and fit this in the bottom. Fit the wedges, trimming where necessary so that an exact fit is achieved with no gaps. Pick over and clean the fruits (do not wash them). Put them into a large pan, sprinkle over the sugar and liquor, and toss over a low heat until evenly coated and the juices just start to run. Spoon the warm fruits into the lined mould, pressing gently down with the bowl of the spoon. The basin should be completely filled so it is a good idea to test by piling the fruits into the basin before you line it. Fit the bread lid. Select a plate or cake tin base that fits just inside the top of the basin (a piece of foil-covered card is a good idea). Place a heavy weight on top, stand the basin in a dish in case any juices overflow and refrigerate for at least 24 hours. To unmould the pudding, place a deepish serving platter on top of the pudding and invert them together, giving the sides of the basin a sharp smack. Test to see that the pudding is released but leave the basin in place until you are ready to serve the pudding as the sides will be completely saturated with the rich cold fruity syrup and will sag somewhat. Summer Pudding must always be served cold (it freezes admirably) and accompanied by lashings of thick pouring cream.

Note:
If you choose to make a Gooseberry Summer Pudding, which is delicious, crush
3 lb (1.4 kg) of gooseberries with the sugar and liquor in a pan over a low heat
until they *just* begin to fall into a pulp. Allow to cool before filling the basin.

Everlasting Syllabub

Serves 4–6

Derived from the French town of Sille and 'bub', an Elizabethan word for 'drink', the early mixtures consisted of white wine or sherry with cream and were drunk rather than eaten. Later mixtures were beaten, producing a buttery top. 'Everlasting' here means that the syllabub can be safely kept for up to a week or so.

rind and juice of 1 lemon
1 wine glass white wine
½ pt (275 ml) double cream
sugar to taste

Steep the rind and juice of the lemon overnight in the white wine. Next morning, pour this into a deep pan and gradually stir in the cream, adding sugar to taste. Whip until very thick, and put into glasses. This dish is better if made the day before use.

Basic Vanilla Ice Cream

Serves 4–5

This is a very rich ice cream; for a somewhat plainer, but equally delicious form, substitute milk for cream.

8 egg yolks
3 oz (75 g) caster sugar
1 pt (575 ml) single cream
vanilla pod

Beat the egg yolks and sugar until they are creamy and thick and all the sugar has dissolved. Bring the cream to the boil, together with the vanilla pod. Remove the pod and pour the cream on to the eggs and sugar, whisking well all the time. Arrange this bowl over a pan of boiling water and, stirring all the time, thicken the 'custard' until it well coats the back of a wooden spoon. Leave the custard to cool completely, then chill; either follow the instructions for your particular machine, or place in a suitable container in the ice-making compartment of your refrigerator, or in the deep-freeze.

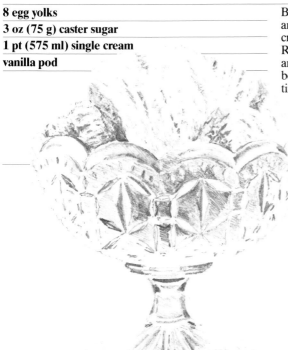

Brown Bread Ice Cream

Serves 4–5

A blissful variant on the ice cream theme - and very British!

1 pt (575 ml) basic ice cream (see above)
2 tbsp Madeira
3 oz (75 g) wholemeal breadcrumbs
2 oz (50 g) unsalted butter
3 oz (75 g) caster sugar

Add the Madeira to the basic ice cream at the custard stage. Fry the breadcrumbs in the butter until crisp. Add the sugar and let this caramelize. Cool completely. Crush with a rolling pin. Add to the basic ice cream as it is beginning to set. Proceed as in the 'basic' recipe.

Flummery
Serves 4–5

A fine old English dish, one of the most delicate you could wish for and simplicity itself to make.

1 pt (575 ml) double cream
scant $\frac{3}{4}$ oz (20 g) gelatine dissolved in a little water
2 oz (50 g) caster sugar
1 tbsp orange flower water
grated rind and juice of 1 lemon

Put all the ingredients into a double boiler or into a basin which will fit into the top of a pan of boiling water. Stir gently but continuously until the sugar and gelatine are completely dissolved. Pour into custard cups and allow to cool before putting into the refrigerator to set. I sometimes omit the orange flower water and the orange rind and juice and substitute 4 oz (110 g) ground almonds which I infuse in the cream.

Old English Sherry Trifle

Perhaps the party dish to end them all, trifle in its many and sometimes elaborate forms seems to have been with us since the eighteenth century. The use of sherry could be controversial, leading, as I remember, to Church Trifle, which had it, and Chapel Trifle which did not.

Base

2 × 7 in (18 cm) fatless sponge cakes or 1 packet small sponge cakes
1 lb (450 g) apricot puree, apricot jam, or quince jelly

Topping

1 pt (575 ml) double cream
4 oz (110 g) glacé cherries
4 oz (110 g) blanched or toasted almonds
2 oz (50 g) each crystallized apricots, crystallized pears or Carlsbad plums
2 oz (50 g) crystallized chestnuts
4 oz (110 g) ratafia biscuits
angelica

Custard Sauce (see page 23)

Use good-quality sponge cakes. First make up the custard. Split the sponge cakes in half across their middles: liberally spread them with puree, jam or jelly, sandwich them together and cut into 1 in (2.5 cm) fingers. Arrange these in a shallow trifle dish, about 12 in (30 cm) across the top and 3 in (7.5 cm) deep. Sprinkle the sponge fingers with plenty of sherry and pour the waiting custard over them. Cool the trifle base completely. (If the bowl is glass, wipe away any condensation from the sides, as this will look unsightly when the trifle is cold.) Prepare all the topping ingredients – the actual quantities will depend on the area of trifle to be covered and this is bound to vary slightly. Cut the crystallized apricots or pears and chestnuts and Carlsbad plums into attractive quarters. Cut long spikes of angelica. Empty the packet of ratafias to free them from biscuit crumbs. Make sure that the blanched or toasted almonds are cold or they will melt the cream. Put each topping ready on a separate plate. Whip the cream until it just stands in peaks but doesn't look as though it will be cheese at any minute! Spread a thick layer over the trifle. Decorate at will with the other topping ingredients. You may like to make a fresh fruit trifle and in this case use fresh fruits only for decoration and stick them into the bed of whipped cream at the last moment so that the juices do not draw and spoil the look of the trifle. A puree of fruit can replace the jam in the sponge cakes. Particularly suitable fruits to use are strawberries or raspberries and fresh apricots. If you are using raspberries, substitute Kirsch for sherry.

Cakes, Breads and Biscuits
Fruit Slab Cake

6 oz (175 g) margarine or butter

6 oz (175 g) caster or light soft brown sugar

2 eggs

8 oz (225 g) self-raising flour, sifted

2–3 tbsp milk

a few drops of almond essence

6 oz (175 g) mixed dried fruits

Line a 8–9 in (20–23 cm) square cake tin with greased greaseproof paper. Cream the fat and sugar together until light and fluffy then beat in the eggs one at a time. Fold in the flour followed by sufficient milk to give a soft dropping consistency. Add the essence and dried fruit and turn into the tin. Level the top and bake at 350°F (180°C) Reg 4 for about 1¼ hours or until well risen and golden brown, and a skewer inserted in the centre comes out clean. Cool for 10–15 minutes in the tin, then turn out on to a wire rack and leave until cold. Store in an airtight container.

Saffron Cake
Makes 2 cakes

Now both scarce and expensive, saffron was once in more abundant supply, usually from the Saffron Walden area and from Cornwall where this recipe originated.

2 lb (900 g) strong plain flour

12 oz (350 g) butter or margarine

1 lb (450 g) currants

8 oz (225 g) chopped mixed candied peel

6 oz (175 g) sugar

1 tsp salt

1 oz (25 g) fresh yeast or ½ oz (15 g) dried yeast

½ tsp saffron

¾ pt (450 ml) lukewarm water

Grease 2 deep round 8 in (20 cm) cake tins. Sift the flour into a warm mixing bowl. Take out 4 oz (100 g) flour and put into a smaller bowl. Rub the fat into the larger quantity of flour until the mixture resembles fine breadcrumbs. Stir in the currants, peel, sugar and salt. Mix the yeast with the smaller quantity of flour, 1 tsp sugar and the warm water. Mix well, cover and leave to stand for 20 minutes in a warm place until the yeast mixture is frothy. Meanwhile, just cover the saffron with hot water. Add the yeast sponge to the flour mixture with the strained saffron liquid and mix to form a dough. Knead well, cover and leave to prove for about 1 hour in a warm place until the dough has doubled in size. Knead again until smooth and divide between the cake tins. Put to rise for 20 minutes. Bake at 350°F (180°C) Reg 4 for 1¼ hours. Turn out on to a wire rack.

Malt Bread
Makes 2 × 1 lb (450 g) loaves

A side-effect of our great national brewing industry was that malt found its way into foods, occasionally being used in place of treacle.

1 lb (450 g) strong plain white flour

1 tsp salt

1 oz (25 g) fresh yeast or ½ oz (15 g) dried yeast

1 tsp sugar

6 fl oz (175 ml) warm water

3 oz (75 g) malt extract

2 tbsp black treacle

1 oz (25 g) butter

8 oz (225 g) sultanas

a little clear honey

Sieve the flour and salt into a bowl. Mix the fresh yeast with the sugar and add to the lukewarm water (or sprinkle dried yeast on the water with the sugar and leave until frothy). Warm together the malt extract, treacle and butter until the fat has melted, and leave until lukewarm. Add to the flour with the yeast liquid and work to a soft dough. If it is very sticky, add a little more flour, but be sure that the dough remains soft and spongy. Cover and leave to prove for 45 minutes. Heat the oven to 400°F (200°C) Reg 6. Knead the sultanas into the dough and divide into two pieces. Knead each piece and shape to fit two greased 1 lb (450 g) tins. Cover and leave to prove for 45 minutes. Bake for 45 minutes. While the loaves are hot, brush the tops with a wet brush dipped into a little clear honey. Cool on a wire rack.

Seed Cake

8 oz (225 g) plain flour	
1 tsp baking powder	
6 oz (175 g) butter or margarine	
6 oz (175 g) caster sugar	
3 eggs, beaten	
1–2 tbsp milk	
2 tsp caraway seeds	

Line a 7 in (18 cm) cake tin. Sift the flour and baking powder. Add the caraway seeds to the flour. Cream the butter or margarine with the sugar until light and fluffy. Beat in the egg, gradually. Fold in the flour, adding a little milk if necessary, to give a dropping consistency. Put into the tin and bake in the centre of the oven at 350°F (180°C) Reg 4 for $1\frac{1}{4}$–$1\frac{1}{2}$ hours.

Date and Walnut Loaf

An exotic import, favoured by Victorian society who made it into a seasonal speciality.

6 oz (175 g) plain flour	
pinch salt	
$\frac{1}{2}$ tsp bicarbonate of soda	
2 tsp baking powder	
$1\frac{1}{2}$ oz (40 g) soft brown sugar	
$1\frac{1}{2}$ oz (40 g) shelled walnuts, chopped	
3 oz (75 g) stoned dates, chopped	
$1\frac{1}{2}$ oz (40 g) black treacle	
$\frac{3}{4}$ oz (20 g) butter or margarine	
$\frac{1}{4}$ pt (150 ml) milk	

Grease and line a 1 lb (450 g) loaf tin with greased greaseproof paper. Sift the flour, salt, bicarbonate of soda and baking powder into a bowl. Mix in the sugar, dates and walnuts. Warm the black treacle, butter and milk until melted. Stir into the flour mixture and beat until the batter is smooth. Pour into the prepared tin. Bake at 350°F (180°C) Reg 4 for 1–$1\frac{1}{2}$ hours. Turn out on to a wire rack. When cold, serve in slices, either plain or spread with butter.

Gobbet Cakes

Makes approx 48

So called because they perfectly fit that eighteenth-century phrase for 'a mouthful'. Flavoured with lemon and ginger, these little cakes go well with coffee after dinner.

4 oz (110 g) unsalted butter	
4 oz (110 g) caster sugar	
finely grated rind and juice of 1 lemon	
3 oz (75 g) self-raising flour	
1 tsp baking powder	
2 eggs	
slices of stem ginger (about 4 pieces)	

Cream the butter and sugar with the lemon rind. Sieve the flour and baking powder together. Beat the eggs and gradually incorporate into the creamed mixture. Incorporate the sieved flour using a little of the lemon juice to arrive at a dropping consistency. Well butter your tins. Put teaspoons of the mixture into them, pop a slice of the stem ginger on top, and bake at 350°F (180°C) Reg 4 for 12–15 minutes, or until done.

Victoria Sponge

The source of the name could not be simpler: Queen Victoria liked it. (And when Queen Victoria liked something, you didn't argue!)

4 oz (110 g) butter or margarine	
4 oz (110 g) caster sugar	
2 eggs	
4 oz (110 g) self-raising flour, sifted	
1 tbsp cold water	
raspberry jam	
caster or icing sugar for dredging	

Grease and line the base or flour 2 × 7 in (18 cm) sandwich tins. Cream the butter and sugar until light and fluffy. Beat in the eggs, one at a time, following each with a spoonful of flour. Add the water, then fold in the flour. Turn into the prepared tins. Bake at 375°F (190°C) Reg 5 for about 20 minutes or until well risen, golden brown and just firm to the touch. Turn out on to wire racks and leave to cool. When cold, sandwich together with raspberry jam and dredge the top with caster or icing sugar.

Teacakes

Makes 6–9

The Duchess of Bedford, appalled by the lengthening wait for her evening meal, took to eating small delicacies in her boudoir in the afternoon and so invented the English tea ceremony that we now revere.

8 oz (225 g) strong plain flour

½ oz (15 g) butter or margarine

½ oz (15 g) fresh yeast or ¼ oz (7 g) dried yeast

1 tsp caster sugar

¼ pt (150 ml) milk

1 egg, beaten

1½ oz (40 g) mixed dried fruit

Glaze

1 tbsp sugar

2 tbsp milk

Grease 2 baking sheets. Sift the flour into a bowl and rub in the butter. Blend the fresh yeast with the sugar and add the lukewarm milk (or sprinkle dried yeast on the milk with the sugar and leave until frothy – about 10 minutes in a warm place). Add the yeast liquid to the flour with the egg and dried fruit, mix thoroughly and knead well. Cover and put to rise in a warm place for 45 minutes until doubled in size. Turn on to a floured surface, knead until smooth and divide into 3 pieces. Knead each piece until smooth and round and then shape into flat round cakes. Place on the baking sheets, cover and leave to prove for 15 minutes in a warm place. Bake at 450°F (230°C) Reg 8 for 12 minutes. Remove to a wire rack and while the buns are still warm, brush over with a glaze made from the sugar melted in the milk. Cut each teacake into 2 or 3 pieces.

Sponge Cake

Many people make this type of cake without butter. The odd ounce of unsalted butter makes it just that bit moister.

4 whole eggs

4 oz (110 g) caster sugar

4 oz (110 g) self-raising flour, sieved

1 oz (25 g) unsalted butter, melted but cold

1 tsp finely grated lemon rind (optional)

Beat the eggs and sugar together (with the lemon rind if used) until quite stiff and thick. Fold and cut in the sieved flour, incorporating lightly but thoroughly. Pour in the butter and incorporate well. Now well butter and fully dredge with caster sugar your cake tin or mould (which should be a lightweight metal one). Spoon in the mixture and bake at 375°F (190°C) Reg 5 for 20–25 minutes. Serve with jam, cream cheese, whipped cream or clotted cream.

Marble Cake

The name comes from the marbled appearance obtained by building up the contents of the baking tin using three separate mixtures.

1½ × recipe quantity Victoria Sandwich (see page 36)

vanilla essence

1 oz (25 g) cocoa, sifted

cochineal

Grease and line an 8 in (20 cm) deep round cake tin with greased greaseproof paper. Make up the Victoria Sandwich mixture as directed then beat in a few drops of vanilla essence. Divide the mixture into 3 bowls. Add the cocoa to 1 bowl, a few drops of cochineal to another and leave the third portion plain. Put spoonfuls of each of the 3 mixtures into the tin in sequence to give a marbled effect. Bake at 350°F (180°C) Reg 4 for about 45–50 minutes or until well risen and firm to the touch. Turn on to a wire rack to cool. The top of the cake may be covered with pink or chocolate butter cream. The mixture may also be baked in 2 × 8 in (20 cm) sandwich tins allowing about 25 minutes.

Simnel Cake with Yeast

This is traditionally eaten at Easter and should be made at least two weeks in advance to allow it to mature. A layer of marzipan is baked in the middle of the cake and another covers the top. The 11 marzipan balls decorating the top of the cake represent the 11 faithful apostles and a decoration of tiny eggs or flowers may be added as well.

8 oz (225 g) strong plain white flour

½ tsp mixed spice

4 oz (100 g) butter

4 oz (100 g) sugar

½ oz (15 g) fresh yeast or ¼ oz (7 g) dried yeast

¼ pt (150 ml) warm milk

3 egg yolks

4 oz (100 g) sultanas

4 oz (100 g) currants

1 lb (450 g) almond paste (see below) or bought marzipan

2 tbsp apricot jam

a little beaten egg white to glaze

Sieve the flour and spice into a warm bowl and rub in the butter until the mixture resembles fine breadcrumbs. Reserve 1 tsp of sugar and stir the rest into the flour. Mix the fresh yeast with the reserved sugar and add to the milk (or sprinkle dried yeast on the milk with the sugar and leave until frothy). Add to the flour with the egg yolks and knead until smooth. Cover and prove for about 1 hour until doubled in size. Heat the oven to 375°F (190°C) Reg 5. Knead the dough again, working in the fruit. Put half the dough into a greased and floured 7 in (18 cm) diameter cake tin. Take one-third of the almond paste and roll into a circle to fit the tin exactly. Place this on the dough and cover with the remaining dough. Prove for 30 minutes. Bake for 1½ hours. Leave in the tin for 30 minutes so that the almond paste firms up, and turn out on to a wire rack to cool. Roll out half the remaining almond paste to fit the top of the cake. Brush the top of the cake with apricot jam and use the marzipan to cover the cake. Make the remaining almond paste into 11 balls and press them round the top of the cake. Brush with a little beaten egg white and put under a hot grill until the almond paste is lightly coloured (this happens very quickly, so keep an eye on the cake all the time). If liked, put a frill or ribbon around the cake, and a decoration of tiny 'eggs' or 'flowers'.

Almond Paste

4 oz (100 g) ground almonds

12 oz (350 g) icing sugar

2 egg whites

water to mix

Makes 1 lb (450 g)
Mix the ground almonds, icing sugar and egg whites to a smooth paste, adding a little water if necessary.

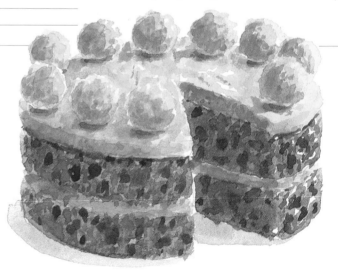

Brandy Snaps
Makes approx 25

4 oz (110 g) butter or margarine

4 oz (110 g) sugar

4 oz (110 g) golden syrup

4 oz (110 g) plain flour

½ tsp mixed spice (optional)

½ tsp ground ginger

Line 2 baking sheets with non-stick parchment. Put the fat, sugar and syrup into a pan and heat gently until melted. Remove from the heat. Sift the flour, spice and ginger together, then add to the melted mixture. Mix well and drop teaspoonfuls of the mixture on to the lined sheets, allowing plenty of room for the mixture to spread. Bake at 350°F (180°C) Reg 4 for 7–10 minutes until bubbly and golden brown. Remove from the oven and as the mixture begins to firm up, roll each quickly around a greased wooden spoon handle. Leave until set then twist slightly and remove to a wire rack to cool. Repeat with remaining mixture. If liked, fill with whipped cream.

Mince Pies
Makes 20

These have more than a passing association with Christmas. At one time they were oval in shape, the pie representing the crib and the filling the good things bought by the three Kings.

12 oz (350 g) shortcrust pastry (see page 252)

12 oz (350 g) mincemeat

1–2 tbsp brandy (optional)

egg white or milk

caster sugar

Roll out two-thirds of the pastry on a floured surface and cut into about 20 plain rounds approx 3 in (7.5 cm) in diameter. Use to line patty tins. Fill with mincemeat which can be mixed with brandy, if liked. Roll out remaining pastry and cut into fluted rounds approx 2½ in (6 cm) in diameter. Damp edges and position lids on the pies. Brush each pie with egg white or milk and make a small slit in the top of each. Bake at 400°F (200°C) Reg 6 for about 20 minutes until a light golden brown. Remove to a wire rack and dredge with caster sugar. Serve hot, warm or cold.

Flapjacks

4 oz (110 g) butter

1 oz (25 g) caster sugar

2½ tbsp golden syrup

8 oz (225 g) rolled oats

pinch salt

Put butter and sugar into a basin and beat until smooth. Heat the syrup in a saucepan, stir into the butter and sugar, then add the oats and a pinch of salt, and mix well. Spread the mixture into a well-greased shallow tin, approx 8 in (20 cm) square, pressing well into the corners and flattening the top. Bake at 375°F (190°C) Reg 5 for 30–40 minutes until crisp and golden brown. Mark into bars immediately on removal from oven. Leave in the tin to cool before removing and breaking into bars.

Swiss Roll

Once a delicate Swiss confection, this was captured by travelling Victorians, brought home and adopted as our own. No Swiss would now recognize it for what it was!

3 eggs

4 oz (110 g) caster sugar

4 oz (110 g) plain flour, sifted

1 tbsp hot water

warmed jam

caster sugar (for dredging)

Grease and line a Swiss Roll tin 12 × 9 in (30 × 23 cm) with greased greaseproof paper. Whisk the eggs and sugar in a bowl over a saucepan of hot water until very thick and the whisk leaves a heavy trail. Sprinkle the flour over the mixture and fold in using a metal spoon until the flour is evenly distributed. Finally stir in the hot water. Pour the mixture into the tin spreading evenly, especially in the corners. Bake towards the top of the oven at 425°F (220°C) Reg 7 for 7–9 minutes until golden brown, well risen and firm to the touch. Meanwhile have ready a sheet of greaseproof paper placed over a damp tea towel and dredge with caster sugar. Turn the cake on to the paper, peel off paper lining and trim off the crusty edges. Spread the surface with warmed jam and roll up quickly and carefully with the help of the greaseproof paper. Cool on a wire rack and dredge with more caster sugar.

Quick Mix Victoria Sandwich

4 oz (110 g) self-raising flour

1 tsp baking powder

4 oz (110 g) soft margarine

4 oz (110 g) caster sugar

2 eggs

Grease and line the base of 2 × 7 in (18 cm) sandwich tins. Sift the flour and baking powder into a bowl. Add all the other ingredients and beat for 2 minutes with a spoon or an electric beater until thoroughly blended and smooth. Divide between the tins, level the tops and bake at 350°F (180°C) Reg 4 for 25–30 minutes or until well risen and just firm to the touch. Turn out on to wire racks and leave to cool. Fill with jam, jam and cream or butter cream and sprinkle the top with caster sugar.

Melting Moments

Makes 20–24

Small confections, these, with a bounden duty to vanish on entering the mouth.

4 oz (110 g) butter or margarine

3 oz (75 g) caster sugar

1 egg yolk

a few drops vanilla essence or a little grated lemon rind

5 oz (125 g) self-raising flour, sifted

porridge oats or crushed cornflakes

glacé cherries

Cream the fat and sugar together until light and fluffy, then beat in the egg yolk and flavouring. Work in the flour and mix to a smooth dough. Wet the hands and divide mixture into small balls. Roll these in porridge oats or crushed cornflakes and put on 2 greased baking sheets. Top each with a small piece of glacé cherry and bake at 375°F (190°C) Reg 5 for 15–20 minutes. Cool on a wire rack and store in an airtight container.

Macaroons
Makes 16–20

One of our oldest delicacies, the macaroon was enjoyed mainly by the well-to-do, for almonds were not cheap. The name comes from the Neapolitan dialect word maccarone, *a dumpling or small cake.*

2 egg whites
4 oz (110 g) ground almonds
8 oz (225 g) caster sugar
1 oz (25 g) ground rice
1 tsp orange flower water or water
$\frac{1}{4}$ tsp vanilla essence
split almonds

Line 2 baking sheets with rice paper. Whisk egg whites fairly stiffly. Mix together the almonds, sugar, rice and flavouring. Add to the egg white and mix well to form a firmish consistency. Place the mixture in small heaps on the baking sheets, leaving room for them to spread. Place a split almond on each and glaze with a little egg white. Bake at 350°F (180°C) Reg 4 for 20–25 minutes until pale golden. It is important to cook macaroons rather slowly to allow them to colour evenly and to get a good texture. Tear the paper away from round the macaroons and cool on a wire rack.

Ginger Nuts
Makes 20–24

4 oz (110 g) self-raising flour
$\frac{1}{2}$ tsp bicarbonate of soda
1–2 tsp ground ginger
1 tsp ground cinnamon
1 tbsp caster sugar
2 oz (50 g) butter or margarine
3 oz (75 g) golden syrup

Grease 2 baking sheets. Sift together the flour, bicarbonate of soda, ginger, cinnamon and sugar. Melt the butter in a pan and stir in the syrup. Add this mixture to the dry ingredients and mix well. Roll the mixture into small balls and place well apart on the baking sheets. Flatten each slightly with the back of a spoon and bake at 375°F (190°C) Reg 5 for 15–20 minutes. Cool slightly before removing carefully to a wire rack to get cold. Store in an airtight container.

Plain Scones
Makes 8–12

8 oz (225 g) self-raising flour
1 tsp baking powder
pinch salt
1$\frac{1}{2}$–2 oz (40–50 g) butter or margarine
1$\frac{1}{2}$ oz (40 g) caster sugar (optional)
$\frac{1}{4}$ pt (150 ml) milk (preferably sour)

Grease or flour a baking sheet. Sift the flour, baking powder and salt into a bowl. Rub in the fat until the mixture resembles fine breadcrumbs then stir in the sugar, if used. Add sufficient milk to mix to a fairly soft dough and knead very lightly. Turn on to a floured surface and roll or pat out to 1 in (2.5 cm) thick. Cut with 1$\frac{1}{2}$–2 in (4–5 cm) rounds and place on the baking sheet. Alternatively divide dough in half and shape into 2 rounds. Cut each into quarters and place on the baking sheet. Brush tops with milk or dredge with flour. Bake at 450°F (230°C) Reg 8 for about 10 minutes until well risen and golden brown. Cool on a wire rack. Serve split and buttered.

Variations

Fruit Scones. Add 2 oz (50 g) currants, sultanas or raisins to the dry ingredients.

Cheese Scones. Omit the sugar and add $\frac{1}{2}$ tsp dry mustard and 3 oz (75 g) finely grated mature Cheddar Cheese.

Note: To sour fresh milk, add 1 tbsp lemon juice to $\frac{1}{4}$ pt (150 ml) fresh milk.

The West Country

All of us have our romantic idea of England. As a lad mine was always 'The West Country', even though I had never been further south than Doncaster nor west of Manchester. Yet I had a clear image about everything: the greenness of it all; its moors, some purple-clad, others bleak and awesome where evil men lived out the rest of their lives in solitary confinement behind the walls of Dartmoor, the one prison everyone has heard of.

The 'countryness' of much of it rang a happier note, with a rubicund cider-drinking people walking down sunlit lanes – the sun *always* shone in the West Country – high-bordered by well-kept hedgerows abundant with hips and haws, blackberries and wild strawberries. Rosy-cheeked women tended the needs of their spouses in picture-postcard thatched cottages, a profusion of roses in each garden with gooseberry jam in the kitchen cupboard and cake in the tin.

Then there was the Atlantic Ocean with its rollers and breakers washing sandy beaches in smugglers' coves; tall sailing ships were moored in picturesque harbours where artists sat in front of easels painting pictures of their England. At the other end of the scale was the Cornish Riviera and the exotic Devon resorts crowned by Torquay and its Imperial Hotel – some think of this as Arnold Bennett's *Imperial Palace* – overlooking England's Bay of Naples where Royalty and the gentry swam and lazed in the sun on golden beaches wafted by unexpected palms, sipping champagne before dancing the nights away under a star-spangled sky.

I wasn't far wrong in my dreams, except that in my fantasies I had only seen the tip of it all, and the clichés were far from adequate for there is so much more than my young imagination could conceive at that time.

Avon, at least a happier name than some given to our new counties, is perhaps where I would begin a brief West Country journey, for here is found Europe's finest eighteenth-century city: *Aquae Sulis* – Bath.

To read Jane Austen's satirical *Persuasion* or *Northanger Abbey* will give an excellent insight into the life and manners of the times as her characters paraded and pirouetted at the 'New' Assembly Rooms or the Pump Room, visited Mrs Sally Lunn's cake shop or Mollands in Milsom Street and later attended a performance of Mr Sheridan's *The Rivals* or *School for Scandal* at the Royal Theatre.

Bath has given its name to many foods still with us: Bath Buns, spiked with candied peel; succulent Bath Chaps; and the buttery-crisp biscuits of Dr Oliver, that eighteenth-century physician who, in his efforts to relieve the agues and fevers of his patients, created this plain biscuit now so popular on our twentieth-century tables with a handsome nugget of the West Country's mature Cheddar Cheese.

Bristol has always been the handsome big brother to Bath's elegant younger sister. Now the centre of the county of Avon, it was a county in its own right as far back as 1373. At that time it was England's second city, trading in sugar, tobacco, rum, wine, chocolate and spices, making the merchants prosperous as they forged links with the New World.

The temptation to stay in this area is great, but we must move on, taking first a southwards route to Wiltshire before going deeper west. Here we find an inland agricultural county noted for its dairy farming, its sheep and, of course, its excellent sausage, bacon, and black-skinned hams from Bradenham.

The spacious chalk uplands of Salisbury Plain contain Britain's most important prehistoric monument – Stonehenge – and a few miles south lies the town of Salisbury. The 400-ft spire of the cathedral can be seen from many miles around and it is not difficult to understand why Constable was inspired to paint it. In nearby Wilton the carpet trade grew and flourished and if a carpet is out of reach, who knows, you might be lucky and come across a Salisbury Steak or take home a half truckle of the finest Wiltshire Cheese – sometimes known as Wiltshire 'loaves' – with a flavour and colour balanced between that of Cheddar and Gloucester.

Still heading south, the landscape becomes more hilly as you enter Dorset. This somewhat remote county is considered by many to be one of the most unspoilt in England and much of it remains as it was depicted by Hardy in his Wessex novels. Like Wiltshire, Dorset is an agricultural county with fertile valleys yielding milk for the famous Dorset butter, and the one-time more famous Dorset Blue Vinney. It was during the Second World War that the Ministry of Food forbade the making of this excellent cheese, for reasons too complicated to go into. However, by the time you read this, local farmers will have overcome the red-tape difficulties and once again this stiff-crumbed heavily blue-veined cheese will be available to enjoy with that local 'crispbread,' the Dorset Nob.

Dorset is full of delightful towns and villages: Cerne Abbas, Sherborne, Poole with its pottery – and one mustn't forget all those villages with a 'piddle' or a 'puddle' incorporated in their names after the River Piddle. The prudish Victorians, preferring the 'u', created many a local controversy in their attempts to have decorum restored.

As we move deeper west, there is more evidence of regional dishes for the visitor to taste. Somerset, home of that beauty spot the Cheddar Gorge, produces our most famous cheese. It is, moreover, a cheese copied (badly) by much of the rest of the world. The character of this well-known cheese varies from farm to farm, season to season, cheesemaker to cheesemaker – sweet, sharp, moist, dewy, hard; the choice is individual, but *Farmhouse* Cheddar it must be.

Formerly one of England's larger counties, Somerset has lost the territory between the Mendips and Bristol, including Weston and Bath, to the new county of Avon. But to many of us Somerset *is* the Mendips and the gently rounded Quantocks, Cheddar Cheese and cider, tall perpendicular church towers, handsome towns and villages, many with traces of the county's own dialect, *Zummerzetsheer,* and of course to many it is the home of Apple Dumplings.

We come to Wells, whose cathedral is one of my favourites, with its exquisite inverted scissor arches and a whole regiment of twelfth- and thirteenth-century sculptures parading on parapets on the west front, looking out to the moat of the Bishop's Palace where elegant swans have inherited the trick of ringing a bell for food. This novel bit of entertainment is said to have been taught them by the daughter of a Victorian bishop of that see.

Before leaving Somerset, try to find a restaurant where Crocky Pie and Priddy Oggies are still on the bill of fare. The ubiquitous faggot, too, has reason to believe that Somerset is the county of its birth; a well-seasoned faggot with a pint of scrumpy will set you up for the journey across the border into Devon.

There's no shortage of regional goodies here in what can be said to be England's most popular holiday county. Devonshire Splits, Apple Cake, Black Cake, Honiton Fairings, Ikky Pie and many other dishes have survived the onslaught of foreign foods. Incredibly picturesque chocolate-box villages with steep, winding cobbled streets, flower-decked houses and cob-cottages abound in Devon, and of course no-one leaves this county without partaking of a Devon Cream Tea, where light scones and home-made strawberry jam are served – ideally oven fresh – with thick rich clotted cream.

And so to Cornwall, England's foot, with its toe in the sea at Land's End. Here *is* the land of smugglers and legends; of early saints with over a hundred holy wells to give ample evidence of strong beliefs in strange powers. The well at St Cleer on the edge of Bodmin Moor is reputed to cure madness; Celtic crosses are a regional feature, and an ancient relic of Celtic Christianity. The River Tamar flows along all but a few miles of Cornwall's border with Devon, creating almost an island of this county and helping to keep out the Saxons until the ninth century. A strong Celtic heritage is reflected in the Cornish language which was still widely spoken as late as the nineteenth century and is not dead today, though more commonly encountered in so many of the place names.

If you're hungry in Cornwall there is an abundance of fresh fish and

other seafoods: Mevagissey lobsters and crabs, oysters from Helford, or you might like to try a piece of Stargazey Pie with pilchard or mackerel heads peering upwards through the rich pastry crust, or perhaps you'll slip a torpedo-shaped Tiddy Oggie into your pocket before tramping across the moors or setting off on a cliff-top hike. The Tiddy Oggie is the Cornishman's name for the regional pasty packed with meat and vegetables. Saffron Cakes, Cornish Splits, Crab Soup and Black Cake still make regular appearances on many a table in this part of England.

Soups

Cornish Broth
Serves 2

8 oz (225 g) stewing beef (in one piece)
1 medium onion, cut in half
1 bouquet garni sachet
2 carrots, diced
1 parsnip, diced
4 oz (110 g) turnip, diced
6 oz (175 g) flatpoll or other cabbage
salt and pepper
1 tbsp chopped parsley
2 slices bread, diced into ½ in (1 cm) cubes

Place the stewing beef (in one piece), onion and bouquet garni in a saucepan and cover with 1½ pt (850 ml) cold water. Season with 1 tsp salt. Bring to the boil and simmer for 1-1½ hours. Add diced vegetables and continue cooking. Shred the cabbage and add to the pan, cooking for a further 15 minutes. Strain stock into another pan and reduce to ¾ pt (425 ml). Slice meat and keep warm with vegetables. Place the diced bread into bowls and pour the soup over, sprinkle well with milled pepper and parsley. Serve the meat separately on plates together with the remaining vegetables and a modicum of the soup. A jacket potato with sour cream or butter would be an ideal accompaniment.

Watercress Soup
Serves 4

Watercress beds are to be seen frequently in the West Country and many farmhouses and antique shops have those pierced china watercress dishes (don't say you thought they were over-large soap trays!). This dark green soup is delicious served iced or hot.

3 bunches watercress, picked over
1 lb (450 g) floury potatoes
1½ pt (850 ml) chicken stock (use cube if necessary)
½ pt (275 ml) single cream
¼ tsp ground mace or nutmeg
salt and pepper
juice of half a lemon

Wash the watercress and reserve a few small sprigs for garnish. Dice the potatoes and cook in the chicken stock for 25 minutes. Add lemon juice and nutmeg. Put into a blender with the watercress and blend until smooth (10-15 seconds). Return to the pan. Reheat the soup, add seasoning to taste. Pour into serving bowl or individual dishes, stir in cream and garnish with the reserved watercress leaves.
Note: Watercress soup discolours if kept hot for too long; this does not impair the flavour.

Crab Soup
Serves 4-5

Whilst this is very much a twentieth-century recipe it pays excellent homage to an area where crabs abound and were at one time commonplace at the high-tea table.

8 oz (225 g) crab meat (half dark and half white)
1 large onion
1 clove garlic
2 pt (1.2 l) fish stock
2 oz (50 g) butter
1 oz (25 g) white flour
grated rind of 1 orange
½ pt (275 ml) double cream
1 glass dry sherry
salt and freshly ground white pepper

Fish Stock Simmer 2 lb (900 g) of washed sole bones in 2 pt (1.2 l) of cold water. (There is little gain in ever simmering fish bones for more than 25-30 minutes.) Drain this stock through a fine muslin and put aside for use.
Soup Slice the onion and crush the garlic. Melt the butter in a heavy-bottomed pan. When just foaming, but not coloured, add the onion and garlic. Cover with a lid and soften the onion without colouring. Add the dark crab meat and work in well. Add the flour, stirring in well to avoid lumping. Slowly add the fish stock, stirring all the time until the soup boils. Simmer for 30 minutes. Strain the soup into a clean pan. Season with salt and pepper; add the cream, sherry and orange rind. Chop the white crab meat and remove any skin or 'blades'. Add the fish to the soup, re-heat and serve immediately.

Fish/Seafood

Red Mullet
Serves 4

Although we live on an island surrounded by fish we eat relatively little of it. Mullet is not commonly eaten outside the West Country, and this dish is an example of locally caught fish being put to good use.

4 × 10–12 oz (275–350 g) red mullet

flour

For each fish

1 small finely chopped shallot, or equivalent piece of onion

1 tsp chopped parsley

1 tsp chopped fennel frond

1 chopped mushroom

1 tbsp sherry

butter

salt and pinch cayenne pepper and milled black pepper

anchovy essence

lemon juice

Prepare 4 pieces of oiled foil, large enough to wrap the fish completely. Butter the foil. Roll the fish in flour and place on the paper. Add the other ingredients and wrap each fish into a secure packet by folding the long edge over twice; bend the ends up and twist once. Place in a baking tin and bake in a preheated oven at 400°F (200°C) Reg 6 for 30 minutes. Serve each fish in its foil, and pass round a small jug of melted butter, flavoured with a little anchovy essence and a good squeeze of lemon juice.

Stargazey Pie
Serves 6–8

This is Cornwall's most famous dish.
'Mawther used to get a herring, clean 'un, and put same stuffin' as what yow do have in mabiers (chicken); sew 'en up with niddle and cotten, put 'en in some daugh made of suet and flour; pinch the daugh up in the middle and lave the heid sticking out one end, and tail t'other. They was some nice pasties, too, cooked in a fringle fire with crock and brandis and old furzy tobs.'
Edith Martin, 1929

8 pilchards or herrings

4 oz (110 g) white breadcrumbs

2 fl oz (50 ml) milk

1 tbsp chopped parsley

juice and grated rind of 1 lemon

4 oz (110 g) chopped onions

salt and pepper

2 chopped hard-boiled eggs

4 oz (110 g) chopped bacon

$\frac{1}{4}$ pt (150 ml) cider

8 oz (225 g) shortcrust pastry (see page 252)

1 egg

Gut, clean and bone the fish leaving the heads on. Soak the breadcrumbs in the milk; squeeze out. Add the parsley, lemon juice and rind and half the onions to the soaked breadcrumbs. Season with salt and pepper. Stuff the fish with this mixture and spread any remaining filling over the base of a 9 in (23 cm) pie plate. Arrange the fish on top with the heads sticking up towards the edges. In the spaces between arrange the hard-boiled eggs, bacon and remaining onions; season and pour over the cider. Roll out the pastry, place over the fish so that the heads stick out and point upwards. Brush with egg beaten with a little water. Bake for 40–50 minutes at 400°F (200°C) Reg 6.

Portland-Style Mackerel

Serves 4

The sharpness of the gooseberry marries well with the oiliness of the mackerel.

4 × 8–10 oz (225–275 g) fresh mackerel
salt and pepper
butter or olive oil
Sauce
8 oz (225 g) gooseberries, topped and tailed
2 oz (50 g) sugar
2 tbsp water
1 tbsp lemon juice
1 oz (25 g) butter
pinch ground rosemary or bay leaf

Clean and split the mackerel, season well with salt and pepper, brush with butter or oil. Place under grill and grill until golden brown, turning carefully after 10 minutes. Place gooseberries with sugar, lemon and water in a pan and cook until tender. Rub through a sieve, return to the pan and add the butter and herb. Re-heat and simmer for 5 minutes. Serve with the mackerel, either hot or cold.

Elvers Omelet

Serves 2–3

Elvers (young eels) are very small thread-like fish that stream up the River Severn on a few days each year. They are scooped out of the river by local fishermen and are considered a great delicacy. They rarely arrive in the shops; you have to know an elver fisherman to obtain any. In the kitchen, elvers are often treated as whitebait or made into a traditional 'omelet' or elver cake. This is best made as an open-faced 'egg cake', as people did in the eighteenth century.

8 oz (225 g) elvers
6 frying bacon rashers
6 eggs, beaten
salt and milled pepper
1 tbsp chopped chives and/or parsley
red wine vinegar

Strictly, although we suggest proportions, there are no set quantities. The number of elvers to bacon rashers is a personal matter, and enough eggs are needed to make the pan of elvers into an omelet. Wash the elvers thoroughly to get rid of grit and slime. Do this in a fine sieve or muslin cloth, scald them with boiling water and drain well. Fry the bacon in a frying pan, take it out and keep warm. Put the elvers into the bacon fat, season and fry for a minute or so over a brisk heat. Pour over the beaten eggs, and stir round using a fork until the mixture begins to set. Lower the heat and cook until the eggs are as soft (or hard!) as you like them. Using a palette knife, slide the omelet on to a dish. Sprinkle with the herbs, cut into portions and serve with the bacon and a splash of red wine vinegar.

Marinated Mackerel

Serves 4

Typically, a fisherman's high-tea dish. There is also evidence that fishermen in the West ate fish for breakfast as they do in the Netherlands and Scandinavia.

4 × 8–10 oz (225–275 g) mackerel
1 onion, sliced
2 sprigs parsley
2 bay leaves, broken into bits
6 cloves
1 blade mace
10 peppercorns
salt
vinegar

Clean and prepare the mackerel and arrange in a pie-dish, chop the onion and parsley and sprinkle over the fish. Add other ingredients with salt to taste. Pour over sufficient vinegar to cover well and bake in a moderate oven for 40–50 minutes. Leave to cool. Arrange the fish on a serving dish and strain vinegar over them. Serve cold with brown bread and butter.

Trout, Oyster and Eel Pie

Serves 4

*'Clean, wash and scale them, lard them with Pieces of a Silver Eel rolled up in spice and sweet Herbs, and
Bay Leaves powder'd; lay on and between them the bottoms of slic'd Artichokes, Mushrooms, Oysters,
Capers and slic'd Lemon; lay on Butter, and close the Pye.'
From a recipe of 1738.*

4 × 8 oz (225 g) trout, skinned and filleted
1 × 8 oz (225 g) tin smoked eel fillets
1 × 8 oz (225 g) jar artichoke bottoms or hearts, drained
4 oz (110 g) mushrooms, sliced
4 oz (110 g) tin oysters in brine, drained
1 tbsp capers, drained
juice of 1 lemon
1 tbsp each of chopped parsley and chives
8 oz (225 g) shortcrust pastry (see page 252) or frozen
1 egg, beaten

Butter a 2 pt (1.2 l) pie-dish. Line the edge with pastry. Arrange all the ingredients in the dish, seasoning and sprinkling with herbs as you go along. Brush the edge with beaten egg. Fit the lid. Brush all over with egg. Bake at 400°F (200°C) Reg 6 for 45–50 minutes.

Potted Crab

Serves 4–5

Potting was an excellent way of preserving, before the days of refrigeration. The butter, after being clarified, acted as a seal when set. Potted foods were not only eaten in their own right, but used in other dishes as well.

1 large dressed crab (frozen crab is excellent)
⅓ pt (190 ml) double cream
2 oz (50 g) butter
a little lemon juice
1 sherry glass Madeira
salt and freshly ground black pepper
clarified butter to cover (see page 251)

Chop the white meat and pound well together with the dark meat. Melt the butter in a pan and add the crab. Cook very slowly for 15 minutes, stirring all the time. Add the cream and continue cooking until you have the consistency of a very thick sauce. Pass through a Mouli or blender and allow to cool. Beat in the Madeira, add a little lemon juice and seasoning to taste. Fill into little pots or wax cartons and cover with a film of clarified butter. Set in a refrigerator.

Ham Olive Pie

Serves 4

The 'olive' is so-called because of its shape. Sometimes olives were called 'birds'. They are made from thin slices of meat, stuffed and shaped, then pot-roasted or braised.

1 lb (450 g) ham, yielding approx 8 slices

Filling

3 eggs, hard-boiled

12 dates, stoned

12 button mushrooms

2 tbsp currants

2 tsp chopped parsley

2 tsp chopped lovage (optional)

6 gooseberries

1 tbsp caster sugar

pinch nutmeg and cinnamon

salt and pepper

milk

½ pt (275 ml) cider

2 tbsp butter

8 oz (225 g) shortcrust pastry (see page 252)

Cut each slice of ham in half. Mix together the hardboiled egg yolks and other ingredients for the filling and divide the mixture between the ham pieces. Roll up to form 'olives.' Place the olives close together in a deep pie-dish. Pour over the cider and add the chopped egg white, and dot with the butter. Roll out the pastry and cover the pie-dish. Brush the top with a little milk. Bake at 350°F (180°C) Reg 4 for about 45 minutes. Eat either hot or cold.

Poacher's Pie

Serves 4–6

Rabbits were the easiest of game to poach; no doubt every poacher's wife had her special recipe for cooking these illegal gifts from the countryside.

2 small rabbits, jointed

1 small onion, sliced

1 small carrot, sliced

salt and milled pepper

stock (use stock cube if necessary)

2 eggs, hard-boiled and sliced

½ oz (15 g) gelatine crystals

8 oz (225 g) shortcrust pastry (see page 252)

1 egg, beaten

Place the rabbit joints in a pan or casserole with the onion and carrot. Season well. Add sufficient stock to just cover. Cook gently until tender. Remove the joints from cooking liquor, strip the meat from the bones, but leave on largish pieces and arrange in a pie-dish together with the sliced hard-boiled eggs. Dissolve the gelatine in some of the cooking liquor, add the rest. Season to taste and pour enough over the rabbit to just cover. Roll out the pastry and rim and cover the pie-dish. Decorate with pastry leaves and brush all over the beaten egg. Bake at 400°F (200°C) Reg 6 for approx 30 minutes. Serve hot or cold.

Wiltshire Porkies

Serves 4

An interesting way to cook sausage in a batter – almost the Wiltshire form of Toad-in-the-Hole.

Batter
8 oz (225 g) plain flour
½ tsp salt
1 egg yolk
1 tbsp oil
water
Filling
1 lb (450 g) sausage meat
1 egg white
oil for deep frying
apple rings
2 oz (50 g) butter
1 tbsp parsley, finely chopped

Mix together the flour, salt, egg yolk, oil with sufficient water to make a 'coating' batter. Beat well and leave to stand for 30 minutes. Divide the sausage meat into eight and form into meat balls (lightly floured hands will help). Whisk the egg white stiffly and fold into the batter. Coat each sausage meat ball with batter and fry in deep oil until golden brown. Fry the apple rings in the butter. Pile the porkies on a hot dish and garnish with the apple rings and chopped parsley.

Cornish Under Roast

Serves 4-6

The Cornish way of preparing a pot roast, not unlike a hot pot.

4 × 6 oz (175 g) slices rump steak, cut thinly
seasoned flour
2 oz (50 g) butter or bacon fat for frying
crushed bay leaf
2 large onions, thinly sliced
4 medium potatoes (4 oz/110 g), thinly sliced
salt and milled pepper
chicken or beef stock (use cube if necessary)

With a wetted rolling pin give each steak a few sharp bangs to break down sinews. Season well on both sides. Roll up the steaks and turn each roll in a little seasoned flour. Shake away surplus. Melt butter (or bacon fat) in a large frying pan, and when foaming and very hot quickly fry the steaks to brown them. Transfer them to an ovenproof pot just large enough to contain them in one layer. Sprinkle the bay leaf over the steaks. Cover with the onions, seasoning lightly. Arrange the potatoes over in layers, again seasoning lightly. Pour over enough stock to come half way up the potato layer. Bake, uncovered at 400°F (200°C) Reg 6 for 50–60 minutes or until the potatoes are cooked through.

Dorset Jugged Steak

Serves 4

Jugging is a method of slow-cooking ideal for hares and rabbits, or, as in this recipe, steak.

1½ lb (700 g) braising steak, trimmed of fat and sinew
1 oz (25 g) plain flour
1 onion
6 cloves
4 fl oz (110 ml) wine glass port
1 bouquet garni sachet
salt and pepper
forcemeat balls (see page 21)
redcurrant jelly
beef or chicken stock (use cube if necessary) to cover

Cut the beef steak into 1 in (2.5 cm) cubes, dust with flour and place in a casserole. Stick an onion with cloves, place in a casserole together with the port, stock, bouquet and seasoning. Cook gently at 350°F (180°C) Reg 4 for 45–60 minutes until the meat is tender. Serve from the casserole with small forcemeat balls and redcurrant jelly.

Purbeck Meat Balls

Serves 4

From the eastern frontiers of cider country, a tasty way to use up roast meat; even more delicious when made from a freshly bought breast of lamb.

1 breast of lamb
1 pt (575 ml) stock or dry cider
1 egg
1 tbsp fresh white breadcrumbs
salt and pepper
1 tbsp freshly chopped parsley
$\frac{1}{2}$ level tsp ground nutmeg
$\frac{1}{4}$ pt (150 ml) milk
4 tbsp oil (or melted butter)
1 medium onion, chopped
2 tomatoes, skinned, de-seeded and chopped
1 tbsp plain flour
1 beef stock cube
$\frac{3}{4}$ pt (425 ml) cooking liquor
2 lb (900 g) mashed potatoes

Cut the breast of lamb into large pieces, place in a pan with the stock and simmer gently until tender (approx $1\frac{1}{2}$ hours). Remove the meat and mince it. Mix the minced meat with the beaten egg, breadcrumbs, parsley, seasoning and nutmeg. Add sufficient milk to bind and make into balls. Heat oil (or butter) in a frying pan, and lightly fry the chopped onion, remove to a casserole, together with the chopped tomatoes. Brown the meat balls and place in the casserole. Add the flour to the remaining fat in the pan and cook for 1 minute. Add the stock cube, pour in the cooking liquor. Cook for 2 minutes and then strain through a sieve into a $2\frac{1}{2}$–3 pt (1.5–1.75 l) casserole. Arrange the mashed potato round the meat and bake at 350°F (180°C) Reg 4 for 30 minutes.

Raw Fry

Serves 3–4

An old-fashioned Cornish dish so-called because the potato remains white, although cooked, and still appears to be raw.

8–12 oz (225–350 g) lamb's liver
bacon dripping
2–3 potatoes
1 large onion
stock (use stock cube)
seasoning

Bacon and egg can be used instead of liver if preferred (suggest 2 rashers and 1 egg per person). Fry the liver in the dripping in a frying pan. When cooked, place on a plate and keep warm. Add a small amount of water to the frying pan, then fill the pan with sliced potato and onion and season to taste. Cover the pan and cook gently for about 20 minutes or until vegetables are tender. Serve the contents of the pan with the cooked liver, pouring over the remaining gravy. Serve with any green vegetables.

Devon Huntsman's Pie

Serves 4

A goodly pie to sustain the Devonshire huntsman on a cold day.

1 lb (450 g) minced meat (cooked)
2 lb (900 g) cooked potatoes, diced
2 onions, very thinly sliced
2 large cooking apples, cored and sliced
$\frac{1}{2}$ pt (275 ml) stock (use stock cube)
salt and pepper
nutmeg
4 oz (110 g) breadcrumbs
butter

Arrange layers of potato, meat, onion, apple in a deep casserole, beginning and ending with potato. Season the stock and pour into the dish. Sprinkle with breadcrumbs. Dot with butter. Bake for 1 hour at 300°F (150°C) Reg 2.

Crocky Pie

Serves 3

This is known in other parts of the country as Pot or Crock Pie.

1 lb (450 g) lamb or beef diced into 1 in (2.5 cm) cubes

1–2 oz (25–50 g) seasoned flour

2 large onions, sliced

12 oz (350 g) carrots, diced into 1 in (2.5 cm) cubes

1 lb (450 g) turnips, diced into 1 in (2.5 cm) cubes

4–6 oz (110–175 g) suet crust pastry (see page 253)

2 tbsp dripping or nut oil

salt and pepper

$\frac{3}{4}$ pt (425 ml) stock (use stock cube)

1 bouquet garni sachet

Roll the meat in seasoned flour and fry in 1 tsp of dripping or oil. Remove the meat. Fry the seasoned vegetables and bouquet garni in the rest of the dripping or oil. Put the meat and vegetables in alternate layers in a deep casserole or crock, and almost cover with stock. Put the lid on the casserole and cook in the oven at 350°F (180°C) Reg 4 for 1–1¾ hours or until tender. Remove the casserole lid, and cover the meat and vegetables with the suet crust. Return to the oven, increase the temperature to 400°F (200°C) Reg 6. Cook for 25–30 minutes until crust is golden brown and cooked through.

Cornish Pasty

Makes 2 large or 4 small pasties

Originally a Cornish Pasty was fish wrapped in pastry made by the wives of Cornish tin miners for their husband's meal in the mines. Today it is internationally known for its filling of sliced meat, onion, potato (and in some areas turnip). Its torpedo shape made it ideal for stuffing into the pocket and for eating held in one hand. Each member of the family had his or her initial imprinted at one end so that any piece of uneaten pasty would find its rightful owner for later delectation!

8 oz (225 g) shortcrust pastry (see page 252)

6–8 oz (175–225 g) potato, finely sliced (not diced)

6–8 oz (175–225 g) onion and/or turnip, finely cut

6–8 oz (175–225 g) steak, chuck or skirt

seasoning

Roll the pastry into rounds. Pile up the sliced potato on about half the pastry. Put the onion and/or turnip on the potato. Cut the meat into small pieces and spread over. Season with salt and pepper. Place a few thin pieces of potato on top to save the meat drying. Damp the edges of the pastry. Fold over to a semi-circle and crimp the edges. (Crimp by pinching the pastry with the left hand and fold over with the right hand, forming a rope-like effect on the side of the pastry.) Place on a greased baking tray and bake at 425°F (220°C) Reg 7 for 10–15 minutes, reducing to 350°F (180°C) Reg 4 for a further 30 minutes.

Ashburton Open Pasty

This pasty uses a different method of folding the pastry which results in the pasty opening during cooking; it also uses a pre-cooked filling.

flaky pastry (see page 253)

any pre-cooked filling – meat, fish or sweet

garnish

For each pasty roll the pastry into an oblong twice as long as it is wide. Lay the filling lengthwise, leaving a space all round for folding. Fold the two ends towards the centre, covering each end of the filling. Bring the two sides to the centre and just pinch them closed. Do not close too firmly. Cook at 400°F (200°C) Reg 6 for about 20 minutes until the filling is heated through and the pastry is golden brown. As the pasty cooks the case will open at the top and it can be garnished as desired.

Herby Pasty

Prepare the pastry as for ordinary pasty. Thoroughly wash equal quantities of parsley, watercress, shallots (early) or leeks, and a half quantity of spinach. Prepare 2–3 slices of bacon cut into small pieces, and an egg well beaten. Pour boiling water over the parsley, watercress and spinach that have been cut into small portions, and let stand for 30 minutes. Squeeze all the moisture out and put on the pastry with the shallots cut finely and the bacon, pinch up the edges of the pasty allowing a small portion left open for the egg to be added, finish pinching and bake.

Apple Pasty

Peel some apples, slice thinly, and lightly sprinkle with brown sugar. In summer, blackberries are usually mixed with the apple.

Broccoli Pasty

Boil the broccoli until nearly cooked, but still quite firm, strain it, and fill pasty in usual way, adding salt.

Eggy Pasty

For this you need diced bacon, parsley, and 1 or 2 eggs according to the size of pasty required.

Jam Pasty

These are usually made smaller than a savoury pasty; any kind of jam may be used.

Mackerel Pasty

Allow 1 or 2 mackerel to each pasty, and clean and boil them in the usual way. Then remove the skin and bones and lay on the pastry; fill up with washed parsley, and add pepper and salt.

Squab (Pigeon) Pie
Serves 4-6

Squabs (pigeons) were at one time used for this dish. As they became more difficult to obtain over the years and the tougher wild pigeon grew less acceptable to our twentieth-century palates, other meats were substituted. Today, tender young pigeons are available in the shops again and so this recipe can be restored and updated.

8 oz (225 g) shortcrust pastry (see page 252)
4 small young pigeons (cut in half)
oil for frying
4 rashers bacon, diced
1 onion, finely sliced
2 oz (50 g) butter
2 oz (50 g) currants
8 dates, pitted
4 Cox's apples, cored, sliced but not peeled
grated rind of $\frac{1}{2}$ orange
4 cloves
salt and milled pepper
$\frac{1}{2}$ pt (275 ml) dry cider

Have your butcher cut the pigeons in half. Make the pastry. Rim a deep pie dish with the pastry. Heat a little oil in a large frying pan. Fry the pigeons, a few at a time, to brown them. Transfer them to the pie-dish. Fry the bacon and onion in the butter until browned. Scatter over the pigeon pieces. Pack the fruits in and around, add the rind and cloves and seasoning. Pour over the cider to cover. Fit a pastry lid. Bake at 350°F (180°C) Reg 4 for $1\frac{1}{4}$–$1\frac{1}{2}$ hours.

Priddy Oggies
Makes 15

The Cornish Tiddy Oggie or potato pasty was popular during the depression that followed the closure of the tin mines. It was adapted in Somerset to include local pork and Cheddar Cheese and took the name of the village of Priddy.

12 oz (350 g) pork fillet
4 thin rashers smoked bacon
6 oz (175 g) grated Cheddar Cheese
1 tsp chopped parsley
salt and pepper
1 egg, beaten
Cheese Pastry
12 oz (350 g) plain flour
6 oz (175 g) butter or margarine
4 oz (110 g) grated Cheddar Cheese
pinch salt, pepper and dry mustard
cold water

Slice the pork fillet lengthwise *almost* through, and with a wetted rolling pin beat very thin. Lay on the bacon to cover the meat. Mix the 6 oz (175 g) grated cheese and parsley, seasoning and beaten egg to a spreading consistency and spread this over the bacon. Roll up the pork fillet into a long swiss-roll shape. Wrap in damp greaseproof paper and refrigerate to firm up. Make cheese pastry (see page 252 for method) and roll it out to an oblong and cut into pieces approx 6 in × 3 in (15 cm × 7.5 cm). Cut the meat into pieces about $1\frac{1}{2}$ in (4 cm) long and place one on each piece of pastry. Press the sides together and brush with beaten egg. Bake at 350°F (180°C) Reg 4 for about 30 minutes until crisp and brown.

Note:
As an alternative to pork fillet, lean slices from a leg of pork can be used. In this case the temperature should be raised to 375°F (190°C) Reg 5 and the baking time increased to 45 minutes.

Exeter Stew
Serves 4

The herby savoury dumplings in this stew make this well worth the extra effort demanded by the recipe.

1–1½ lb (450–700 g) chuck steak

dripping or oil

2 medium onions, sliced

2–3 carrots, sliced

1 oz (25 g) plain flour

salt and pepper

bouquet garni sachet

1¼ pt (850 ml) stock

Savoury Dumplings

4 oz (110 g) self-raising flour

2 oz (50 g) suet

4 tsp chopped parsley

¼ tsp ground thyme

¼ tsp ground sage

1 tsp grated lemon rind

salt and pepper

1 egg, beaten

water

Remove any fat from meat and cut into a large square. Heat dripping or oil in frying pan and fry meat until brown, remove and place in a casserole. Fry the onions and carrots, add to the meat, add the flour to the pan and gradually stir in the stock. Bring to the boil, add seasoning and bouquet garni. Pour over the meat and vegetables in the casserole. Cook at 350°F (180°C) Reg 4 for 1½–2 hours, or until meat is tender. Make savoury dumplings by mixing together the ingredients and adding sufficient water to make a soft dough. Divide into 8–10 balls. Increase temperature to 400°F (200°C) Reg 6 so that the stew boils, drop the dumplings in and allow to cook for a further 20–30 minutes.

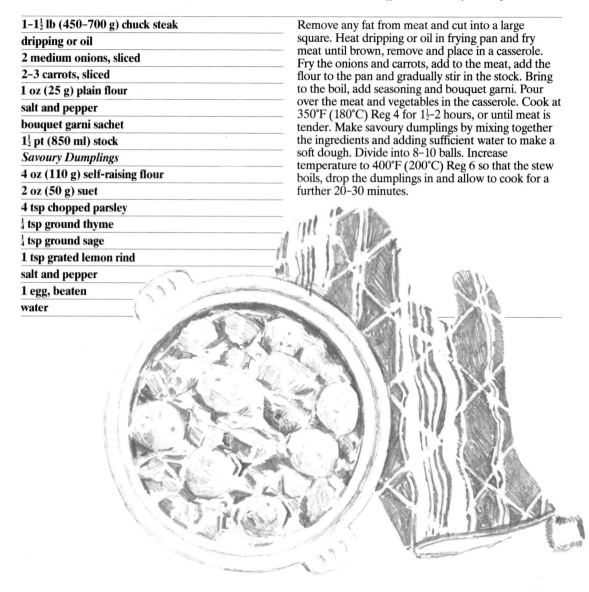

Savouries

Parsley Pie
Serves 3-4

A typically economic dish from the land of the pie and the pasty.

8 oz (225 g) shortcrust pastry (see page 252)	Line a deep, round tin with two-thirds of the pastry. Place half the parsley in the base, cut the bacon rashers into small pieces and lay on the parsley. Break the eggs on top of the bacon. Season well. Place the remaining parsley on top. Cover the whole with the remaining pastry, seal the edges well and make a hole in the centre. Bake at 400°F (200°C) Reg 6 until well browned.
3 tbsp fresh parsley, coarsely chopped	
2 rashers smoked bacon	
3-4 eggs	
salt and pepper	

Artichoke Pie
Serves 4-6

A savoury pie that goes very well with roast beef or lamb.

8 oz (225 g) shortcrust pastry (see page 252)	Make pastry and leave to chill. Peel the artichokes and leave to soak for about 10 minutes in water which has had a squeeze of lemon juice or vinegar added to prevent discoloration. Remove and cut into even-sized pieces and cook in boiling salted water until they are soft – but not mushy! Make a white sauce with the flour, butter and milk, add sherry and stir, then add artichokes, grapes and dates cut in half. Put into a deep pie-dish about 8 in (20 cm) long. Slice hard-boiled eggs on top. Season to taste, damp edges of pie dish, roll out pastry and place on top of mixture, press down edges and notch with a fork. Brush with milk and bake at 400°F (200°C) Reg 6 for about 30 minutes.
1 lb (450 g) Jerusalem artichokes	
lemon juice or vinegar	
1 heaped tbsp butter	
1 heaped tbsp plain flour	
½ pt (275 ml) milk	
1 tbsp sherry	
4 oz (110 g) seedless white grapes	
12 dates	
2 eggs, hard-boiled	
salt and pepper to taste	

Leeky Pie
Serves 4

This is sometimes called Likky Pie.

1½ lb (700 g) leeks	Wash and chop the leeks. Cook for a few minutes in boiling water and drain. Place the leeks and bacon in alternating layers in a casserole. Season to taste. Add sufficient milk to just cover. Bring to the boil on top of the stove and simmer for 30 minutes. Make the pastry. Add the eggs and cream to the leeks. Roll out the pastry to fit the casserole and place on top of the mixture. Cook the pie at 400°F (200°C) Reg 6 for about 30 minutes, until the pastry is firm.
8-12 oz (225-350 g) streaky bacon, finely sliced	
salt and pepper	
milk	
6 oz (175 g) suet crust pastry (see page 253)	
2 eggs, beaten	
1 tbsp cream or butter	

Dorset Flan
Serves 6

8 oz (225 g) shortcrust pastry (see page 252)	Make the pastry, roll it out and line an 8 in (20 cm) flan ring. Line with buttered foil and bake blind for 20 minutes. Beat one of the eggs and brush the pastry base. Lay the ham slices in the flan case. Break the two eggs and place whole on top of the ham. In a basin place the semolina, milk and remaining beaten egg, mix to a smooth paste, season to taste. Pour over the ham and egg. Bake at 375°F (190°C) Reg 5 for 30-40 minutes, until the top is lightly browned. Eat either hot or cold.
4 oz (110 g) sliced cooked ham	
3 eggs	
½ pt (275 ml) milk	
2 tsp fine semolina	
salt and pepper	

Helston Pudding

Serves 4–5

2 oz (50 g) raisins	
2 oz (50 g) sultanas	
1 oz (25 g) candied peel, chopped finely	
2 oz (50 g) suet	
2 oz (50 g) sugar	
2 oz (50 g) breadcrumbs	
2 oz (50 g) ground rice	
2 oz (50 g) plain flour	
$\frac{1}{2}$ tsp mixed spice	
pinch salt	
$\frac{1}{2}$ tsp bicarbonate of soda	
milk	

Mix together all dry ingredients. Dissolve bicarbonate of soda in a little milk. Add this to the dry ingredients, with sufficient milk to produce a stiff batter. Pour into a $1\frac{1}{2}$ pt (850 ml) greased basin. Cover well with greased greaseproof paper, place in a saucepan of boiling water and boil for 2 hours.

Dorset Lemon Tart

Serves 4

True to its place of origin, this is really an apple tart with lemon in it.

Pastry

4 oz (110 g) plain flour	
2 oz (50 g) butter	
1 tbsp caster sugar	
$1\frac{1}{2}$ tbsp milk	

Filling

2 large cooking apples	
2 eggs	
2 oz (50 g) sugar	
grated rind and juice of 1 lemon	

Sieve flour into mixing bowl, add butter cut into small pieces and mix. Dissolve sugar in cold milk, pour into ingredients. Using a fork, stir to make a rough dough, turn out on to a floured working surface and knead until smooth. Roll out and line a 7 in (18 cm) flan ring. To make the filling, peel and grate the apple, add sugar and grated rind and juice of lemon. Beat the eggs and add to the apple mixture. Pour into the flan and bake for about 30 minutes at 350°F (180°C) Reg 4 or until the pastry is well cooked and the top golden. Can be eaten hot or cold.

Oldbury Gooseberry Tarts

Makes 12

Although we do not know why, since it grows freely elsewhere, the gooseberry again comes to the fore in this West Country recipe.

Pastry

1 lb (450 g) plain flour

¼ tsp salt

6 oz (175 g) butter or margarine

approx ¼ pt (150 ml) hot milk and water

Filling

8 oz (225 g) gooseberries

2 oz (50 g) demerara sugar

Prepare pastry by sieving flour and salt into a bowl, adding softened fat and cutting it into the flour. Gradually pour on hot, but not boiling, milk and water, mixing to a stiff dough with a knife. Leave in a cool place to firm up a little. Take pieces of the dough the size of a golf ball, and roll out the pastry to 5 in (12.5 cm) diameter and then pinch the pastry together in 5 places around the edge. Bring up to form a pie shape ready to hold the gooseberries and after filling with fruit and sugar cover this with a round of pastry squeezed well together to form the lid. Dampen under the edge of the pastry lid to seal well. Brush the tarts with beaten egg. Bake for about 25 minutes at 375°F (190°C) Reg 5 until gooseberries are soft.

Marlborough Pudding

Serves 4

This pudding could well have been served as a treat at Marlborough School.

4 oz (110 g) puff pastry (see page 253)

3 oz (75 g) sugar

1½ oz (40 g) mixed candied peel

3 oz (75 g) butter

yolks of 2 eggs, beaten

Line an 8 in (20 cm) flan ring with puff pastry (rolled thinly). Sprinkle the candied peel in the base of the dish. Place the butter in a pan, or melt, add the sugar and well-beaten egg yolks. Heat gently until mixture bubbles, then pour into the flan case. Bake at 375°F (190°C) Reg 5 for 30–45 minutes.

Mazzard Pie

Serves 4

A mazzard was a small wild cherry peculiar, as far as is known, to Devon and Cornwall.

4 oz (110 g) shortcrust pastry (see page 252)

1 lb (450 g) or more mazzards (cherries)

sugar to taste

2 tbsp water

Remove stalks from mazzards and wash, place in pie-dish with water and sugar. Cover with pastry and bake at 400°F (200°C) Reg 6 until golden, and fruit is soft. Serve with Devonshire clotted cream.

Devonshire Apple Pudding

Serves 4–5

Several of these pudding recipes, as may be expected, are made with apples. Responsibility for their profusion in the West lies with the Normans who brought over quantities of apple trees from their native land.

1½ lb (700 g) apples

sugar, to sweeten apples if necessary

4 oz (110 g) breadcrumbs

3 oz (75 g) butter

4 oz (110 g) sugar

3 oz (75 g) ground almonds

1 egg

Peel, core and slice apples. Cook gently in very little water. Sweeten to taste. Mix with the breadcrumbs and place in a greased pie-dish. Cream the butter and sugar until light and fluffy, beat in the egg, and stir in the ground almonds. Pour over the apples. Bake for 45–60 minutes at 325°F (160°C) Reg 3. Serve hot or cold with blackcurrant jam and whipped cream.

Devonshire Junket

Serves 4–5

When made with rich Devon cream this pudding or delicacy is lifted from the ordinary to the sublime.

½ pt (275 ml) milk

½ pt (275 ml) Devonshire cream

1½ oz (40 g) caster sugar

1 tsp rennet

a little ground ginger

Ginger Sauce

2 large pieces stem ginger

1 tbsp caster sugar

1 tbsp Demerara rum

¼ pt (150 ml) double cream

Mix the milk and the cream together and sprinkle in the sugar. Slowly warm this until the sugar is dissolved and the liquid is no more than blood heat. Stir in the rennet, pour immediately into a large shallow serving dish and leave in the kitchen atmosphere to set. Then make the sauce. Chop the ginger very finely and mix with the sugar and rum. Stir in the double cream and continue stirring until it ribbons. Chill the sauce. Sprinkle a little ground ginger on the top of the junket before serving, using a dredger to achieve an even coating. Serve the ginger sauce separately.

Devonshire Tartlets

Makes 6

These are individual tarts, the filling topped with twists of pastry.

4 oz (110 g) shortcrust or puff pastry (see pages 252–3)

3 oz (75 g) spongecake crumbs

4 oz (110 g) apples, finely sliced

2 oz (50 g) caster sugar

2½ fl oz (70 ml) cream

dust of nutmeg

1 egg or milk to glaze

Line patty tins with the pastry. Sieve cake crumbs, and mix together with apples, sugar, cream and nutmeg. Place a spoonful in each tartlet, decorate with twisted strips of pastry. Brush with egg or milk and sprinkle with caster sugar. Bake at 350°F (180°C) Reg 4 for about 30 minutes.

Wiltshire Gooseberry Pudding

Serves 4

A heavy country pudding – not for those watching their waistlines.

4 oz (110 g) self-raising flour

½ pt (275 ml) milk

2 eggs

pinch salt

6 oz (175 g) gooseberries

demerara sugar

butter

Make a batter with the flour, milk, eggs and salt. Beat well, stir in the gooseberries. Pour into a greased 1½ pt (850 ml) basin and cover with greased greaseproof paper. Steam for 1½ hours. To serve, wrap a white napkin round the basin. Cover the top with demerara sugar and butter and cut into small pieces.

Cakes and Biscuits

Figgy Hobbin

'Figs' was the name given at one time to raisins; when currants were used, the recipe was called
Currany 'Obbin.

8 oz (225 g) plain flour	Sift the flour, baking powder and salt together; rub in the lard and stir in the sugar and suet. Add the fruit and mix to a stiff paste with milk. Roll out and cut into 4 in (10 cm) squares $\frac{1}{4}$ in (5 mm) thick. Bake in preheated oven at 400°F (200°C) Reg 6 for approx 30 minutes. Best eaten hot, with butter.
1 tsp baking powder	
pinch salt	
2 oz (50 g) lard	
1 tbsp caster sugar	
2 oz (50 g) suet	
2 oz (50 g) raisins or sultanas	
milk to mix	

Cornish Vinegar Cake

4 oz (110 g) butter or lard	Rub the fat into the flour. Add the fruit, sugar, spices and salt. Add the vinegar and enough milk to achieve a dropping consistency. Place in a greased and lined 8 in (20 cm) tin. Bake at 325°F (160°C) Reg 3 for about $1\frac{1}{2}$ hours. Serve sliced, with butter and jam.
1 lb (450 g) self-raising flour	
8 oz (225 g) dried fruit	
8 oz (225 g) sugar	
2 tsp mixed spice	
pinch salt	
3–4 tbsp vinegar	
8 fl oz (220 ml) milk	

Madeira Cake

In Beau Nash's Bath, ladies and gentlemen calling on each other in the morning would be offered a glass
of Madeira and a finger of this delicate almond cake with a hint of lemon.

6 oz (175 g) butter	Butter and line a 7 in (18 cm) cake tin. Cream butter and sugar until fluffy. Add eggs gradually, beating. Sieve the two flours and almonds on to a paper. Cut and fold in half of this mixture. Add rind and juice. Fold in rest of flour mixture. Pour into tin. Place peel on top. Bake at 325°F (160°C) Reg 3 for $1-1\frac{1}{4}$ hours. Turn on to a rack and cool. Serve on second day.
6 oz (175 g) caster sugar	
3 eggs, beaten	
3 oz (75 g) self-raising flour	
3 oz (75 g) plain flour	
2 oz (50 g) ground almonds	
rind and juice of 1 lemon	
a little milk if necessary	
1–2 slices of candied citron peel	

Shaley Cake (Lardy Cake)

*The two are not dissimilar in their ingredients, but very different in appearance. The latter name for this
rich, sticky, fruity, scone-like cake is more popular in the North, and in particular in Lancashire, where
they are sold as thick round cakes, upside down to reveal their toffee-like bases. Shaley Cakes have their
top specially criss-crossed to resemble shale. With the advent of modern ovens these cakes are rarely made
in the home, where once they were baked on the 'bast' or bottom of the old fire ovens.*

8 oz (225 g) strong flour + 1 tsp salt or
1 lb (450 g) once risen bread dough

½ oz (15 g) fresh yeast

¼ pt (150 ml) milk

6 oz (175 g) lard

4 oz (110 g) granulated sugar

3–4 oz (75–110 g) currants

pinch mixed spice

Glaze

1 tsp milk

1 tsp sugar

Prepare a yeast dough with flour, salt, yeast and milk.
When once risen roll out the dough into an oblong.
Spread half the lard on the dough. Sprinkle on one-
third of the sugar and one-third of the currants. Fold
into three, re-roll and repeat process twice more using
the remaining fat and sugar. Shape dough and place
into a 7 in (18 cm) square tin, ready greased. Prove
for 20–30 minutes. Brush with sugar and milk glaze,
and score with knife. Cook for 15 minutes at 425°F
(220°C) Reg 7 then reduce to 400°F (200°C) Reg 6
for a further 30 minutes.

Bridgwater Manchips

A manchet or manchip was a type of bread roll.

2 oz (50 g) fresh yeast or 1 oz (25 g) dried yeast

2 oz (50 g) sugar

¼ pt (150 ml) water

2 oz (50 g) white fat or lard

12 oz (350 g) plain bread flour

1 tsp salt

2 oz (50 g) butter or margarine

red jam

Glaze

**1 tbsp sugar dissolved in 1 tbsp milk and brought
to boil**

Add warm milk to yeast and sugar and leave in a
warm place to begin to ferment (10–20 minutes). Rub
lard into sieved flour and salt. Mix yeast liquid into
flour and make a pliable dough. Knead well. Leave in
a cool place to rest for about 30 minutes. Meanwhile
soften butter to spreading consistency. Pull dough to
an oblong about ¼ in (5 mm) thick. Spread one-third
of the softened butter on two-thirds of the dough,
then fold up into three as for flaky pastry. Repeat this
twice more, leaving the dough to rest in a cool place
between rollings if the fat is very soft. Having
incorporated all the butter, cool the dough, then roll it
quite thinly to an oblong. Brush it all over with water,
and cut into oblongs about 3 in × 4 in
(7.5 cm × 10 cm). Spread thinly with jam, then fold
over. Place on greased baking trays and leave to prove
in a warm place for about 30 minutes until well-risen.
Bake for 8–10 minutes at 400°F (200°C) Reg 6. As
soon as the manchips are cooked, brush with the hot
sugar and milk glaze, and sprinkle generously with
caster sugar.

Cornish Splits
Makes 14–18

When served with cream and black treacle, these light splits are called 'Thunder and Lightning!'

1 lb (450 g) strong flour
1 tsp salt
$\frac{1}{2}$ oz (15 g) yeast
1 tsp sugar
2 oz (50 g) lard
$\frac{1}{2}$ pt (275 ml) tepid milk

Sieve flour and salt together into a bowl. Rub in the lard. Whisk yeast and sugar in tepid milk and add it to the flour, mix to a soft dough and knead well until the dough becomes smooth. Cover and leave to rise in a warm place until doubled in size. Knock back and knead dough again, divide into 14–18 sections and shape each into a round. Place on a greased and floured baking sheet. Leave to prove again. Bake at 375°F (190°C) Reg 5 for about 15 minutes. When cool, split and serve with jam and cream.

Saffron Cake

It is said that saffron was introduced to Cornwall by the Phoenicians when they came to trade for tin. It is well worth paying the high price asked today for this delicate yellow powder, for the bonus of colour and aroma it gives to Cornwall's greatest cake.

2 tsp dried yeast
1 tsp sugar
$\frac{1}{4}$ pt (150 ml) warm water
$\frac{1}{4}$ tsp saffron strands
3 tsp boiling water
$1\frac{1}{2}$ lb (700 g) white bread flour
1 tbsp milk powder
$\frac{1}{2}$ tsp salt
1 oz (25 g) caster sugar
2 oz (50 g) butter
2 oz (50 g) lard
5 oz (140 g) currants
2 oz (50 g) sultanas
1 oz (25 g) mixed peel
yellow colouring

Put the dried yeast into a small bowl with a teaspoon of sugar. Add warm water, whisk and leave to froth for 10–15 minutes. Put the saffron strands in a separate cup, add 3 tbsp of boiling water and leave to infuse. Sift 7 oz (200 g) flour into a bowl, stir in the milk powder, pour in the frothed yeast and mix to a batter. Cover the bowl with cling film or a cloth and leave in a warm, draught-free place for 30 minutes (this is the ferment or leaven). Now put the balance of the measured flour into a large mixing bowl, add the sugar and salt and rub in the fats until the mixture resembles fresh breadcrumbs. Pour in the frothed mixture followed by the saffron strands and soaking water. Beat for 10 minutes by spoon or hand (5 minutes in an electric mixer). When ready, the dough should be silky and very elastic. Cover again with cling film and leave in a warm place to rise. It should double in bulk, which usually takes about 1 hour. Deflate the dough and beat by hand for 5 minutes. Add yellow colouring if necessary. Work in the dried fruits and peel, and transfer the dough to a well-greased 2 lb/900 g (2$\frac{3}{4}$ pt/1.5 l) loaf tin. Slip the tin inside a plastic bag, trapping a little air inside so it balloons up, and tie with a tie-tag. Leave in a warm, draught-free place for about 40 minutes, or until the mixture has risen to the top of the tin. Bake at 400°F (200°C) Reg 6 for 50 minutes. Turn off the heat, remove the saffron cake from the tin, and return the loaf to lie on one side on the oven rack. Close the door and leave for 5 minutes, then remove and leave to cool on a wire rack.

Devon Apple Fruit Cake

4 oz (110 g) margarine

4 oz (110 g) caster sugar

8 fl oz (220 ml) cooked sieved apple

1 tsp bicarbonate of soda

2 tbsp syrup or honey

6 oz (175 g) plain flour

½ tsp ground cinnamon

¼ tsp ground cloves

good pinch nutmeg

2 oz (50 g) sultanas

2 oz (50 g) raisins

Cream fat and sugar. Dissolve bicarbonate in 1 tbsp water and add to sieved apple. Stir this into the creamed fat and sugar. Beat in the honey or syrup. Sieve the flour and spices and fold this into the wet mixture. Add the dried fruit. Place in a well-greased and lined tin, and bake at 350°F (180°C) Reg 4 for 40–50 minutes until firm in the middle.

Hot Apple Muffins

8 oz (225 g) plain flour

1 tsp baking powder

3 oz (75 g) lard

2 oz (50 g) moist sugar

3 large cooking apples

1 egg

a little butter

a little caster sugar

Mix the flour and baking powder. Rub in the lard and add the moist sugar. Peel, core and mince the apples. Beat the egg well with the minced apples. Add to the flour, etc. Work all well together. Add a little milk if too dry – although the apples moisten in baking. Put into a greased flat tin and bake in a moderate oven at 350°F (180°C) Reg 4 for about 30 minutes. When done, cut into squares, split open and butter, dusting with caster sugar before serving.

Dorset Cider Cake

As with the puddings, so several of the cake recipes profit from the easy availability of West Country apples and cider.

12 oz (350 g) plain flour

1 tsp ground cinnamon

1 tsp baking powder

1 tsp bicarbonate of soda

8 oz (225 g) butter

4 oz (110 g) sugar

grated rind of 1 orange

3 eggs

6 fl oz (170 ml) cider

2 in (5 cm) piece of candied orange peel cut into strips

Lightly grease an 8 in (20 cm) cake tin. Sift together the flour, cinnamon, baking powder and soda. Cream butter until soft. Add sugar and orange rind. Beat until mixture is light and fluffy. Beat in eggs, one at a time, adding 1 tbsp flour mixture with each egg. Stir in remaining flour mixture. Pour in cider slowly, beating constantly with a spoon. When batter is smooth and thoroughly combined, spoon into prepared tin. Arrange strips of peel over the batter. Bake for 1¼–1½ hours at 325°F (160°C) Reg 3.

Sally Lunn Teacakes

*Probably called after Mistress Sally Lunn who touted her special buns in the streets of Georgian Bath.
An alternative explanation has it that the name comes from the Old French Sol et Lune (sun and moon)
and refers to the golden top of the bun and the white base.*

1 lb (450 g) plain flour
2 tsp salt
½ oz (15 g) fresh yeast
½ tsp sugar
2 oz (50 g) fat
4 fl oz (110 ml) milk
2 eggs, beaten

Sift flour and salt and add the yeast creamed with sugar, the fat melted in the warm milk and 1 beaten egg. Mix to a smooth dough of dropping consistency and leave to rise and double in size. Knock the dough back and shape to fit greased round baking rings about 6 in (15 cm) wide; leave to rise until the rings are full, then bake for 15–20 minutes at 425°F (220°C) Reg 7. Brush with beaten egg halfway through baking. Serve hot, filled with whipped cream and sprinkle with crushed sugar.

Bath Buns

Makes 12–16

No doubt these light textured buns were sold in Mistress Sally Lunn's shop in the Georgian city.

1 lb (450 g) plain flour
1 tsp salt
1 oz (25 g) fresh yeast or ½ oz (15 g) dried yeast
2 oz (50 g) sugar
3 oz (75 g) margarine or butter
3 eggs
½ pt (275 ml) milk approx
2 oz (50 g) chopped peel
2 oz (50 g) currants
lump sugar to decorate

Warm the milk and pour a little on the yeast with 1 tsp sugar. Allow to begin to ferment. Take 4 oz (110 g) flour and add this to the fermenting yeast, beating well to produce a soft but elastic dough. Drop this dough into a bowl of just warm water and leave for about 10 minutes, until it rises to the top of the water and begins to look like the curd of a cauliflower. Meanwhile rub the fat into the rest of the flour and add the sugar and salt. Make a well in the flour and drop in the eggs. When the fermenting dough has expanded lift it carefully out of the water, drain for a minute and drop it on to the eggs in the flour. Beat by hand to produce a soft elastic dough. Leave to rise in a greased bowl in a warm place till doubled in size (approx 50 minutes). Beat in the fruit and peel. Divide into 12–16 small rounds. Shape, brush with milk and sprinkle with crushed lump sugar. Place on a greased baking sheet, leave in a warm place till well-risen and bake at 375°F (190°C) Reg 5 until firm and brown. Glaze if required with sugar and milk glaze.

Cornish Heavy Cake (Fuggan)

Purely regional, and mostly from the area south of Truro, these cakes were made in the fishing villages where seine nets were used. When the net was being hauled in and the men were shouting 'Heave' with every pull, the wives knew the men would soon be in for their tea and would make this quick flat cake to be eaten warm or cold. The diamond criss-cross pattern marked on the top with a knife depicts the fishing net.

6 oz (175 g) plain flour

1½ oz (40 g) sugar

3 oz (75 g) currants

3 oz (75 g) lard

¼ tsp salt

1–2 oz (25–50 g) peel, if liked

approx 2 tbsp milk or water to mix

Mix the flour, salt and sugar roughly together. Add the other ingredients and mix with a little milk or water to make a stiff dough. Roll to approx ½ in (1 cm) thick. Criss-cross with a knife. Bake on a greased baking sheet at 375°F (190°C) Reg 5 for 25–30 minutes.

Cornish Sandwiches

A traditional Cornish way of filling scones – almost the poor sister of the Cornish Split, using scones instead of splits which need yeast baking to make the soft dough buns.

2 tsp damson, whortleberry or blackberry jam

clotted cream

8 or 9 little scones, very fresh but cold (see page 220)

Rub the jam through a sieve, split the scones and remove part of the soft inside. Spread a little jam on each half of the scone, and 1 tsp of thick cream on the lower half of each, press each scone together. These are best prepared only a short time before they are to be eaten.

Ginger Fairings

Fairings were at one time gifts or trinkets sold at all local fairs. Later, in the seventeenth and eighteenth centuries these gifts became cakes or biscuits sold at the gingerbread stalls. The Gingerbreads or Parkins of the North contained oatmeal. In the South and Scotland, the more expensive white flour was used. Gingerbreads in Cornwall became known as Fairings and are a thin, crisp, ginger biscuit.

4 oz (110 g) plain flour

2 oz (50 g) margarine

2 tbsp syrup

¼ tsp salt

2 oz (50 g) granulated sugar

1 level tsp each of baking powder, ground ginger, mixed spice, bicarbonate of soda, ground cinnamon

Mix all the dry ingredients except the sugar. Rub in the fat, add the sugar. Heat the syrup until it runs and add to the mixture. Roll into balls the size of a walnut and place on a greased tin on the top shelf of a fairly hot oven, 375°F (190°C) Reg 5. When the biscuits begin to colour, remove to a lower shelf where they will flop and crack.

Launceston Cake

6 oz (175 g) butter

6 oz (175 g) sugar

$\frac{1}{2}$ tbsp black treacle

1 tbsp golden syrup

3 eggs

2 oz (50 g) lemon peel

1 lb (450 g) currants

8 oz (225 g) self raising flour

2 oz (50 g) ground almonds

Prepare an 8 in (20 cm) cake tin. Cream the sugar and butter, add syrup and treacle, then the beaten eggs one at a time, followed by the fruit, flour and almonds, folding in carefully. Bake for about $1\frac{3}{4}$ hours at 350°F (180°C) Reg 4.

Colebrooke Revel Cakes

Makes about 12

One of the original meanings of the word 'revel' was a riot. Later the word came to mean a party or a fair at which revel or rout cakes were offered. This recipe is adapted from an old Devonshire version.

$2\frac{1}{2}$ tbsp white wine

$\frac{1}{4}$ tsp saffron (optional)

1 egg yolk

$\frac{1}{4}$ pt (150 ml) double cream

$\frac{1}{2}$ oz (15 g) fresh yeast or $\frac{1}{4}$ oz (7 g) dried yeast

4 oz (110 g) caster sugar

4 oz (110 g) butter or margarine

1 lb (450 g) strong plain flour

$\frac{1}{4}$ tsp nutmeg

$\frac{1}{4}$ tsp cinnamon

Warm the wine with the saffron. Leave to cool and then strain, discarding the saffron. If not using the saffron, the wine need not be warmed. Mix the egg yolk, cream, cooled wine, yeast and 1 tsp of the sugar and leave in a warm place until the mixture begins to bubble. Sift the spices and the flour together. Rub the fat into the flour, then add the rest of the sugar. Make a well in the flour mixture and pour in the yeast mixture. Do not mix, but take about 1 tbsp of the flour and sprinkle it across the surface of the yeast mixture. Leave for about 30 minutes in a warm place. Blend the mixture well and knead thoroughly (for about 10 minutes). The mixture will be very slack and sticky, so if a mixer is available, this makes the job much easier. Carefully turn out the dough on a well-floured table and roll to a thickness of $\frac{1}{2}$ in (1 cm). Take care not to allow the rolling pin to get too sticky – sprinkle with more flour if it does. Cut out 2 in (5 cm) circles of dough and place on greased baking sheets. Cover and leave in a warm place until the buns look 'spongy'. Bake at 400°F (200°C) Reg 6 for 15–20 minutes. Turn the oven down after 10 minutes if the buns start to get over-brown. Cool on a wire rack and dredge lightly with icing sugar. These are delicious while still warm from the oven or heated up the next day, buttered and spread with jam and Devonshire clotted cream.

Widecombe Fair Gingerbread

The annual fair, held on the second Tuesday in September, is now a popular tourist attraction made specially famous by the 'Uncle Tom Cobleigh' song associated with it. These gingerbread biscuits would have been bought as gifts by people at the fair to take home to mother.

2½ oz (60 g) butter or margarine

3 oz (75 g) soft dark brown sugar

3 oz (75 g) black treacle

5 oz (150 g) plain flour

1 tsp ground ginger

2 tsp milk

pinch bicarbonate of soda

pinch salt

Cream butter or margarine until softened, cream in the sugar and black treacle until fluffy. Sieve flour, ginger and salt and stir in. Gently warm the milk and add the bicarbonate of soda. Stir until dissolved then add to the mixture and mix in thoroughly. With floured hands, divide into small walnut-sized pieces, roll into a ball and place several inches apart on a baking sheet. Bake at 375°F (190°C) Reg 5 for 15 minutes. Place on a cooling tray.

Cornish Black Cake

This is an excellent regional variation of a rich fruit cake, 'black' with fruit and spices.

6 oz (175 g) butter

6 oz (175 g) caster sugar

4 oz (110 g) plain flour and 4 oz (110 g) ground rice or 8 oz (225 g) plain soft flour

3–4 eggs

½ tsp mixed spice

½ tsp bicarbonate of soda

1 lb (450 g) currants

4 oz (110 g) mixed peel

2–4 oz (50–110 g) chopped almonds

2 oz (50 g) chopped raisins

2 oz (50 g) chopped sultanas

¼ tsp nutmeg

½ tsp baking powder

½ tsp cinnamon

1 tbsp brandy (approx)

milk to mix (if required)

Line an 8 in (20 cm) cake tin. Cream fat and sugar, add flour, spices, eggs, fruit, brandy and milk. Bake for 3–3½ hours as follows: 1 hour at 325°F (160°C) Reg 3, then at 275°F (140°C) Reg 1 until cooked.

London and the South East

Someone once said 'The custard stops at Hatfield', the implication being that the South is all cream and roses. Well, to many this might appear to be so, albeit it unjustly. It has to be observed that the perforce grubby evidence of the industrial might of the Midlands, North and South Wales, Northern Ireland and Southern Scotland seems light years away when you simply recite the romantic names of the southern counties. Each shire conjures up magical visions of orchards, hop fields and fecund gardens, the landscape pierced by spearing spires, oasthouses, warm brick-hued farms and manors and hedgerows abundant with nature's wild flowers, shrubs and ferns.

Kent, so often by-passed on our journey to the Channel Ports as it bulges out into the North Sea, is known to most as The Garden of England. Like its far-off sisters Hereford and Worcester, Kent is the home of the apple and, more importantly to the male of the species, of the hop, the Doric 'vine' of beer-making. Swathes of hops are as visually attractive as the Bacchanalian garland of the grape vine which is fast reclothing the land, as the southern counties of England redevelop a vinicultural heritage lost since Roman times and the early days when those Conquerors encouraged wine-making in England. A delightful, fresh, light, German-type wine it is too.

Whether you are a Maid of Kent or a Kentish maid is difficult to establish, and even local inhabitants cannot tell you accurately on which side of the River Medway you have to be born to claim which title. However, you will probably, though maybe as a novelty at harvest time, produce an Oast Cake, Kentish Apple Cake or even a Biddenden Biscuit. In adjacent Sussex, home of two of our great British institutions – the twentieth-century Glyndebourne

Opera Festival (restorer of the high-quality picnic, without doubt) and the ancient custom in Lewes of lighting massive bonfires and the burning of Papist effigies on November 5th – you *will* be confident of eating a Sussex Pond Pudding in some farmstead or other. Whether the recipe includes the (to me) all-essential seedless raisins in the buttery 'pond' surrounding the pin-pierced lemon in its pastry crust, is a matter for the cook's individual conjecture, but taste it you must. It ranks high as an unusual English speciality.

On the other hand Surrey, perhaps because of its proximity to the capital, offers little in the way of country delights – with two major exceptions. It appears that our fat-breasted capon had its origins here, and we can be sure it was reared for use in the kitchens of the royal palaces of Hampton Court, Nonsuch, Bushey, Kew and Richmond. It is also beyond question that it was from this last palace that the ladies-in-waiting to Henry VIII's various queens were sent along to the local pastry shop in the Kew Road for the light-crusted cheesecakes now known as Maids of Honour Tarts. Newens shop is there to this day baking, so they claim, these tarts to the original recipe. Well worth a taste when next you visit the world's greatest horticultural gardens at Kew, with its elegant hothouses and rare flowering plants, shrubs and trees.

The Home Counties form almost a rural lace collar around the world's most exciting city, London. To William Dunbar, London was 'the flower of cities all'. I wonder what London means to you? Is it a town of humorous East Enders trading in street markets with their attendant food stalls selling saveloys, cockles, mussels and jellied eels? Or a London of music halls and comedians, of pubs with their unique 'island' bars, chased glass windows, gasoliers and red plush banquettes whose clients partake of pie and liquor or a bowl of steaming London Particular? Is your city the 'clearing house of the world', steeped in history, where Christopher Wren's St Paul's is at the fulcrum surrounded by the many fine city churches built before and after the Great Fire, the Guild Halls and courts and the renowned food markets of Smithfield, Billingsgate and Leadenhall? Or do you think of the new-fangled development at Covent Garden, where in Bernard Shaw's imagination Eliza Doolittle was to be found peddling violets under the portico of Inigo Jones's church on the edge of the famous piazza?

The revitalization of this area around the beautiful Opera House in Bow Street is a sight for resident and tourist alike. Food shops abound amid arts and crafts studios, galleries, pubs, restaurants and bistros – though this is hardly the name one would readily apply to these eateries with their strong American-style menus. Where, you may rightly ask, is there a decent honest fish and chip shop or a pies, peas and mash stall? All gone, I fear, in the name of 'progress'. Oh yes, you'll find plenty of glamorous cocktail bars where once stood an honest pub, and hot dogs and hamburgers where once the aforementioned street food would have abounded.

Of course, for many, London is the place for good eating, and there are countless luxurious hotels and chic restaurants, nightclubs and discothèques to serve you, if this is where your purse allows you to be. Winging into the mind come such international names as The Savoy Hotel, built by Richard d'Oyley Carte and on whose board of directors to this day sits a member of that famous family. César Ritz was responsible at the turn of the century for giving London its first steel-framed building, housing the most beautiful dining room in the world overlooking verdant Green Park. High on the list comes my own favourite, The Connaught (always first to serve grouse on the Glorious Twelfth), whose rich-panelled dining room is for the quieter guest who enjoys faultless service. Then comes the Dorchester, now leaping ahead in the *Nouvelle Cuisine* stakes, and elegant Brown's, just as it always was, or the plush new Berkeley with its fashionable bar. Tucked away discreetly in Brook Street is the mecca for princes, Claridges, where legend has it that the staff wear mufflers on their shoes so as not to disturb the kings and queens slumbering in its elegant suites.

For me London is SHOPS: handsome stores such as Harrods with its unique food halls garlanded with exotic vegetables and fruits, stacked with cheeses, jams and butters, pelmets of poultry and game and a veritable mosaic of fish patterning the cool, wet, marble slabs – a three-dimensional still-life. In Jermyn Street it's the festival of silks and poplins in the many gentlemen's outfitters, or following one's nose into the odorous depths of Paxton and Whitfield to purchase the finest English cheese to be found in this country, and the luxury of having it wrapped in brown paper and tied with real waxed string. Then, round the corner, the fabulous jewel of a store, Fortnum and Mason, now three hundred years old and still on the same site. My pound of honeycomb or pot of Gentlemen's Relish will still be served to me under glittering chandeliers by an assistant clad in full morning dress. Outside Fortnums and across the road, through the Burlington

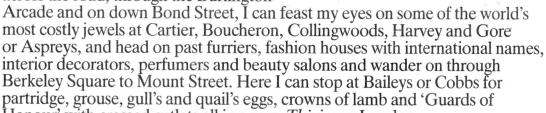

Arcade and on down Bond Street, I can feast my eyes on some of the world's most costly jewels at Cartier, Boucheron, Collingwoods, Harvey and Gore or Aspreys, and head on past furriers, fashion houses with international names, interior decorators, perfumers and beauty salons and wander on through Berkeley Square to Mount Street. Here I can stop at Baileys or Cobbs for partridge, grouse, gull's and quail's eggs, crowns of lamb and 'Guards of Honour' with crossed cutlets all in a row. *This* is my London.

But perhaps for you the fact that London is the hub of the theatre world is its most important aspect? Here your choice is almost limitless, from the *avant garde*, where, crushed into the back room of Islington's Kings Head Theatre or in the Mile End Road you can sit uncomfortably through some thought-provoking new play bound (it is hopefully claimed) for a West End stage, or you may prefer the elegance of the regency Theatre Royal in the Haymarket with a play by Shaw, Ibsen, Sheridan or Chekhov. Or there's the excitement of the South Bank complex, where the National Theatre has its three homes. Difficult as it is to find, the new Barbican Centre is worth the search. Adventurous are the programmes and excellent the acoustics.

How can one give more than a cocktail snack of a taste of this great city in so little space? If New York is The Big Apple, then London is The Big Cake, and there's surely a slice for every one of us.

Soups

Brown Windsor Soup

Serves 8

A thick brown soup that once seemed an indispensable part of the traveller's menu; carefully made, it is both rich and tasty.

8 oz (225 g) shin of beef
8 oz (225 g) mutton
2 oz (50 g) butter
6 oz (175 g) onions, sliced
4 oz (110 g) carrots, sliced
2 oz (50 g) plain flour
4 pt (2.25 l) brown meat stock
faggot of herbs
salt and pepper
$\frac{1}{4}$ pt (150 ml) Madeira
2 oz (50 g) boiled rice (optional)

Cut the meat into 1 in (2.5 cm) cubes. Melt the butter in a pan and fry the meat and vegetables until they are lightly browned. Add the flour and cook until brown. Add the stock gradually, bring to the boil, add the faggot of herbs and simmer for approx 2 hours until the meat is tender. Season, then take out the meat and remove the bones and skin. Return the meat to the soup and rub through a sieve or blend in a liquidizer. Bring the puree back to the pan, add the Madeira, reheat and add the rice if liked. Adjust seasoning and serve hot.

London Particular

Serves 8

This thick green pea soup with bacon, also known as 'London Peculiar', takes its name from the near-impenetrable 'pea-souper' fogs that were once a regular part of winter life in the capital.

2 oz (50 g) bacon, diced
4 oz (110 g) carrots, diced
2 oz (50 g) celery, diced
4 oz (110 g) onions, chopped
1 oz (25 g) butter
1 lb (450 g) split dried peas
4 pt (2.25 l) ham stock
salt and pepper
diced meat to garnish (optional)

Put the bacon, carrots, celery and onions in a saucepan with the butter, cover and cook for 5–10 minutes. Add the peas and cook for 2–3 minutes. Pour the stock over these ingredients, add salt and pepper and bring to the boil, then simmer for 2–3 hours, skimming as necessary. Rub the soup through a coarse sieve or blend in a liquidizer. Return to the pan and heat through; adjust seasoning. Serve hot, with additional diced meat if liked, and sippets of bread.

Watercress Soup

Serves 4

Watercress is widely grown in Hampshire, an area rich in cooling streams.

1 bunch watercress
1 small onion, chopped
1 oz (25 g) butter
8 oz (225 g) potatoes, peeled and sliced
12 fl oz (325 ml) water
10 fl oz (275 ml) milk
salt and pepper
1 tbsp cream or top of milk

Wash the watercress and remove the coarse stalks. Chop the watercress and cook gently with the onion in melted butter for about 7 minutes. Add the sliced potatoes and water and cook till tender. Sieve or liquidize. Add the milk and bring the mixture just to the boil. Cool a little and season well. Stir in the cream. Serve hot.

Fish/Seafood

Amberley Trout

Serves 4

Amberley is on the River Arun in West Sussex, where there is good trout fishing to be had.

4 trout, each approx 12 oz (350 g)
2 oz (50 g) plain flour
salt and pepper
4 oz (110 g) butter
1 tbsp finely chopped parsley
1 tsp finely chopped fresh sage

Clean the trout under a running tap. Keep the heads on. Rinse well and dry. Sieve the flour, salt and pepper together. Dust the fish with this seasoned flour and fry them in 2 oz (50 g) butter until crisp. Drain on kitchen paper. Keep hot in the serving dish. Fry the parsley and sage in the remaining butter. Pour the mixture over the trout and serve at once.

Arundel Mullet

Serves 4

This is a seventeenth-century recipe from West Sussex, traditionally served in soup plates with a supply of bread on hand to mop up the wine sauce.

4 mullet
$\frac{1}{4}$ pt (150 ml) white wine
2 tbsp finely chopped onions
small bunch of fresh herbs
scrape of nutmeg
2 anchovy fillets, chopped
lemon juice
black pepper

Simmer 2 mullet at a time in $\frac{1}{2}$ pt (275 ml) salty water, until cooked. Drain each fish carefully. Keep hot in a serving dish until all 4 are cooked. Take $\frac{1}{4}$ pt (150 ml) of the water and add the white wine, onions, herbs, nutmeg, anchovy fillets, lemon juice and black pepper. Simmer for 15 minutes. Remove the herbs. Pour the sauce over the hot mullet and serve at once.

Lent Pie

Serves 4

A tasty fish pie that you need not feel guilty about eating in Lent.

1 lb (450 g) cod fillet
3 eggs
2 large onions
3–4 potatoes
seasoning and mustard
mushroom ketchup
anchovy essence
2 oz (50 g) butter
4 oz (110 g) shortcrust pastry (see page 252)

Steam and flake the fish, discarding the skin and bones. Hard boil the eggs then slice them. Peel and slice the onions and potatoes. Layer these ingredients in an oven-dish, seasoning to taste and sprinkling a pinch of mustard over each layer. Combine a little mushroom ketchup with anchovy essence, as liked, and mix this into 5 fl oz (150 ml) water. Pour over the fish. Put knobs of butter all over the top and cover with a pastry lid. Bake until the fish is tender (about 1 hour) at 350°F (180°C) Reg 4.

Jellied Eels

Serves 4–6

Eels have always been popular in London, particularly in the East End which is on the estuary side where the eels proliferate.

1½ lb (675 g) eels

seasoning

1 tbsp vinegar

1 medium onion

2 cloves

½ oz (15 g) gelatine

Clean and skin the eels and place in a saucepan with 1½ pt (850 ml) water, salt, pepper, vinegar and the onion with 2 cloves stuck in it. Simmer over a low heat until the eels are tender, then cut the eels into small pieces, removing the bones. Strain ¾ pt (425 ml) of the liquid in which the eels were cooked into a saucepan. Melt the gelatine with a little of the liquid in a bowl over hot water. Add to the liquid and stir well. Put the eels in a bowl or mould. Pour the jelly over them. Set in a cool place overnight. Turn out into a flat dish and serve.

Stewed Thames Eels

Serves 4

2 × 8–12 oz (225–350 g) eels

salt and pepper

4 cloves

2 blades mace

¼ pt (150 ml) beef gravy

2 fl oz (50 ml) port

2 fl oz (50 ml) Madeira

1 oz (25 g) butter

1 oz (25 g) plain flour

2 fillets anchovy

Soak the eels overnight in salt water. Rinse in several clear waters. Clean and skin the eels. Season them well with salt and pepper. Put them in a stewpan with the cloves and mace. Add strong beef gravy, port and Madeira. Cover the stewpan tightly. Stew until tender. Remove the eels and keep them hot in their serving dish. Remove the cloves and mace. Melt the butter in a pan. Stir in the flour, and cook for 1–2 minutes. Slowly add the gravy, stirring all the time. Finely chop the anchovy fillets and add to the thickened gravy. Arrange the eels in their hot dish, and pour the gravy over them. Serve at once.

Meat

Hertfordshire Pork Pie

Serves 4

A dish made at pig-killing time. Instead of the usual hot water crust pastry, this recipe is made with rough puff pastry, using lard from the pig.

1 lb (450 g) rough puff pastry (see page 253)

2 lb (900 g) pork, including the trimmings after the pig has been cut into joints, together with some meat cut from the leg

seasoning

Cut the pork into small pieces and partly cook with a little water and seasoning. Allow to cool. Make the pastry and roll it into 2 rounds about the size of a dinner plate. Place the pork in the middle of the pastry, damp the edges and crimp them together in a pasty shape. Brush with milk and bake at 400°F (200°C) Reg 6 for about 45 minutes. Serve cold with pickles, or hot with vegetables.

Ashdown Partridge Pudding

Serves 6–8

The combination of game and meat is found in the earliest known records. The medieval cook probably discovered that old game birds (too tough for roasting and grilling) became tender and succulent when cooked for hours under a pastry covering. Rabbit and pigeon are equally suitable for this type of steamed game pudding. Ashdown Forest no doubt provided the main ingredient when this recipe was first set down in writing.

1 brace partridge

4 oz (110 g) sliced rump steak

2 lb (900 g) suet crust pastry (see page 253)

4 oz (110 g) sliced mushrooms

$\frac{1}{2}$ tsp finely chopped mixed herbs

$\frac{1}{2}$ tsp finely chopped parsley

salt and pepper

5 fl oz (150 ml) claret

1 pt (575 ml) beef or game stock

Joint each partridge into 4 or 6 portions and dice the beef. Line a 3–4 pt (1.75–2.25 l) pudding basin with two-thirds of the suet pastry. Put the partridge joints and meat into the basin, add the mushrooms, herbs and parsley and season with salt and pepper. Pour in the claret and enough stock to cover the contents. Cover with the remaining pastry and tie down with buttered greaseproof paper and a pudding cloth or foil. Steam for 3 hours.

Berkshire Hog

Serves 6

From the homeland of the eponymous black pig, a dish of chops in wine with sour cream.

1 oz (25 g) butter

1 tbsp oil

6 pork chops

4–8 button onions

1 clove garlic, crushed

$\frac{1}{2}$ pt (275 ml) white wine or stock

bouquet garni

4 oz (110 g) mushrooms

1 tbsp plain flour

$\frac{1}{4}$ pt (150 ml) sour cream

Heat the butter and oil in the pan; add the pork chops and brown lightly. Remove the chops and place them on a plate. Put the onions and garlic in the pan and cook gently until pale gold in colour. Add the wine or stock and return the pork chops to the pan. Add the bouquet garni and seasoning. Bring to the boil, cover with a tightly fitting lid and cook gently for 1 hour. Add the mushrooms and continue cooking for about 15 minutes. Mix the flour with a little of the sour cream, stirring gently to a smooth mixture. Pour this into the pan over the pork (off the heat). Return to the heat and bring back to the boil. Boil for 1–2 minutes to cook the flour; add the rest of the cream, re-season and serve.

Chiddingly Hot Pot
Serves 6

From East Sussex, an all-in-one family stew of shoulder or chuck steak with vegetables and spicy flavours.

2 lb (900 g) stewing steak (shoulder or chuck steak)
seasoned flour
2 oz (50 g) dripping
2 oz (50 g) chopped celery
2 oz (50 g) chopped onion
¼ tsp ground allspice, salt and pepper
8 oz (225 g) sliced potatoes
3 cloves
2 tsp tarragon vinegar
1 oz (25 g) melted butter
¾ pt (425 ml) brown stock

Chop the meat into cubes of about 1 in (2.5 cm) and dust with seasoned flour. Brown the meat in the dripping, remove from the pan and fry the celery and onions lightly. Put a layer of onions and celery in a casserole dish, sprinkle with allspice, salt and pepper; cover with a layer of meat and a thin layer of potatoes. Repeat these layers, adding seasoning and the cloves and vinegar. Finish with a layer of potatoes and brush with melted butter. Add enough stock to come just below the potatoes; cover with a lid. Cook in the oven at 325°F (160°C) Reg 3 for 1½ hours. Remove the lid and continue cooking for another hour to brown the potatoes.

Harvest Rabbit
Serves 2

A reminder that cornfields are no place for rabbits to linger once the harvester comes to whittle their cover away.

1 small rabbit
dripping
3 prunes, stoned and soaked
bunch fresh herbs
seasoned flour
1 large onion
1 thin slice fat bacon
stock
forcemeat balls (see page 21)

Skin, draw and wash the rabbit. Leave in salt water for 15 minutes. Drain, dry and fry until golden brown all over. Drain the rabbit and then stuff under the ribs the well-soaked, stoned prunes and the bunch of fresh herbs. Coat with seasoned flour. Cover the bottom of a deep pie-dish with the sliced onion. Lay the rabbit and slices of bacon on top. Cover with stock and bake slowly for 2 hours at 300°F (150°C) Reg 2. Make the forcemeat balls, bind them with the egg and fry until deep brown. Serve the rabbit on a hot dish garnished with onions and plenty of large forcemeat balls. Serve strained gravy separately.

Buckinghamshire Rabbit Pie

Serves 4

2 lb (900 g) rabbit, jointed

bouquet garni

1 onion, stuck with 3–4 cloves

salt and pepper

2 oz (50 g) short cut macaroni

2 oz (50 g) onion, finely chopped

2 oz (50 g) grated Cheddar Cheese

1 tsp dried thyme

$\frac{1}{2}$ pt (275 ml) double cream

8 oz (225 g) puff pastry (see page 253)

Soak the rabbit in cold salted water and cover for 1 hour or more. Drain. Cover with fresh water and bring to the boil; skim and add bouquet garni, onion stuck with cloves, $\frac{1}{2}$ tsp salt and a few peppercorns or milled pepper. Cover and simmer gently for $1\frac{1}{4}$–$1\frac{1}{2}$ hours until the rabbit is tender. Remove the joints and strain the stock into another saucepan. Cut all the meat off the bones. Heat the stock again. Drop the macaroni into boiling stock and boil until tender. Drain the macaroni and mix with the rabbit meat, chopped onion, cheese and thyme. Season to taste with salt and pepper and pack into a 2 pt (1.2 l) pie-dish with a funnel or egg cup in the centre. Pour the cream over it.

Make the pastry, roll it out and cut a narrow band out of it. Brush the edge of the dish with cold water and press the band of pastry on it. Brush that also with water and cover the whole dish with the pastry. Trim round the edges and pinch them. Cut slits in the centre to allow the steam to escape; brush all over with beaten egg or milk and bake at 425°F (220°C) Reg 7 for 35–40 minutes until nicely browned.

Sussex Huffed Chicken Breasts

Serves 4

'Huff crust' describes a very old way of making a flour-and-water crust which is wrapped round meat, as clay was in still earlier times, and baked. The word turns up in various guises, among them 'hough' and 'haugh'.

4 chicken breasts

1 lb (450 g) suet crust pastry (see page 253)

Stuffing

4 oz (110 g) dried prunes

4 oz (110 g) cooking apples, peeled, cored and chopped

2 small onions, chopped

1 oz (25 g) breadcrumbs

a little lemon rind

salt and pepper

beaten egg to bind

Mix the stuffing ingredients with a little egg to bind. Make a pocket in the chicken breasts and fill this with the mixture. Make the pastry and roll it out. Divide it in two and wrap the pastry around each chicken breast to make a parcel. Brush with beaten egg. Bake on a baking sheet at 400°F (200°C) Reg 6 for 30–40 minutes.

Bacon Badger

Serves 4-6

First and foremost a suet pudding, this dish can be prepared by steaming in a pudding basin or by boiling in a cloth.

8 oz (225 g) suet crust pastry (see page 253)
1 lb (450 g) bacon
1 large potato
1 onion
$\frac{1}{2}$ tsp dried sage
pepper

Roll the pastry out into a rectangle. Prepare the bacon, chop it with the potato and onion. Spread this mixture over the pastry to within $\frac{1}{2}$ in (1 cm) of the edge. Season with the sage and pepper. Damp the edges. Roll up firmly, pressing the edges well together. Tie in a floured cloth, leaving room for expansion, put into boiling water and boil steadily for $2\frac{1}{2}$-3 hours, topping up the pan with boiling water when necessary. Unwrap. Serve on a hot dish with gravy and a green vegetable. Alternatively, steam in a basin for the same length of time.

Aylesbury Game Pie

Serves 6

A rich pie from the fringes of hunting country.

12 oz (350 g) shortcrust pastry (see page 252)
4 pigeons
$\frac{1}{2}$ oz (15 g) butter
1 small onion, finely chopped
1 glass sherry
2 oz (50 g) salt belly pork
3 oz (75 g) fresh white breadcrumbs
8 oz (225 g) minced beef or veal
2 tsp chopped fresh parsley or herbs

Make the pastry, and put to chill. Brown the pigeons slowly in butter in a casserole. Take them out and cut away the back carcase, leaving the breasts whole. Add the onion to the casserole, cook for 1 minute and then replace the breasts. Flame with the sherry, season and lay the carcases back on top. Cover and cook slowly for 40-50 minutes, then cool.

Meanwhile, simmer the pork (start in cold water) until tender, then bone and chop (or mince coarsely). Turn the pork into a bowl with the breadcrumbs and the beef or veal, season and moisten with juice from the pigeons. Cut the meat from the pigeon breasts. Line a spring form mould or tin with some of the shortcrust pastry. Fill with the meat and breadcrumb mixture, layering it with the pigeon meat. The top layer should be the breadcrumb mixture. Cover with the pastry, brush with egg and bake for about 1 hour at 400°F (200°C) Reg 6. When the pastry is brown, lower the oven heat to 350°F (180°C) Reg 4 and complete the cooking (about 30 minutes).

Pigeons in Pimlico
Serves 6

This is a modern version of a recipe dated 1800. The original contained truffles and morels (mushrooms).
It is a complicated recipe, but is absolutely delicious.

4 oz (110 g) puff pastry (see page 253)

4 prepared pigeons

4 oz (110 g) dripping

4 slices veal escallop

8 rashers streaky bacon

Stuffing

4 pigeon livers

6 oz (175 g) open cap mushrooms

1 small onion

2 tbsp chopped parsley

1 tsp mixed herbs

pinch powdered mace

8 oz (225 g) fresh brown breadcrumbs

1 egg

seasoning

Ragoût (in this recipe, a stew of mushrooms)

6 oz (175 g) open cap mushrooms

1 tbsp chopped parsley

1 pt (575 ml) good rich stock

2 tbsp butter

2 tbsp beurre manié (butter and flour worked together)

Make 8 small tartlets from the puff pastry and bake at 450°F (230°C) Reg 8 for 15–20 minutes. Turn the oven down to 400°F (200°C) Reg 6 ready for the pigeons. Put the tartlets aside. Spread the pigeons with dripping.

To make the stuffing, chop the livers and mushrooms together with the onion. Stir in the parsley, herbs, mace and breadcrumbs. Bind with the egg and season to taste. Stuff the pigeons with this mixture, reserving 8 tsp for the tartlets.

Beat out the veal and wrap a piece around each pigeon. Wrap 2 bacon rashers, carefully rinded and with any bone removed, around the veal (joins underneath). Wrap each pigeon in foil and roast at 400°F (200°C) Reg 6 for 1 hour. Check at 40 minutes as they may be done (poke with a carving fork). Put the reserved stuffing into the tartlets and put into the oven for the last 5 minutes of cooking.

To make the ragoût, sizzle the mushrooms in butter. Add the stock. Work in the beurre manié, stirring all the time. Simmer for 1–2 minutes until the ragoût thickens. Put the pigeons in a serving dish. Pour the ragoût over them. Serve with the tartlets around the pigeons.

Sussex Cheese and Potato Cakes

Makes 8

12 oz (350 g) mashed potato
2 oz (50 g) butter
2 oz (50 g) Cheddar Cheese
2 oz (50 g) plain flour
1 tsp dry mustard
2 oz (50 g) minced cooked ham (optional)
1 egg, beaten

Beat the butter into the potato. Stir in the cheese, mustard and flour and minced cooked ham if liked. Beat the egg into the mixture. Season well. Drop spoonfuls of the mixture on a well greased hot griddle or heavy frying pan. Cook, turning once, for 10 minutes – 5 minutes each side – or bake at 400°F (200°C) Reg 6 for 15 minutes. Minced cooked ham can be added to the mixture. Serve hot.

Sussex Fritters

Serves 4

8 oz (225 g) cold boiled potatoes
2 oz (50 g) butter
4 oz (110 g) minced cooked ham
1 tbsp parsley, finely chopped
seasoning
2 eggs
2 oz (50 g) fresh brown breadcrumbs

Mash the potatoes with the butter. Mix in the ham, parsley and seasoning. Beat the egg into the mixture. Shape into small balls. Beat the second egg well. Put the breadcrumbs on a plate. Pass the balls through the egg. Roll them in breadcrumbs and fry. Serve very hot.

Hampshire Haslet

Serves 6

'Haslet' comes from the Old French hastelet, *meaning entrails or innards, and here refers to the finely chopped or minced mixture of pork, bread, sage and onion.*

8 oz (225 g) stale white bread
2 lb (900 g) fairly lean pork, coarsely minced
1 small onion, chopped
1 tsp sage
1 tsp salt
½ tsp pepper

Cut the bread into cubes and soak in milk or water to cover. When soft, squeeze the excess moisture out and add the bread to the meat, onion, sage and seasonings. Mix well. Mince them all together through a fine plate. Grease a large loaf tin. Shape the mixture into oblongs and fill the tin. Bake at 375°F (190°C) Reg 5 for about 1½ hours until well done. (Pork needs to be well cooked and no longer pink.) Serve cold with salad.

Buckinghamshire Dumpling

Serves 6

The word is a diminutive form of 'dumpy', a word coined in the mid-eighteenth century for something dumpy in shape.

1 lb (450 g) flour
6 oz (150 g) suet
2 large onions, grated
2 tsp chopped sage
8 oz (225 g) fat bacon, cut into strips
8 oz (225 g) liver, cut small
salt and pepper to taste

Mix the flour and suet into a stiff dough, adding a little salt. Roll out on to a floured surface. Cover the dough with the small pieces of liver and bacon, the onion, sage and seasonings. Roll up tightly in floured cloth and boil for about $2\frac{1}{2}$ hours. Serve with a good brown gravy.

Spinach with Cream and Eggs

Serves 4

This is a modern version of a recipe credited to William Verral of Lewes in 1759.

2 lb (900 g) spinach
2 oz (50 g) butter
$\frac{1}{2}$ pt (275 ml) single cream
1 oz (25 g) plain flour
seasoning
scrape of nutmeg
1 medium onion
4 eggs

Wash the spinach in several waters. Strain. Cook carefully with just the water clinging to the leaves and 1 oz (25 g) of the butter. When tender, drain and chop finely. Put the spinach into a pan with the cream, the rest of the butter and the flour, and cook over a very low heat (the cream will curdle if it is overheated). Stir gently to blend all the ingredients. Taste and season. Add a scrape of nutmeg. Put the skinned whole onion into the pan. Put the lid on and leave for 10 minutes over the same very low heat. Hard boil the eggs. Remove the onion from the pan. Put the creamy spinach on a hot serving dish and garnish with hot sliced hard-boiled eggs.

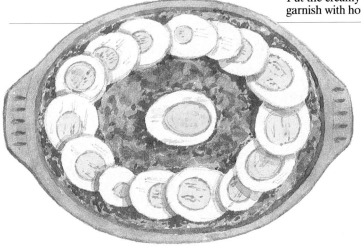

Boodle's Orange Fool

Serves 4

A tempting dessert from the famous London club.

grated rind and juice of 4 large oranges

grated rind and juice of 2 lemons

2 tbsp caster sugar

6 sponge cakes

1 pt (575 ml) single cream

Mix the grated rinds together. Squeeze the juice of all the fruit, sweeten to taste, and mix together. Extra sugar may be needed, as oranges vary in sweetness. Cut the sponge cakes into 4 and place the pieces in the bottom of the serving dish. Pour the cream into the fruit juice and rind, stirring very lightly. Then pour the mixture over the sponge and leave for at least 2 hours. Decorate with extra cream if desired.

Stone Cream

Serves 6

½ pt (275 ml) double cream

whites of 2 eggs

½ pt (275 ml) milk

1 oz (25 g) sugar

2 drops vanilla essence

3 tsp gelatine

jam

nuts, preserved ginger or cherries to decorate

Whip the cream. Whip the egg whites until fairly stiff. Mix with the cream. Add the milk, vanilla and sugar. Dissolve the gelatine in 2 tbsp water in a bowl over a pan of hot water. Pour in a thin stream into the mixture. Put some jam in the bottom of 6 small dishes; pour the cream mixture over, and leave to set. Decorate according to taste.

Solid Syllabub

Serves 4

A sherry syllabub, based on a recipe of 1854 from Bowcombe in the Isle of Wight.

½ pt (275 ml) sherry

rind and juice of 1 lemon

4 oz (110 g) loaf sugar

1 pt (575 ml) double cream

a little grated nutmeg

Put the sherry into a bowl. Grate the rind and squeeze the juice of the lemon over the loaf sugar. Add this to the sherry. Stir until the sugar has dissolved. Whip the cream. Fold lightly into the sherry. Spoon into glasses, and serve with just a little grated nutmeg on top.

Christmas Cheesecake

Serves 10

Two very British ideas are here married together in a modern recipe.

6 oz (175 g) sweet shortcrust pastry (see page 252)
6 oz (175 g) mincemeat
8 oz (225 g) cottage cheese
2 oz (50 g) caster sugar
$\frac{1}{4}$ pt (150 ml) evaporated milk
2 eggs, separated
grated rind and juice of 1 orange
icing sugar to decorate

Make the pastry and line one 8 in (20 cm) and one 5 in (13 cm) flan ring. Cover the bases with a layer of mincemeat. Sieve or liquidize the cottage cheese. Beat into the cottage cheese the orange rind and juice, the sugar, evaporated milk and egg yolks. Whisk the egg whites stiffly and fold them into the mixture. Pour over the mincemeat and bake at 375°F (190°C) Reg 5 for 40–45 minutes or until the filling is set. Cool. Decorate with sieved icing sugar and a sprig of holly.

Chichester Pudding

Serves 4

The wealthy always used to eat white bread thinking it was purer than wholemeal. Unfortunately the poorer people believed it to be true and they too gave up their wholemeal flour. This recipe dates from the period when white bread was considered best.

4 slices white bread
2 eggs, separated
2 oz (50 g) caster sugar
9 fl oz (250 ml) milk
grated rind and juice of 1 large lemon

Butter an oven dish well. Cut the crusts off the bread and make into breadcrumbs (not too fine). Beat the egg yolks with the sugar and milk. Add the breadcrumbs, grated rind and juice of the lemon. Whisk the whites until soft and fold into the mixture. Turn into the dish. Bake at 350°F (180°C) Reg 4 for 35–40 minutes until set and well risen. This is best served like a soufflé, straight from the oven. When cut, it is marbled yellow and white.

Chiltern Hills Pudding

Serves 4–6

4 oz (110 g) seed tapioca
$\frac{1}{4}$ pt (150 ml) milk
4 oz (110 g) suet
4 oz (110 g) raisins
1 tsp bicarbonate of soda, dissolved in a little milk
4 oz (110 g) breadcrumbs
3 oz (75 g) sugar

Soak the tapioca in the milk for 2 hours. Mix the suet with the raisins. Dissolve the bicarbonate of soda in a little milk and add to the tapioca, with the other ingredients. Beat well. Put in a greased pudding basin, cover with greaseproof paper or foil and steam for 3 hours.

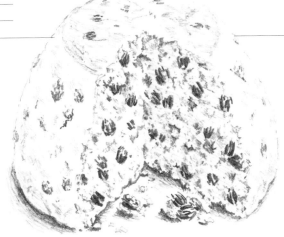

Sussex Pond Pudding

Serves 6–8

This pudding is so called because the luscious buttery mixture flows out into a 'pond' when the pudding is turned out and cut.

8 oz (225 g) suet crust pastry (see page 253)

2 oz (50 g) seedless raisins or sultanas

2 oz (50 g) currants

4 oz (110 g) demerara sugar

1 large, juicy, thin-skinned lemon

4 oz (110 g) unsalted butter

Make the pastry, adding 1 tsp grated lemon rind to the dough. Well butter a $2\frac{1}{2}$ pt (1.5 l) pudding basin. Line with the pastry, reserving about one-third of it for the lid. To make the filling, mix the dried fruit and sugar together in a bowl. Prick the lemon all over with a bodkin. Cut the refrigerator-hard butter into small cubes. Disperse half of this with half the fruit and sugar into the lined basin. Press the lemon into the centre of this, then pack the remaining ingredients around it. The basin should be full. Wet the pastry edges, fit the lid and seal well. Cover with buttered foil, making a pleat across the top to allow the crust to rise. Steam for $2\frac{1}{2}$ hours.

Sussex Apple Pie

Serves 6

1 lb (450 g) spiced shortcrust pastry (see page 252)

8 oz (225 g) cooking apples, peeled, cored and sliced

2 oz (50 g) currants

2 oz (50 g) raisins

2 oz (50 g) sugar

1 tsp ground cinnamon

1 tsp mixed spice

2 tbsp water

Make the pastry. Roll out two-thirds of it and line an 8 in (20 cm) flan ring set on a baking sheet. Arrange layers of apples, currants and raisins over the pastry base, sprinkling each layer with the sugar mixed with the cinnamon and spice. Spoon over the water, cover with the remaining pastry and bake for 45 minutes at 425°F (220°C) Reg 7 for 10–15 minutes, and then at 350°F (180°C) Reg 4 for a further 30 minutes.

Lord John Russell's Pudding

Serves 8

This iced pudding is based on a recipe from Rusley Lodge, Esher, dated 1863. It is a nineteenth-century version of an Italian Cassata or French Bombe.

6 egg yolks

$1\frac{1}{2}$ pt (850 ml) milk

2 oz (50 g) caster sugar

grated rind of 1 lemon

$\frac{1}{2}$ oz (15 g) gelatine

$\frac{1}{2}$ pt (275 ml) single cream

2 tbsp brandy

2 drops almond essence (not 'flavouring')

3 tbsp mixed peel

2 oz (50 g) glacé cherries, cut in half

Beat the egg yolks into the milk; add the sugar and grated rind of the lemon. Heat in a bowl over hot water, stirring all the time until the mixture thickens so that it firmly coats the back of a spoon. Take off the heat. Dissolve the gelatine in 2 tbsp water in a bowl over hot water. Pour into the custard in a thin stream. Stir in the cream, the brandy and the almond essence. Fold in the mixed peel and glacé cherries. Pour into a 3-4 pt (1.75–2.25 l) bowl and cover tightly. Put in the freezer. Take out after 2 hours and beat well with a wooden spoon to break down the ice crystals. (Do not use an electric beater.) Return to the freezer for 3–4 hours or until needed.

Note:
An ice-cream maker can be used.

Cherry Suet Pudding

Serves 4–6

4 oz (110 g) suet crust pastry (see page 253)	Make the pastry. Stir the cherries into the mixture and put into a greased 1½ pt (850 ml) pudding basin. Cover with greaseproof paper or foil and boil for 2½ hours. Serve with sugar.
2 large handfuls black cherries, pitted	

Note:
Gooseberries can be used instead of cherries, in which case serve with golden syrup and custard or cream.

Bucks Cherry Turnovers

Serves 4

8 oz (225 g) shortcrust pastry (see page 252)	Make the pastry. Divide the dough, cherries and sugar into 4 equal parts. Roll out the dough into 4 circles and place the cherries and sugar on each. Moisten the edges of the pastry with water and draw the edges of each circle together. Crimp firmly together to hold in the juice, keeping the join along the top. Place on a baking tray and bake at 450°F (230°C) Reg 8 for 20 minutes. Reduce the heat to 350°F (180°C) Reg 4 for a further 20 minutes.
8 oz (225 g) small black cherries, pitted	
4 oz (110 g) sugar	

Hunt Pudding

Serves 6–8

A welcome filler after a winter's day spent chasing the inedible.

8 oz (225 g) plain flour	Sift the flour, baking powder and spices together. Add the sugar, suet, raisins and milk and blend thoroughly. Put the pudding mixture in a floured cloth. Tie the ends securely, leaving room for expansion, and boil for 2½–3 hours. Serve, if liked, with melted redcurrant jelly poured over the pudding.
2 tsp baking powder	
1 tsp mixed spice	
3 oz (75 g) caster sugar	
4 oz (110 g) suet, finely chopped or shredded	
6 oz (175 g) raisins	
¼ pt (150 ml) milk	
8 oz (225 g) redcurrant jelly (optional)	

Friar's Omelet

Serves 4–6

4 cooking apples, peeled, cored and sliced

2 oz (50 g) sugar

2 oz (50 g) butter

grated rind and juice of $\frac{1}{2}$ lemon

1 egg

2 oz (50 g) breadcrumbs

Stew the apples with the sugar, 1 oz (25 g) of the butter, and the rind and juice of $\frac{1}{2}$ lemon until tender. Stir in the well-beaten egg. Put half the breadcrumbs at the bottom of a buttered pie-dish. Pour in the apple mixture and cover with the rest of the breadcrumbs. Dot the remaining butter on top and bake at 350°F (180°C) Reg 4 for 15 minutes.

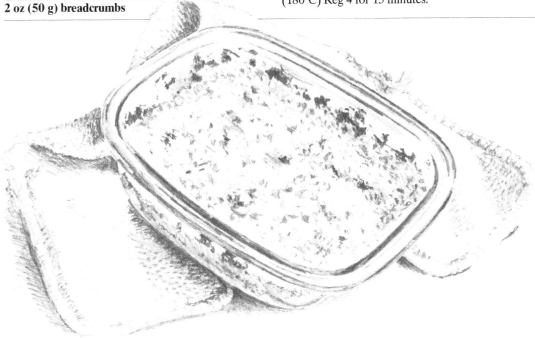

Cakes, Breads and Biscuits

Maids of Honour Tarts

Makes 6–8

These famous cheesecakes, a speciality of Kew, Surrey, are made from a sixteenth-century recipe. This one is from Hampton Court Palace. They were said to have been a favourite delicacy of Anne Boleyn, the name being given to them by Henry VIII when he saw her eating them while she was a Maid of Honour to Catherine of Aragon, Henry's first wife.

8 oz (225 g) puff pastry (see page 253)
1 pt (575 ml) fresh milk
1 tsp rennet
pinch salt
4 oz (110 g) butter
2 egg yolks
2 tsp brandy
$\frac{1}{2}$ oz (15 g) sweet almonds
a little sugar
a little ground cinnamon
rind and juice of $\frac{1}{2}$ lemon
currants to decorate

Make the pastry. Warm the milk to blood heat. Add the rennet and the salt. When the curds have set, drain through a fine muslin overnight. Rub the curds through a sieve with the butter. Beat the yolks of the eggs to a froth with the brandy. Add to the curds. Blanch and chop the almonds and add them to the curds with a little sugar and cinnamon. Add the rind and juice of $\frac{1}{2}$ lemon. Line patty tins with puff pastry. Fill them with the mixture and sprinkle with currants. Bake in the oven at 425°F (220°C) Reg 7 for 20–25 minutes, or until well risen and golden brown.

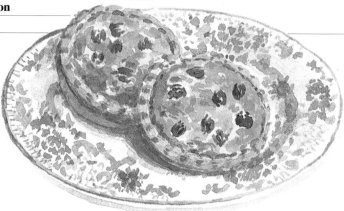

Kent Flead Cakes

Makes 20

Flead, flaire or flare is the fat lining the abdominal wall and running up round the kidneys of a pig. It is from the flead that the best lard is obtained. In other counties, such as Hampshire, it is known as 'veil'. Flead is not now easy to obtain but suet may be used as a substitute.

1 lb (450 g) plain flour
7 oz (200 g) flead
2 oz (50 g) butter
pinch salt
cold water

Remove the skin from the flead and shred it as thin as possible into the flour, sifted with the salt. Moisten with sufficient cold water to work into a smooth paste. Lay the paste on a board and beat with a heavy rolling pin until the flead is perfectly blended with the flour. Roll it out and add the butter in small pieces; fold it once and roll it out for use to a thickness of $\frac{3}{4}$ in (2 cm). Cut into small diamond-shaped pieces, about 2×2 in (5×5 cm). Bake in the oven at 425°F (220°C) Reg 7 for 20 minutes.

Beer Cake

The quantities below will make a reduced-size version of a gigantic Victorian fruit cake designed to fill families of a dozen or more.

5 oz (150 g) butter
8 oz (225 g) sugar
$\frac{1}{4}$ pt (150 ml) old ale or draught beer
12 oz (350 g) plain flour
8 oz (225 g) currants
2 oz (50 g) candied peel
1 tsp baking powder
pinch nutmeg or mace
$\frac{1}{2}$ tsp salt
2 small eggs

Cream the butter and sugar together. Add the beer. Mix the dry ingredients together and add to the mixture. Mix well. Beat the eggs, and add to the mixture. Grease and line a 7 in (18 cm) baking tin. Pour in the mixture and bake for 3 hours or more at 325°F (160°C) Reg 3 for 1½–2 hours.

Chelsea Buns

Makes 12

These tea cakes, a cross between a bread and a bun, were made as a treat for Pensioners at the Royal Hospital.

10 oz (275 g) plain flour
3 oz (75 g) butter
3½ oz (85 g) caster sugar
$\frac{1}{2}$ oz (15 g) fresh yeast
$\frac{1}{4}$ pt (150 ml) milk (sour if possible)
2 large eggs
2 oz (50 g) currants
large pinch mixed spice

Warm the flour and sift into a warm basin. Rub in half the butter roughly, and add half the sugar. Cream the yeast with 1 tsp of the sugar; warm the milk to blood heat, pour it on to the beaten eggs and add all the yeast. Pour into the centre of the flour, beat well, and allow to rise for 1¼–1½ hours, until the dough doubles its bulk. Turn out on a floured board, knead lightly to shape, and roll out to a square with a rolling pin. Spread with the remainder of the butter and sprinkle with some of the sugar; fold up. Roll out again thinly and sprinkle with the remaining sugar, the currants and the spice. Roll up with the hands as for a Swiss roll. Cut off 12 slices about 1½ in (4 cm) thick, and stand them close together on a well-greased warmed tin, with the cut side downwards. Allow to prove for 15–20 minutes. Sprinkle with sugar and bake in the oven at 450°F (230°C) Reg 8 for about 20 minutes.

Wigs

Makes approx 24

These were eaten at the Kattern and Tandra Festivals in north Bedfordshire. Wigs in this context are wedges (from the Middle English wigge*), because they were cut in wedges from the round – and not, as some will have it, because they curl over the edge of the tin and look like wigs.*

1 lb (450 g) treacle	Put the treacle in a pan. Add the butter and melt gently. Stir in the cold milk. Take off the heat and sift in the flour; do this slowly, stirring all the time to prevent it going lumpy. Add the sugar, bicarbonate of soda, ginger and caraway seeds. Pour into three 7–8 in (18–20 cm) well-greased sandwich tins. Bake at 350°F (180°C) Reg 4 for about 40 minutes, or until a skewer comes out clean.
4 oz (110 g) butter	
$\frac{1}{4}$ pt (150 ml) milk	
1 lb (450 g) plain flour	
3 oz (75 g) caster sugar	
1 tsp bicarbonate of soda	
2 tsp ground ginger	
$\frac{1}{2}$ oz (15 g) caraway seeds	

Brighton Rocks

Makes 20–25

A South Coast member of the craggy rock cake/bun family.

4 oz (110 g) butter	Cream the butter and sugar. Work in the ground almonds and currants. Add the flour with the beaten eggs and rose water. Mix to a stiff dough. Form into small balls and place on greased baking trays. Glaze with a little beaten egg. Bake at 425°F (220°C) Reg 7 for about 7 minutes.
4 oz (110 g) caster sugar	
2 oz (50 g) ground almonds	
2 oz (50 g) currants	
8 oz (225 g) plain flour	
2 eggs, beaten	
1 tsp rose water	
egg to glaze (save a little from the mixture)	

Brighton Buns

Makes 12–16

4 oz (110 g) butter	Cream the butter and sugar until white and fluffy. Add the beaten egg. Sift the flour. Fold lightly into the mixture. Fold in the almonds. Make into rocky heaps on a greased baking tray using a dessertspoon. Bake at 425°F (220°C) Reg 7 for about 15 minutes, until the buns are a warm honey-brown.
4 oz (110 g) sugar	
1 egg	
8 oz (225 g) plain flour	
2 oz (50 g) ground almonds	
$\frac{1}{2}$ oz (15 g) bitter almonds	

St Albans (Father Rocliff's) Buns or Hot Cross Buns or Pope Lady Cakes

Makes 12

Pope Ladies or Nuns obviously take their name from their shape; at least one source has it that Pope Lady means the Virgin Mary; another has it that the buns were named after the fictional Popess Joan of the ninth century. Father Rocliff was a fourteenth-century monk who introduced the custom of giving a small spiced cake to the poor of St Albans on Good Friday, in addition to their usual basin of soup.

1 lb (450 g) strong plain flour

½ tsp salt

2–3 tsp mixed spice

1 oz (25 g) fresh yeast

3 oz (75 g) sugar

4 oz (110 g) butter

milk to mix

2 eggs

6 oz (175 g) dried fruit

2 oz (50 g) candied peel

currants to decorate

2 tbsp granulated sugar to glaze

3 tbsp milk to glaze

Sift together the flour, salt and spices. Cream the fresh yeast with 1 tsp sugar and 1 tbsp milk. Leave to froth. Rub the butter into the flour mixture. Pour the frothy yeast and 2 beaten eggs into the mixture, with about ¼ pt (150 ml) milk to make a dough. Beat and knead well until the dough is smooth and the basin and hands are clean. Cover the basin and stand in a warm place until the dough has doubled in size. Beat in the remaining sugar and fruit and knead again until smooth. Divide the dough into 12 equal pieces. Shape into 'Pope Ladies' (see drawing) and use currants to represent the eyes. Place on greased tins and allow to rise again until double in size. Alternatively, shape into buns and before putting in the oven, make a really deep cross on each with a sharp knife dipped in oil. The oil keeps a faint division in the dough. Bake at 450°F (230°C) Reg 8 for about 15 minutes. Glaze with sticky bun glaze (2 tbsp granulated sugar dissolved in 3 tbsp milk). Return to oven for 3 minutes.

Hampshire Drops

Makes 30

4 oz (110 g) butter

4 oz (110 g) caster sugar

1 egg

4 oz (110 g) self-raising flour

4 oz (110 g) cornflour

a little raspberry jam

Cream the butter and sugar together until white and fluffy. Add the well beaten egg. Sift the flours together and fold gently into the mixture. Put teaspoonfuls, spaced well apart, on to non-stick baking paper on a baking tray. Bake at 350°F (180°C) Reg 4 for about 10 minutes. Cool on a wire tray. Sandwich well together with raspberry jam.

Kent Oast Cakes
Makes 18–20

8 oz (225 g) plain flour
3 oz (75 g) butter or lard
pinch salt
1 tsp baking powder
1 oz (25 g) sugar
3 oz (75 g) currants
1 tsp lemon juice
5 tbsp water

Sieve together the flour, salt and baking powder. Rub in 2 oz (50 g) butter or lard, add the sugar and currants and mix to a soft dough with the lemon juice and water. Shape with the fingers into small pieces and roll into $\frac{1}{4}$ in (5 mm) rounds on a floured board. Fry on both sides in the remaining butter or lard, adding a little at a time until golden brown (about 6–8 minutes). Eat hot instead of scones for tea.

Sussex Plum Heavies
Makes approx 20

$1\frac{1}{4}$ lb (550 g) butter
$1\frac{1}{2}$ lb (675 g) self-raising flour
8 oz (25 g) currants
$2\frac{1}{2}$ tbsp caster sugar
$\frac{1}{2}$ pt (275 ml) water

Rub 6 oz (175 g) butter into the flour and make it into a stiff dough with cold water, having added the currants and sugar. Roll it out on a floured board. Take another 6 oz (175 g) butter and spread it in knobs over the dough. Flour it and fold it up, then roll out again. Repeat this twice using the remaining butter. Roll out the dough to a rectangle 1 in (2.5 cm) thick and score the surface to make a diamond pattern. Brush over with milk and bake on a tray at 400°F (200°C) Reg 6 for 45 minutes. Divide into pieces. Eat fresh or store in an airtight container for later use. They will keep for several weeks.

Muffins

Makes 8

1 lb (450 g) strong plain flour
1 tsp salt
$\frac{1}{2}$ oz (15 g) fresh yeast or $\frac{1}{4}$ oz (7 g) dried yeast
1 tsp sugar
$\frac{1}{2}$ pt (275 ml) lukewarm water
plain flour or fine semolina

Sieve the flour and salt into a bowl. Mix the fresh yeast with the sugar and add to the water (or sprinkle dried yeast on the water with the sugar and leave till frothy). Add to the flour and mix well. Knead to a firm dough. Cover and leave to rise for 1 hour. Knead lightly again and roll out on floured board to $\frac{1}{2}$ in (1 cm) thick. Cover and leave to stand for 5 minutes. Cut into 3 in (7.5 cm) rounds. Place on a well-floured baking sheet and dust the tops with flour or fine semolina (this gives a golden and slightly crisp finish). Cover and leave to rise for 40 minutes. Cook on a hot greased griddle or in a thick frying pan for about 6 minutes each side until golden brown or bake for 10 minutes at 450°F (230°C) Reg 8, turning after 5 minutes. To serve, pull the muffins open all the way round, leaving the halves joined in the middle. Toast on both sides, then pull apart and butter. Put together again and serve hot.

Gipsy Bread

10 oz (275 g) self-raising flour
pinch salt
pinch mixed spice
4 oz (110 g) soft brown sugar
6 oz (175 g) sultanas
$\frac{1}{2}$ tsp ground ginger
2 oz (50 g) chopped peel
6 oz (175 g) black treacle
1 tbsp milk
1 egg
$\frac{1}{4}$ tsp bicarbonate of soda, dissolved in 2 tsp milk

Grease a 2 lb (900 g) loaf tin. Mix the dry ingredients. Warm the treacle with the milk. Add the egg and whisk the mixture. Dissolve the bicarbonate of soda in 2 tsp of milk, and add to the mixture. Mix well and pour into the tin. Bake at 350°F (180°C) Reg 4 for about 45 minutes. Reduce the heat to 325°F (160°C) Reg 3 for 30 minutes more. Cool in the tin for 10 minutes. Eat sliced, spread with butter.

Sussex Oaty Slices

8 oz (225 g) soft margarine	Cream the margarine and sugar well. Add the honey and marmalade, then stir in the oats. Press the mixture into a greased Swiss Roll tin, and smooth the top. Bake at 325°F (160°C) Reg 3 for 30–35 minutes. Leave to cool in the tin for 10 minutes. Cut into fingers or squares.
8 oz (225 g) soft brown sugar	
2 heaped tbsp thick marmalade	
2 tbsp clear honey	
14 oz (400 g) rolled oats	

Wholemeal Fruit Scones
Makes 18

8 oz (225 g) plain wholemeal flour	Stir together the flour, baking powder and spice. Rub in the fat until the mixture is like fine breadcrumbs. Stir in the sugar and fruit. Mix with the milk and egg to a soft dough. Roll out on a lightly floured board $\frac{3}{4}$ in (2 cm) thick. Cut into rounds and place close together on a greased baking sheet. Bake for 15 minutes at 425°F (220°C) Reg 7. Cool on a wire rack.
3 tsp baking powder	
1 tsp ground mixed spice	
4 oz (110 g) butter or margarine	
1 oz (25 g) light soft brown sugar	
4 oz (110 g) mixed dried fruit	
$\frac{1}{4}$ pt (150 ml) milk	
1 egg	

Almond Slices

6 oz (175 g) shortcrust pastry (see page 252)	Roll out the pastry and use to line an oblong or square flat baking tin. Mix the icing sugar, ground almonds and semolina. Add 1 egg yolk, the almond essence and a little water to bind the mixture. Beat 2 egg whites, add the caster sugar and continue beating. Fold into the almond mixture, and spread on the pastry. Sprinkle with flaked almonds. Bake at 300°F (150°C) Reg 2 for 30 minutes. Cut into fingers when cold.
4 oz (110 g) icing sugar	
4 oz (110 g) ground almonds	
2 oz (50 g) semolina	
2 eggs, separated	
a few drops almond essence	
a little water	
a few flaked almonds	

Sussex Honey Bread
Makes 1 × 1 lb (450 g) loaf

6 oz (175 g) plain flour	Sieve the flour into a bowl. Stir in the sugar, soda, spice and salt. Rub in the margarine. Beat the egg and honey together with the water and beat into the dry mixture. Add the currants or sultanas. Put into a greased and lined 1 lb (450 g) loaf tin. Bake for 1 hour at 350°F (180°C) Reg 4. Cool on a wire rack.
3 oz (75 g) demerara sugar	
1 tsp bicarbonate of soda	
1 tsp mixed spice	
pinch salt	
1 oz (25 g) margarine	
3 oz (75 g) clear honey	
1 egg	
$\frac{1}{4}$ pt (150 ml) water	
2 oz (50 g) currants or sultanas	

Kent Huffkins

Makes 8

1½ lb (675 g) strong plain flour

1½ tsp salt

2 oz (50 g) lard

½ oz (15 g) fresh yeast or ¼ oz (7 g) dried yeast

1 tsp sugar

¾ pt (450 ml) milk and water

Sieve the flour and salt into a bowl and rub in the lard until the mixture is like fine breadcrumbs. Mix the fresh yeast and sugar and add to the lukewarm milk and water (or sprinkle the dried yeast on the liquid with the sugar and leave until frothy). Add to the flour and mix to a soft dough. Knead, cover and leave to rise for 1 hour. Knead well and divide mixture into 8 pieces. Form each piece into a ball and roll out 1 in (2.5 cm) thick. Put on a greased baking sheet, cover and prove for 20 minutes. Press each piece of dough firmly in the centre with a floured thumb. Bake for 20 minutes at 450°F (230°C) Reg 8, turning the huffkins over half-way through baking. Wrap in a clean tea towel while cooling so that they remain soft.

East of England

My first impression of East Anglia was the quality of the light – a pale, soft, silvery gold. It is not difficult to understand how Constable and Gainsborough,

having been born within half a century of each other under the same 'sweet circle' of East Anglian sky, came to fall under its magic. It is also important to know that in spite of Constable's portrayals of cloudy skies and rain-drenched landscapes, this eastern hump of land records the lowest rainfall in the whole of Britain.

A rapid tour of this part of England might well start in Colchester, the oldest registered town in Britain and still the home of oysters and other shellfish. Perhaps it was the excellent quality of these native molluscs that made Old King Cole such a merry old soul! It is a happy thought, though I fear the price charged today for the aphrodisiac oyster is well beyond the reach of most of us, and I doubt whether one would light upon a hostelry offering an oyster stew, unless perhaps it be in Orford. Elsewhere you might, if lucky, find the odd oyster slipped into a steak and kidney pie – but I hazard you would need to be *very* lucky, for this delightful habit has died with the shooting skywards of the price of oysters. It's hard to believe that at one time a pint of them could be bought for a mere penny, and that it was common to serve one's traditional turkey with oyster sauce.

A Dunmow Flitch is also a thing of the past, apart from the ceremonial award on Whit Monday of a flitch, or side of bacon, to the married couple who can prove that they have not quarrelled or (quaint official term) 'repented' their marriage for one year and a day. Today's housewife, ignoring her annual prospects at Dunmow, prefers to buy her bacon pre-packed and wrapped in the supermarket.

It seems but a pace from Roman Colchester to Ipswich and then along the coast with its attractive inlets and rivers and tiny fishing ports. There is still a good variety of smoked fish to be had in painterly Orford, where a bowl of stewed eel in a delectable, delicate parsley'd sauce is one of the delights of the Orford Oysterage. This coastal village, of course, was the inspiration for Benjamin Britten's *Peter Grimes* and *Curlew River*, though Aldeburgh is probably the town which first comes to mind when our most famous twentieth-century composer is given a fleeting thought. Although this is not an area remarkable for regional dishes, you may be lucky and light upon an Epping Sausage or a helping of Colchester Pudding.

The seaports of Lowestoft and Great Yarmouth were at one time known for grand fleets of trawlers and smacks which brought in immense catches of herring, bloaters, mackerel, cod and haddock, yet no regional dishes appear to be fish-based, and whilst the herring was kippered in abundance, it is not of this area that we think when the succulent kipper is a breakfast-time prospect. (I always think of British Rail, for they do cook a good kipper in the Breakfast Car!).

Inland only a few miles, and Norfolk offers us one of Britain's most beautiful cities – Norwich. The fifteenth-century spire of its magnificent Norman Cathedral, built from stone brought over from Caen in France, soars over this gem of a city which has more than thirty parish churches for the enthusiast of ecclesiastical architecture to feast his mind and eyes upon. Centuries ago this city offered 24 of its special spiced eel pies to the King as a form of rent. I doubt if there's an eel pie to be found today!

Between Norwich and the sea come the whispering reeds of an area to which devotees return year after year – the Norfolk Broads. Here is provided an unique network of waterways for boating and sailing enthusiasts, and as you leave Norwich heading along the northern coast for Kings Lynn, you may well decide to abide awhile and gather samphire in the shallow sandy waters. Samphire, or poor man's asparagus, is gathered in slim short spears and is still eaten with melted butter  in that part of the country and pickled for winter use in some of the old farmsteads. Were you to travel inland, vast panels of yellow, rimmed with poppies, stretch to the horizons to delight the eye: this is mustard, and not to be confused with fields of rape cultivated for cattle-feed and the making of rape seed oil.

Round the corner of the Wash, Lincolnshire, once England's second largest county, slots readily alongside its cousins in East Anglia. In an area bounded by Horncastle, Louth and Spilsby, nothing much has changed since Tennyson's childhood days there at the beginning of the nineteenth century. Flat as far as the eye can see, it's here in New Holland that much of our table produce is grown: potatoes, peas, beans, lettuces, cucumbers – in fact, all those vegetables which appear most regularly on our menus. There is a timelessness about Lincolnshire villages and hamlets. Ancient remains have emerged from

Bronze Age long barrows, Iron Age hill forts, Roman roads and remains of medieval villages deserted in Tudor times. The city of Lincoln, the setting for our most handsome medieval cathedral, also has evidence of earlier days in its Norman bridge and intact Roman arch.

The Romans linked East Anglia to their Northern capital city, Eboracum (York), with a sophisticated system of canals traversing Lincolnshire en route. It is here – in Grantham with its special Gingerbread and high-spired parish church – that a luscious slice of Stuffed Chine can be found in any self-respecting butcher's shop. Deep slashes are cut into a chine of pork or bacon and an abundance of parsley and other herbs are crammed into the gashes before the meat is simmered to a succulent turn. Eaten cold with a crisp salad it is one of the underestimated delights of the English table. It is a wonder to me that this recipe hasn't been fully developed to rival its French relative and counterpart, *Jambon Persillé*, but such are the conservative ways of our countrymen. Change is slow, even when for the better.

Back down to Cambridgeshire, to find the home of the Burn't Cream at Trinity College in the university city. It is said that students used searing hot salamanders, or branding irons, to mark these rich custards by imposing a caramel symbol on their sugary tops. Many people would argue that a good Cambridge Sausage is the best that money can buy, and they're probably right, particularly when served with a spoonful of Cambridge Sauce and a wedge of light Cambridge Tart to follow.

Travelling through the southern part of Cambridgeshire brings the traveller back into Essex, passing through Saffron Walden. There can be few English towns that have retained the medieval street layout as distinctly as here. Dating from the Neolithic and Bronze Ages, Saffron Walden thrived in the Middle Ages through the wool trade, the Dutch weavers having spread their influence from the Suffolk town of Lavenham. The crop of saffron predominant at that time gave its name to the town and was used primarily as a dye, then as a medicine, before folk realized it had a culinary use, flavouring such delights as Saffron Cake, or a savoury custard or cream.

Today as you reach what is also one of the most distant stations on London Transport's Central Line, it is hard to imagine that Epping was once a bustling East Anglian market town, complete with a Butter Market and its attendant cross, supplying London with its favourite butter. Much of the capital's butter came from Essex and Suffolk, where the grazing was good and the cows had browsed the fresh young grass, their milk yielding rich, golden butter – albeit the colour was often helped with the addition of marigold petals or even carrot juice.

So there you have it. The East of England, too flat for many, a fertile nursery of artistic, agricultural and academic skills for others, a verdant land which produces much of our butter and milk, our plump ducklings, turkey and pigs. It is one of the gardens of England.

Soups

Spring Soup
Serves 4–5

An early nineteenth-century recipe from Cambridge that features, among other herbs,
purslane, more frequently used in those days as a salad and pot-herb.

1 lb (450 g) frozen small peas
3 large onions
1 medium lettuce
4 tbsp parsley, sorrel, chervil, purslane (freshly chopped and mixed)
1 oz (25g) butter
seasoning
3 egg yolks, beaten
½ pt (275 ml) milk

Prepare the vegetables, chop the herbs and put all in a pan with butter for a few minutes. Turn, using a spoon, and cook until the onion is soft and golden brown. Barely cover with approx ½ pt (275 ml) warm water, season, and cook until tender (about 3 minutes). Strain off the liquid and mix a little of it with the well-beaten eggs and milk. Heat this, stirring continuously until it thickens. Sieve the vegetables into the remaining liquid, re-heat and add the milk mixture, stirring constantly; do not boil again.

Westerfield White Soup
Serves 4–5

This recipe was collected in Ipswich. The original was dated 1876 and described as 'an
excellent and nourishing dish which is particularly suitable for invalids'.

1 lb (450 g) veal bones and pieces
2 pt (1.2 l) water
1 small onion
4 peppercorns
salt to taste
⅛ blade mace
¼ pt (150 ml) cream (or top of milk)
3 tsp arrowroot (approx)
1 oz (25 g) vermicelli

Wash the bones and pieces of veal; place them in a large saucepan with the water. Bring them to the boil and simmer very gently with the onion, salt, peppercorns and mace until the liquid is reduced by one-third. This will take 3–4 hours; Then strain the soup and set it aside to cool. When it is cold, skim off the fat and return the soup to a clean saucepan, add the cream and when it boils thicken it with the arrowroot mixed with a little cold milk. Just before serving add 1 oz (25 g) vermicelli which has been boiled in slightly salted water and well drained.

Gravy Soup
Serves 3–4

8 oz (225 g) lean beef shin, cut into cubes
8 oz (225 g) gammon of bacon, cut into cubes
1 large carrot, chopped
1 large onion, chopped
3 sticks celery, chopped
pepper and salt

Put the meat and bacon in a saucepan. Wash and add the chopped vegetables, cover with cold water and bring slowly to the boil. Simmer for 2–3 hours. Then strain and put the meat on one side (it can be used for meat loaf). Rub the vegetables through a sieve or liquidize them and add to the soup. Season well and serve very hot.

Fish/Seafood

Aldeburgh Sprats

Aldeburgh has long been noted for its sprats and at one time the first catch of the season was always sent to London for the Lord Mayor's banquet.

3–4 oz (75–110 g) sprats (per person – as a starter) fine oatmeal to dust salt	Wash the sprats well, draw them and dust with fine oatmeal. Sprinkle a frying pan with salt, heat it and then put the sprats in and fry until golden brown. No fat should be added as the salt draws the fat from the fish.

Eel Pie

Serves 4–6

Eels formed a large part of the economy of East Anglia for many years, and rents for land might be paid to the church or state in 'booklets of eels'.

8 oz (225 g) rough puff pastry (see page 253) 2 lb (900 g) eel 2 oz (50 g) plain flour salt and pepper 2–3 tbsp oil or 2 oz (50 g) butter 1 onion, chopped 2 tsp chopped herbs (fennel, tarragon, parsley) 1 tbsp lemon rind, grated juice of 1 lemon 1 glass sherry or white wine $\frac{1}{4}$ pt (150 ml) single cream (or top of milk) 1–2 eggs, hard-boiled	Make the pastry. Cut the eel into 2 in (5 cm) pieces. Dip these in flour seasoned with salt and pepper and fry lightly until browned. Drain. Fry the onion in the butter or oil. Add seasoned flour which is left over (approx 2 tsp), the chopped herbs, the lemon rind and juice and the sherry or white wine. Season this sauce and stir in the cream or milk. Put the eel into a 2 pt (1.2 l) pie-dish; strain over the sauce. Put sliced hard-boiled egg over the eel and cover with a pastry top. Decorate with pastry leaves, glaze and bake at 425°F (220°C) Reg 7 for 20 minutes, reducing temperature to 350°F (180°C) Reg 4 for 30–40 minutes.

Southend Whitebait

Serves 4

Whitebait are the 'fry' of young herring and sprat and are best eaten between March and August. Until recently you could buy whitebait on the sea front at Southend and eat them like fish and chips.

1 lb (450 g) whitebait 2 oz (50 g) plain flour salt and pepper fat for deep-frying 1 lemon, cut into wedges	Wash and dry the whitebait. Toss lightly in flour seasoned with salt and pepper and fry in deep fat; drain well, return to the basket and fry crisp in very hot fat. Drain and serve sprinkled with salt and decorated with lemon wedges. Eat with brown bread and butter.

Note:
Whitebait can also be baked in the oven or grilled.

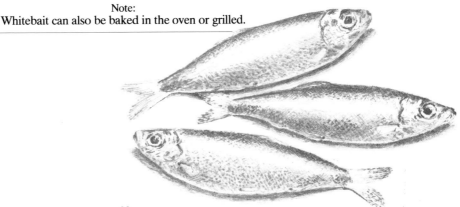

Meat

Suffolk Oysters
Serves 4

This Suffolk Hot Pot, though rather pricey to assemble, is both tasty and filling.

1½ lb (700 g) casserole steak

2 oz (50 g) dripping

2 sheep's kidneys

12 or more oysters

1 small onion

1 oz (25 g) plain flour (approx)

1 pt (575 ml) hot water

1½ lb (700 g) potatoes (approx)

seasoning

Cut the steak into thin pieces ½ in (1 cm) thick. Fry them brown in a little of the dripping. Put in the bottom of a casserole. Skin and slice the kidneys and arrange on top of the steak. Fill in round the meat with the oysters. Slice and fry the onion in the meat dripping. Sprinkle with flour and cook until brown. Add 1 pt (575 ml) of hot water and any liquor from the oysters and bring to the boil to thicken slightly. Fill the casserole with thickly-sliced potatoes and pour the gravy and onion over. Season. Cover and bake for 1½ hours at 350°F (180°C) Reg 4. Remove the lid and brown the potatoes for 20–30 minutes. Serve direct from the casserole.

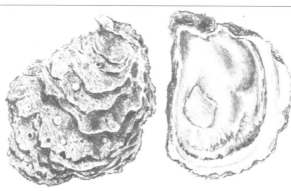

Boston Royal Swan Pie
Serves 3–4

We do not know for certain whether this pie was originally made from swan flesh, or whether it was named after a local inn where it was the speciality of the house. Probably the latter, because royal swans are chiefly associated with the River Thames. One very old set of instructions makes no mention of swans. It begins as follows: 'Take the flesshe of fatte hen, pound it well and add to it the same amount of pork, fat and leane and halfe the weighte both of gammon and of pigges liver – to them adde half a cuppe of anchovy pounded in a mortar with ginger and green herbes.' Such a large quantity, as well as the laborious method, are unsuitable for these days, but the modern version tastes just as good. If you have the time to cut off raw chicken meat, this improves the taste a great deal.

4 oz (110 g) pig liver

8 oz (225 g) chicken meat (raw or cooked)

8 oz (225 g) belly pork

4 oz (110 g) gammon

1½ oz (40 g) fine white breadcrumbs

¼ pt (150 ml) cream

2 tsp anchovy essence

good pinch each of chervil, thyme, rosemary, ground ginger, ground allspice

salt and pepper

8 oz (225 g) shortcrust pastry (see page 252)

Blanch the liver by pouring boiling water over it. Cut all the meat into pieces and mince together. To this add the fine white breadcrumbs soaked in the cream, the anchovy essence and the herbs and spices. Mix together thoroughly, season with salt and pepper and let it rest in a cool place for 1–2 hours before making into a pie or pies. Make the pastry, then place the meat mixture in a 1½ pt (850 ml) pie-dish and cover with the pastry. Bake at 400°F (200°C) Reg 6 for 20 minutes.

Norfolk Pork Cheese
Serves 6–8

The word 'cheese' is here used to describe the texture or consistency of this pork dish which is served in bowls.

1 salt pork hock with trotter
pepper
powdered sage or finely chopped fresh sage

Simmer the hock in enough water to cover for about 1½ hours or until the meat falls off the bones. Cut the meat into pieces and toss lightly in the pepper and sage. Put the bones back in the liquid and boil them until the stock is reduced to about ½ pt (275 ml). Strain the liquid over the meat, mix well and put into bowls. When cold and beginning to set like jelly, mix again and pack into bowls. Cover and place light weights on top until fully set.

Norfolk Stew and Norfolk Dumplings (Autumn Rabbit)
Serves 4

The ubiquitous East Anglian rabbit is here put to good use in alliance with tasty dumplings.

Norfolk Stew

1 rabbit, jointed
1 oz (25 g) dripping
1 oz (25 g) plain flour
½ pt (275 ml) ale
1 onion, sliced
1 carrot, sliced
2 oz (50 g) mushrooms, sliced
2 eating apples, peeled, cored and sliced
thyme, parsley, bay leaves
salt and pepper

Norfolk Dumplings

6 oz (175 g) self-raising flour
⅓ tsp salt
¼ tsp pepper
milk/water to mix

To make the stew, clean and wipe the rabbit joints and fry in the dripping until golden brown. Remove the joints to a casserole; stir the flour into the hot fat in the pan, then add the ale. Simmer for a few minutes, then pour over the rabbit and add the onion, carrot, mushrooms, apples, herbs and seasoning. Cover and cook for 1¼–2 hours at 350°F (180°C) Reg 4.

To make the dumplings, mix the flour and seasonings with enough water to make a stiff dough. Divide into portions and cook on top of the rabbit for the last 20 minutes of the cooking time.

Huntingdon Fidget Pie

Serves 4

The name of the dish probably derives from 'fitchet', meaning brindled, as in Fitchet-cat.

1 lb (450 g) streaky bacon

8 oz (225 g) onions, chopped

1 lb (450 g) cooking apples, peeled, cored and chopped

seasoning

$\frac{1}{4}$ pt (150 ml) cider

8 oz (225 g) shortcrust pastry (see page 252)

1 egg, beaten, to glaze

Remove the rind from the bacon and dice it. Mix the bacon, onions and apples together and season. Put into a 2 pt (1.2 l) pie-dish and pour over the cider. Make the pastry. Roll it out and cover the pie. Make four cuts out from the centre about 3 in (7.5 cm) long. Fold back triangles of pastry to expose the filling. Roll out trimmings and cut out crescents using a fluted cutter. Brush with beaten egg and place round the edge of the pastry. Brush the pie with egg and bake at 450°F (220°C) Reg 7 for 20 minutes and then lower the heat to 350°F (180°C) Reg 4 for 30 minutes until the pastry is crisp and golden.

Hen On Her Nest

Serves 6

A nineteenth-century farmhouse recipe that looks quite spectacular when served.

1 boiling fowl, 3–4 lb (1.4–1.8 kg)

2 onions, sliced

2 carrots, sliced

1 tsp ground ginger

1 tsp black peppercorns

pinch dried mixed herbs

pinch salt

3 oz (75 g) butter

12 oz (350 g) long grain rice

4–6 eggs, hard-boiled

2 oz (50 g) plain flour

$\frac{1}{4}$ pt (150 ml) chicken stock or milk

$\frac{1}{4}$ pt (150 ml) double cream

Place the chicken in a large saucepan with the carrots, onions, spices and herbs. Add enough water to cover the fowl. Salt well and bring to the boil. Cover and simmer for 2–2$\frac{1}{2}$ hours depending on the weight of the chicken. When cooked, transfer the chicken to a baking tin, spread 1 oz (25 g) butter over the skin and put into an oven at 400°F (200°C) Reg 6 for 10 minutes to brown. Keep warm. Cook the rice in salted water and hard boil the eggs. Melt the remaining butter in a separate pan, add the flour and make a roux and gradually add the chicken stock or milk, stirring over a low heat. Finally stir in the cream and season. Arrange the cooked rice on a flat dish. Place the chicken in the centre and tuck the shelled eggs underneath. Pour a little of the sauce over the bird; serve the remainder separately.

Old Norfolk Partridge Stew

Serves 4

East Anglia is very much partridge country and this recipe makes a welcome change from the roasting which these birds generally receive.

1 brace partridges	
2 oz (50 g) oil or dripping	
1 or 2 slices lean ham	
1 clove garlic	
1 tomato	
6 small mushrooms	
4 cloves	
6 peppercorns	
salt	
water or stock	
1 glass port (optional)	
2 oz (50 g) plain flour	
2–8 slices toast to garnish	

Cut up the birds into joints or halves, fry in a little oil or dripping, then put them into a stew-pan with the slices of ham, clove of garlic, tomato, mushrooms, cloves, peppercorns, salt and enough water or stock to cover them. A glass of port may be added if desired. Simmer the birds very slowly for 2 hours. Serve them on a dish, heaped up, surrounded by the gravy, which has been freed from fat, thickened with the flour and made very hot. Garnish the dish with triangles of toast.

Pigeon Pie

Serves 6

Formerly known as Rook Pie, this dish was prepared annually on 14 May for the maids at the start of their holiday.

8 oz (225 g) rough puff pastry (see page 253)	
6 pigeons	
1 lb (450 g) braising steak	
1 oz (25 g) flour	
pepper and salt	
1 oz (25 g) butter	
1 pt (575 ml) warm water	
3 eggs, hard-boiled	
$\frac{1}{2}$ oz (15 g) gelatine	
1 onion, chopped	
thyme and parsley, chopped	

Make the pastry. Skin the pigeons. Cut into neat joints and cut the steak into pieces. Toss in seasoned flour and fry in butter until golden brown. Add warm water and simmer for $1\frac{1}{2}$ hours. Put the meat and eggs into a $1\frac{1}{2}$ pt (850 ml) pie-dish. (If the meat is removed from the bones, more can be packed into the pie-dish.) Dissolve the gelatine in a little water over a bowl of very hot water. Add in a thin stream to the gravy, stirring all the time. Add the chopped onion and herbs. Pour over the meat. When cold, cover with pastry. Bake for 30 minutes at 425°F (220°C) Reg 7. Serve cold.

Norfolk Rabbit Pie

Serves 4

1 × 2–$2\frac{1}{2}$ lb (900 g–1.1 kg) rabbit, jointed	
$\frac{1}{2}$ onion, chopped	
salt and pepper	
4 eggs, hard-boiled	
8 oz (225 g) rough puff pastry (see page 253)	

Cook the rabbit, onion, salt and pepper in enough water to cover until the rabbit is tender. Allow to cool, then remove the flesh from the bones. Place the flesh in a $1\frac{1}{2}$ pt (850 ml) pie-dish. Place the hard-boiled eggs in the dish and enough juice from the rabbit to come halfway up the pie-dish. Make the rough puff pastry. Roll it out and cover the pie-dish. Cook for 25–30 minutes at 425°F (220°C) Reg 7 until the pastry is cooked and brown.

Note:
A large rabbit will require a larger pie-dish.

Oxtail Brawn

Serves 6

1 oxtail
plain flour to dust
1 oz (25 g) butter
1 onion
3 cloves
1 bunch mixed herbs
salt and pepper
2 tbsp vinegar
1 egg, hard-boiled

Wash the oxtail, cut it into joints, dry it well and flour it. Melt the butter in a saucepan and fry the oxtail, turning it until it is brown all over. Add the onion (stuck with 3 cloves), the herbs, seasonings and the vinegar and cover with cold water. Bring to the boil and simmer for 3–4 hours or longer until the meat leaves the bones. When it has cooled a little, chop the meat and put it into a mould previously well buttered and decorated with sliced hard-boiled egg. Return the bones to the saucepan and boil rapidly until the stock is reduced to $\frac{1}{2}$ pt (275 ml). Cool slightly and fill the mould with it. When very cold, turn out on to crisp lettuce leaves and serve with potato salad (see, for a change, Ipswich Poet's Potato Salad, in the section on Savouries).

Lincolnshire Stuffed Chine

Pork chine was very popular in the eighteenth century. It was thought then that pork came into season at Bartholomewtide and remained good until Lady Day. Sometimes known as Neck of Chine Bacon, it is now a purely local cut and is taken from the back of a fat pig, cuts being made on either side of the bone. The joints of meat on the bone are then called chines. If you are unable to obtain a chine you can use a shoulder of bacon.

In Rosemary Ruddle's Rutland Recipes the author reports that a Mrs Smith of Hambledon described the dish to her in this way: 'It was a tradition that it was served in farmhouses (together with rook pie) during May Week, ie the first week in May when the farmhouse servants were on holiday. Unmarried farmworkers used to have this week's holiday too, when they attended May Fair and changed jobs, shepherds wearing a tuft of wool in their caps, waggoners two or three ears of corn, etc. Stuffed Chine was also served at christenings – each of my four children were christened traditionally, though this didn't happen annually as it used to in Victorian times!'

1 pork chine (or shoulder of bacon) soaked for 12 hours
several sprigs parsley
several sprigs mint
a few lettuce leaves
1 nettle
3 or 4 spring onions (including green part)
celery (optional)
1 leaf from a rose bush
1 or 2 dandelion leaves
sage

Weigh the chine and soak it for 12 hours in cold water. Wipe it dry. To make the stuffing, mince all the remaining ingredients. Score the chine deeply and stuff it with the mixture, pressing it well down into the cuts. Sew a cloth round it (or just tie it tightly in a cloth, as for a suet roll). Boil it, allowing 30 minutes for the first pound (450 g) and 15 minutes for each pound thereafter. Serve cold with vinegar. It can be eaten with a salad and has a fine, sharp, prickly flavour.

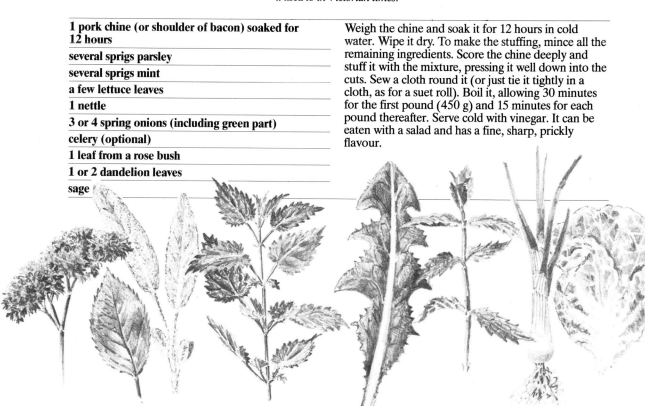

Lincolnshire Potato Cheesecake

Serves 4–6

From the heart of a great potato-growing region, here is a filling variation on the cheesecake theme.

6 oz (175 g) shortcrust pastry (see page 252)
8 oz (225 g) hot mashed potatoes
salt
pinch nutmeg (optional)
4 oz (110 g) softened butter
4 oz (110 g) caster sugar
2 eggs, beaten
grated rind and juice of 1 lemon

Cook the potatoes (steamed or pressure-cooked are best). While they are cooking, make the pastry and roll it out on a floured board. Line an 8 in (20 cm) flan ring on a baking tray. Prick the base and leave to rest. To make the filling, sieve the potatoes with the salt and nutmeg. Add the butter, sugar, eggs and grated lemon rind and juice; beat together well. Fill the flan case almost to the top. Bake on the middle shelf at 400°F (200°C) Reg 6 for 15 minutes. Remove the flan ring and bake for 10 minutes until the filling is set and browning on top.

Ipswich Poet's Potato Salad

This rhyming recipe was found written on a yellowed sheet of paper between the papers of an old cookery book bought at a Saxmundham auction. Chilled and garnished with the chopped egg whites, tomatoes and watercress, it makes a delightful and unusual salad. In the previous section we suggested trying it with Oxtail Brawn.

2 large potatoes
1 tsp mustard
2 tsp salt
3 tsp olive oil
1 tsp vinegar
2 egg yolks, hard-boiled
1 clove garlic
1 tsp anchovy

Two large potatoes passed through the kitchen sieve
Unwanted softness to the salad give.
Of mordant mustard add a single spoon –
Distrust this condiment which bites so soon.
But deem it not, good cook, a fault
To add a double quantity of salt.
Three times the spoon with oil of olive fill,
But once with vinegar, for more will kill
Its true flavour. And now your poet begs
Add pounded yolks of two hard-boiled eggs.
Let garlic clove be rubbed around the bowl
And scarcely suspected, animate the whole.
And lastly in this flavoured compound toss
A magic teaspoon of anchovy sauce.

Yarmouth Straws

Makes 36 (approx)

This recipe has close parallels with the group of French Dartois *recipes, and especially with* Dartois aux Anchois *in which anchovies are wrapped in cheese pastry.*

8 oz (225 g) shortcrust pastry (see page 252)
2 oz (50 g) grated Cheddar Cheese
8 oz (225 g) kipper fillets
cayenne pepper

Make the pastry and roll it to a thickness of $\frac{1}{4}$ in (5 mm). Sprinkle half the cheese and a shaking of cayenne pepper over the pastry. Fold in three and roll out again. Shake over the rest of the cheese and fold in three. Roll out $\frac{1}{8}$ in (3 mm) thick. Cut into strips about 3 in (7.5 cm) long and $\frac{1}{4}$ in (5 mm) wide. Divide the kippers into strips the same size. Put a strip of kipper and pastry together and twist them round each other, joining the ends well. Bake at 375°F (190°C) Reg 5 for 20 minutes.

Epping Sausages

Serves 4

Epping and sausages have a long association which may go back to the Middle Ages, when the monks of Waltham Abbey grazed their pigs in Epping Forest.

1 lb (450 g) fresh belly of pork, boned
12 oz (325 g) butcher's suet or beef dripping
salt and pepper
pinch sage
pinch thyme
grated rind of 1 lemon
pinch nutmeg
1 egg, beaten

Wash the pork, mince it twice, put it into a large bowl and mix with all but 1 oz (25 g) of the suet or dripping. Put this remainder into a large frying pan and heat gently until the suet or dripping melts (remove the membranes from the melted suet). Leave the fat in the pan. Season the pork with salt and pepper; add the sage, thyme, lemon rind and nutmeg. Add the egg to the pork mixture. Beat well using a wooden spoon until smooth. Divide the mixture into 8 portions and roll each into a sausage shape. Re-heat the suet or dripping. Fry the sausages gently for 15–20 minutes, turning frequently until golden and well cooked. Drain on absorbent paper. Serve hot or cold.

Norfolk Treacle Custard Tart

Serves 4-6

4 oz (125 g) shortcrust pastry (see page 252)	Make the pastry. Roll it out thinly and line an 8 in (20 cm) metal plate. Prick the base and leave to rest. Warm the syrup and the lemon rind in a saucepan. Cut the butter into small pieces and stir into the syrup until it has melted. Beat the cream and egg together and blend into the syrup. Pour into the pastry case. Bake in the centre of the oven at 375°F (190°C) Reg 5 for 20–25 minutes until the pastry is crisp and the filling set. Allow to shrink before removing and slide on to a serving plate. Serve hot or cold.
4 tbsp golden syrup	
1 tsp finely grated lemon rind	
$\frac{1}{2}$ oz (15 g) butter	
2 tbsp single cream	
1 large egg, beaten	

Million Pie (Norfolk Marrow Tart)

Serves 4-5

This was a great favourite in the days when, until quite recently, marrow was considered a fruit rather than a vegetable. Currants or raisins were sometimes added to the filling. Another version was simply made with marrow slices cooked with sugar, raisins and water in a pie-dish until tender, then covered with a pastry crust and baked until golden. The word 'million' is a local name for marrow.

8 oz (225 g) shortcrust pastry (see page 252)	Make the pastry and line a 7 in (18 cm) sponge sandwich tin with the pastry, keeping the trimmings for decoration. Spread with jam. Boil the marrow until soft and drain in a colander to remove all the liquid. Leave until cold and beat in the egg, nutmeg and sugar. Put into the flan and sprinkle a little more nutmeg on top. Decorate with strips of reserved pastry. Bake at 400°F (200°C) Reg 6 for 10 minutes, then at 350°F (180°C) Reg 4 for 20 minutes until golden. Serve hot or cold.
2 oz (50 g) jam	
1 lb (450 g) prepared vegetable marrow (peeled and seeded)	
1 egg	
pinch ground nutmeg	
$1\frac{1}{2}$ tbsp sugar	

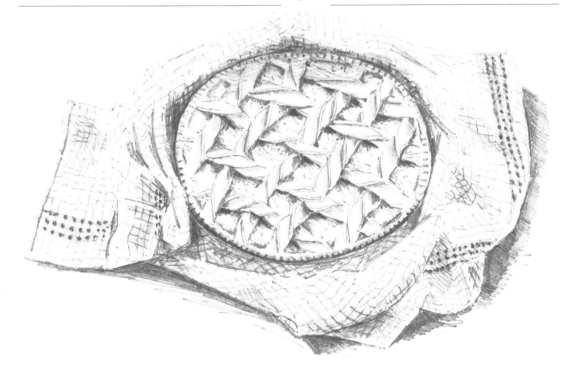

Norfolk Bread Pudding

Serves 4–6

8 oz (225 g) bread scraps (crusts as well)	Soak the bread in water until soft. Squeeze out until quite dry. Mix together all the ingredients. Place in a bowl and beat with a fork. Grease a 1½ pt (850 ml) pie-dish with margarine or butter. Press the mixture into the dish. Dot with margarine or butter. Cook for 1 hour at 375°F (190°C) Reg 5.
4 oz (110 g) suet	
2 oz (50 g) soft brown sugar	
4 oz (110 g) currants	
nutmeg and spices	
grated lemon rind	
2 oz (50 g) margarine or butter	

Felixstowe Tart

Serves 6–8

This fifty-year-old family recipe can be used with other seasonal fruit fillings, or jam.

1½ lb (675 g) Bramley apples with sugar to taste	Cook the apples with a little water and sugar to taste. Leave to cool. Rub the butter into the flours. Add the sugar and baking powder. Add the yolks of the eggs and mix. Roll out on to a 10 in (25 cm) ovenproof tart plate. Prick the base and crimp the outer edge with a fork. Bake for 20 minutes at 350°F (180°C) Reg 4 until golden brown. Leave to cool. Pile the cooked apple (when cold) on to the centre of the tart leaving a 1½–2 in (4–5 cm) border uncovered.
3 oz (75 g) butter or margarine	
4 oz (110 g) plain flour	
4 oz (110 g) cornflour	
3 oz (75 g) sugar, plus 3 oz (75 g) caster sugar	
1 tsp baking powder	
2 eggs, separated	

Whip the whites of the eggs with 3 oz (75 g) caster sugar to a stiff meringue. Cover the whole tart with this meringue. Bake at 275°F (140°C) Reg 1 until the meringue is set and slightly browned. Serve hot or cold with cream.

Lincolnshire Curd Tart

Serves 6–8

This is a Lincolnshire version of the seventeenth- and eighteenth-century cheesecake, made with spices.

6 oz (175 g) shortcrust pastry (see page 252)	Make the pastry and line a 9–10 in (23–25 cm) flan ring. Set the oven at 375°F (190°C) Reg 5. Choose one of the alternatives listed and mix the ingredients together in the given order. Pour into the pastry case. Bake for 30 minutes until risen and slightly browned. Bring to the table quickly while still risen.
10 oz (275 g) cottage cheese	
3 oz (75 g) double cream or melted butter	
3 egg yolks	
either 4 oz (110 g) sugar, 1 generous tbsp wholemeal breadcrumbs, and cinnamon to taste	
or nutmeg to taste, salt, freshly ground pepper and 3 egg whites, stiffly beaten	

Lincoln Tart
Serves 4-6

4 oz (110 g) shortcrust pastry (see page 252)

2 oz (50 g) margarine

1 rounded tbsp golden syrup

4 oz (110 g) desiccated coconut

1 egg, beaten

1 rounded tbsp raspberry jam

Make the pastry. Roll out and line a 7 in (18 cm) flan ring set on a baking sheet. To make the filling, put the margarine, sugar and syrup into a saucepan and stir over a low heat until melted. Add the coconut and egg and mix well. Spread the jam in the base of the flan case, spread the coconut mixture on top and bake in the centre of the oven at 400°F (200°C) Reg 6 for 15 minutes. Reduce the temperature to 350°F (180°C) Reg 4 for a further 15-20 minutes or until the filling has set. Cover the top with foil if the mixture becomes too brown. Serve warm or cold.

Cambridge Gooseberry Pudding
Serves 4-6

4 oz (110 g) puff pastry (see page 253)

1 lb (450 g) green gooseberries

$\frac{1}{4}$ pt (150 ml) water

2 oz (50 g) brown sugar

1 oz (25 g) butter

grated rind of $\frac{1}{2}$ lemon

1 egg, separated

sugar to taste

1 stale sponge cake, made into crumbs

1 tbsp caster sugar

Make the puff pastry. Top and tail the gooseberries and put into a pan with the brown sugar and water. Cover and stand on the edge of the stove to cook slowly. When tender, press through a sieve (or liquidize) and stir in the butter, grated lemon rind and a well-beaten egg yolk. Add sugar to taste and a stale sponge cake made into crumbs. Blend well. Line an 8 in (20 cm) pie plate or flan ring with the puff pastry. Place the mixture on the pastry. Bake for 25 minutes at 400°F (200°C) Reg 6. Meanwhile, beat the egg white until stiff and dry; fold in the caster sugar. Cover the pudding with this meringue and return to the oven for 5 minutes to brown.

Colchester Pudding
Serves 6-8

$\frac{3}{4}$ pt (425 ml) stewed fruit

1 pt (575 ml) milk

rind of 1 lemon, thinly peeled

2 oz (50 g) tapioca

$4\frac{1}{2}$ oz (115 g) caster sugar

$\frac{1}{4}$ tsp vanilla essence

$\frac{1}{2}$ pt (275 ml) custard (see page 23)

2 egg whites

cochineal

Put a layer of any stewed fruit in a glass dish. Put the milk in a saucepan; add the thinly peeled lemon rind. Bring slowly to the boil. Strain out the rind and sprinkle on the tapioca. Simmer this very slowly until soft and creamy, keeping the lid on but stirring frequently. Add 1$\frac{1}{2}$ oz (40 g) of the sugar and vanilla, then pour on to the fruit; it should be just thick enough to flow easily, but if too thick, a little milk can be added. Let this get cold, then pour over the custard. Beat the egg whites to a stiff froth, sweeten with 3 oz (75 g) caster sugar and add a few drops of vanilla. Colour the froth with cochineal to a pale pink. Heap on to the custard. Brown the meringue in the oven for 20 minutes at 275-300°F (140-150°C) Reg 1-2.

Clee Saucer Cheesecakes
Serves 8

This Lincolnshire recipe demonstrates the useful art of making small cheesecakes.

1 lb (450 g) shortcrust pastry (see page 252)	Grease 8 ovenproof saucers well and line them with the pastry. Mix together all the remaining ingredients except the peel and place in the pastry cases. Decorate with the peel. Bake at 350°F (180°C) Reg 4 for 45 minutes. Serve hot.
8 oz (225 g) curds	
6 oz (175 g) caster sugar	
pinch salt	
pinch ground nutmeg	
grated rind of $\frac{1}{2}$ lemon	
6 egg yolks	
2 oz (50 g) citron peel, chopped	

Note:
With today's problems of obtaining ingredients, these could be made with curd cheese, in which case 2 egg yolks could be omitted or the mixture will be over-rich. Chopped mixed peel could be used instead of the slightly rarer citron peel.

Norfolk Apple Pudding
Serves 4-5

6 oz (175 g) suet crust pastry (see page 253)	Grease a $1\frac{1}{2}$ pt (850 ml) pudding basin. Put the golden syrup in the bottom. Make the suet crust pastry, keeping back one-quarter for the lid. Roll the other three-quarters out thinly and line the pudding basin. Slice the cooking apples finely and put into the lined basin with the brown sugar. Add the grated lemon peel. No liquid is necessary. Put on the top crust. Cover with greaseproof paper. Cover with a pudding cloth or foil. Place in a saucepan of boiling water. Shut the lid tight and steam for 3–$3\frac{1}{2}$ hours. When ready, turn out. This is a pudding that can be brought straight to the table.
2 rounded tbsp golden syrup	
1 lb (450 g) prepared cooking apples	
1 oz (25 g) brown sugar	
grated rind of 1 lemon	

Boston Apple Pudding
Serves 6-8

This is a fine recipe that can hold its own with the most elegant French flan.

8 oz (225 g) puff pastry (see page 253)	Make the pastry. Prepare the apples and stew them in a little water with the cinnamon and cloves. When the apples are soft, remove the spices and sieve the fruit until you have a smooth pulp. Add the butter, beaten eggs and sugar and mix well. Finally stir in the lemon juice. Line a 9 in (23 cm) pie-dish with puff pastry and spoon in the apple mixture. Bake at 400°F (200°C) Reg 6 for 20 minutes.
2 lb (900 g) cooking apples, peeled, cored and sliced	
1 piece stick cinnamon	
4 cloves	
4 oz (110 g) butter	
2 eggs	
2 oz (50 g) demerara sugar	
juice of $\frac{1}{2}$ lemon	

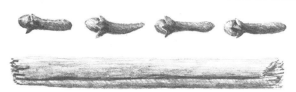

Burn't Cream

Serves 4

An English custard with a sugared top, this is associated with Trinity College, Cambridge, where the college crest was impressed on the top of the cream with a branding iron.

4 egg yolks
1 oz (25 g) caster sugar
1 vanilla pod
1 pt (575 ml) double cream
extra caster sugar

Beat the egg yolks with the sugar until light and fluffy. Put the vanilla pod into the cream in the top of a double saucepan, or a basin over a saucepan of hot water. Bring the cream almost to the boil (but it must not boil). Remove the vanilla pod. Pour the cream on to the egg yolks, stirring all the time. Return to the double saucepan and gently thicken, stirring all the time. Pour into a shallow dish and leave to stand for several hours. Before serving, dust with caster sugar and brown under the grill.

Ipswich Pudding

Serves 3-4

1½ oz (40 g) breadcrumbs
¾ pt (425 ml) full cream milk
4 egg yolks
2 oz (50 g) granulated sugar
¾ oz (20 g) butter
4 oz (110 g) blanched almonds
2 egg whites
2 oz (50 g) caster sugar

Steep the crumbs in cream, then add the 4 egg yolks, beaten, and the granulated sugar, butter and almonds. Put the mixture in a pudding dish and bake for 30 minutes at 350°F (180°C) Reg 4. Having whisked the egg whites, add the caster sugar and put this on top after the base is set. Return to the oven and brown the meringue for approx 8 minutes.

Newmarket Pudding

Serves 4-6

2 eggs
3 oz (75 g) sugar
½ pt (275 ml) milk
5 individual sponge cakes
2 oz (50 g) finely chopped peel
2 oz (50 g) Muscatel raisins, halved
1 oz (25 g) currants
3 tbsp redcurrant jelly

Beat together the eggs and sugar and stir in the milk. Slice the sponge cakes and place them in layers in a greased basin alternating with a mixture of peel, raisins and currants. Pour in the custard mixture, cover with greased paper and a pudding cloth or foil and steam gently for 1-1¼ hours until set. Warm the redcurrant jelly, turn out the pudding and coat with the jelly just before serving.

Norwich Tart

Serves 4–6

6 oz (175 g) shortcrust pastry (see page 252)

2 oz (50 g) butter

4 oz (110 g) icing sugar

3 oz (75 g) ground almonds

grated rind and juice of ½ lemon

walnut halves and glacé cherries to decorate

Make the pastry and line an 8 in (20 cm) sponge sandwich tin. Prick lightly, cover with greaseproof paper and baking beans and bake at 400°F (200°C) Reg 6 for 15 minutes. Remove the beans and paper. Cream together the butter and icing sugar and work in the ground almonds and the grated rind and juice of the lemon. Put the mixture into the pastry case and arrange walnut halves and glacé cherries on top. Bake at 350°F (180°C) Reg 4 for 25 minutes.

Cakes, Breads and Biscuits

Lincolnshire Dripping Cake

This cake was traditionally made for lunch breaks during harvesting. It is delicious cut into thin slices and buttered.

1 lb (450 g) plain flour
½ tsp salt
1 tsp ground cinnamon
6 oz (175 g) lard or dripping
2 oz (50 g) chopped mixed candied peel
8 oz (225 g) raisins
6 oz (175 g) soft brown sugar
½ pt (275 ml) milk (approx)
1 tbsp black treacle
1 tsp bicarbonate of soda
2 eggs, beaten

Grease a deep 8 in (20 cm) square tin and line the base with greased greaseproof paper. Sieve the flour, salt and cinnamon into a bowl. Rub in the lard or dripping with the fingertips, until the mixture resembles fine breadcrumbs. Stir in the fruit and sugar. Warm ¼ pt (150 ml) of the milk; stir in the treacle to dissolve. Add the bicarbonate of soda to 1 tbsp of the milk. Add these liquids and eggs to the dry ingredients with sufficient extra milk to make a mixture which will just drop from the spoon. Pour into the tin and bake in the centre of the oven at 325°F (160°C) Reg 3 for 1½–2 hours or until the cake springs back when pressed lightly with the fingers. Cool in the tin for 10 minutes, turn out, remove the paper, and cool on a wire rack.

Old Lincolnshire Plum Bread

8 oz (225 g) lard or 4 oz (110 g) lard and 4 oz (110 g) margarine
2 lb (900 g) plain flour
1 oz (25 g) yeast
12 oz (350 g) sugar
spice (optional)
1 tsp salt
8 oz (225 g) currants
8 oz (225 g) raisins
8 oz (225 g) sultanas
4 oz (110 g) mixed peel
2 eggs, beaten
milk to mix

Rub the fat into the flour. Cream the yeast with a little water and sugar and allow to froth. Add the yeast to the dry ingredients, mix into a soft dough with the eggs and warm milk, knead and allow to rise for 3 hours; put into 4 × 1 lb (450 g) greased and lined cake tins and allow to rise again. Bake at 400°F (200°C) Reg 6 for 1 hour.

Grantham Gingerbreads

These are a creamy-coloured biscuit, renowned for the wholly enjoyable scrunching sound they make when eaten.

9 oz (250 g) self-raising flour
1 rounded tsp ground ginger
4 oz (110 g) butter or margarine
12 oz (350 g) caster sugar
1 egg

Sieve the flour and ginger together. Cream the butter and sugar until light and fluffy and beat in the egg gradually. Stir in the flour and ginger until a fairly firm dough is obtained. Roll into small balls about the size of a walnut and place well apart on 2 greased baking trays. Bake towards the top of the oven for 40–45 minutes at 300°F (150°C) Reg 2 until crisp and very lightly browned.

Norfolk Rusks

8 oz (225 g) self-raising flour

1 tsp baking powder

1 tbsp sugar

1 small egg, beaten

good pinch salt

milk to bind – approx $\frac{1}{4}$ pt (150 ml)

Mix all the dry ingredients and rub in the fat. Add the egg and enough milk to make an elastic dough. Roll out $\frac{1}{2}$–$\frac{3}{4}$ in (1–2 cm) thick and cut into small rounds 1$\frac{1}{2}$ in (4 cm) in diameter. Bake (as for scones) at 425°F (220°C) Reg 7 for 8 minutes. Remove from the oven, split and replace in the oven to dry for approx 3 minutes. If a very crisp texture is required, lower the oven to 325°F (160°C) Reg 3 to prevent burning. Serve with butter, jam or cheese, or as they are.

Suffolk Rusks, Grandmother's Receipt

At one time Suffolk Rusks were made from pieces of dough taken from the main baking of the day. Now the recipe below is more usual. 'Receipt' is the old name for recipe.

1 lb (450 g) plain flour

2 oz (50 g) fat

4 oz (110 g) sugar

1 oz (25 g) yeast

2 eggs, beaten

$\frac{1}{4}$–$\frac{1}{2}$ pt (150–275 ml) warm milk and water

The flour must be slightly warm, and mixed where there are no draughts. Rub the fat into the flour and add the sugar leaving 1 tsp to mix with the yeast in equal parts of warm milk and water. When all the ingredients, including the eggs, are combined, leave in a bowl to rise in a warm place. When risen, cut into small pieces, make into balls and put on a warm tin to rise again. Cook at 425°F (220°C) Reg 7 for 10 minutes. When cooked, split the rusks in half with a fork and return to the oven to crisp at 250°F (120°C) Reg $\frac{1}{2}$. Fill with jam and/or cream or serve them as they are. Another option is to eat them as buns, in which case they do not need to be split and crisped.

Brandy Butter or Senior Wrangler Sauce

A Wrangler is a title, dating from 1750, given to Cambridge Undergraduates who were awarded a 1st Class pass in their Maths Tripos. The Senior Wrangler is the student obtaining the highest honours and who thus ranks first among the Wranglers. The name was applied also to Brandy Butter by Dr Whewell, a Senior Wrangler who became Master of Trinity in the mid-nineteenth century.

4 oz (110 g) unsalted butter

4 oz (110 g) caster sugar

2–3 tbsp brandy to taste

Cream the butter; beat in the sugar by degrees and beat until white. Beat in the brandy 1 tbsp at a time. Chill before serving with Mince Pies, Christmas Pudding, etc.

Suffolk Kitchels

These cakes were traditionally made during the Twelve Days of Christmas, and kept for visiting godchildren. The old saying 'Ask me a blessing and I will give you a kitchel' still survives among some of the older generation.

1 lb (450 g) puff pastry (see page 253)

2 oz (50 g) butter

8 oz (225 g) currants

3 oz (75 g) chopped peel

2 oz (50 g) ground almonds

½ tsp cinnamon

½ tsp nutmeg

caster sugar to decorate

Make the pastry. Melt the butter and add the currants, chopped peel, ground almonds, cinnamon and nutmeg. Divide the puff pastry in half and roll each piece into a thin square. Moisten round the edge of one piece and spread the filling evenly on the top. Cover with the second piece of pastry and press the edges well together. With the back of a knife, mark the pastry into about 2 in (5 cm) squares without cutting through the pastry or filling. Bake at 450°F (230°C) Reg 8 for 25 minutes. Sprinkle with caster sugar while still hot and divide along the squares already marked.

Suffolk Fourses

These cakes were traditionally served at four o'clock to the harvesters, accompanied by beer or cider.

1 oz (25 g) yeast

1 tsp sugar

½ pt (275 ml) milk

2 oz (50 g) lard

2 lb (900 g) plain flour

½ tsp salt

2 oz (50 g) sugar

2 oz (50 g) raisins

pinch spice

6 oz (175 g) butter

3 eggs

Cream the yeast and sugar together; warm the milk and add the yeast mixture. Rub the lard into the flour and salt, then add the sugar, raisins and spice. Melt the butter, and mix with the well-beaten eggs; add to the warm milk mixture, and put all together into the flour to make a light dough. Cover with a cloth and set in a warm place to rise. When the dough has doubled its bulk, put it on a floured board and knead. Roll out ¾ in (2 cm) thick and cut into rounds with a 4 in (10 cm) cutter. Put on greased baking trays and leave to prove. When risen, bake in a hot oven for 15-20 minutes at 425°F (220°C) Reg 7.

Bible Cake

1. **8 oz (225 g) butter** - *8 oz Judges V, verse 25 (last clause)*
2. **8 oz (225 g) sugar** - *8 oz Jeremiah VI, 20*
3. **1 tbsp honey** - *1 tbsp I Samuel XIV, 25*
4. **3 eggs** - *3 of Jeremiah XVII, 11*
5. **8 oz (225 g) raisins** - *8 oz I Samuel XXX, 12*
6. **8 oz (225 g) figs, chopped** - *8 oz Nahum III, 12, chopped*
7. **2 oz (50 g) almonds, blanched and chopped** - *2 oz Numbers XVII, 8, blanched and chopped*
8. **1 lb (450 g) plain flour** - *1 lb I Kings IV, 22*
9. **season to taste with spices** - *season to taste with Chronicles IX*
10. **pinch salt** - *pinch Leviticus II, 13*
11. **1 tsp leaven baking powder** - *1 tsp Amos IV, 5*
12. **3 tbsp milk** - *3 tbsp Judges IV, 19*

Beat Nos 1, 2 and 3 to a cream; add 4, one at a time, still beating; then 5, 6 and 7, and beat again; add 8, 9, 10 and 11, having previously mixed them, and lastly No 12. Bake at 325°F (160°C) Reg 3 for 1½ hours.

Note: References are to passages in the Authorized Version

Newmarket Cake

8 oz (225 g) butter

12 oz (350 g) caster sugar

12 oz (350 g) self-raising flour

3 oz (75 g) grated chocolate

4 eggs

¼ pt (150 ml) strong black coffee
or ¼ pt water and 3 heaped tsp instant coffee

3 oz (75 g) almonds, blanched and finely chopped lengthways, or flaked almonds

Beat the butter and sugar together until very soft and creamy. Beat in the egg yolks. Sift the flour and add the grated chocolate. Fold this into the creamed mixture with the coffee. Add the almonds and fold in with the stiffly beaten egg whites. Bake in a greased 8 in (20 cm) tin lined with greaseproof paper. Bake for 2 hours at 325°F (160°C) Reg 3 until the centre is firm to the touch. Turn out and cool on a wire rack.

Brown Fair Buttons

8 oz (225 g) plain flour

4 oz (110 g) dark soft brown sugar

$\frac{1}{2}$ oz (15 g) ground ginger

pinch bicarbonate of soda

2 oz (50 g) lard

4 oz (110 g) golden syrup

a few drops lemon essence

Mix together the flour, sugar, ginger and bicarbonate of soda. Rub in the lard and pour in the syrup and essence. Mix very well. Roll out thinly and cut into rounds. Bake at 350°F (180°C) Reg 4 for 12 minutes. Lift off and cool on a wire tray.

Cambridge Tea Loaf

6 oz (175 g) butter

8 oz (225 g) self-raising flour

pinch salt

2 oz (50 g) caster sugar

4 oz (110 g) sultanas

4 oz (110 g) currants

1 oz (25 g) chopped mixed peel

$\frac{1}{4}$ tsp cinnamon

a few chopped nuts

just under $\frac{1}{4}$ pt (150 ml) milk

Rub the butter into the flour and add the rest of the ingredients. Bake in a 2 lb (900 g) greased loaf tin for 1 hour 20 minutes at 350°F (180°C) Reg 4.

Midlands

What a shame the Midlands has to have such a bald title. For although that's exactly what it is – the very middle of England (and to pinpoint things more acutely, the village of Meriden near Coventry lays claim to be the bull's eye) – the various areas which comprise 'the Midlands' have much more glamorous titles: The Heart of England, or The Cotswolds, The Wrekin, and even The Avon Valley. Technically, the area designated here to bear the title of Midlands stretches from Derbyshire in the north to the edge of the new county of West Midlands and Warwickshire in the south and across from the Staffordshire/ Shropshire borders in the west to Leicestershire and what was once Rutland in the east.

The Midlands is the home of England's second city, Birmingham. Though teeming with a million and a half people whose lilting accent and friendliness is a joy to the soul, Birmingham has produced only one regional dish which could be called truly *Brummiger* in origin, unless we allow the development of chocolate at Bourneville. They'll try to have you believe that Black Pudding is theirs, but it has to be said that whilst it commands a certain popularity in working-class homes, this delicacy belongs further north than the West Midlands. But, hard by in Coventry, where it could be said that the British set eyes on their most famous 'streaker' (for didn't Lady Godiva ride naked through the streets in protest against taxes back in the eleventh century?), you could well taste a Coventry Godcake, or a Warwick Chop with Chestnuts, and a dribble or so of Warwick Sauce.

Let me not delay too long in this area of the Midlands for, attractive, lush and pink-hued as it is, and home as it also is of our greatest poet, at Stratford-upon-Avon, we must in the name of food and our national reputation move to the easternmost part of the area. Here lies the home of our greatest and most famous cheese – Stilton. There are also other well-known cheeses here, such as Leicester, Red Leicester and Sage Derby, and many other names spring to mind of cheeses, alas, no longer made – Cottenham, Banbury and Colwick are but three of them.

There can be few people who don't know the story of our great national cheese, made in the heart of these hunting shires. One Elizabeth Scarbrow,

housekeeper at Quenby Hall in the early 1700s, made an excellent cheese which she sold on market days at the nearby Bell Inn in the village of Stilton in the now-extinct county of Huntingdonshire. Other housekeepers and farmer's wives quickly jumped on this bandwagon, for Stilton village was but a half mile or so from the major road running from London to Edinburgh. Passengers who tasted it on a stop-over soon learned to like Stilton. The cheese, however, was never actually made in the village which gives it its name. Today, praise be, there are cooks – and I like to think I'm one of them – who use Stilton in new ways, such as Stilton Tart, Stilton Pancakes, Chilled Stilton Soup and so on, and I always serve Stilton and Raisin Butter with Yorkshire Yule Cake at Christmas time.

The hunt does keep English traditions alive, and those who follow the Fernie, Cottesmore, Quorn or Belvoir may well see goodly wedges of rich Melton Hunt Cake being passed around, and the succulent pot-bellied hand-raised pies of Melton Mowbray are evident at every hunt breakfast or meet and also in demand at such great London food shops as Harrods, Fortnum and Mason, and Paxton and Whitfield.

Before moving over to the west of this region, we must not forget the county of squires, spires, spinsters and springs – Northamptonshire. Whilst the geographical and even architectural features of many of the Midland counties are confused and blurred at the edges, this handsome county has some fine runners in the regional food stakes: Leek and Onion Pie (from Earls Barton), Bacon and Onion Roll, and Raspberry Vinegar! Just why that condiment was peculiar to Northamptonshire is difficult to trace. Raspberries, as garden fruits, were first recorded in England as early as 1548, and any self-respecting country house would have an abundant kitchen garden containing rows of canes. Such a house would have been the home of Sir John Blencowe, who represented Brackley in Northants in Parliament from 1690 to 1695, and whose wife, Ann, wrote an excellent 'receipt' book in 1694. I am the proud possessor

of a copy of this magical little volume, in which my now-famous recipe for Butter'd Orange had its origins.

For reasons given in the introduction to this book, England was a country of haves and have-nots. Sadly, few of the recipes and teachings of the haves were passed down to us, or if they were, they were certainly quickly lost over the years. Mistress Blencowe's delicious recipes make one seriously ponder the extent of that loss. We have only to think of her Potted Tongue, where ginger, mace, nutmeg and good sweet butter were used, and of her Honeycomb Cakes, Boiled Carp, Peaches in Brandy, Flummery, and her Hodge Podge (Hot Pot) which contained beef, onions, mace, cloves, celery, turnips, fresh herbs and 'crusts' fried in butter (the precursors to today's frenchified croûton), and her Oyster Pye with anchovies, parsley, cream and eggs topped with a 'flacky' crust. Ah well!

On we must go. It has often been said that the best scenery found in Derbyshire is in Staffordshire! Certainly these two beautiful counties still have traces of regional goodies for the table. Bakewell Pudding – tart or pie, call it what you will – is Derbyshire's donation to a national repertory. Debased as it is today, it should be remembered that the eighteenth-century recipe specified that an egg, cream and almond mixture be spooned over rich, fruity strawberry jam and baked in a crisp, *buttery*, flaky pastry. Where is *that* combination available now, except in the home of some gifted amateur cook in a well-fed household?

Staffordshire is the home of Oat Cakes, still eaten for breakfast with Bacon and Eggs. And Chicken Hot Pot, for inexplicable reasons, also has no mean reputation in this county, which is the clearly-divided home of both the

Potteries around Stoke-on-Trent and The Black Country around Wolverhampton (now, of course, part of West Midlands).

One would have thought that Stratford-upon-Avon might have cottoned on to Shakespeare's reference to 'Apricocks' in *Richard II*. But no, the use of apricots, oranges and other fruits, so popular in our Elizabethan kitchens, has fallen out of favour over the years, hence we must lose out on such luscious dishes as pork simmered in wine or cider together with various spices, dates, walnuts, celery and many other delights. The 'spoon foods' of the Middle Ages – that is what I like to call these forgotten dishes. Don't, however, get too depressed about things, for, if you really search, there may be a Plum Shuttle lurking around in some remote corner of Rutland. Remember, we have lost not only dishes in the Midlands, but three counties as well.

Soups

Butter Bean Soup
Serves 3–4

1 lb (450 g) dried butter beans

4 pt (2.3 l) water

2 leeks or onions

1 small carrot

bunch mixed herbs

1 pt (575 ml) milk

seasoning

bunch parsley to garnish

Soak the beans all night in cold water. Put them on to boil for 1 hour in 4 pt (2.25 l) fresh water with a little salt. Chop the vegetables finely. Add them and the herbs and seasoning to the beans and simmer for another hour. Add the milk. Rub through a sieve. Garnish with parsley and serve.

Farmhouse Soup
Serves 3–4

1¼–1½ lb (560–675 g) mixed vegetables (onion, carrot, artichoke, parsnip, leek, potato, etc)

2 oz butter or beef dripping

1 pt (575 ml) bonestock

1 bouquet garni sachet

flake of mace

1 bay leaf

seasoning

salt and pepper

Prepare all the vegetables and chop roughly. Avoid strongly-flavoured vegetables like turnip or celery to keep a balanced flavour. Melt the fat in a saucepan and cook the vegetables until they are starting to get soft and the fat has been absorbed. Add the stock, herbs and seasonings and simmer gently until the vegetables are tender and the stock reduced. Adjust the seasoning. Liquidize or pass through a sieve and then heat through. Serve with tiny herb dumplings.

Rabbit Broth
Serves 4–5

This is an elegant consommé rather than a broth; it has a delicate flavour and lovely clear pale colour.

2 rabbit legs

4 oz (110 g) beefsteak

3 pt (1.7 l) water

salt

4 black peppercorns

bunch parsley

½ onion

¼ turnip

½ bay leaf

extra parsley to garnish

Wash the rabbit well and joint it. Put it with the beefsteak, cut into small pieces in a pan with the water. Bring slowly to the boil and add the salt and peppercorns just before it boils. Skim carefully. Add the vegetables and herbs. Simmer for 3½ hours. Strain and put in a cool place to get cold before skimming off the fat. For serving add a little chopped parsley.

Devilled Grilled Cod

Serves 4

4 cod cutlets or steaks about 1 in (2.5 cm) thick	Put the fish in a greased ovenproof dish and place under a very hot grill for 2–3 minutes on one side. Cream the margarine with the chutney, curry powder, seasonings, mustard, and anchovy essence. Turn the fish over and spread the uncooked side with the devilled mixture. Return to the grill and reduce the heat slightly. Cook for 10–12 minutes until the coating is brown and the fish is cooked through. Serve at once.
1 oz (25 g) margarine, softened	
1 tsp chutney	
1 tsp curry powder	
seasonings	
1 tsp dry mustard	
1 tsp anchovy essence	

North Staffordshire Swallows

Serves 2

These small fritters may be made with any firm white fish and served at breakfast or high tea.

6 oz (175 g) white fish	Slice the uncooked fish thinly and cut the peeled potatoes into slices, about $\frac{1}{8}$ in (3 mm) thick. Place a slice of fish on a slice of potato; season with salt and pepper and cover with another slice of potato. Dip the fish sandwiches in batter, and fry in hot deep fat until golden brown, about 5–7 minutes.
4 oz (110 g) potatoes	
salt and pepper	
1 portion plain coating batter (see page 251)	
fat for deep-frying	

Plaice with Cucumber Sauce

Serves 4

4 plaice fillets, skinned	Reserve half the shrimps or prawns for decoration and divide the remainder between the fillets. Fold the fillets in half and place in a buttered ovenproof dish. Mix the seasonings with the white wine or lemon juice and pour over the fish. Bake at 375°F (190°C) Reg 5 for 15 minutes. Cut 6 slices of cucumber for decoration and peel and dice the remainder. Blanch for 1 minute in boiling salted water. To make the sauce, melt the margarine or butter in a saucepan and stir in the flour. Cook for 1 minute then add the milk, the white wine and the diced cucumber. Bring to the boil, stirring continuously, until it thickens. Cook for 1–2 minutes and season. Remove the fish with a slotted spoon to a serving dish. Take 2 tbsp of the fish liquor and add it to the sauce, then pour over the fish. Garnish with shrimps or prawns, slices of cucumber and watercress.
2–4 oz (50–100 g) shrimps or prawns, shelled	
salt and pepper	
pinch dry mustard	
3 tbsp white wine or lemon juice	
watercress to garnish	
Sauce	
$\frac{1}{2}$ cucumber	
1 oz (25 g) margarine or butter	
1 oz (25 g) plain flour	
$\frac{1}{2}$ pt (275 ml) milk	
2 tbsp white wine	
salt and pepper	

Meat

Love in Disguise
Serves 6-8

This dish of baked stuffed veal hearts was popular in the eighteenth century. The coating of vermicelli and breadcrumbs disguises the hearts.

4 calf hearts

8 oz (225 g) veal forcemeat

10–12 rashers bacon

4 oz (110 g) vermicelli

2 oz (50 g) breadcrumbs

1 egg

2 oz (50 g) lard

Cut off flaps, gristle and tubes from the hearts and snip out membrane which divides the hearts inside. Soak in cold water for 2 hours, wash and soak in fresh water for 30 minutes. Stuff with veal forcemeat and sew up the opening with fine string. Wrap the bacon round the hearts and secure with wooden skewers. Wrap in foil and bake for 1½ hours in the oven at 375°F (190°C) Reg 5. Break the vermicelli into small pieces and boil until soft in salted water. Drain, cool and mix with breadcrumbs. Remove hearts from the oven, cool slightly and brush with beaten egg. Coat the hearts with the vermicelli and breadcrumb mixture. Return the hearts, without foil, to the roasting tin, add the lard and bake for a further 30 minutes or until the coating is crisp and brown.

Mutton (Lamb) Collops
Serves 4

Mutton is fairly rare these days, but lamb which is anyway more tender makes a splendid substitute. This recipe was found in Stratford-upon-Avon in 1820.

12 oz (350 g) chump end leg of lamb (off the bone)

1 tbsp plain flour

2 oz (50 g) onion, finely chopped (optional)

⅓ pt (200 ml) meat stock or water

2 tsp mushroom ketchup

1–2 tbsp Worcestershire Sauce (optional)

pinch cayenne pepper

salt and pepper

strip lemon rind

1–1½ lb (450–675 g) mashed potato

Mince the meat finely and mix well together with the flour (and onion if used). Place in a saucepan. Mix together the remaining ingredients, except the potato, and gradually stir into the meat mixture. Bring to the boil, cover, and simmer gently for ¾–1 hour, shaking the pan occasionally. Pipe the potato round the edge of a serving dish, and place the meat mixture in the centre.

Quorn Bacon Roll
Serves 4

Another excellent example of 'hunt' food which, like the Pork Pie, is easy to consume one-handed.

12 oz (350 g) savoury suet crust pastry (see page 253)

6–8 rashers bacon (collar, preferably)

1 large onion, chopped

2 tsp fresh sage, chopped

Make the suet pastry. Roll the pastry into a square ¼ in (5 mm) thick. Lay the rashers of bacon on the pastry and sprinkle with the chopped onion and sage. Roll up into a sausage shape, wrap in a pudding cloth (or alternatively in greased greaseproof paper and kitchen foil) and place in a pan of hot water and 'boil' gently for approx 2 hours. Serve with potatoes, carrots and turnips.

Staffordshire Beefsteaks

Serves 4-6

1½ lb (700 g) beef steak, eg chuck, shoulder, rump or sirloin
2 large onions
2 oz (50 g) dripping, lard, or 2 tbsp oil
¾ pt (425 ml) stock or water
1 tbsp plain flour
1 tbsp mushroom or walnut ketchup
seasoning

Cut the steaks into portion-size pieces. Slice the onions. Melt the fat in a flameproof casserole, add the steak and onions and fry gently until lightly browned. Add the stock, bring to the boil and simmer gently for 20-30 minutes depending on the cut of meat (the shorter time for sirloin and rump). Make a thick gravy with the flour and cooking liquor, flavouring it with the ketchup and seasoning. Pour the gravy over the meat. Place the casserole in a moderately hot oven at 325°F (160°C) Reg 3 and cook until the meat is tender (½-1½ hours depending on the cut of meat).

Earls Barton Leek Pie

Serves 4-6

12 oz (350 g) chuck steak
12 oz (350 g) belly pork
¾ pt (425 ml) stock or water
salt and pepper
1½-2 lb (700-900 g) leeks
8 oz (225 g) shortcrust pastry (see page 252)

Dice the beef and pork, place in a casserole together with stock and some seasoning. Place casserole in oven and cook at 350°F (180°C) Reg 4 for approx 1½ hours, until tender. Allow to cool, so that surplus fat may be removed. Wash, slice thickly, and boil the leeks. Prepare the pastry. Fill a pie-dish with alternate layers of meat and leeks, with leeks on top. Add a little of the stock from the meat. Cover with the pastry and bake at 400°F (200°C) Reg 6 for 25-30 minutes, until pastry is pale golden brown.

Staffordshire Supper

Serves 4

Though once popular elsewhere, this dish is now most strongly associated with Staffordshire.

8 oz (225 g) young broad beans (weighed after podding)
8 oz (225 g) peas (weighed after podding)
4 rashers bacon or ham (home cured, if possible)

Sauce
1½ oz (40 g) plain flour
1½ oz (40 g) butter/margarine
1 pt (600 ml) milk
2 tbsp fresh parsley, finely chopped
salt and pepper

Cook the beans and peas in lightly salted, boiling water until just tender. Grill or fry the bacon until crisp. Meanwhile make the sauce by melting the butter in a pan, stir in the flour to make a roux, cook gently for 1-2 minutes. Gradually stir in the milk, bringing to the boil between each addition, add the parsley and season to taste. Place the vegetables in a serving dish, lay the cooked bacon over, and cover with the parsley sauce. The dripping from the bacon may be poured over the top, if liked. Serve with crusty new bread, or tiny new potatoes.

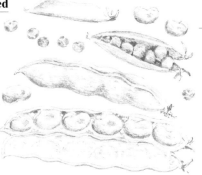

Jugged Rabbit or Chesterfield Stew

1 rabbit
12 oz (350 g) beef (thick flank, sliced thinly)
1 large onion
1 carrot
$\frac{3}{4}$ pt (450 ml) beef stock
bouquet garni sachet
salt and pepper
$\frac{1}{4}$ pt (150 ml) port or red wine
2 oz (50 g) butter or 2 tbsp oil

Forcemeat Stuffing

4 oz (110 g) breadcrumbs
1$\frac{1}{2}$ oz (40 g) suet or melted margarine
1 tbsp fresh parsley, chopped
2 tsp fresh thyme, chopped
salt and pepper
beaten egg to bind

Cut rabbit into joints and place in a casserole. Cut beef into pieces approx 5 × 3 in (13 × 7.5 cm). Make forcemeat stuffing, by mixing together the ingredients and adding sufficient egg to bind. Place a little stuffing on each piece of beef, roll up, and tie with string. Place beef rolls in casserole with the rabbit. Coarsely chop the vegetables, and add to the casserole, together with the stock, bouquet garni and seasoning. Cover tightly, place in the oven and cook at 325°F (160°C) Reg 3 for 2–2$\frac{1}{2}$ hours until meat is tender. Meanwhile, form remaining stuffing into balls and fry in butter or oil. When meat is tender, stir in the wine and place the stuffing balls on top. Return casserole to the oven for a further 10–15 minutes.

Spinster's Veal Pot Pie

Serves 6–8

2$\frac{1}{2}$ lb (1.1 kg) stewing veal
1 veal kidney
seasoned flour
3 oz (75 g) dripping or lard or 3 tbsp oil
$\frac{1}{2}$ pt (275 ml) beef stock
$\frac{1}{2}$ pt (275 ml) dry white wine
1 clove garlic, stuck with 2 cloves
6 peppercorns, crushed
bouquet garni sachet
12 small onions
12 carrot balls or slices
12 turnip balls or slices
12 button mushrooms
8 almonds, blanched and chopped
12 oz (350 g) flaky pastry (see page 253)
milk
$\frac{1}{4}$ pt (150 ml) single cream

Cut veal and kidney into small pieces. Toss in seasoned flour. Heat dripping/oil in a frying pan, and brown the meat, turning constantly. Transfer the meat to an ovenproof casserole. Add the stock, wine, garlic, peppercorns and bouquet garni. Cover, bring slowly to the boil, and simmer gently for 1$\frac{1}{4}$ hours. Add the vegetables and continue cooking for a further 30 minutes. Allow to cool. Discard bouquet garni. Stir in the almonds. Meanwhile make the flaky pastry and allow to rest. Roll out the pastry and place over the casserole, brush with milk. Make a small hole in the centre (or use a pie funnel). Bake at 450°F (230°C) Reg 8 until the crust is golden brown. Warm the cream, and pour into the pie through a funnel. Return the pie to the oven and bake for a further 5 minutes, or until the gravy bubbles up.

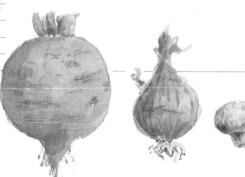

Melton Mowbray Pork Pie

Serves 6-8

Melton Mowbray lays claim to be the originator of the plump-bellied pork pie. Other areas produce equally good pies – some with apples, some with eggs, some with herbs and spices – but the simple filling of Melton's pork butchers continues to satisfy the Leicestershire people to this day.

Crust

12 oz (350 g) hot water crust pastry (see page 252)

Filling

1 lb (450 g) pork (failing flitch, use shoulder; get 1¼ lb (560 g) to allow trimming)

1 tsp salt

½ tsp pepper

2 tbsp water

1 egg

Make the dough, knead well by hand and leave to cool for about 1 hour, kneading once or twice during this time. The dough must not get really cold otherwise it will crack and crumble. Turn on to a floured board, flour the mould (the Leicestershire Pie Mould is wooden, but a 2 lb (900 g) jam jar will do), put the crust on top of the mould and shape it from the top some way down the sides: the crust should be about ⅓ in (8 mm) thick. Leave to set for approx 20 minutes, then turn crust off mould and trim top with scissors.

To make the filling, mince the meat on the coarse knife of the mincer, add salt and pepper and mix well, add water and mix again. Press meat well into corners of pastry case, filling case to within ¾ in (2 cm) of the top. Make the lid out of pastry trimmings, and press the edges together. Cut round with scissors to neaten off – this cutting also helps to bind the top and sides together. Make a hole in the centre of the top. Cut a length of greaseproof paper about 1 in (2.5 cm) higher than the pie. Wrap it round the pie, making sure it goes right down to the bottom, and stick the ends together with flour paste. The pie need not be baked on the same day – in fact it is improved by standing overnight. To cook, stand pie in a sandwich cake tin or on a baking tray. Brush top with beaten egg. Cook at 375°F (190°C) Reg 5 for 1 hour, then at 325°F (160°C) Reg 3 for another 45–50 minutes. Remove the paper collar, brush the sides with beaten egg and return the pie to the oven for a few minutes to brown. Remove from the oven and when pie is nearly cold, pour jelly through hole in top of crust.

Jellied Stock Makes 1 pt (575 ml)

ham bones

2 pig's trotters

2 pt (1.2 l) water

salt

1-2 sprigs thyme

Pig's trotters with a few ham bones make a wonderful jelly. Put the ham bones with two pig's trotters into 2 pt (1.2 l) water. Add salt and a sprig or two of thyme. Bring to the boil and simmer for several hours, reducing the jelly to 1 pt (575 ml) or less. Strain, cool and leave overnight in the refrigerator. Remove the fat when the jelly is set. Melt when needed.

Warwickshire Chops and Chestnuts

Serves 4–6

These oven-baked chops with chestnuts and onions are equally delicious when made with pork chops.

8 × 4 oz (110 g) lamb chops
2 oz (50 g) dripping
12 oz (350 g) onions, finely chopped
1 oz (25 g) plain flour
1 pt (575 ml) brown stock
1¼ lb (560 g) chestnuts, boiled and peeled
salt and pepper

Fry the chops lightly in the dripping until sealed. Remove and arrange in an ovenproof dish. Add the onions to the dripping and fry until soft. Stir in the flour and cook for a few minutes, gradually blend in the stock and bring to the boil. Add the chestnuts and season to taste with salt and pepper. Pour this sauce over the chops, cover with a tightly fitting lid and simmer. Bake in the oven at 350°F (180°C) Reg 4 for 1 hour.

Savoury Sausage Casserole

Serves 4

1 large onion, chopped
1 lb (450 g) pork sausagemeat
pinch mixed herbs
salt and pepper
1 tbsp seasoned plain flour
1 oz (25 g) lard
2 tsp curry powder
¾ pt (425 ml) stock
4 oz (110 g) carrots
4 oz (110 g) mushrooms

Mix the onion with the sausagemeat and herbs, and season well. Divide the mixture into 16 pieces, roll each piece into a ball and toss in the seasoned flour. Melt the lard in a large frying pan, add the meat balls and fry them quickly until brown all over. Transfer them to a plate. Stir the curry powder and the rest of the flour into the fat in the pan and cook for a few seconds, then remove the pan from the heat and stir in the stock. Return to the heat and, stirring all the time, bring the sauce to the boil for 2 minutes to thicken. Peel the carrots and cut into small sticks. Wipe and roughly chop the mushrooms and stir them with the carrots into the sauce. Put the meat balls into the sauce and cover with a lid or foil. Simmer for about 30 minutes until the meat balls are cooked. Serve with rice.

Cheese and Pork Casserole

Serves 4

4 pork chops or 4 slices shoulder pork
seasoning
fat or oil for frying
4 oz (110 g) cheese, grated
4 small onions, finely chopped
4 large cooking apples, peeled and finely chopped

Season the pork and fry until well browned on both sides. Make a bed with a third of the grated cheese in the bottom of an oven tin large enough to hold the pork in one layer. Place the pork on top of the cheese. Mix together the chopped onion and apple and spread the mixture over the pork. Season and cover with the remainder of the cheese. Cover with foil and cook at 400°F (200°C) Reg 6 for 40–45 minutes. Remove the foil and cook for a further 10 minutes.

Savouries

Chicken Creams

Serves 2 (main course)
Serves 4 (starter)

2 tsp parsley, finely chopped	
4 oz (110g) chicken breasts	
2 tbsp breadcrumbs	
2 oz (50 g) potato, cooked and mashed	
1 egg	
Sauce	
1 oz (25 g) butter or margarine	
1 oz (25 g) plain flour	
¼ pt (150 ml) stock	
salt and pepper	

Grease some dariole moulds or ramekin dishes, and place finely chopped parsley in base of each. Mince the chicken, mix together with breadcrumbs and potato. To make a binding sauce, melt butter, stir in flour to make a roux, and cook gently for 1 minute. Gradually stir in the stock, bring to the boil between each addition. Cool. Stir in lightly beaten egg and the chicken mixture. Place in the prepared moulds. Cover with greased greaseproof paper. Steam for 30 minutes. If cooked in dariole moulds, turn out and serve with chicken gravy or sauce. If cooked in ramekin dishes, serve in the dishes, garnished with chopped parsley.

Brummy Bacon Cakes

Serves 4

This is probably the only recipe in the book which can really claim to have come from our Second City - to which I am nonetheless greatly attached.

2 oz (50 g) streaky or cooked leftover bacon	
8 oz (225 g) self-raising flour	
¼ tsp salt	
1 oz (25 g) butter	
3 oz (75 g) Cheddar Cheese, grated	
¼ pt (150 ml) milk	
1 tbsp tomato ketchup	
dash Worcestershire Sauce	
milk for glazing	
watercress for garnish	

Grill the bacon until crisp and cut into small pieces. Sieve flour and salt together, rub in butter finely. Add the bacon and one-third of the cheese. Mix milk, ketchup and Worcestershire Sauce together. Add to dry ingredients to make a soft dough. On a floured board, roll out a 7 in (18 cm) circle. Brush with milk and cut into 8 wedges. Arrange on a greased baking sheet and sprinkle with remaining cheese. Bake at 400°F (200°C) Reg 6 for 30 minutes.

Oxford Sausages

Serves 8

In Oxford, sausages were at one time made with a mixture of different meats - and were all the tastier for that.

1 lb (450 g) lean shoulder of pork	
1 lb (450 g) shoulder of veal	
1 lb (450 g) beef suet	
8 oz (225 g) white breadcrumbs	
grated rind of ½ lemon	
2 tsp grated nutmeg	
1 tsp chopped sage	
pinch each thyme, savory, marjoram, finely chopped	
salt and pepper	
2 egg yolks	
2–3 oz (50–75 g) butter	

Mince or finely chop the pork, veal and beef suet, add the breadcrumbs, lemon rind, nutmeg, sage, thyme, savory, marjoram, salt and pepper. Bind the mixture with egg yolks. Mix thoroughly, divide the mixture into 16 pieces and roll each portion between floured hands into sausage shapes. Fry in butter for about 10 minutes, turning 2 or 3 times.

Stuffed Tripe with Mushy Peas

Serves 4

1½ lb (675 g) tripe, prepared in 1 or 2 pieces

2 large onions

4 oz (110 g) fresh breadcrumbs

salt and pepper

1 tbsp mixed herbs (sage, parsley, thyme, marjoram, etc)

4 rashers bacon

Boil the onions, then chop coarsely and mix with the breadcrumbs, seasonings and chopped herbs to form a paste. Spread a thick layer over half the tripe, fold or place the other half over and sew the edges together with fine string. Place in a greased tin, with the bacon rashers on top. Bake for 1 hour at 350°F (180°C) Reg 4. Serve with mushy peas and freshly made mint sauce (see page 23)

Cheese Pinwheels

Serves 4

8 oz (225 g) plain soft flour

pinch salt

½ tsp dry mustard

2 oz (50 g) lard

2 oz (50 g) margarine

4 oz (110 g) strong cheese, coarsely grated

8–12 oz (225–350 g) sausagemeat

Sift the flour with the salt and mustard into a bowl. Rub in the fats until the mixture resembles fine breadcrumbs. Add the grated cheese and about 8 tsp water to bind. Knead very lightly and roll out to form an oblong about 8 × 11 in (20 × 28 cm). Spread the sausagemeat over the pastry leaving about ¾ in (2 cm) clear along one short side. Moisten the edges with water and roll the pastry up as for a Swiss Roll. With a sharp knife, cut slices from the roll, form them into rounds and place on a baking tray. Bake at 400°F (200°C) Reg 6 for about 20 minutes until lightly browned. Serve hot with beans and grilled tomatoes or cold with a green salad.

Stuffed Onions

Serves 4 as an accompaniment or starter.

4 even-sized onions

2 oz (50 g) cheese, grated

2 oz (50 g) breadcrumbs

¼ tsp dry mustard

salt and pepper

a little margarine

parsley to garnish

Boil the onions for 20-30 minutes according to size, after removing the papery outer skins. Do not allow to become too soft. Combine the grated cheese, breadcrumbs and mustard in a bowl. When the onions are cooked, scoop out their centres with a small spoon and mix them with the ingredients in the bowl. Season. Fill the cavities in the onions with the stuffing mixture and place in a greased ovenproof dish. Dot the tops with margarine and cook at 425°F (220°C) Reg 7 for about 30 minutes, until tender. Sprinkle the top of each onion with parsley and serve with a white sauce, a tomato sauce, or gravy.

Buxton Pudding

Serves 4–6

4 oz (125 g) shortcrust pastry (see page 252)
4 oz (125 g) butter or margarine
4 oz (125 g) caster sugar
2 eggs, beaten
4 oz (125 g) breadcrumbs
2 tbsp raspberry jam

Make the pastry. Cream fat and sugar. Add eggs gradually, then fold in crumbs. Line sides of a pie-dish with the pastry, place jam in bottom and cover with mixture. Bake at 375°F (190°C) Reg 5 until set – approx 30 minutes.

Bakewell Pudding

Serves 4–5

That these delicacies are called puddings and not tarts is agreed by all locals. As to their origin, I suspect they are a version of seventeenth- or eighteenth-century cheesecake, but the following anecdote is worth an airing. Legend has it that the puddings were first made at the Rutland Arms Hotel in Bakewell about the middle of the nineteenth century, when Mr and Mrs Greaves were the proprietors. One day, when special visitors were expected, the cook misunderstood Mrs Greaves's instructions. Instead of mixing the egg mixture into the flour and spreading the jam on top, the pudding was made as in this recipe, thus converting what should have been a rich strawberry tart into a pudding. Fortunately for the cook, the visitors much enjoyed the new pudding and congratulated Mrs Greaves on it. It is of interest to note that Mrs Greaves was the sister-in-law of Sir Joseph Paxton who was head gardener at Chatsworth House for many years and also designed the Crystal Palace.

6 oz (175 g) puff pastry (see page 253)
3 tbsp strawberry jam
4 oz (110 g) melted or clarified butter (see page 251)
6 oz (175 g) caster sugar
5 egg yolks
3 egg whites
almond essence

Line an 8 in (20 cm) flan ring or baking tin (traditionally oval) with the puff pastry. Spread the jam over the pastry base. Cream together butter and sugar, then mix in the egg yolks and whites. Add almond essence to taste. Pour over the jam. Bake at 425°F (220°C) Reg 7 for 15 minutes then at 350°F (180°C) Reg 4 for a further 20–25 minutes.

Mansfield Goooseberrry Pie

Serves 6

This traditional pie was sold every year at Mansfield Fair.

8 oz (225 g) hot water crust pastry (see page 252)
Filling
1 lb (450 g) green gooseberries
sugar to taste
Sugar Glaze
1 tbsp sugar dissolved in 1 tbsp water
warm apple jelly

Take warm pastry and knead until smooth. Cut off a quarter of the pastry for the lid. Keep warm. Mould the rest of the pastry round a jar. Leave until cool. Remove pastry. Place on a baking tray. Fill pastry with gooseberries and sugar. Put on lid. Make a hole in top of pie. Brush top and sides with glaze. Bake at 425°F (220°C) Reg 7 for 1 hour or until pie is cooked. Brush the top and sides with the glaze during cooking. Add jelly when the pie has cooled but is still warm.

Welbeck Pudding

Serves 4

6 Bramley apples	Line a pie-dish with the jam. Peel and slice the apples and place in alternate layers with the jam. Blend the arrowroot with a little milk. Add the egg yolk to the mixture. Lastly add the remainder of the milk. Pour over the apples. Whisk the egg white to a peak, add the sugar and place over the apples. Bake at 350°F (180°C) Reg 4 for about 1 hour, on the lower shelf of the oven.
2 tbsp apricot jam	
1 tbsp arrowroot or cornflour	
$\frac{1}{4}$ pt (150 ml) milk	
1 egg, separated	
1 oz (25 g) sugar	

Gotham Pudding

Serves 4

The little country town outside Nottingham is the accredited source of this recipe in a book published about 1870.

3 eggs	Beat the eggs, and gradually beat into the flour in a bowl. Add the milk. Beat for about 10 minutes, then add the salt, peel and baking powder. Pour into a greased 1 pt (575 ml) basin. Cover and steam gently for 1½ hours or until cooked. Stand a few minutes to allow the pudding to shrink.
2 large tbsp plain flour	
½ pt (275 ml) milk	
pinch salt	
4 oz (110 g) candied peel	
1 tsp baking powder	

Leicestershire Curd Tarts

Makes 8

This is one of the better surviving recipes for the formerly ubiquitous cheesecake.

8 oz (225 g) curds or 2 pt (1.2 l) milk plus 2 tsp rennet	To make curds, heat the milk until tepid, and add the rennet. When firm, strain curds from whey through butter muslin and leave overnight to strain. Soften the curds with a fork, beat in softened butter, then add sugar, breadcrumbs, lightly beaten eggs, fruit, flavourings and cream. This is a very liquid mixture. Line deep patty pans with the puff pastry which has previously been rolled out thinly and cut with a 3 in (7.5 cm) cutter. Prick the bottom of the pastry and fill with the mixture. Bake for 10–15 minutes at 425°F (220°C) Reg 7, then for 10–15 minutes at 325°F (160°C) Reg 3 until cooked.
4 oz (110 g) butter	
4 oz (110 g) sugar	
2 oz (50 g) fine breadcrumbs	
4 egg yolks	
3 egg whites	
12 oz (350 g) currants and sultanas, mixed	
finely grated nutmeg	
½ tsp finely grated lemon rind	
a little rum or brandy	
2 tbsp cream	
8 oz (225 g) puff pastry (see page 253)	

Speaker's Pudding
Serves 6

I have not been able to discover whether this recipe was a favourite of Nottinghamshire's 'Mr Speaker' Denison, or whether the pudding had the power to encourage a reluctant speaker, but it appears in several books written around 1840. It bears no resemblance to the more mundane Bread and Butter Pudding, and is well worth trying. Don't forget the brandy!

slices white bread

3 oz (75 g) butter

12 oz (350 g) stoned raisins

4 egg yolks

1 pt (575 ml) milk or ¾ pt (425 ml) milk and ¼ pt (150 ml) single cream

1 tbsp sugar

1 tbsp rose water

1 wine glass brandy or rum

Butter a mould and dredge with sugar (Charlotte mould or a seamless cake tin best). Line with buttered slices of stale bread. Add the raisins alternately with the bread, buttering each slice, until the mould is full. Beat up the eggs and add the milk. Stir in the cream, sugar and rose water. Pour over the contents of the mould. Lastly, pour over the brandy and leave to soak for 15 minutes. Bake at 350°F (180°C) Reg 4 for approx 1 hour or it may be steamed for 1½–2 hours.

Nottingham Pudding
Serves 6

The Bramley cooking apple originates from Southwell, Nottinghamshire, where the first tree still flourishes. Both Nottingham and Welbeck Puddings use this excellent apple as their main ingredient.

6 even-sized Bramley apples

3 oz (75 g) butter

3 oz (75 g) caster sugar

pinch nutmeg

pinch cinnamon

6 tbsp plain flour

3 eggs, beaten

milk to mix

pinch salt

Peel and core apples. Cream butter and sugar, add a pinch each of nutmeg and cinnamon. Fill the centre of each apple with this mixture. Place in a well-buttered dish. Blend flour with a little cold water and add 3 well-beaten eggs to it with a pinch of salt and sufficient milk to make a thick creamy batter. Pour over the apples and bake at 350°F (180°C) Reg 4 for 1½ hours.

Newark Pudding
Serves 4

2–3 oz (50–75 g) fresh white breadcrumbs

1 pt (575 ml) milk

2 eggs, separated

1 tbsp ground rice

2 tbsp sugar

1 tbsp melted butter

4 oz (110 g) raisins

vanilla essence to taste

¼ tsp bicarbonate of soda

Place the crumbs in a bowl, cover with ½ pt (300 ml) milk, and leave to soak. Beat the egg yolks lightly and add to the soaked breadcrumbs. Soak the ground rice in a little milk and add to the crumbs. Gradually add the rest of the milk, beating well, until a smooth batter is obtained. Stir in the sugar, butter, raisins, flavourings and bicarbonate of soda. Whisk the egg whites until stiff, fold carefully into the mixture. Pour into a buttered pie-dish, and bake at 350°F (180°C) Reg 4 for 1 hour. Turn out and serve with a sweet sauce, eg a Melba-type sauce (see page 23) made with fresh fruit.

Feast Plum Pudding
Serves 4–5

*These worthy puddings could be bought ready-made in cake shops until the
Second World War.*

1 small loaf bread
4 oz (110 g) suet
8 oz (225 g) raisins
4 oz (110 g) currants
2 oz (50 g) candied lemon peel
4 oz (110 g) sugar
2 eggs, beaten

Remove the crusts from the bread, slice thickly and soak with water, leave overnight. Strain the water off, and mix in the remaining ingredients. Mix well. Place in a well-buttered deep dish or tin, cover and bake at 275°F (140°C) Reg 1 for 3–4 hours. Usually this pudding is eaten cold but it may be warmed up before serving.

Staffordshire Yeomanry Pudding
Serves 6

8 oz (225 g) sweet shortcrust pastry (see page 252)
raspberry jam
Filling
2 egg yolks
1 egg white
8 oz (225 g) butter
8 oz (225 g) caster sugar
1 oz (25 g) ground almonds
¼ tsp almond essence

Roll two-thirds of the pastry until ¼ in (5 mm) thick and line a shallow pie-dish, trim and damp edge with water. Spread on jam and then filling. Roll out remaining pastry and place on top. Trim, seal and flute edges. Make 4 or 6 small cuts in top with point of knife. Bake at 350°F (180°C) Reg 4 for 40 minutes. Cover with foil for last 10 minutes as this pastry browns quickly. It is good eaten just warm, but not too hot, and is also very good cold.

High Church or Stir-in Pudding
Serves 4–5

This recipe appears under both names, and is included in all the manuscript books I have read. The oldest, dated 1770, uses fresh blackcurrants, and the later ones, blackcurrant jam. I much prefer the fresh fruit. Notts Children's Dinner Association Book, dated 1883, states that this was a great favourite with the children. I recommend it on a cold day, when the first course has been light.

8 oz (225 g) plain flour
pinch salt
4 oz (110 g) suet or margarine
1 tsp bicarbonate of soda
¼ pt (150 ml) milk
fresh or frozen blackcurrants, with sugar to taste, or 6 oz (175 g) blackcurrant jam
2 oz (50 g) demerara sugar

Mix salt with flour, add suet or rub in margarine if used. Dissolve bicarbonate of soda in the milk. Add the jam or fruit to the flour, with the sugar. Lastly add the milk to make a stiff paste. Place in a greased basin, cover and steam for 2½–3 hours.

Banbury Apple Pie
Serves 4–5

6 cooking apples	Peel and slice 6 medium apples, place in a layer in a well-buttered pie-dish, add a sprinkling of peel and a few currants, pour on a little butter, add a sprinkling of sugar and spices and repeat the layers until the dish is full. Cover with shortcrust pastry, and glaze with milk and sugar. Place in the oven at 400°F (200°C) Reg 6 and bake for 30 minutes. Sprinkle caster sugar over the top of the pie, and serve it hot or cold, with whipped cream or custard.
2 oz (50 g) candied peel	
4 oz (110 g) currants	
3 oz (75 g) butter, melted	
pinch ginger and cinnamon	
sugar	
8 oz (225 g) shortcrust pastry (see page 252)	

Brown Betty
Serves 4

1½ lb (675 g) apples (before preparing)	Peel, core and slice the apples. Put a layer of breadcrumbs in a 2 pt (1.2 l) pie-dish, add a layer of apples, sprinkle with sugar and spices and dot with butter. Add another layer of crumbs, apples, etc, and continue until dish is full. Mix golden syrup and water and pour over. Cover top with buttered crumbs. Bake at 325°F (160°C) Reg 3 for 45 minutes or until apples are soft.
6 oz (175 g) breadcrumbs	
3 oz (75 g) sugar	
½ tsp cinnamon	
¼ tsp cloves	
2 tbsp butter	
2 tbsp golden syrup	
⅛ pt (80 ml) water	

Bloxham Statute Plum Pudding

The Bloxham Statute, or Hiring Fair, took place on the first Thursday after old Michaelmas Day. It was recorded by Dr Plot in 1677 and mentioned by Daniel Defoe when he passed through the village c 1724. It was the time when young people and servants offered themselves for hire, carrying badges to show their qualifications. The Sunday following the hiring fair was the statute feast when Bloxham Statute Plum Pudding would be eaten. Until late into the 1800s the day was still marked by a special service in church. This recipe is from an 1820 recipe book.

1 lb (450 g) sliced white bread	Soak the bread in cold milk for 12 hours, then drain away milk which has not been absorbed and crumble the bread. Steep the ground rice in milk until it is quite thick then add melted butter. Then add the bread, flour, raisins, currants, sugar, nutmeg, cinnamon, mace, the glass of liquid and the eggs, well beaten. Butter the dishes well, shake a little flour over them, fill 3 parts full and bake at 350°F (180°C) Reg 4 for 1 hour or until firm.
cold milk	
1 lb (450 g) ground rice	
1¼ lb (560 g) butter, melted	
2 oz (50 g) plain flour	
1 lb (450 g) stoned raisins	
8 oz (225 g) moist sugar	
1¼ lb (560 g) currants	
1 nutmeg, grated	
cinnamon	
mace	
1 glass brandy and rum, mixed	
5 eggs	

Warwick Pudding
Serves 6

This delicious recipe was discovered waiting patiently for its resurrection between the pages of an old history book housed at the Warwickshire Record Office. Named after the county town, it would make a delightful dish for any occasion and is easy to make.

crystallized or stem ginger for decoration	
1 oz (25 g) gelatine	
2 tbsp milk	
3 egg yolks	
6 egg whites	
4 oz (110 g) caster sugar	
1 pt (575 ml) single cream	
1 wine glass rum	

Butter a 2 pt (1.2 l) mould, and decorate it with the ginger. Dissolve the gelatine in the milk. Beat the egg yolks and whites with the sugar and gradually stir in the cream. Gently cook in a double saucepan (or in a bowl over a pan of hot water), stirring constantly until the mixture coats the back of the wooden spoon. Cool, stir in the dissolved gelatine and the rum, pour into the mould and allow to set in a cold place. Turn out to serve.

Rhubarb Charlotte
Serves 4

6 oz (175 g) breadcrumbs	
2 oz (50 g) butter, melted	
1 lb (450 g) rhubarb	
2 oz (50 g) brown sugar	
$\frac{1}{2}$ tsp ground ginger	
$\frac{1}{4}$ tsp ground cinnamon	
$\frac{1}{4}$ tsp grated nutmeg	
grated rind of 1 orange	
2 tbsp golden syrup	
2 tsp orange juice	
2 tsp lemon juice	

Toss the crumbs in the melted butter, shaking the pan so that they absorb it evenly. Spread some of the crumbs in a thin layer over the bottom of a buttered 2 pt (1.2 l) ovenproof dish. Cut the rhubarb into 1 in (2.5 cm) lengths and use some of it to make one layer on top of the crumbs. Mix together the sugar, spices and grated orange rind. Sprinkle some of this over the rhubarb. Repeat the layers of crumbs, rhubarb and sugar until the dish is full, ending with the layer of crumbs. Heat the syrup with the fruit juices and 2 tbsp water. When it is melted, pour over the Charlotte. Cover with a piece of greaseproof paper and bake in the centre of the oven at 400°F (200°C) Reg 6 for 20–30 minutes, depending on the age and thickness of the rhubarb. Uncover and cook for a further 10 minutes or so until the top is golden and crisp. Serve with single cream.

Cakes, Breads and Biscuits

Ashbourne Gingerbreads

This speciality of the charming little town close to Dovedale is still made by several local bakeries, one of which has been making the biscuits for over 100 years. The candied peel makes them that bit different from other gingerbreads.

8 oz (225 g) butter	Cream together the butter and sugar until soft. Sift in the flour, ginger and salt, and add the rind or peel. Knead with the hands until a smooth dough is obtained. Roll out into a long roll about 2 in (5 cm) in diameter and cut into slices. Place the slices on a greased baking sheet, mark by pressing with 3 fingers across each. Bake at 350°F (180°C) Reg 4 for about 20 minutes.
5 oz (140 g) caster sugar	
10 oz (275 g) plain flour	
2 tsp ground ginger	
pinch salt	
grated lemon rind or finely chopped candied peel	

Langley Wakes Cakes

Many Derbyshire villages marked their annual Wakes or Fair Week by baking their own versions of these biscuits.

12 oz (350 g) plain flour	Sieve together the flour, baking powder and ground ginger, add the caraway seeds and the finely grated lemon rind. Rub the butter into the flour, add the sugar and the currants. Mix to a stiff paste with the beaten egg. Roll out on a floured surface approx $\frac{1}{4}$ in (5 mm) thick, and cut into 4 in (10 cm) rounds. Place on a greased baking sheet, sprinkle lightly with caster sugar. Bake at 375°F (190°C) Reg 5 for about 15–20 minutes. Leave the cakes to cool for a few minutes on the baking sheet; this will help them to crisp.
1 tsp baking powder	
$\frac{1}{2}$ tsp ground ginger	
$\frac{1}{2}$ oz (15 g) caraway seeds	
finely grated rind of $\frac{1}{2}$ lemon	
8 oz (225 g) butter	
6 oz (175 g) sugar	
4 oz (110 g) currants	
1 egg, beaten	
caster sugar for sprinkling	

Note:
Although called cakes, these should be crisp like biscuits.

Lincolnshire Buns

Makes 12

8 oz (225 g) plain flour	Mix together the flour, salt, ground almonds and baking powder. Rub in the butter. Beat the egg, add to the mixture with the milk to make a very stiff paste. Place in 12 tall heaps on a greased baking sheet, bake at 400°F (200°C) Reg 6 for 15–20 minutes. Cut the tops off each and place a knob of butter on the cut surface, press the top back on again. Serve hot.
$\frac{1}{2}$ tsp salt	
2 tsp ground almonds	
2 heaped tsp baking powder	
3 oz (75 g) butter	
1 egg	
$\frac{1}{8}$ pt (80 ml) milk	

St Catherine's Cakes

St Catherine's Day was formerly kept as the Feast of the Lacemakers. These cakes are connected with Catherine of Aragon, who, to lighten her sorrows when she was banished from the court of Henry VIII, taught lace-making to the Bedfordshire villagers near where she stayed; these little cakes are said to have been a great favourite with her.

4 oz (110 g) plain flour

½ tsp bicarbonate of soda

4 oz (110 g) caster sugar

1 heaped tbsp ground almonds

4 oz (110 g) butter

hazelnuts, walnuts or almonds

glacé cherries

Mix together the flour, bicarbonate of soda, sugar and ground almonds. Melt butter and stir into the dry ingredients. This makes a stiff paste. Pinch off small pieces of the same size, roll into balls and place these well apart, on a lightly floured baking sheet. Press them with a fork, taking care to keep them an even size. Handle the mixture lightly. Into each cake press half a hazelnut, walnut or almond, or glacé cherry. Bake for 10–12 minutes at 400°F (200°C) Reg 6. They are delicious when served hot, but they will also keep well in an airtight tin.

Coventry Godcakes

These were made by godmothers to be eaten at Christenings. The name comes from their triangular shape which represents the Trinity.

8 oz (225 g) puff pastry (see page 253)

mincemeat

egg white

caster sugar

Make the puff pastry, and allow to rest for 30 minutes before using. Roll the pastry ¼ in (5 mm) thick, and cut into 4 in (10 cm) squares. Place a good teaspoon of mincemeat on each square, damp the edges, fold together to form a triangle. Brush with lightly beaten egg white and sprinkle with caster sugar. Bake in a hot oven at 450°F (230°C) Reg 8 for approx 15 minutes, until lightly browned.

Staffordshire Oatcakes

Makes about 24

Staffordshire and Derbyshire homesteads still serve oatcakes at breakfast time with their bacon and eggs. Elsewhere this habit seems to have fallen into decline. Many of the old farmhouses had a built-in 'bakestone,' made of gritstone and capable of withstanding heat from the fire below. This was used for cooking the oatcakes. Some farms had a large wooden rack for drying them; an example can be seen in the museum at Bakewell.

8 oz (225 g) fine oatmeal

8 oz (225 g) plain white flour

1 tsp salt

1 tsp sugar

½ oz (15 g) fresh yeast

1½ pt (850 ml) warm milk and water

Add salt to flour and oatmeal and stir. Dissolve yeast with a little of the warm liquid and add sugar. Set aside to work in a warm place. Mix the dry ingredients with the yeast and the rest of the warm liquid to make a batter. Cover with a clean cloth and leave in a warm place for about 1 hour. Then bake on a well-greased bakestone, griddle or thick-based frying pan. Turn each oatcake after 2–3 minutes when the upper side appears dry; the underside should be golden brown. Bake for a further 2–3 minutes.

Orange Tea Bread

Makes one 1 lb (450 g) loaf

6 oz (175 g) self-raising flour

½ tsp salt

3 oz (75 g) caster sugar

grated rind of 1 medium orange

2 tbsp coarse cut marmalade

1 tbsp cooking oil

1 egg, beaten

3 tbsp milk

Sift the flour and salt into a bowl and add the sugar and orange rind. Make a well in the middle and stir in the marmalade, oil, egg and milk. Mix well. Turn into a greased 1 lb (450 g) loaf tin. Bake for 40–45 minutes at 350°F (180°C) Reg 4. Cool on a wire rack. Serve sliced with butter.

Rutland Plum Shuttles

These cakes, with their sausage shape and pointed ends, are named after the weaver's shuttle.

1½ lb (675 g) plain flour

4 oz (110 g) butter

4 oz (110 g) caster sugar

4 oz (110 g) currants

2 oz (50 g) candied peel

1 oz (25 g) fresh yeast or ½ oz (15 g) dried yeast

1 tsp sugar

½ pt (275 ml) milk

½ pt (275 ml) water

Sieve the flour into a warmed bowl. Rub in the butter until it resembles fine breadcrumbs. Add the sugar, currants and peel. Mix well. Whisk yeast with sugar and some of the liquid warmed to tepid (or sprinkle dried yeast on water with sugar and leave until frothy). Stir the yeasted liquid into the flour mixture, adding more liquid during the mixing to form a soft dough. Knead well. Leave, covered, in a warm place until doubled in size (approx 45–60 minutes). Turn the dough on to a floured board and knead until smooth. Pull into small pieces and shape into ovals about the size of a sausage, with pointed ends. Place on a greased baking sheet. Leave, covered, in a warm place for 20 minutes to prove. Bake at 425°F (220°C) Reg 7 for 15–20 minutes.

Northamptonshire Seblet Cake

Makes 8

In the days when wheat was sown by hand, these large caraway cakes were a favourite with the farm labourers who named them after the basket that held the seed they were strewing.

6 oz (175 g) butter
6 oz (175 g) caster sugar
3 large eggs, beaten
1–2 tbsp (15–30 ml) milk
4 oz (110 g) plain flour
4 oz (110 g) self-raising flour
2 tsp (10 ml) caraway seeds

Grease and line the bases of eight 4 in (10 cm) Yorkshire Pudding tins (if you have a sheet of 4, bake in 2 sessions). Cream butter and sugar until light and fluffy, gradually beat in eggs. Fold in flour and caraway seeds, adding milk to give a soft mixture. Divide between the tins and bake at 350°F (180°C) Reg 4 for about 35 minutes, or until firm to the touch. Eat fresh.

Note:
To make a cake for slicing, a 7 in (18 cm) round cake tin can be used instead of the individual tins. Bake for 1–1½ hours.

Thor Cakes

Wirksworth, the centre of the lead-mining industry since Roman times, is the home of these biscuits which are traditionally eaten on 5 November. These cakes are not dissimilar to Ockbrook Foggies, of which it was once said that 'in the Countie of Derbyshire no sweetmeat of more fame exists.'

8 oz (225 g) fine oatmeal
8 oz (225 g) plain flour
8 oz (225 g) granulated sugar
8 oz (225 g) treacle
1 oz (25 g) candied peel, chopped
6 oz (175 g) margarine
2 tsp baking powder
1 tsp salt
1 tsp ginger
1 tsp mixed spice

Mix together the dry ingredients. Rub in fat. Mix to a stiff paste with slightly warmed treacle. Knead lightly. Roll out to ¼ in (5 mm) thickness. Cut into large rounds, as big as a saucer. Place on greased oven sheet and bake at 350°F (180°C) Reg 4 until golden brown (20–30 minutes).

Belvoir Castle Buns

*These buns are associated with the seat of the Dukes of Rutland, and were apparently a
special favourite of the Seventh Duke (1818–1906). They are not unlike Chelsea Buns.*

1 lb (450 g) plain flour

2 oz (50 g) butter

4 oz (110 g) sugar

4 fl oz (150 ml) milk and water

$\frac{1}{2}$ oz (15 g) yeast

4 oz (110 g) chopped dried fruit

Rub the fat into the flour and add sugar. Cream the yeast with a little sugar and add to it the warm milk and water. Pour the liquid into the centre of the flour, sprinkle dry mixture over the top, cover with a cloth and leave in a warm place until bubbles appear on the surface. At this stage, mix well and knead until the dough is smooth. Put to rise in a warm atmosphere until its size is doubled. Knead again and roll out thinly. Sprinkle the fruit over the top and roll up like a Swiss Roll. Cut into pieces 1 in (2.5 cm) wide. Place on a greased tin and allow to rise for 30 minutes. Brush with milk. Bake for 10 minutes at 425°F (220°C) Reg 7.

Bosworth Jumbles

*This is one of a group of recipes, all of which are said to have been dropped from the pocket
of King Richard III's cook on the battlefield at Bosworth.*

5 oz (150 g) butter

5 oz (150 g) caster sugar

1 egg

10 oz (275 g) plain flour

1 tsp grated lemon rind

2 oz (50 g) ground almonds

Cream the butter and sugar together and work in the egg, flour, lemon rind and ground almonds. Form the mixture into a long sausage shape and break off into small pieces. Form these into S shapes and bake on a greased baking sheet at 350°F (180°C) Reg 4 for 10 minutes. Lift off carefully and cool on a wire rack.

Fig Pie

*Fig Pie has been made in Draycott-le-Moors, Staffordshire, and the neighbouring villages for
a long time. One theory says it dates back to the time of the Crusaders, who may have
introduced figs to the area; as there is a Crusader's tomb in Draycott-le-Moors, this could well
be true. This recipe was traditionally eaten on Mothering Sunday, known to local people as
Fig Pie Wakes.*

8 oz (225 g) shortcrust pastry (see page 252)

8 oz (225 g) packet of figs

2 oz (50 g) sultanas

1½ tbsp black treacle

1 tbsp golden syrup

1 pt (575 ml) water

1–1½ tbsp cornflour to thicken the mixture

Line two 7 in (18 cm) flan rings with the shortcrust pastry and bake blind. Take stalks off figs and cut up small, put the figs, sultanas, black treacle, golden syrup and water (minus 2 tbsp) into a medium saucepan, bring to the boil and simmer with lid on for approx 20 minutes until fruit is tender. Mix the cornflour with the remaining water, pour into the mixture and stir continuously until it is thick and cooked. Pour into pastry cases and leave until set. Serve cold cut in slices.

Kattern Cake

These cakes are associated both with St Catherine's Day and with Catherine of Aragon who was born on Old St Catherine's Day, 6 December. In many places a bell man went round in the morning crying:
'Rise maids, rise!
Bake your cattern pies,
Bake enough and bake no waste,
And let the bell man have a taste.'

1 lb (450 g) strong plain white flour

2 tsp salt

2 oz (50 g) lard

½ oz (15 g) fresh yeast or ¼ oz (7 g) dried yeast

1 tsp sugar

½ pt (275 ml) tepid water

2 oz (50 g) butter or lard

1 oz (25 g) caraway seeds

2 oz (50 g) sugar

1 egg, beaten

Sieve flour and salt into a bowl. Rub the lard into the flour. Whisk the fresh yeast together with the sugar into half the measured tepid water. (If using dried yeast, sprinkle the yeast on to ¼ pt (150 ml) of the tepid water and allow to reconstitute for 15 minutes.) Make a well in the centre of the flour, pour in the yeasted liquid. Gradually stir the flour into the liquid, adding the remaining water a little at a time, until a soft dough is produced. Knead well for at least 5 minutes. Cover the bowl and leave in a warm place for the dough to double in size (30–45 minutes). Turn the dough out on to a floured surface and knock back to its original size. Knead into the dough the butter or lard, caraway seeds, sugar and egg. Knead well. Place in a greased and floured 9 in (23 cm) cake tin. Cover with a cloth and leave in a warm place for 30 minutes. Bake at 400°F (200°C) Reg 6 for 35–40 minutes.

Tandra Cake

Makes 2 × 1 lb (450 g) loaves

This is a richer version of Kattern Cake and was traditionally eaten on St Andrew's Day. It was also known as St Andrew's Cake.

1 lb (450 g) plain flour

1 tsp salt

½ oz (15 g) fresh yeast or ¼ oz (7 g) dried yeast

1 tsp sugar

½ pt (275 ml) water

4 oz (110 g) currants

4 oz (110 g) sugar

1 oz (25 g) chopped candied peel

1 egg

4 oz (110 g) melted lard

Sieve flour and salt. Whisk fresh yeast and sugar into warmed water (or sprinkle dried yeast on water with sugar and leave until frothy). Add the yeasted liquid to the flour, and knead well. Leave the dough, covered, in a warm place to rise until twice its size (45–60 minutes). Knock back dough, and knead the remaining ingredients into it. Knead thoroughly. Divide into two, and shape, set into 2 × 1 lb (450 g) greased loaf tins. Allow to prove in a warm place, covered for approx 30 minutes. Bake at 350°F (180°C) Reg 4 for 1–1½ hours.

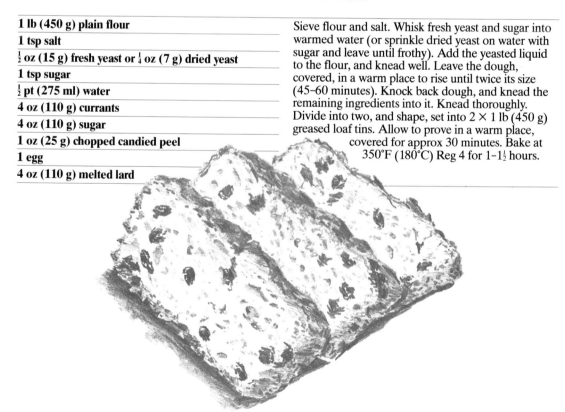

Northamptonshire Cheesecakes
Makes 12

*These cheesecakes were eaten with frumenty, a creamy porridge,
at sheep-shearing time.*

8 oz (225 g) shortcrust pastry (see page 252)
1 pt (575 ml) milk
rind and juice of 1 lemon
1 oz (25 g) butter
1½ oz (40 g) caster sugar
1 egg
2 oz (50 g) currants
grated nutmeg

Make the pastry, roll out and cut 12 circles with a 3½ in (9 cm) cutter. Use to line 12 deep bun tins. Prick bases with a fork and bake blind at 400°F (200°C) Reg 6 for 10 minutes. Grate lemon rind and set aside; pour milk into saucepan and add 2 tbsp lemon juice. Bring gently to boil so that the milk separates into curds and whey. Allow to cool, strain and press well. Place butter, sugar and egg in basin over pan of hot water and cook gently, stirring, until mixture thickens slightly and coats the back of a spoon – do not boil. Remove from heat and add lemon rind, currants and curds. Divide mixture between the cases and sprinkle with grated nutmeg. Return to oven at 350°F (180°C) Reg 4 for about 20 minutes or until filling has set. Serve warm.

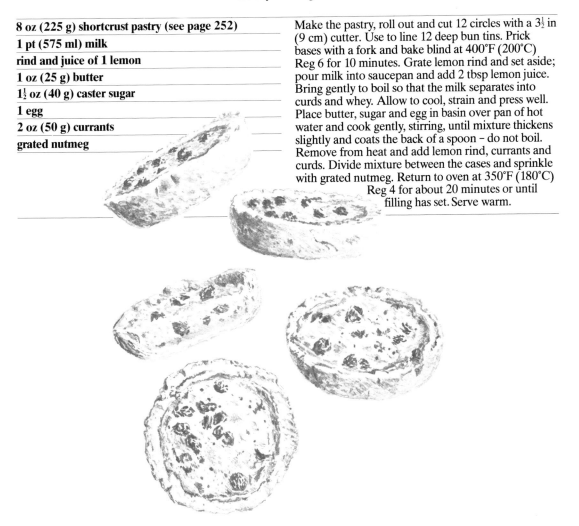

Pump Cake

*This probably gets its name from the days when there was a pump at the kitchen sink.
The cook would have held the filled cake tin under the pump and run water over it.*

2 oz (50 g) butter or margarine
3 oz (75 g) sugar
2 tsp almond essence
1 egg, well beaten
5 oz (150 g) self-raising flour
apricot jam

Beat together the fat and sugar. Add egg and essence. Add flour and make a dough. Divide into two. Press half into a greased sandwich tin. Spread with the jam. Place second round of dough on top of jam. Put under 'pump' and run water over. Drain off. Brush with water, sprinkle with sugar and bake at 350°F (180°C) Reg 4 for about 30 minutes.

Odell Biscuits

From the Bedfordshire village of Odell, these are another good local example of ginger fairings.

8 oz (225 g) plain flour	Sieve together the dry ingredients. Add the butter and rub in. Warm the treacle and add to the rubbed-in mixture. Knead until free of cracks, roll into small balls, place on a greased baking sheet. Bake at 350°F (180°C) Reg 4 for 10–15 minutes.
1 tsp bicarbonate of soda	
1 heaped tsp ground ginger	
2 oz (50 g) butter	
2 tbsp black treacle	

Derbyshire Moorland Tarts

These tarts, rather similar to Mince Pies, come from the village of Ashover between Chesterfield and Matlock, and not, as the name suggests, from the northern moors of the county. Anthony Babbington, one of the Gunpowder Plot conspirators, had family links with Ashover. The tarts are especially good eaten with Derbyshire Stilton Cheese made at Hartington.

4 oz (110 g) shortcrust pastry (see page 252)	Make up the pastry and roll out to fit a 7in (18 cm) flan ring. Melt the butter gently. Stir in the other ingredients to form a spread. Fill the pastry case, and bake at 400°F (200°C) Reg 6 until set, approx 30 minutes. This recipe may also be made as small tarts, which will take 15–20 minutes to cook. Eat them hot or cold.
3 oz (75 g) butter	
2 eggs, hard-boiled and finely chopped	
4 oz (110 g) sugar	
4 oz (110 g) candied peel	
4 oz (110 g) currants	
$\frac{1}{4}$ nutmeg, grated	

Banbury Cakes

These are similar to Coventry Godcakes, though oval-shaped, and probably have a common origin.

8 oz (225 g) rough puff pastry (see page 253)	Make rough puff pastry using milk to give the old-fashioned texture. Melt butter and add the flour and spice to heat in a pan. Remove. Add fruit, sugar and rum or sherry and lemon juice. Cut pastry into 5 in (13 cm) rounds, $\frac{1}{4}$ in (5 mm) thick. Put filling on the rounds, damp edges, draw up and flatten to an oval or oblong shape. Put on baking tin. Turn over and make 3 slits across top. Bake at 475°F (240°C) Reg 9 for 15–20 minutes. Just before the cakes are ready, brush with egg whites and sprinkle with sugar.
Filling	
1 oz (25 g) butter	
$\frac{1}{2}$ oz (15 g) plain flour	
grated nutmeg	
4 oz (110 g) currants	
$\frac{1}{2}$ oz (15 g) peel	
2 oz (50 g) brown sugar	
1 tsp lemon juice	
2 tbsp rum or sherry if liked	

Miscellaneous

Lumpy Tums

A recipe for porridge written by Joseph Allen, a shoemaker of Onecote, near Leek, Staffordshire, in 1855. Fine oatmeal was stirred into boiling milk, stirred with a pinch of salt added and was eaten either as it was or with treacle.

Taters they are windy meat,
Un Frumity it is a treat,
Puddin's good, when stuffed wi' plums,
But gie mi plenty lumpy-tums.

Its put yer kettle* on th' fire,
Un bring the meal a little higher,
When the milk it boils and foams
Then's yer time for lumpy-tums.

Bafe, mutton, veal, poke, ducks or gase,
Fresh fish or fowl or bread un chase,
O! Gie mi thase when dinner comes
Bu' at supper gie mi lumpy-tums.

Would yo ya tender offspring rear,
Wi' bodies fit fatigues t'bear,
Paumper 'um not wi' deenty crums,
But bring 'em up on lumpy-tums.

Just view our labourers robust race
Theer rosy chakes, theer ruddy face;
They'n nerves loike stale, they'n hearts liek droms
Because they were reared on lumpy-tums.

Just view those healthy country girls
Theer rosy chakes, theer glossy curls;
Th' rosiest chakes un reddest combs
Han girls ut's reared on lumpy-tums.

Th' plow lad when his work war done,
Returned wom wi' th' settin' sun,
Some fag end of a song he hums,
When he think o' wom un lumpy-tums.

Wae well remember Robert Peel,
Who kindly lowered th' price o' meal.
Its a poor look out at folks' woms,
If they had no meal for lumpy-tums.

Jim Shaw†, that valiant man who slew
Ten of th' French at Waterloo,
His powerful arms dealt them theer dooms,
For hae wor reared on lumpy-tums.

Let pale-faced wimmin sip aw dey,
On slape-destroyin' strung grane tey,
Th' acrid juice th' nerves benums.
They's non such juice i' lumpy-tums.

Koind heavens, listen too mi prayer,
Un grant mi whoile oi tarry here,
Oi eks no' wealth's uncounted sums
But health un' peace on lumpy-tums.

*saucepan
†born at Cossall, nr Nottingham

Wales and the Welsh Borders

If we approach this charming region from the landward side, a logical place to start our journey is in the north, in Cheshire. A favourite county for me, Cheshire is at once inextricably mixed up with Manchester and yet its residential satellites of Altrincham, Bowdon, Wilmslow, Sale and Hale are firmly entrenched in Cheshire's rich red soil with buildings as rosy-pink as the local cheese is golden. Indeed, a slim wedge of Blue Cheshire with a glass of light Sauternes is a gastronomic marriage that few gourmets can resist, and there are those of us who might suggest that Cheshire Cheese is disputably better than the harder nuttier Cheddar in far-off Somerset.

But Manchester and Cheshire have, for me, a much more intimate connection with our tables and kitchens, for here it was, at Arley Hall near Knutsford, that an eighteenth-century Yorkshire lass, Elizabeth Whitaker, married the gardener of Lady Warburton, became Mistress John Raffald and, having wed and moved to Manchester's Bull's Head Inn, went on to write in 1769 *The Experienced English Housekeeper.* This is the *one* book which was to open my eyes to the exciting dishes which were prepared in the England of those far-off days, and inspired me to write *my* first book, *Fine English Cookery.*

Sadly, there is little left of Elizabeth Raffald's recipes (except in my book!) and one wonders what happened to such delights as Green Fricassee of Chicken, Marbl'd Veal and the true liquor-soaked trifles and syllabubs she served to her guests. But lost they are, and sad it is, and much I could write about it. However, this present book exists to help prevent other national and regional dishes from sliding imperceptibly into oblivion: so on with our cook's tour, southwards through the border counties.

I often call these the 'quiet' counties, particularly Shropshire, for the hurly-burly of modern life by-passes its rather melancholy landscape, leaving much of it untouched. 'Clunton and Clunbury, Clungunford and Clun are the quietest places under the sun,' wrote A. E. Housman in *A Shropshire Lad.*

The rich English fare, at one time served by 'comelye and

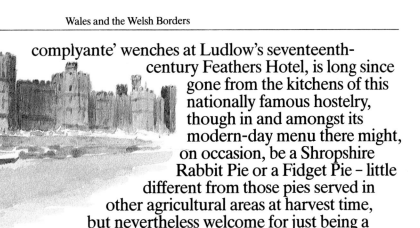

complyante' wenches at Ludlow's seventeenth-century Feathers Hotel, is long since gone from the kitchens of this nationally famous hostelry, though in and amongst its modern-day menu there might, on occasion, be a Shropshire Rabbit Pie or a Fidget Pie – little different from those pies served in other agricultural areas at harvest time, but nevertheless welcome for just being a regional favourite.

You will, for sure, get a Shrewsbury Biscuit in the county's capital town, and for those who are attracted to timber-framed buildings with exotic Tudor chimneys, an hour or two at Much Wenlock won't go amiss, and there is nothing to stop one dreaming of the dishes which would have been served up by the cooks from their ancient kitchens – a dish of pork with 'apricocks', a 'fysshe in jelly', a rich almond tart or a winey syllabub.

Further south you come to cider country and Hereford, whose handsome cathedral is one of the trio which, with Gloucester and Worcester, forms the famous Three Choirs Festival. The Wye Valley, arguably one of the

most beautiful spots in our country, joins the Black Mountains of Wales to the west with the Malvern Hills to the east, and runs south to Gloucestershire's Forest of Dean.

Regional dishes may not abound in this area of England, but a threefold *international* trademark remains for all time in the rich golden wheels of Double Gloucester Cheese, the ciders of Hereford and the piquancy of Worcestershire Sauce, the latter used in its home county for spicing up sausage, meat and fish, and across the world as an essential ingredient of those Bloody Marys served with American Sunday brunch anywhere from New York's fashionable Plaza Hotel to San Francisco's even more fashionable Mark Hopkins.

And so to the Principality of Wales, for a brief taste of a prince of regions, stuffed with places of historical and visual interest. Those of us non-Welsh who spent childhood holidays paddling the long sands of

Penmaenmawr, or whose teenage knees trembled on the Crib Goch Ridge at the sight of the distant navy-blue Llyn Llydaw, now return to indulge a spectrum of grown-up interests.

In a holiday mood, one could start at Colwyn Bay, the Victorian holiday resort to which families return year after year for every sort of holiday fun, from fishing to archaeology. But one could also pay a visit inland to Rhyd-y-Foel, the home of the Llandulas Male Voice Choir. This fine choir is only one among hundreds. Just *think* of the music that abounds in Wales! Not just at the International Eisteddfod, when about 10,000 competitors converge on Llangollen to continue a tradition rooted before the age of Christianity, but in every likely hall throughout the land, week in, week out. And of course there is the internationally-famous Welsh National Opera Company.

Across from Bangor lies the 'island of Druids', Anglesey, famous for its Dark Cake, and stretching over the Menai Strait soars a marvel of engineering, one of the many bridges and viaducts built by Thomas Telford. At the time it was opened, in 1826, it was the longest single-span bridge in the world.

Turning inland, one's appetite whetted if not by Snowdon Pudding then by the distant backdrop of Snowdon from Bodnant, it is only sensible to head for the climber's paradise. Here in the changeless villages of North Wales, hungry walkers and mountaineers replenish their energies at tables laden with such delights as Lamb Stew with Trollins (dumplings), Leek Pasties, Spiced Potato Bakes, and maybe Bara Brith (currant bread). It is the very nature of the rugged Welsh countryside that makes sheep the principal livestock, and tender Welsh lamb a staple dish. To have eaten Welsh Lamb Pie or Mutton Cawl means you will seldom eat lamb any other way!

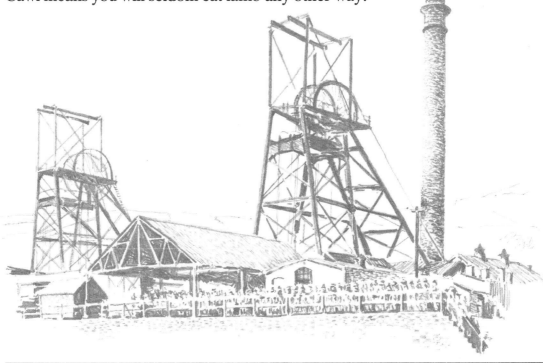

Fish appears too, because the 750 miles of Welsh coastline is a gateway to a paradise of mullet and bass, of codling, plaice and flounder. And Swper Scadan (herring supper) or Pennog Picl (pickled herrings) and Cockle Pie make good use of these fruits of the sea.

South-west we go through a wealth of beauty and historical landmarks to the smallest of the National Parks, Pembrokeshire, from where are said to have been quarried the stones for Stonehenge! But Wales is not just a scenic paradise, it also holds an important place in the industrial history of Britain. Local iron-ore supplies meant the development of a one-time thriving steel industry at Port Talbot, and we should go southwards to visit Merthyr Tydfil, which to the Welsh means iron, coal and railways. Dowlais was once the largest ironworks in the world, and employed 10,000 men, and Richard Trevithick tested his early steam locomotives on the tramway to Abercynon. Surely it was amongst the thrifty folk of this area that the tasty Cow Heel Brawns, Faggots, Welsh Onion Pie and Welsh Cheese Pudding were born? Cheese lovers must travel on south again to Caerffili, home of the mild, crumbly cheese that many of us like to eat with fruit or Christmas Cake, though a tasty Glamorgan Sausage slots well into any menu today as a savoury cheese dish.

These, then, are a mere few blobs from the rich cream that is Wales. It only remains to sample a little of the regional food that goes with that cream.

Soups

Cheshire Potato Soup
Serves 6

By the Napoleonic Wars, potatoes were grown extensively as a main field crop in Wirral and Frodsham. They were shipped by barges up the Mersey and later the Bridgewater Canal to the industrial towns of Lancashire as well as to Liverpool.

1 lb (450 g) potatoes

1 lb (450 g) leeks

1 onion

2 oz (50 g) margarine

1¼ pt (725 ml) stock

½ pt (275 ml) milk

salt and pepper

fried bread cubes

Wash, peel and roughly dice the potatoes. Thoroughly wash and trim the leeks and cut into slices. Peel and slice the onion. Melt the margarine in a saucepan, add vegetables, cover and cook gently for 5 minutes. Add a little seasoning and stock, and bring to the boil. Cover and simmer for 20 minutes. Put the mixture into a liquidizer or pass through a fine sieve. Rinse the saucepan and return the soup to the saucepan. Add milk, and season again if necessary. Re-heat the soup and serve piping-hot with fried bread cubes.

Chicken Broth
Serves 6

1 oz (25 g) haricot beans

1 oz (25 g) lentils

1 oz (25 g) pearl barley

1 oz (25 g) dried peas

1 chicken carcase

2½ pt (1.5 l) water

1 leek, chopped

mixed herbs

seasoning

Soak the dry ingredients overnight. Simmer the carcase in the water for 2 hours. Remove bones from stock and add the other ingredients except the leek. Simmer gently for 2–3 hours. Add the leek. Simmer for a further 10 minutes. Garnish with chopped parsley. Serve with freshly baked wholemeal bread rolls and butter.

Cawl
Serves 4–6

Cawl is a traditional dish. The broth was served with bread and the meat and vegetables as the main course. This is sometimes known as 'Lobsgows' and may originate from 'Lobscouse' (lob-sheep, scouse-broth) a North of England derivation, but over the years it has been absorbed into traditional Welsh cooking, at least in North Wales; it is almost unknown in South Wales.

2 lb (900 g) neck of lamb

1 small swede

8 oz (225 g) carrots

8 oz (225 g) parsnips

1 large onion, diced

8 oz (225 g) potatoes

2 large leeks

seasoning

parsley, chopped

Dice the vegetables. Cover the meat with salted water, bring to the boil and skim. Add all the vegetables except the leeks and potatoes. Simmer gently for 2–2½ hours or pressure-cook for 30 minutes. Skim fat. Remove bones. Add potatoes. Cook for a further 30 minutes. Add chopped leeks and cook for 10 minutes. Before serving, add parsley.

Leek Soup – Cawl Cennin A Hufen
Serves 8

$1\frac{1}{4}$ lb (560 g) leeks

2 oz (50 g) butter

12 oz (350 g) onions, chopped

1 head celery

3 pt (1.75 l) mutton stock

1 oz (25 g) chopped parsley

diced meat (optional)

salt and pepper

$\frac{1}{4}$ pt (150 ml) double cream

diced fried bread cubes or toast

Clean the leeks thoroughly to remove all grit, etc, chop them roughly and keep aside a small amount of the green tops for garnishing. Melt the butter and cook the vegetables without browning them. Add the stock, bring to the boil and simmer for 1 hour, skimming off fat if necessary. Rub the soup through a sieve or blend in a liquidizer. Re-heat the soup, stir in the chopped parsley, the chopped green tops of leek, and some diced meat if desired. Season with salt and pepper. Stir in the cream, adjust the seasoning if necessary and serve with fried bread cubes or toast.

Oyster Soup
Serves 6

Oystermouth, on the shores of Swansea Bay, was once the centre of a flourishing oyster industry in the Gower peninsula. Smacks would dredge the lower waters of Swansea Bay and the oysters when lifted would then be deposited in shallow waters to mature. After a succession of poor harvests, the dredging smacks were no longer required and the industry ceased in Mumbles in the 1930s.

6 shallots

2 oz (50 g) butter

$1\frac{1}{2}$ oz (40 g) plain flour

2 pt (1.2 l) fish stock or any white stock such as mutton

24 oysters

1 sprig thyme

salt and pepper

1 bay leaf

$\frac{1}{4}$ pt (150 ml) cream

Peel and chop shallots, melt butter in pan, add shallots, cook for 2 minutes without browning, add flour, stir well. Add stock, oyster beards and liquid, thyme, bay leaf and seasoning. Simmer gently for 2 hours. Skim off fat, add cream, put through strainer. Adjust seasoning. Blanch oysters, keep liquid and put into soup just before serving.

Lettuce Soup
Serves 4-5

2 lettuces

1 onion

1 oz (25 g) butter

$\frac{3}{4}$ pt (425 ml) milk

$\frac{3}{4}$ pt (425 ml) chicken stock

salt and pepper

4 fl oz (100 ml) double cream

$\frac{1}{2}$ tsp chopped chives

Shred the lettuce and chop the onion. Cook in the butter in a saucepan with the lid on for 5 minutes until soft but not coloured. Add the milk and chicken stock and cook for a further 20 minutes. Put through a blender, adjust seasoning and add the cream, reserving a little for garnish. Serve cold with a little whipped cream and chives to garnish.

Cockle Pie – Pastai Gocos

Serves 4-6

For many centuries vast cockle beds have stretched into the Burry Estuary at Penclawdd, Gower. Cockle women rode out on ponies or donkeys to gather their harvest which lay a few inches deep in the muddy sand. These they prepared and sold at Swansea Market. This pie may be made with limpets instead of cockles.

8 oz (225 g) shortcrust pastry (see page 252)
3 pt (1.75 l) prepared cockles
3 tbsp chives or spring onions
8 oz (225 g) streaky bacon
pepper
$\frac{1}{2}$ pt (275 ml) cockle or fish stock
a little milk

Line a deep 2 pt (1 l) pie-dish with shortcrust pastry, leaving enough for thin strips on top. Put a layer of cockles on the bottom, then chives, then bacon and seasoning. Repeat until dish is full. Pour over the cockle stock. Lay pastry strips lattice-fashion over the pie. Brush with milk. Bake at 400°F (200°C) Reg 6 for 30 minutes. Serve hot or cold with salad.

Wye Baked Salmon

Serves 8

The exquisite taste of salmon from the River Wye is enhanced with oysters, eels and wine, and all are cooked together on a pastry base.

12 oz (350 g) shortcrust pastry (see page 252)
8 × 6 oz (175 g) salmon steaks
2 oz (50 g) fresh white breadcrumbs
2 oz (50 g) chopped mushrooms
2–3 oz (50–75 g) melted butter
4 oz (110 g) cooked flaked salmon
4 oz (110 g) cooked flaked eel
salt, pepper, ground cloves, nutmeg
2 eggs, beaten
milk
8 oysters
2 tbsp red wine
juice of 1 lemon

Line a 3 pt (1.75 l) pie-dish with pastry. Place the salmon steaks in boiling water for a few minutes; drain and remove the skin. Cook the breadcrumbs and mushrooms in 1 oz (25 g) butter; blend in the cooked flaked salmon and eel and season to taste with salt, pepper, ground cloves and nutmeg. Remove from the heat and bind this stuffing with lightly beaten eggs and a little milk. Arrange the salmon steaks over the pastry base, cover with the stuffing and sprinkle with a few breadcrumbs and a little melted butter. Place the cleaned oysters round the salmon. Boil the remaining butter with the wine and lemon juice and pour over the salmon. Bake at 350°F (180°C) Reg 4 for 45 minutes.

Potted Salmon

Serves 8

This recipe for potting Wye salmon dates from the eighteenth century.

8 × 6 oz (175 g) salmon steaks
1 oz (25 g) mixed nutmeg, mace, ground cloves and white pepper
4 oz (110 g) butter
4 oz (110 g) finely chopped onions
6 bay leaves
6 chopped anchovy fillets (optional)
4 oz (110 g) clarified butter (see page 251)

Wipe the salmon steaks clean and season with the spices. Arrange the steaks in a well-greased baking dish with butter between the layers; sprinkle with the onions and lay the bay leaf and anchovies, if used, on top. Dot with butter, cover with foil and bake for 30–40 minutes. Lift out and drain the salmon. Remove skin and bones and pound or flake the flesh. Pack tightly in pots, pour over clarified butter and leave to set.

Earl Sefton's Salmon

Serves 4

Having caught your salmon, here is a splendid way to serve it. This recipe, for Flaked Cooked Salmon, is a family one passed down from a Cheshire aunt to her niece, and to her daughter. It was a favourite dish of the nineteenth-century gourmet, the Earl of Sefton, who lived at Croxteth Hall, Liverpool.

Stage 1
4 salmon steaks
or 1½ lb (700 g) piece of salmon cut into 4 steaks
½ oz (15 g) of nutmeg, ground cloves, mace and pepper
2 oz (50 g) butter
2 oz (50 g) onion, finely chopped
2–3 bay leaves

Clean the salmon and toss the steaks in the spicy mixture. Place them in a well-greased dish dotting the butter over and around the steaks. Sprinkle over with the chopped onions and put in the bay leaves. Cover with foil and bake at 300°F (150°C) Reg 2 for 40 minutes. The next stage is to make Flaked Cooked Salmon.

Stage 2
1 pt (575 ml) milk
6 eggs
extra seasoning if required
a little salt
2 tsp chopped parsley to garnish

Place the flaked salmon in a buttered ovenproof dish. Heat the milk. Beat the eggs in a large basin, pour over these the hot milk, stirring all the time. Strain, then pour over the salmon. Place in a 2½ pt (1.5 l) bain-marie and cook at 300°F (150°C) Reg 2 until set. Serve hot or cold, garnished with parsley.

Note:
One of the most important ingredients in the cooking of salmon is the bay leaf. These should be gathered in advance, dried and stored in a jar with a piece of muslin soaked in olive oil.

Shropshire Salmon Pie

Serves 6–8

3 lb (1.5 kg) salmon
1 pt (575 ml) white sauce (see page 23)
4 tsp cream
1 small onion
seasoning
8 oz (225 g) puff pastry (see page 253)

Boil the salmon in $\frac{1}{2}$ pt (275 ml) water for 10 minutes, so that it is not much cooked, take it up and cut into good-sized pieces. Then make a white sauce of the fish stock, add the cream, a little onion partly cooked, and seasoning. Mix that well with the salmon, then put it into a pie-dish and let it get cold. When cold, cover it with the puff pastry and bake. Tinned salmon may be used, but should not then be boiled.

Laverbread

Serves 6

Laver is a kind of edible seaweed which can be bought ready-prepared in Swansea market and elsewhere along the western coast of Wales. It is traditionally prepared using silver or wooden spoons, and an aluminium saucepan.

$\frac{1}{2}$ plastic carrier-bagful of laver
salt
margarine
wine vinegar
about 8 fl oz (220 ml) water
fine oatmeal
bacon fat or oil for shallow-frying

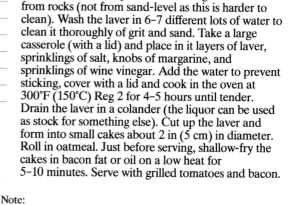

Gather about half a plastic carrier-bagful of laver from rocks (not from sand-level as this is harder to clean). Wash the laver in 6–7 different lots of water to clean it thoroughly of grit and sand. Take a large casserole (with a lid) and place in it layers of laver, sprinklings of salt, knobs of margarine, and sprinklings of wine vinegar. Add the water to prevent sticking, cover with a lid and cook in the oven at 300°F (150°C) Reg 2 for 4–5 hours until tender. Drain the laver in a colander (the liquor can be used as stock for something else). Cut up the laver and form into small cakes about 2 in (5 cm) in diameter. Roll in oatmeal. Just before serving, shallow-fry the cakes in bacon fat or oil on a low heat for 5–10 minutes. Serve with grilled tomatoes and bacon.

Note:
If you want to gather your own laver be sure to identify it correctly with the help of a field guide (latin name *Porphyra umbilicalis*). Also be careful to avoid polluted beaches.

Potted Lampreys

lampreys
salt and pepper
butter
mace
nutmeg (optional)
clarified butter (see page 251)

Take the lampreys and run a stick through their heads. Slit their tails then hang them by their heads and they will bleed at the tail end. When they have stopped bleeding, cut them open and gut them. Wipe them inside and out until they are clean and dry (do not wash with water). Rub over with a mixture of pepper and salt, leave overnight. Next day, wipe dry again, then sprinkle with a pinch of pepper, salt and mace, and a little nutmeg if liked. Roll up tight, place in a buttered pot and cover with dabs of butter. Cover with foil and bake at 350°F (180°C) Reg 4 until done – test with skewer. When cool, drain out the butter from them and replace with clarified butter to cover.

Meat

Welsh Roast Lamb
Serves 5-6

3-4 lb (1.5-1.8 kg) joint of lamb
fresh rosemary sprigs (dried is not so good)
2-3 garlic cloves
2 tbsp honey

Make slits in skin of joint and insert 1-2 in (2.5-5 cm) pieces of rosemary in slits. Pound cloves of garlic to a paste and rub over skin. Leave for 2-3 hours or overnight, wrapped loosely in foil. Preheat oven to 350°F (180°C) Reg 4. Cook meat in foil for 25 minutes per lb. Remove foil, reserve juices for gravy. Spread honey over joint and return to oven at 400°F (200°C) Reg 6 for approx 20 minutes to brown top. Make gravy of all the juices.

North Cheshire Dumpling
Serves 5-6

1 lb (450 g) self-raising flour
6 oz (175 g) suet
milk to mix
8 oz (225 g) fat bacon, cut into thin strips
8 oz (225 g) liver, cut small
2 large onions, grated
2 tsp sage, chopped
salt and pepper to taste

Mix the flour and suet to a stiff dough with milk, adding a little salt; roll out on a floured pastry-board. Cover the dough with the cut-up bacon. Now cover the bacon with the small pieces of liver, spread over with the grated onion and sage; add pepper and salt. Roll up tightly in a floured cloth and boil for about 2½ hours. Serve with a good brown gravy.

Hereford Pigeon Pie
Serves 4

2 medium or 3 small pigeons
12 oz (350 g) stewing beef
2 carrots
2 onions
salt and pepper
6 oz (175 g) shortcrust pastry (see page 252)

Pluck, clean and joint pigeons. Cut up beef into fairly small pieces. Dice onions and carrots and put all into stew-pan. Cover with water and simmer slowly for about 2½ hours or a little longer for older birds. Remove meat and vegetables from liquid, put into 1½ pt (850 ml) pie-dish with salt and pepper to taste, and a little of the liquid to moisten. Cover with pastry and cook at 375°F (190°C) Reg 5 for 30-40 minutes.

Fidget Pie
Serves 4

No-one seems to know how Fidget or Fitchett Pie acquired its name, but it is well loved among Shropshire families. It was traditionally served as a substantial meal when the harvesters came in late from the fields, and was almost certainly served throughout the year; in hard times it was made with vegetables only. The addition of mutton chops was a special treat.

1 lb (450 g) potatoes

2 large onions

3 large cooking apples

12 oz (350 g) lean gammon or 6 oz (175 g) lean gammon and 4 scrag ends of mutton chops

2 tsp sugar

½ tsp dried thyme

½ pt (275 ml) stock

salt and pepper

8 oz (225 g) shortcrust pastry (see page 251)

Peel and thickly slice the potatoes. Peel and thinly slice the onions and apples. Dice the gammon, and clean the chops (if used). Put a layer of sliced potatoes in the bottom of a 2 pt (1.2 l) pie-dish. Cover this with a layer of gammon, a layer of sliced onion and then a layer of apple. Sprinkle with a little sugar. Repeat for 3 layers until the dish is full, ending with a layer of gammon. If mutton chops are used they should be added in the middle layers of the pie. Sprinkle with thyme and season well. Pour over just enough stock to cover the filling. Roll out the pastry to make a fairly thick pie crust and cover the top of the dish. Bake at 350°F (180°C) Reg 4 for 20 minutes until the pastry is brown. Either transfer to a lower shelf in the oven or reduce heat to 325°F (160°C) Reg 3 for a further 55 minutes. If the pastry crust becomes brown too quickly, cover with greaseproof paper or foil. If the pie is to be served cold, the stock must be strong enough to set to a jelly.

Cheshire Pork Pie
Serves 4

This pork pie with apple was recorded in 1770 by Hannah Glasse as 'Pork and Pippin Pie'.

2–3 lb (900 g–1.5 kg) loin of pork

salt and pepper

grated nutmeg

8 oz (225 g) shortcrust pastry (see page 252)

8 oz (225 g) medium-size pippins

1 tsp sugar

½ pt (275 ml) white wine, or stock flavoured with a little vinegar

a little butter

1 egg, beaten

milk to glaze

Skin the loin of the pork and cut it into steaks. Season with salt, pepper and nutmeg. Make the pastry. Put in a layer of pork then a layer of pippins, cored and pared, a little sugar, then another layer of pork. Put in the white wine or stock flavoured with vinegar and some butter on the top. Cover with the pastry. Glaze with the beaten egg and milk. Bake at 350°F (180°C) Reg 4 for 1-1¼ hours.

156

Harvest Pudding

Serves 6–8

Rabbits were the most abundant form of meat at harvest time; breaking cover by the dozen as the corn was cut, they were easy victims for the hungry farmworkers.

1 large or 2 small rabbits, jointed

1 lb (450 g) suet crust pastry (see page 253)

4 oz (110 g) chopped onions

8 oz (225 g) mushrooms, sliced

8 oz (225 g) bacon, diced

seasoning

pinch sage

$\frac{1}{4}$ pt (150 ml) stock or water

Make the pastry and line a $3\frac{1}{2}$–4 pt (2–2.25 l) pudding basin with three-quarters of it. Layer the rabbit joints, onions, mushrooms and bacon in the basin, seasoning each layer with salt, pepper and sage. Pour over the stock, cover with a pastry lid and seal the edge firmly. Cover with foil or greased greaseproof paper and a pudding cloth. Place in a pan with a small amount of boiling water and steam for 2 hours. Replenish the boiling water as required but do not allow the water to boil over the top of the pudding. To serve, turn the pudding out into a deep rimmed dish.

Gloucestershire Cottage Pie

Serves 6

1 lb (450 g) cooked beef, cold

4 oz (110 g) cooked bacon or fat ham

salt and pepper

2 onions, finely chopped

1 oz (25 g) butter

$\frac{1}{2}$ pt (275 ml) gravy

1 egg

4 oz (110 g) cold potatoes

2 oz (50 g) fresh breadcrumbs

Mince the beef and bacon, season well. Fry chopped onion in butter until brown, then add gravy and simmer for approx 10 minutes. Mix egg, meat, bacon, potatoes and breadcrumbs. Add to the gravy, etc. Mix well. Turn into a greased pie-dish and bake for 30 minutes at 375°F (190°C) Reg 5. Serve cold with salad.

Shrewsbury Lamb Cutlets

Serves 4

8 lamb cutlets

1 pt (575 ml) aspic jelly (approx)

8–12 oz (225–350 g) cooked green vegetables, eg young peas, broad beans, asparagus tips

2 oz (50 g) butter or dripping

mayonnaise or French dressing (see page 22)

Bone, trim and flatten cutlets before grilling in fat. When cooked, press beneath a heavy weight until they are cold. Pour half the aspic jelly into a large dish. When set, arrange the cutlets in it. Cover with another layer of aspic and allow to set in a cool larder or refrigerator for at least 1 hour. Remove the cutlets with a sharp knife and arrange them on a round dish. Fill the centre of the dish with the cooked green vegetables tossed in mayonnaise or French dressing. Garnish with neatly cut cubes of aspic jelly and serve.

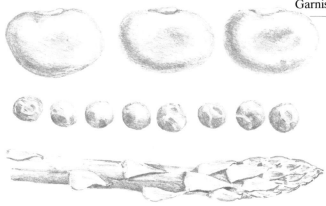

Welsh Faggots

Serves 6

This is a typical Welsh dish although found in similar form in France and the North of England. Faggots contain valuable protein and are easy to transport, making them a great favourite in the past with miners, quarry-workers, etc. They are economical, tasty, freeze well and are still very popular today.

8 oz (225 g) white breadcrumbs
1¼ lb (560 g) pig's liver or fry
8 oz (225 g) fat pork or bacon
2 large onions
8 sage leaves
1 tsp mixed herbs
salt and pepper
pig's caul

Moisten the breadcrumbs with cold water until quite soft, then squeeze as dry as possible and beat with a fork. Wash liver and wipe it dry, cut the pork (or fat bacon) into small pieces. Peel and chop the onions. Run all the ingredients through a mincer. Mix the breadcrumbs, chopped sage and mixed herbs, season liberally with pepper and add salt to taste. Put the caul in cold water to soak, then cut with scissors into roughly 6 in (15 cm) squares. With the ingredients mixed together, form into balls and cover with the caul. Pack closely into a greased dripping pan, sprinkle with a little cold water before baking at 400°F (200°C) Reg 6 for 1 hour or so. The faggots should be well browned and are delicious hot or cold.

Shropshire Pie

Serves 5-6

1 rabbit – 2¼–2½ lb (1–1.1 kg) approx, including liver and kidneys
8 oz (225 g) fat green bacon or pork
1 tsp mixed herbs
½ oz (15 g) currants
1 small apple, peeled and cored
1 small egg yolk
¾–1 oz (20–25 g) white breadcrumbs
8 oz (225 g) small onions, peeled
½ tsp grated nutmeg
salt and pepper
8 fl oz (220 ml) red wine and stock, mixed
1 lb (450 g) puff, flaky or shortcrust pastry (see pages 252–3)

Cut the rabbit into small joints and finely chop the liver and kidneys. Cut the bacon into small pieces. Make a forcemeat with the liver and kidneys, half the herbs, the currants, finely chopped apple, salt, pepper, egg yolk, and enough breadcrumbs to bind the mixture. Roll into small balls. Place the rabbit, bacon, forcemeat balls, and onions cut into halves or quarters in a 3 pt (1.8 l) pie-dish, seasoning with salt and pepper, the rest of the herbs and the nutmeg. Pour in the red wine and stock. Cover the dish with the pastry rolled fairly thickly, cut a hole in the centre, brush with beaten egg yolk and milk or water and bake at 400°F (200°C) Reg 6 for 1½ hours. Cover the pastry with a double thickness of greaseproof paper or foil when it has browned sufficiently.

Welsh Chicken Pie

Serves 4

This is an attractive chicken pie, usually served with broccoli.

4 tbsp chopped parsley
3 rashers bacon
1 lb (450 g) cooked chicken, cut into small pieces
1 onion
1 tsp sugar
¼ tsp mace
chicken stock
8 oz (225 g) wholemeal pastry (see page 252)

Cover bottom of pie-dish with chopped parsley, then the bacon cut into small pieces, followed by the cooked chicken. Chop onion finely and mix with sugar and mace; sprinkle over chicken. Pour on chicken stock to cover. Roll out pastry and cover pie-dish. Bake for 40 minutes at 350°F (180°C) Reg 4.

Chicken and Leek Pie

Serves 5–6

Pastry

4 oz (110 g) puff pastry (see page 253)

4 oz (110 g) shortcrust pastry (see page 252)

1 egg, beaten for glazing

Filling

8 leeks, washed, trimmed and finely sliced

2 oz (50 g) butter

2 chicken breasts, about 12 oz (350 g) together

$\frac{1}{2}$ tsp ground mace

salt

1–2 oz (25–50 g) butter

2 tsp soy sauce (optional)

Sauce

1 oz (25 g) flour

1 oz (25 g) butter

$\frac{1}{2}$ pt (275 ml) milk infused with a piece of onion, bay leaf and a sprig of thyme

Butter a lipped 9–10 in (23–25.5 cm) tin 1$\frac{1}{2}$ in (4 cm) deep and loose-bottomed. Line it with the shortcrust pastry. Roll out the puff pastry and cut a lid to fit. Soften the sliced leeks in the butter in a lidded pan, stirring from time to time. Leave on one side. Cut the chicken breasts into $\frac{1}{2}$ in (1 cm) cubes. Season with a little salt and the mace. Melt 1 oz (25 g) butter in a large frying pan until it is lightly browned and foaming. Fry the chicken in 2 batches for a couple of minutes only. Bring the fried chicken together. Splash over the soy sauce (if used) and mix well in, coating each bit lightly. Remove with a draining spoon. Mix the leeks with the white sauce. Mix in the chicken cubes. Fill into the pie case. Wet the edges. Fit the puff pastry lid and brush all over with the beaten egg. Add decorations and brush these with the egg. Bake at 425°F (220°C) Reg 7 for 25–30 minutes, or until the pastry is puffed up crisp and golden brown. Serve hot or cold.

Planked Salt Brisket

Planked Brisket was one of the earliest Cheshire 'takeaways'. It was cooked and then pressed between two pieces of wood (planks) by the travelling grocers who visited the villages once a week and offered their pink spiced salted brisket ready to be carved thick or thin as requested by their customers – thick for family, thin for harvester's baggin. Most farmer's wives pickled (or wet salted) several pieces of beef and shoulder pork in one large crock. The meat had a pinky colour when cooked because of the small amount of saltpetre used in the 'pickle' recipe. A brisket becomes salt beef in 7–10 days if submerged in the following brine. Make it in a plastic dustbin if you are not lucky enough to possess an authentic crock.

Brine **(enough for 4 × 4 lb/1.8 kg pieces of meat)**

2 gal (9 l) water

5 lb (2.2 kg) salt

1 lb (450 g) brown sugar

2 oz (50 g) saltpetre

Boil all the ingredients together for 15 minutes. Skim. Cool and pour into the crock. Place pieces of meat in the crock and weight them down in the pickle with an old dinner plate. Turn the meat each day for 7–10 days. Remove the brisket from the brine. Wash well and dry. String well to keep in shape.
Place meat in an ovenware dish to fit size of joint. Cover with either $\frac{1}{2}$ pt (275 ml) claret or good stock. Cover with a well-fitting lid and cook at 350°F (180°C) Reg 4 for 3$\frac{1}{2}$–4 hours. Remove from heat and, taking meat, press it between two weighted boards.

Katt Pie
Serves 4–5

Mutton or Katt Pies were traditionally made and sold at fairs for over 200 years. One such was Templeton Fair, Pembrokeshire, held on 12 November.

Pastry

8 oz (225 g) grated suet

6 fl oz (170 ml) boiling water

½ tsp salt

1 lb (450 g) plain flour

or 1½ lb (675 g) shortcrust pastry (see page 252)

Filling

8 oz (225 g) currants

6 oz (175 g) brown sugar

1 lb (450 g) lean minced lamb or mutton

seasoning

a little milk or beaten egg to glaze

To make the pastry, boil the suet in the water for 5 minutes. Stir in salt and flour quickly until mixture leaves sides of pan. Roll out quickly to just under ½ in (1 cm) thick. Cut 2 large circles and use one to line a deep 9–10 in (23–25.5 cm) ovenproof plate. Arrange filling in layers of currants, sugar, and lamb/mutton with seasoning to taste. Place pastry lid on top, make an incision, brush with milk or egg and cook for 30–40 minutes at 375°F (190°C) Reg 5.

Braised Duck
Serves 5–6

1 duck about 4 lb (2 kg)

1 large onion

2 medium carrots

2 oz (50 g) mushrooms

1 rasher bacon, roughly chopped

2 oz (50 g) butter

rind of 1 orange

1 bouquet garni sachet

seasoning

stock

¼ pt (150 ml) red wine

1½ oz (40 g) plain flour

parsley, croûtons and orange rings to garnish

Joint the duck and trim excess fat. Prepare the vegetables and chop up roughly. Melt the butter in a large pan and lightly brown the vegetables and bacon. Add the grated orange rind, herbs and seasoning, and enough stock to barely cover the vegetables. Put in the duck joints, cover with greaseproof paper and a tightly fitting lid. Cook gently for about 45 minutes. Remove the lid, pour in the wine and cook uncovered in the oven for about 35 minutes at 350°F (180°C) Reg 4. Arrange the joints on a heated serving dish. Strain the liquid and make a gravy using the flour and orange juice. Strain the gravy over the duck and garnish.

Savouries

Leek and Bacon Pasty – Pastai Cennin
Serves 4

9 oz (250 g) shortcrust pastry (see page 252)

2 or 3 medium leeks

4 rashers streaky bacon

seasoning

water

sage, chopped (optional)

2 eggs, beaten (optional)

Line an 8–9 in (20–23 cm) ovenproof plate with the pastry, cover with finely chopped washed leeks. On top lay some strips of bacon; season and add an eggcupful of water, then cover with a pastry lid. Make slits in the pastry, and bake at 400°F (200°C) Reg 6 for 30–45 minutes. Serve hot. A little chopped sage may be added to the filling, which also may be enriched by adding 2 beaten eggs.

Badminton Eggs
Serves 3

3 eggs

2 truffles

1 tbsp stock

2 heaped tbsp breadcrumbs

6 pickled mushrooms

1 tbsp mushroom ketchup

1 tbsp port

seasoning

cayenne pepper

Boil the eggs quite hard, and when cooked place for a minute or so in cold water. Boil the truffles until tender in good stock. Fry the breadcrumbs. Remove the eggshells, and cut the eggs in half lengthways; take out the yolks and chop them finely with the mushrooms and the truffles. Put the yolk mixture in a saucepan with a wineglassful of the stock that the truffles were cooked in, the ketchup, port and pepper and salt. Let all simmer together for 10 minutes, then thicken with a little fresh butter that has been rolled in flour. Lay the whites of the eggs hollow part up, fill them with fried breadcrumbs, dust lightly with cayenne, and pour over them the mixture from the saucepan.

Welsh Rarebit – Caws Pobi
Serves 3

4 oz (110 g) single Gloucester or Cheshire Cheese

2 oz (50 g) butter

1 tbsp cream

1 egg, beaten

seasoning (salt, pepper and dry mustard)

3 slices toasted bread (one side only)

small quantity ale

Cut the cheese into small pieces. Heat cheese, butter and cream slowly in a saucepan, stirring continuously. Bring to the boil and beat until smooth. Add a little ale. Allow to cool slightly before adding the egg. Put on to untoasted side of bread and brown under the grill.

Tart of Green Sprouts and Herbs
Serves 3

8 oz (225 g) green sprouts

1 tsp mixed herbs

salt to taste

1 medium onion stuck with 6–8 cloves

4 thin slices bacon

6 oz (175 g) shortcrust pastry (see page 252)

milk to glaze

$\frac{1}{4}$ pt (150 ml) gravy

Drain and mince the sprouts then add the herbs and salt. Place in a 7 in (18 cm) shallow pie-dish. Add the onion stuck with cloves and thin slices of bacon. Cover with pastry, glaze with milk and bake for 30 minutes at 375°F (190°C) Reg 5. When the pie is cooked put in the hot gravy, and then return to the oven for a few minutes to heat through.

Cheshire Onion Pie

Serves 4

6 oz (175 g) shortcrust pastry (see page 252)
2 oz (50 g) butter
1–1¼ lb (450–560 g) onions, peeled and sliced
1 oz (25 g) plain flour (scant weight)
1 tsp salt
black pepper
grated nutmeg
¼ pt (150 ml) top of milk or cream
1 large egg

Make the pastry and roll out on to a floured board. Line an 8 in (20 cm) flan ring on a baking tray. Leave to rest while preparing filling. Melt the butter in a saucepan, add onions, cook gently until soft, about 15 minutes. Do not brown. Add flour, let it sizzle then add salt, good quantity of pepper and a little nutmeg. Stir in the milk, bring to the boil and cook for 2 minutes. Remove from heat. Beat the egg lightly, spoon into it a little mixture from the pan and stir in, then return to pan and mix in. Taste for seasoning. Spoon into flan case, level and grate a little more nutmeg on top. Bake at 400°F (200°C) Reg 6 for 45–50 minutes. After about 30 minutes, when pastry is set, remove flan ring to allow crust to brown. Cool on a wire tray.

Glamorgan Sausages

Makes 10–12

This is a cheese-flavoured savoury which takes its name from the shape of the rolled-out pieces.

a little very finely chopped onion
pinch mixed herbs
pinch mustard
pepper and salt
5 oz (150 g) fresh white breadcrumbs
3 oz (75 g) grated cheese, preferably strong Cheddar
1 egg, separated
plain flour
crisp breadcrumbs for coating
pork fat or oil for shallow-frying

Mix together the onion, mixed herbs, mustard, salt and pepper, breadcrumbs and cheese. Bind together with yolk of egg. Divide into small sausages and roll in flour. Dip each into white of egg, then roll in crisped breadcrumbs and fry in pork fat or oil. Serve with creamed potatoes or chips. Can also be eaten cold – excellent with fresh green salad.

Puddings and Desserts

Threshing Day Pudding

Serves 6

6–8 oz (175–225 g) carrots, grated

4 oz (110 g) suet

6 oz (175 g) breadcrumbs

4 oz (110 g) brown sugar

8 oz (225 g) sultanas

4 oz (110 g) self-raising flour

1½ tsp mixed spice

½ tsp salt

1 egg

½ pt (275 ml) milk

Bring a deep pan of water to the boil. Mix the carrots, suet, breadcrumbs, sugar and fruit together in a large bowl. Sift flour, salt and spice into the bowl and mix well. Beat the egg and milk and stir thoroughly. Place in a 2 pt (1.2 l) basin, cover with foil or a square cloth securely tied with string, then bring the two opposite corners of the cloth over the top of the basin and knot firmly, then the other two likewise. Lower the basin into the boiling water – it should come more than halfway up the sides of the basin. Steam for 3½–4 hours. Top up boiling water as necessary. Serve with custard.

Victoria Plum Charlotte

Serves 4–5

1 small sliced loaf bread

2 oz (50 g) butter

4–6 oz (110–175 g) brown sugar

12 oz–1 lb (350–450 g) plums

Grease a shallow 1pt (500 ml) pie-dish and line base and sides with slices of buttered bread. Sprinkle sugar, cover with halved plums, cut side uppermost, layering with sugar. Cover with remaining bread and butter. Bake at 350°F (180°C) Reg 4 for 20–30 minutes. Turn out and serve hot or cold with cream.

Tewkesbury Saucer Batter

Serves 3–4

This recipe dates back to the days before teacups. Saucer batters are native to the Welsh Marches and the fruit-growing districts of the West Midlands. Soft fruit is the customary filling, but occasionally a savoury batter filled with young vegetables is served as an accompaniment to meat.

8 oz (225 g) soft fruit, eg raspberries or strawberries

2 oz (50 g) sugar

4 oz (110 g) plain flour

¼ tsp salt

1 egg, separated

½ pt (275 ml) milk

caster sugar

Put the fruit in an ovenproof dish, sprinkle with sugar and cover with a lid to start the juices running. Put on one side. Mix the flour and salt together, beat in the egg yolk and milk and whip to a batter. Allow to stand for 30 minutes. Grease 2 deep ovenproof saucers with butter. Whip the egg white until stiff and standing up in peaks, then fold it into the batter. Pour half the batter into each greased dish and put the 2 saucers and the dish of fruit into the oven. Bake at 450°F (230°C) Reg 8 for 10–20 minutes until the batter comes away from the edges of the saucers. Remove from the oven and slide the batter from one saucer, hollow side up, on to a warmed serving dish. Fill it with the hot fruit and then cover with the inverted batter from the second saucer. Sprinkle with caster sugar and serve hot.

Gloucestershire White Pot

Serves 8–10

8 oz (225 g) plain flour

4 eggs

8 oz (225 g) golden syrup

1 nutmeg, grated

mixed spice to taste

4 pt (2.2 l) milk

1 oz (25 g) butter

This is best baked in a deep earthenware bowl or pan. Beat up in the pan the flour, eggs, syrup and spice. Boil the milk and stir it boiling into the other ingredients, forming a paste. Dot the butter in pieces on the top, and at the last moment pour ¼–½ pt (150–275 ml) cold water into the middle of the pan and put into the oven without stirring. Bake at 375°F (190°C) Reg 5 for the first hour, turn the oven down gradually and bake gently for 4 hours. The ideal oven for this dish is the old farmhouse bread oven.

Tarporley Oatmeal Pudding

Serves 4–6

8 oz (225 g) self-raising flour

8 oz (225 g) fine oatmeal

8 oz (225 g) shredded suet

1½ tsp ground ginger

4 oz (110 g) sugar

1 egg, beaten

3 tbsp syrup

milk to mix

Mix all the dry ingredients together. Add beaten egg to warmed-up syrup and stir into mixture. Mix to a cake consistency with as much milk as needed. Put into a buttered dish. Bake at 350°F (180°) Reg 4 for 1½ hours. Serve hot with hot syrup, fruit (jam) sauce or custard sauce.

Speech House Pudding
Serves 4

This is named after the Speech House in the Forest of Dean, now a hotel. The Verderers' (Foresters') Court was a local law court and its sessions were held in what is now the hotel dining room.

2 oz (50 g) butter or margarine	Cream fat and sugar well. Separate eggs and beat in the yolks. Fold in the flour and jam. Dissolve the bicarbonate of soda in the milk. Whisk the egg whites stiffly. Fold in the dissolved bicarbonate of soda and lastly the egg whites. Place in a greased basin, cover and steam for approx 3 hours. Serve with jam sauce.
1 oz (25 g) caster sugar	
2 eggs	
2 oz (50 g) plain flour	
1 tbsp raspberry jam	
$\frac{1}{2}$ tsp bicarbonate of soda	
1 tbsp milk	

Gooseberry Amber
Serves 4

No collection using recipes from Cheshire would be complete without the famous Marton and Goostrey Gooseberries. Each year a Gooseberry Show is held to find the largest and heaviest berry, which is then auctioned – not for eating but for its seed.

2 oz (50 g) butter	Melt the butter in a pan, add the gooseberries, break down and cook until the skins are tender. Add the sugar, cook until a thick puree, stir in the fine breadcrumbs and the beaten egg yolks. Pour into a buttered pie-dish and bake at 350°F (180°C) Reg 4 until set, about 30 minutes. Beat the egg whites to a stiff froth with 1 tbsp caster sugar and few drops of vanilla essence. Heap meringue on top of fruit, sprinkle with sugar and replace in oven at 325°F (160°C) Reg 3 until meringue is crisp and golden brown.
1 lb (450 g) gooseberries, washed	
4 oz (110 g) sugar	
1 oz (25 g) fine breadcrumbs	
2 eggs, separated	
3 tbsp caster sugar	
vanilla essence	

Snowdon Pudding – Pwdin Eryri
Serves 8

Pudding

8 oz (225 g) suet	Mix all the ingredients except a handful of the raisins, beat the eggs and add. Pour into a large greased basin already spread with the remainder of the raisins. Cover and boil for $1\frac{1}{2}$ hours. Serve with a white sauce (see page 23), or on special occasions a wine sauce. To make this, boil the sugar and lemon rind in about a wine glass of water for about 15 minutes and then remove the rind, reserving the water. Beat the flour into the butter and stir in the water. Add $1\frac{1}{2}$ wine glasses of sherry, Madeira or white wine and serve really hot.
$1\frac{1}{2}$ oz (40 g) cornflour or ground rice	
6 oz (175 g) brown sugar	
8 oz (225 g) breadcrumbs	
4 oz (110 g) raisins, stoned	
6 oz (175 g) lemon marmalade	
grated rind of 2 lemons	
pinch salt	
6 eggs	

Wine Sauce

$1\frac{1}{2}$ oz (40 g) sugar
rind of $\frac{1}{2}$ lemon
$\frac{1}{2}$ tsp plain flour
1 oz (25 g) butter
$1\frac{1}{2}$ glasses sherry, Madeira or white wine

Cakes, Breads and Biscuits
Bara Brith

Makes 3 × 1 lb (450 g) loaves.

The words mean 'speckled bread' and this recipe and its variants are common to all Celtic countries.

1 oz (25 g) fresh yeast

milk to mix

12 oz (350 g) lard or butter or mixed

3 lb (1.4 kg) plain flour

12 oz (350 g) brown sugar

1 lb (450 g) currants

4 oz (110 g) candied peel

1 lb (450 g) raisins

½ tsp mixed spice

1 tsp salt

2 or 3 eggs

Mix yeast with warm milk. Rub the fat into the flour, then add all the remaining ingredients except the eggs and yeast mixture. Make a well in the centre and add eggs and the yeast and warm milk. Mix into a soft dough, then cover and leave in a warm place for 1½ hours to rise, till twice its original size. Turn on a floured board, place in 3 greased 1 lb (450 g) loaf tins, stand again in a warm place for approx 20 minutes then bake at 400°F (200°C) Reg 6 for 1–2 hours. When cold, cut into thin slices and serve with plenty of butter.

Plate Cake – Teisen Lap

4 oz (110 g) butter

8 oz (225 g) plain flour

4 oz (110 g) sugar

4 oz (110 g) dried fruit

1 heaped tsp baking powder

½ tsp grated nutmeg

2 eggs

¼ pt (150 ml) milk

Rub fat into flour, add sugar, fruit, baking powder and nutmeg. Mix in beaten eggs. Gradually add milk to make a fairly soft mixture. Turn on to a well-greased 9–10 in (23–25 cm) ovenproof plate and spread evenly. Cook at 350°F (180°C) Reg 4 for about 20 minutes. Reduce heat to 300°F (150°C) Reg 2 for a further 35 minutes. The cake should be lightly browned and firm to touch. Test with a skewer before removing from oven. Turn out on a wire rack to cool.

Tinker Cakes – Teisen Tincar

Makes 22–24

8 oz (225 g) self-raising flour

4 oz (110 g) butter

3 oz (75 g) sugar

1 medium apple

milk to mix

lard to grease pan

Sift flour into bowl, rub in butter, stir in sugar, peel and core the apple and then grate it into this mixture. Add sufficient milk to make a soft dough. Knead quickly into a soft ball, roll to ¼ in (5 mm) thick, cut into 2 in (5 cm) rounds, cook on a lightly greased griddle or thick frying pan for 4 minutes on each side until golden brown. Serve either buttered or sugared, hot or cold.

Pikelets – Pice'r Pregethwr

Makes 18–20

The bakestone, girdle or mâm is the traditional place for cooking these pancakes and the
Welsh Cakes that follow.

8 oz (225 g) self-raising flour	Sieve flour and add sugar. Add egg and enough milk to make a thick batter. Melt margarine, add bicarbonate of soda and vinegar and mix into the batter. Drop 2 tsp on to a hot greased bakestone or greased thick frying pan. Cook until bubbles appear and bottom is brown then turn and cook other side. Serve well buttered.
4 oz (110 g) sugar	
1 egg	
milk to mix	
2 oz (50 g) margarine	
$\frac{1}{4}$ tsp bicarbonate of soda	
1 tsp vinegar	

Welsh Cakes – Pice ar y Maen

Makes 48–50 2 in (5 cm) cakes

The old way to cut out shapes, before pastry cutters became universal, was to use a cup or a
saucer. A tea cup, for instance, gave a 3 in (7.5 cm) circle – or near enough.

12 oz (350 g) plain flour	Sift dry ingredients, rub in fats, add sugar and currants. Mix with beaten eggs. Roll out and cut into circles or triangles. Bake on a greased bakestone or in a cast-iron frying pan until lightly browned on each side. Serve hot or cold; they are lovely with Welsh butter.
1 tsp baking powder	
pinch salt	
$\frac{1}{2}$ tsp mixed spice	
3 oz (75 g) margarine	
3 oz (75 g) lard	
$4\frac{1}{2}$ oz (125 g) sugar	
4 oz (110 g) currants	
2 eggs	

Fanny's Gingerbread

Although many gingerbreads originate from the North, the following recipe has been made
for many years in Chedworth and Withington, Gloucestershire, where it was considered
extravagant and was only made at Easter and Christmas.

8 oz (225 g) butter	Cream butter with sugar. Add warmed treacle and eggs and beat well. Mix all the dry ingredients together. Dissolve bicarbonate of soda in beer. Mix all thoroughly. Put in a large square greased tin with a layer of greaseproof paper at the base and bake at 300°F (150°C) Reg 2 for 2 hours or more. Keep for a week or more in a tight-fitting tin before cutting.
4 oz (110 g) sugar	
8 oz (225 g) black treacle	
2 eggs	
1 lb (450 g) plain flour	
$\frac{1}{2}$ oz (15 g) mixed spice	
a little cinnamon	
$\frac{1}{2}$ oz (15 g) ground ginger	
a little ground cloves	
4 oz (110 g) currants	
4 oz (110 g) sultanas	
3 oz (75 g) mixed peel	
3 oz (75 g) ground almonds	
1 tsp bicarbonate of soda	
$\frac{1}{2}$ pt (275 ml) beer or ale	

Shrewsbury Cakes
Makes 18

*Shrewsbury Cakes are first mentioned in a document of 1561, though they were probably
made well before this date. The cakes, or rather the baker who made them famous, are
mentioned by Richard Barham in his Ingoldsby Legends:
'Palin, prince of cake pounders!
The mouth liquifies at thy very name.'
Palin ran a confectionery shop on the corner of Castle Street and School Lane in Shrewsbury
during the late eighteenth and early nineteenth centuries. He was well known for his
particular mix which included spices and rose water. To reduce the sweetness of the original
recipe, butter has been added and the amount of sugar reduced, giving something that is
more like shortbread.*

6 oz (175 g) butter
8 oz (225 g) plain flour
8 oz (225 g) caster sugar
pinch salt
powdered cinnamon to taste
ground nutmeg to taste
caraway seeds (optional)
1 egg yolk
a few drops concentrated rose water
1 egg yolk

Rub the butter into the flour, sugar, salt and spices.
Work to a breadcrumb state. Mix the rose water with
the egg yolk and add to mixture, bring together with
the hands and knead gently to form a smooth
mixture. Roll the dough out to $\frac{1}{4}$ in (5 mm) thick, then
press out cakes using a 4 in (10 cm) fluted cutter.
Place on greased baking sheets and prick well. Bake at
325°F (160°C) Reg 3 for 15–20 minutes until a light
golden colour. Dredge with caster sugar while still
warm.

Griddle Tart – Tarten Planc
Serves 5–6

*At harvest time these cakes would be made nearly all day. Servings vary according to
appetite. Some recipes include dots of butter, to be put on the fruit when the demerara sugar
was pressed over the apple.*

6 oz (175 g) shortcrust pastry (see page 252)
3 oz (75 g) demerara sugar
12 oz (350 g) cooking apples, very thinly sliced

Roll out pastry to a large circle approx 10 in (25 cm)
in diameter. Place apples on half the circle. Damp
edges and fold 'empty' pastry over apples. Seal edges
well. Grease griddle with bacon fat. Bake slowly for
approx 10 minutes on each side until browned.
Remove from griddle, leave to cool for 5 minutes.
Split in half horizontally. Open out and press
demerara sugar over apple. Cut into 2 in (5 cm) slices.

Berffro Cakes – Teisen Berffro
Makes 8–10

These cakes originated in Anglesey; Berffro is a shortened version of Aberffraw.

1 oz (25 g) sugar
2 oz (50 g) butter or margarine
3 oz (75 g) plain flour

Cream fat and sugar together, add flour, and work
with the hand until soft. Take a small portion of the
mixture and press over a shell sprinkled with sugar,
remove and place on a baking tray, continue until all
the mixture is shaped. Bake at 375°F (190°C) Reg 5
for about 15 minutes until golden brown. These cakes
are good sprinkled with sugar and served with
whipped cream and raspberry jam.

Crempog

Makes 10-12

These are Welsh light cakes or pancakes.

4 oz (110 g) plain flour
pinch salt
2 oz (50 g) sugar
buttermilk (or milk) to mix
2 or 3 tbsp sour cream (if available)
1 egg
1 tsp bicarbonate of soda
1 tsp cream of tartar

Put most of the flour in a large bowl, add salt and sugar and mix well. Make a well in the centre, pour in a little buttermilk and the sour cream and mix with the rest of the flour. Break in the egg and beat well, adding more buttermilk as required to make a dough that will drop easily off the spoon. Get the pan or hot plate very hot, greasing well. Mix soda and cream of tartar with a little water and pour immediately into the mixture in the bowl. Mix all together, beating thoroughly. Drop in spoonfuls on to the hot pan or plate, bake one side, turn over and bake the other. Serve hot with butter in which a little salt has been mixed.

Caerphilly Scones – Sgonau Caerffili

Makes 16-20

12 oz (350 g) plain flour
3 tsp baking powder
$\frac{1}{4}$ tsp salt
1$\frac{1}{2}$ oz (40 g) butter
3 oz (75 g) Caerphilly Cheese, grated
2 oz (50 g) Parmesan Cheese, grated
pepper to taste
$\frac{1}{2}$ pt (275 ml) milk

Sift flour, salt and baking powder. Rub in butter. Grate cheeses finely and add to flour with a pinch of pepper. Mix well. Add enough milk to make a soft dough. Roll out $\frac{3}{4}$ in (2 cm) thick. Cut into rounds and bake on a greased baking sheet at 425°F (220°C) Reg 7 for 15-20 minutes. Serve hot with butter.

Cheshire Souling Cake

Souling Cake was traditionally made for the custom of Hodening, which took place on All Souls' Day, 2 or 3 November. A band went round the streets, accompanied by the 'Soulers', and children went from house to house singing this song:
'Soul! Soul! for a Soul Cake!
I pray you good missis, a Soul Cake,
An apple, a plum, a pear or cherry,
Or any good thing to make us all merry.
One for Peter and two for Paul,
Three for Him that made us all.'

12 oz (350 g) plain flour
$\frac{1}{2}$ tsp cinnamon
$\frac{1}{2}$ tsp mixed spice
pinch nutmeg
6 oz (175 g) sugar
6 oz (175 g) margarine or butter
1 egg
1$\frac{1}{2}$ tsp vinegar

Mix the dry ingredients, rub in the fat, drop in the egg and vinegar, and knead until soft. Roll out $\frac{1}{4}$ in (5 mm) thick, cut into rounds with a big cutter, bake at 350°F (180°C) Reg 4 for 15-20 minutes until it is slightly coloured.

The North

It is often said that 'the Northerner' sets great store by effort, and indeed there is much evidence for this statement today, with baking, jam-making, preserving (albeit by means of a freezer, perhaps) and other culinary jobs still forming part of the household routine, not only in rural areas but also in many urban parts. And where else is the biscuit and cake tin always full, and a choice of three desserts offered if you appear for high tea or supper, if not in areas north of the proverbial Wash! Manufacturers of the ubiquitous 'mixes' will tell you that up North an egg has to be added as well as water or milk to the contents of their packets, and that sales of non-stick pans and bakeware were slow to take off when first they appeared on the market.

There is a clearly-defined line where the North, to the Northerner that is, begins. The Ouse and Humber form a distinct southern boundary for Yorkshire and Lancashire, making a firm base to the area. At the top Hadrian's Wall keeps the Sassenachs safe from the wild Scots!

Landscape in these wonderful parts is more varied than in any other region of the British Isles: from the bleak moors of Brontëland, in south-west Yorkshire, to the eye-stretching horizons of the Plain of York in the east and the Vale of Bowland on the west of the forbidding Pennines to the breathtaking Yorkshire Dales with broad-based valleys contained by hills soaring up to the sky – verdant, lush as green velvet, full of rivers and rivulets, with springs and waterfalls cascading like veils over fossil-full rocks. There are, of course, the mills, but even their chimneys, like tall fingers pointing to the sky, have a particular magic for me.

As you travel further north, so the scenery escalates in drama as you pass through County Durham, where the mining villages have a special scenic backdrop and the dramatic sweep of the River Wear cradles both cathedral and castle high on a 100-foot rock. 'Half church of God, half castle 'gainst the Scot' was Walter Scott's poetic view of the City of Durham.

The Lake District – for, to most, Cumbria will always be known as that – is itself an entity and one of the jewels of our country, with purple-clad mountains, deep lakes, winding passes, romantic woods, in and amongst which lie sleepy towns built with the stones of history and legend. Cumbria! Where dark treacle is used in gingerbreads, and rum finds its way into the rich butter they love so much, and where Kendal Mint Cake survives.

Back over to the east. Northumberland, whose dukes defended us during centuries of border warfare and strife against the marauding Scots, is a dramatic county. History was made to last when in AD 122 the Roman Emperor Hadrian built his Wall, stretching out across the broad countryside and punctuated with mile castles, turrets and forts as it winds forbiddingly across the whole of England from east to west, making it quite clear that no-one enters without being vetted!

In the North there is still much evidence of a regional cookery. Lancashire, with its international Hot Pot, springs quickly to mind. The Hot Pot started in the south of the county in the mill towns where the poor of the Industrial Revolution had to use their skills and thriftiness to manage on a tight budget in households where maximum benefit had to be reaped from minimum input. Whether the folk of this 'cotton county' were responsible for our most famous of roasts – the sirloin of beef – is open to dispute, certainly with a Yorkshireman. It is claimed in legend that James I knighted the succulent loin having dined excellently at Hoghton Tower, near Blackburn no less. Tripe and Onions, the tiny brown Potted Shrimps of Morecambe Bay, Goosnargh Cakes and the renowned Chorley Cake and currant-packed Eccles Cakes are alive, well and regional, and with us to this day.

As a Yorkshireman I cannot concede that Parkin is solely Lancastrian in origin, as many would claim: this richest of ginger cakes, today universally

served on Bonfire Night, was a development throughout the North of the use of oats and oatmeal, the Southerners preferring the lighter texture of wheat flour in their Gingerbread or Cake.

It is indisputable that the world-famous Yorkshire Pudding is from my home county. What a pity that today's economies prevent this king of puddings being made as it once was – in a pan placed under the meat roasting before a glowing fire on a spit, the drippings falling juicily in the spluttering batter until it was crisp and ready to eat. What can and should be restored is the Yorkshire habit of serving it as a first course, proud and puffed-up, with plenty of thin beef gravy and perhaps a splash of the county's dark brown relish to warm things up on a winter's day.

The Curd Tart – derived from the eighteenth-century cheesecake – can often be found in cake shops, though sadly in a debased form. How well I remember the Curd Tart my late mother-in-law used to make from the 'beastings' of the newly-calved cows which grazed on the adjacent farmland!

Continuity in the creative use of the family pig is shown by the pork pies in all the better pork butchers. Once produced as a treat at Christmas time, they now often appear at high tea and in the working man's lunch 'snap'. Polony, chittlings, scratchings, hands and legs of pork and the now-legendary prize-winning Black Puddings, without which no Northern breakfast is complete, are just a few of the good things still around to be enjoyed.

'Apple Pie without the cheese is like a kiss without the squeeze!' How right the Yorkshireman was on this count, as he insisted on a goodly helping of crumbly Wensleydale with his deep-dish pie. Custard was for children and the faint-hearted. And there's many a good tale to be told by those living to this day – me for one – of Funeral Biscuits, which were shortbread affairs wrapped in wax paper and tied with black ribbon, baked to sustain mourners as they followed the slow pace of the funeral hearse from chapel to cemetery. I have also met those who have tasted Hindle Wakes Chicken (Hen de la Wake), an ancient custom, sadly gone, where on wake nights a chicken would be stuffed with prunes and simmered in a pot throughout the night of vigil ready to be consumed at breakfast as a restorative following the fasting.

The Singing Hinnies of Northumberland and Durham abound, and life without these would be unthinkable for any self-respecting Geordie. But where today does one find a Durham Pikelet or Feltham Spice Bread? And what happened to Newcastle Potted Salmon, Westmorland Beer Cake or Yorkshire Yule Cake? Though, come to think of it, I just recall a wedge of this rich fruit yeast cake being left for Father Christmas's reindeer when I was a lad during the Second World War. Many of these goodies, such as Oven Bottom Cake (a bread cake baked on the hot iron base of the old-fashioned fire range, eaten warm, split open and liberally buttered and trailed with treacle), Lardy Cakes, Griddle Cake and Drop Scones and other baked affairs disappeared when fire ovens gave way to the cleaner, trouble-free gas and electric appliances, though many could still be made on the now-even-newer electric grills and griddles.

Perhaps the slower communications and the greater resistance to change explain why much of the regional fare of the North is still in existence, though I like to think it is because the Yorkshireman knows what's good for his inside. Whatever the reason, thanks be for it! In this chapter many recipes are recalled for Southerners and foreigners alike to enjoy. Speaking of whom, I am reminded of a visit I once paid to a luncheon club in the far north of Northumberland, where the lady Chairman said, as she bade me farewell having driven me many miles to the station, 'You're *so* lucky living in the South, where they have so much!' I lived but seven miles from Leeds in those days, so it's all relative!

Soups

Barley Broth
Serves 4

1 lb (450 g) scrag end of mutton
2 pt (1.2 l) water
salt and pepper
½ oz (15 g) pearl barley
2 oz (50 g) turnip, diced
2 oz (50 g) celery, diced
2 oz (50 g) carrot, diced
1 onion, diced
2 tsp parsley, chopped

Wipe and trim the mutton and cut into small pieces about 2 in (5 cm) square. Place in a pan with the water and salt; bring to the boil. Skim well then simmer for 2–3 hours. Wash the barley and add this and the vegetables at least 1 hour before serving. When the broth is ready, remove the meat, season the broth well, then add the finely chopped parsley. Eat the meat separately.

Lancashire Thick Pea Soup with Pig's Trotters
Serves 4

Whenever possible, nineteenth-century households kept a pig in the backyard, using household scraps and vegetable trimmings from the allotments to help feed it. The pig was of great importance to the family diet, providing pork, bacon, ham, brawn, black puddings and other offal. The feet or trotters were cooked with onions and dried peas to give a substantial and delicious meal which, it was said, 'would stick to your ribs'.

4 oz (110 g) dried peas
1 large onion or leek
1 small stick celery
2 pt (1.2 l) water
2 pig's trotters
1 heaped tsp salt
pinch pepper
¼ tsp dry mustard
chopped parsley to garnish

Soak the peas overnight. Drain well. Chop the onion (or leek) and celery finely. Put all the ingredients into a large pan with a lid; bring slowly to the boil, then simmer gently until the trotters are very tender. Carefully lift out the trotters and remove the meat from the bones. Dice the meat and return it to the pan. Adjust the seasonings. Serve very hot, sprinkled with parsley. Eat with slices of crusty bread.

Leek Soup
Serves 6–8

Most Northumbrian villages, particularly in the mining areas, are famous for growing leeks of mammoth proportions for shows which are held annually throughout the county. However, something a little smaller is required for this soup.

2 large potatoes, peeled and sliced
2 large leeks, sliced
1 white stick celery, diced
2 oz (50 g) dripping
3 pt (1.75 l) stock or water
seasoning
chopped parsley to garnish

Prepare the vegetables. Fry them in the dripping in a large saucepan for a few minutes, stirring occasionally to prevent them from browning. Add the stock or water and seasoning. Cover and simmer gently for 1½ hours. Check seasoning. Sprinkle with chopped parsley before serving.

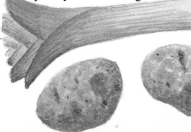

Morecambe Bay Potted Shrimps
Serves 4

Other shrimps may be used for potting, but the best are those small brown ones from Morecambe Bay. The seal of butter should be used for spreading on the brown bread or toast usually served with this dish.

½ pt (275 ml) picked shrimps

3 oz (75 g) butter

pinch powdered mace

pinch grated nutmeg

salt and pepper to taste

Place all the ingredients in a pan and heat them gradually, stirring carefully until they are well coated with butter. Do not overheat. Place in small straight-sided dishes (ramekins, for example) and cover with melted butter to exclude the air. Serve with thinly sliced brown bread or toast and butter, and thin slices of lemon.

Salmon Mousse
Serves 8 as a starter

2 eggs, separated

¼ pt (150 ml) mayonnaise (see page 22)

3 tsp gelatine

1 tbsp white wine vinegar or lemon juice

8-12 oz (225–350 g) fresh salmon, cooked and finely flaked, or canned salmon

¼ pt (150 ml) double or whipping cream

1 tbsp sherry

seasoning

Beat the egg yolks into the mayonnaise. Soften the gelatine in the wine vinegar or lemon juice in a bowl over a bowl containing hot water; stir until dissolved. When cool, add to the egg and mayonnaise mixture. Fold in the fish (if using canned salmon, remove the skin and bones). Half-whip the cream and add, together with the sherry. Beat the egg whites until stiff, and fold into the mixture. Season well. Pour into a lightly buttered mould, and leave to set in the refrigerator. Serve with lettuce, tomato and cucumber.

Pickled Salmon
Serves 4-6

2 lb (900 g) salmon, filleted

1 small onion

2 carrots, sliced

1 sprig each parsley, thyme and tarragon

½ pt (275 ml) white wine vinegar

salt and pepper

Boil the salmon in barely enough water to cover for 15 minutes. Reserve the liquid. Take out the salmon and leave till cold. Place the sliced onion, carrots and chopped herbs in a saucepan with the fish liquor and vinegar. Season well, bring to the boil and simmer for 15 minutes. Place the salmon in a deep dish and, while the liquid is still hot, pour it over the salmon. Leave for a few days in this liquid, turning the salmon night and morning. Take out the salmon, strain the liquid and serve with the cold salmon.

Lancashire Hot-Pot

Serves 4

Hot-Pot cooked in a deep dish has long been associated with Lancashire. At one time it was called Mutton Hot-Pot and the mutton chops were stood up on end instead of being placed in layers, so a deep pot was needed to accept the long chop bones of the large Pennine sheep. In times of great poverty, or when a family was without a breadwinner, a Vegetable Hot-Pot was made instead, and this was known as 'Fatherless Pie'.

4 medium onions, sliced

4 small carrots, sliced

4 thick slices turnip

4 large potatoes, sliced

8 thick middle-neck lamb chops

2 tbsp seasoned flour

1 black pudding

well-flavoured stock or water

Prepare the vegetables. Trim excess fat from the chops. Coat the chops in the seasoned flour. Fill a deep ovenproof dish with layers of onions, carrots and turnip, with the chops and black pudding in the centre, covered with more vegetables. Shake in the surplus seasoned flour. Pour in the stock or water to within $\frac{1}{2}$ in (1 cm) of the top. Finish by covering the top with a layer of overlapping potato slices. Season lightly and brush with melted butter. Cover with a lid and bake at 375°F (190°C) Reg 5 for $2\frac{1}{2}$–3 hours until the meat is tender. Remove the lid and allow the potatoes to brown and crisp for the last 30 minutes.

Pot Pie

Serves 4

12 oz (350 g) suet crust pastry (see page 253)

1¼ lb (560 g) beef steak

4 oz (110 g) kidney

plain flour

1 onion

1 carrot

Make the pastry and line a basin using three-quarters of the dough. Cut the meat into small pieces and dip each piece in flour. Cut up the onion and carrot into small pieces and mix with the meat. Place the mixture in the lined basin and add enough water to three-quarters fill the basin. Roll out the remaining dough, damp the edge and place on top of the pie as a lid. Pinch the edges together well. Cover with a floured cloth or foil, leaving room for the pie to expand. Steam for $3\frac{1}{2}$–4 hours in a saucepan. Keep the water boiling and top up with boiling water as necessary.

Stand Pie

Serves 6

12 oz (350 g)) leg, loin or shoulder of pork
1 pig's foot
8 oz (225 g) hot water crust pastry (see page 252)
salt and pepper
$\frac{1}{4}$ tsp each thyme, sage and marjoram
2 tsp plain flour

Select tender pork, as it has to cook in the same time as the pastry. Make some stock by simmering the pig's trotter and the bone and rind from the pork in just enough water to cover. To make the filling, cut the pork into very small pieces; do not discard any of the fat. Place the meat in a basin; add the seasoning, herbs and the flour. Moisten with 2 tbsp of the stock. Reserve the rest of the stock. Cut off one-third of the pastry to be used for the lid and trimmings. Mould the remainder into the shape of a pie approx 6 in (15 cm) in diameter and 4 in (10 cm) high. Pin around the pastry a double thickness of well-greased greaseproof paper, about 20 in (50 cm) long and 3 in (7.5 cm) high. Press the filling well down inside the pastry case. Roll out the remainder of the pastry into a circle to make the lid. Dampen the edges of the pie with cold water. Make a hole in the centre of the lid, place it on top of the pie and trim the edges. Make a pastry rose and place over the hole in the lid. Cook at 450°F (230°C) Reg 8 for 20–30 minutes, then reduce the heat to 350°F (180°C) Reg 4 for 1 hour. Remove the paper band, glaze with egg or milk and cook for a further 10 minutes. When the pie is cold, remove the 'rose' and pour in some cold stock. Make sure the stock is completely cold (almost to the point of turning to jelly). The stock will gradually sink into the filling, so add extra stock at intervals until full. Leave to set before cutting.

Tripe and Onions

Serves 4

There are various kinds of tripe. White tripe, with its honeycomb and sponge look, is generally used for traditional Tripe and Onions, and dark or black tripe is better for egging and crumbing before being fried. As a Yorkshireman I like honeycomb tripe, served cold with salt, pepper and malt vinegar. (For the squeamish, it has already been cooked in the cleansing process.)

1 lb (450 g) tripe
1 lb (450 g) onions, peeled and sliced
$\frac{3}{4}$ pt (425 ml) milk
$\frac{1}{4}$ pt (150 ml) water
salt and pepper
1 oz (25 g) plain flour
chopped parsley to garnish

Cut the tripe into 2 in (5 cm) squares, place in a saucepan, cover with cold water, bring to the boil, and throw away the water. Add to the tripe the sliced onions, milk, water and seasonings. Bring to the boil and simmer very gently for 1–1½ hours or until the tripe is tender. Mix the flour with a little extra cold milk and stir this into the tripe and onions. Return to the boil for 5 minutes. Serve garnished with chopped parsley.

Lobscouse
Serves 6

The Danes have this dish in their repertoire - called Lobescoves - and it is more than likely that Lancashire Lobscouse has its roots in Scandinavian lands.

1½ lb (675 g) salted silverside of beef, soaked overnight

2 oz (50 g) butter

3 lb (1.4 kg) potatoes, sliced

1 carrot, sliced

1 large onion, quartered

8 oz (225 g) dried peas, soaked overnight

¼ tsp thyme, chopped

¼ tsp mint, chopped

1 tsp black pepper

2 pt (1.2 l) stock, unsalted

Trim the meat and cut into ½ in (1 cm) cubes. Melt the butter in a deep casserole. Put in potatoes, carrots and onion, with the meat on top. Drain the peas and put them on top of the meat. Add the herbs and pepper. Pour on the stock, adding enough water if necessary to cover the peas. Cover with a tightly-fitting lid or with foil. Cook at 300°F (150°C) Reg 2 for 3–4 hours.

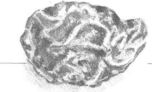

Hindle Wakes
Serves 4–6

'Hen de la Wake' is believed to have been introduced to Lancashire, and Bolton-le-Moor in particular, by the Flemish spinners who settled in that area. There are now many variations of this recipe but the essential stuffing of prunes and spices remains the same.

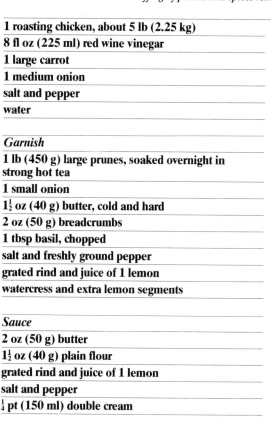

1 roasting chicken, about 5 lb (2.25 kg)

8 fl oz (225 ml) red wine vinegar

1 large carrot

1 medium onion

salt and pepper

water

Garnish

1 lb (450 g) large prunes, soaked overnight in strong hot tea

1 small onion

1½ oz (40 g) butter, cold and hard

2 oz (50 g) breadcrumbs

1 tbsp basil, chopped

salt and freshly ground pepper

grated rind and juice of 1 lemon

watercress and extra lemon segments

Sauce

2 oz (50 g) butter

1½ oz (40 g) plain flour

grated rind and juice of 1 lemon

salt and pepper

¼ pt (150 ml) double cream

Fit the trussed bird into a pot just large enough to contain it. Add the vinegar, carrot, onion, salt and pepper and just enough water to well cover the thighs of the bird. Cover and cook gently on top of the stove for about 45 minutes or until the thighs are tender. Leave to cool for 1 hour in the cooking liquor. Remove the bird, skin it and cut into serving portions, taking out any bones. Arrange the pieces on a dish. Cover with foil so that the meat does not dry up, but let it get quite cold. Skim as much fat as possible from the liquor and reserve it. Soak the prunes in the hot tea overnight. Slit them and remove the stones. Finely chop an onion and fry it in ½ oz (15 g) of the butter. Add the breadcrumbs, herbs and seasoning, lemon juice and rind. Grate the remaining butter and add this. Stuff the pitted prunes with the mixture, arrange in a buttered baking dish and cover with foil. Bake at 350°F (180°C) Reg 4 for 25 minutes. Put to cool and leave on one side.

To make the sauce, melt the butter in a pan, stir in the flour and gradually work in 1 pt (575 ml) of the strained cooking liquor. Cook the sauce for a few minutes, stirring all the time. Add the lemon juice and rind and more salt and pepper if necessary. Cover with oiled paper and cool completely. Half whip the cream and fold into the cold sauce, incorporating it thoroughly. Coat each piece of chicken with this sauce. Garnish with the stuffed prunes, lemon segments and bunches of watercress.

Cumberland Sausage
Makes 5 lb (2.25 kg)

This is a very rich meaty sausage, as made in the local farmhouses. Traditionally, this sausage is made in a long link, or several links about 12 in (30 cm) long, and twisted in a spiral. It is cut into portions for serving after it has been cooked.

5 lb (2.25 kg) pork	Mince the pork, making sure there is a good proportion of fat included. Season, mix well to ensure that the salt and pepper are evenly distributed. Fill the sausage skin. Leave for at least a day to mature. The sausages can be frozen, but are best used within a month.
1 oz (25 g) salt	
$\frac{1}{2}$ oz (15 g) pepper	
sausage skin	

Potato Pie
Serves 4–6

4–5 large potatoes	Peel and slice the potatoes. Cut up the meat into 1 in (2.5 cm) cubes. Take a deep ovenproof dish and put in layers of potatoes, sliced onions and meat. Season, and add a little water. Cover the dish and cook for $1\frac{1}{2}$–2 hours or until tender at 350°F (180°C) Reg 4. Make the pastry and roll out to make a lid. Place on top of the dish and return to the oven. Cook at 400°F (200°C) Reg 6 for 25–30 minutes. Serve with pickled red cabbage.
1 lb (450 g) stewing beef	
6 oz (175 g) beef kidney (optional)	
1 large onion, sliced	
seasoning	
4 oz (110 g) shortcrust pastry (see page 252)	

Cumberland Bacon and Egg Pie
Serves 4

6 oz (150 g) shortcrust pastry (see page 252)	Divide the pastry into two and roll out half to line a 7 in (18 cm) flat ovenproof plate. Cut up the bacon into pieces $2\frac{1}{2}$ in (6 cm) long and place on the pastry, leaving 4 depressions. Break an egg into each depression and season. Roll out the other half of the pastry, moisten the edges and cover the pie. Press the edges together and trim; decorate, using the pastry trimmings. Brush with beaten egg. Bake at 425°F (220°C) Reg 7 for 30–40 minutes.
4 oz (110 g) streaky bacon	
4 eggs	
seasoning	
a little beaten egg to glaze	

Kielder Venison Pot Roast
Serves 4–6

In the preparation of venison, marinating in wine is necessary to prevent drying; it also helps to keep the meat more tender. The original providers for this recipe were the deer in Kielder Forest, north-west Northumberland, where in 1775 the Duke of Northumberland built a castle to serve as a shooting-box.

½ pt (275 ml) salad oil

1 pt (575 ml) mead, white wine or white wine vinegar

1 onion, finely chopped

1 stick celery, finely chopped

pinch black pepper

paprika

salt

3 bay leaves, crushed

2–3 lb (900 g–1.4 kg) venison, cut from thick end of haunch

plain flour

To prepare the marinade, mix together the salad oil and mead, white wine or white wine vinegar in a saucepan. Add the chopped onion, celery, pepper, paprika and salt to taste, and the bay leaves. Bring the marinade to the boil, cool slightly and pour over the meat in a large bowl. Marinate overnight, remove the meat and save the liquid. Dry the meat well, dust with flour, and fry on all sides in a little fat in a frying pan for a few minutes. Place in a covered roasting tin with half the marinade and cook in the oven at 350°F (180°C) Reg 4 for approx 1½ hours or until tender. Thicken the remainder of the marinade with flour to make gravy. When the meat is cooked add the juices from the roasting tin to the gravy. Serve with garden peas, new potatoes and rowan jelly.

Durham Cutlets
Serves 2–3

½ oz (15 g) butter

½ oz (15 g) plain flour

¼ pt (150 ml) stock or milk

salt and pepper

4 oz (110 g) cooked meat, minced

3 oz (75 g) breadcrumbs

½ tsp chopped parsley

1½ tbsp chopped mushrooms

1 tsp Worcestershire Sauce

2 eggs, beaten

macaroni to decorate (optional)

Make a thick sauce with the butter, flour and stock or milk. Add the seasonings, the meat, 2 oz (50 g) of the breadcrumbs, the parsley, mushrooms, Worcestershire Sauce and one beaten egg. Mix well. Spread evenly on a wet plate and leave till firm, then shape into triangular pieces. Flour a board and your fingers and shape the pieces into 'cutlets'. Dip in the remaining beaten egg and then the breadcrumbs. Fry until golden brown. Put a piece of macaroni in one corner to resemble a bone.

Black Dish
Serves 6

8 oz (225 g) stewing steak

1 lamb's kidney

1 black pudding

2 oz (50 g) mushrooms, chopped

1 medium onion, chopped

1 large carrot, chopped

2 tsp barley

4 tsp lentils

½ tsp dried sage; salt and pepper

4 oz (110 g) suet crust pastry (see page 253)

plain flour

Cut the meat into small pieces. Skin the black pudding and cut into small pieces. Put all the ingredients except the dumplings in a large casserole. Cover with water and cook at 300°F (150°C) Reg 2 for 2 hours. To make the suet dumplings, divide the pastry into 8 pieces, each about the size of a small egg. With floured hands, roll each piece into a firm ball; dredge with flour. Put the dumplings into the casserole and cook for a further 30 minutes. Serve with roast or boiled potatoes.

Yorkshire Pudding
Serves 3–4

The typical Yorkshire Pudding is generally made with milk and water to give it lightness and crispness. In some districts it is thought best to use 'blue' or skim milk, in which case the batter is not allowed to stand for any length of time. For a crisp pudding, there must be no fat in the mixture. Other essentials for a good pudding are very hot fat and not too much of it, and a good hot oven. Traditionally, Yorkshire Pudding should be eaten with thick gravy as a separate item before the main meat course. It is now more usual to serve it as an accompaniment to roast beef. The old method of cooking was to place the pudding in the roasting tin underneath the joint which was being roasted on a spit. The juices from the meat would then drip down on to the cooking pudding.

4 oz (110 g) plain flour	Put the flour and salt in a basin. Break the egg into them and add enough milk and water to make a beating consistency. Beat well and leave to stand for 30 minutes. Heat the oven to 450°F (230°C) Reg 8. For small puddings, use a 2½ × 1 in (6 × 2.5 cm) bun tray and put a knob of fat into each tin. Place the tray in the oven until the fat is smoking hot. One large tin may also be used. Meanwhile, add the rest of the milk and water to make a batter. Take the tray from the oven and, using a long-handled spoon, put 2 tbsp of the batter into each part of the tin. Bake for 15–20 minutes at the above temperature until the puddings are risen and golden brown.
1 tsp salt	
1 large egg	
¼ pt (150 ml) milk	
¼ pt (150 ml) water	
cooking fat or dripping	

Yorkshire Pudding (Seasoned)
Serves 4–6

The texture of this variation will not be as light as that of a Yorkshire Pudding. Serve it either separately with gravy before the main course, or with the main course. It is excellent with roast pork.

1 pt (575 ml) basic batter mix (see previous recipe)	Stir the onion and sage into the batter mix just before pouring the batter into hot fat in a Yorkshire Pudding tin. Cook at 400°F (200°C) Reg 6 for 20–30 minutes.
1 large onion, finely chopped	
2 tsp dried sage or 1 tbsp fresh sage	

Sage and Onion Pudding
Serves 4

1 large onion	Grease a 1½ pt (850 ml) pie-dish. Finely chop the onion and place in a pan with sufficient water to just cover. Cook in a closed pan until the onion is soft. Add the breadcrumbs, sage and milk. Dice the butter and stir into the mixture. Season to taste. Pour the mixture into the pie-dish. Cook at 400°F (200°C) Reg 6 for 30–40 minutes or until firm. Serve hot with roast pork.
4 oz (110 g) fresh breadcrumbs	
2 tsp dried sage or 1 tbsp fresh sage	
1 pt (575 ml) hot milk	
2 oz (50 g) butter	
salt and pepper	

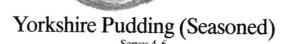

Black Pudding

These now win prizes for our pork butchers as they gain in popularity on the continent. Their black outward appearance (they are red inside) comes from the skins being brushed with blood before cooking.

8 oz (225 g) barley

fat from the pig or lard

3 pt (1.75 l) pig's blood, strained (approx)

3 pt (1.75 l) milk (approx)

$\frac{3}{4}$ standard loaf of white bread, made into breadcrumbs

3 oz (75 g) porridge oats

$1\frac{1}{4}$ oz (30 g) salt

$1\frac{1}{2}$ tsp pepper

3 heaped tsp dried mint

Soak the barley overnight and boil until tender. Drain. Finely cut up some of the fat from the pig and put in the bottom of each dish or roasting tin. (Lard may be cut into small cubes and used if there is not much fat from the pig.) Mix all the ingredients together in a large container. Fill the dishes with blood mixture and bake at 425°F (220°C) Reg 7 until set. To serve, cut into slices, reheat in a frying pan with sausages or add to a Hot-Pot.

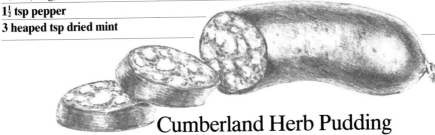

Cumberland Herb Pudding

Serves 4

1 heaped tbsp pearl barley

4 oz (110 g) nettles (optional)

1 lb (450 g) spring cabbage

2 medium onions

2 medium leeks

1 egg, beaten

1 oz (25 g) butter

salt and pepper

Soak the barley overnight in 1 pt (575 ml) water. Boil until tender in the same water and reserve the liquid. Place the washed and shredded vegetables in a large heavy saucepan. Add the cooked barley and liquid in which it was cooked. Add a little more water if necessary. Boil quickly until tender (20–30 minutes) keeping the lid on the pan, and stirring occasionally to prevent the barley from sticking. Drain, discarding the liquid. Put the vegetables back in the pan. Add the butter and egg, season to taste and turn into a 2 pt (1.2 l) heatproof basin. Cover and re-heat in the oven at 350°F (180°C) Reg 4 for about 10–15 minutes. Serve hot. The pudding can be turned out of the basin if desired.

Onion and Apple Pie

Serves 4–6

1 lb (450 g) potatoes

1 lb (450 g) cooking apples

1 lb (450 g) onions

2 eggs, hard-boiled

mace

salt

1–2 oz (25–50 g) butter

6 tbsp vegetable stock or water

6–8 oz (175–225 g) shortcrust pastry (see page 252)

Peel and finely slice the potatoes, apples and onions, and slice the hard-boiled eggs. Place them all in layers in a well-greased pie-dish. Sprinkle with mace and salt to taste. Dot with pieces of butter and pour over the stock or water. Cover with pastry and cook for $1\frac{1}{2}$ hours at 350°F (180°C) Reg 4.

Pease Pudding

Serves 4

'Pease pudding hot, pease pudding cold,
Pease pudding in the pot, nine days old.'
(North Country rhyme)

1 lb (450 g) split peas
1 large potato, diced
2–3 pt (1.2–1.75 l) bacon or ham stock
salt and pepper

Wash the split peas and mix with the potato. Place together in a muslin bag and tie up loosely. Place in a saucepan with the stock, cover, bring to the boil and simmer gently until the peas are soft (about 2 hours). Lift the muslin bag from the stock, allow to drain for 2–3 minutes. Empty the contents into a bowl and mash, adding a little stock to moisten if necessary. Season and place in a serving dish and serve either hot or cold.

Watercress Pie

Serves 4

2 bunches watercress
4 oz (110 g) butter
mace or nutmeg
4 eggs
4–6 oz (110–175 g) shortcrust pastry (see page 252)

Wash and dry the watercress, then chop finely and mix well with the butter. Add the spice to taste. Line a shallow dish with half the mixture. Break the eggs on to the mixture so that the whites run together and the yolks are spread evenly apart. Lightly place the remainder of the mixture on top of the eggs, taking care not to break the yolks. Cover with a thin layer of pastry and cook at 350°F (180°C) Reg 4 for 30 minutes. Serve hot or cold.

Mock Crab

Serves 2–3

3 medium tomatoes
1 medium onion
2 oz (50 g) butter
2 oz (50 g) cheese, grated
1 egg, beaten
salt and pepper

Skin and finely chop the tomatoes. Chop or grate the onions. Cook the onion and tomatoes in a pan with the butter. When tender, add the cheese and stir well. Add the egg and seasoning, and cook slowly until the mixture thickens. Pour onto a plate. Serve hot on toast, or allow to cool and use to make sandwiches.

Lettuce Sauce

This is a great favourite with Roast Beef and Yorkshire Pudding.

1 lettuce	Chop the lettuce (medium fine) and add the mint and/or spring onions. Put them all in a basin and sprinkle with the salt and sugar. Mix well. Leave for 10 minutes, then add the malt vinegar. Serve with hot or cold meats.
1 tbsp finely chopped mint and/or 1 tbsp spring onions, chopped	
1 tsp salt	
2 tbsp sugar	
$\frac{1}{4}$ pt (150 ml) malt vinegar	

Celery Cheese

Serves 4

1 head celery	Wash the celery well and slice finely. Put into a saucepan and barely cover with milk. Season to taste and simmer till cooked. Allow to cool. Mix in the cheese and egg. Place in a greased pie-dish, cover with breadcrumbs and cook at 350°F (180°C) Reg 4 until brown. Serve as a vegetable with the main course.
milk	
salt	
4 tbsp grated cheese	
1 egg, beaten	
breadcrumbs	
salt and pepper	

Thatch

Serves 2

1 cup grated raw potato	Mix all the ingredients together. Melt enough fat to cover the bottom of a large frying pan. When hot, spread the mixture evenly over the base and cook gently until brown and crisp on the base and set on top. Turn and cook the other side. Cut into wedges and serve with grilled tomatoes and garden peas.
1 cup chopped bacon	
1$\frac{1}{2}$ oz (40 g) self-raising flour	
2 eggs, beaten	
salt and pepper	

Puddings and Desserts

John Peel Tart
Serves 6

John Peel, the famous huntsman, lived in the Caldbeck area of Cumberland in the early 1800s. He is immortalized in the song 'John Peel' written by John Woodcock Graves. Today he is toasted all over Cumbria whenever hunting folk meet.

8 oz (225 g) shortcrust or flaky pastry (see pages 252–3)

1 oz (25 g) margarine

4 oz (110 g) golden syrup

1 oz (25 g) chopped peel

1 oz (25 g) ground almonds

6 oz (175 g) currants, cleaned

½ tsp mixed spice

2 tsp lemon juice

Warm the margarine and syrup together; when melted, stir in all the other ingredients. Allow to cool. Line a 7 in (18 cm) ovenproof pie-plate with half the pastry. Put the filling in, and cover with the remaining pastry, sealing edges well. Bake for 40 minutes at 400°F (200°C) Reg 6. Serve warm or cold.

Border Tarts
Serves 6

5 oz (150 g) shortcrust pastry (see page 252)

Filling

2 oz (50 g) margarine

2 oz (50 g) caster sugar

1 egg, beaten

2 oz (50 g) currants

1 oz (25 g) cut mixed peel

1 oz (25 g) ground almonds or chopped nuts

a few drops almond essence

Icing

3 oz (75 g) icing sugar

2 tsp lemon juice

a few drops water

Line an ovenproof plate or sandwich tin with the pastry. Cream the margarine and sugar together. Add the egg, dried fruit, ground almonds or chopped nuts, and the essence. Put the mixture into the pastry case and smooth the top. Roll out the pastry trimmings, cut into strips and cover the mixture in a trellis pattern. Cook at 400°F (200°C) Reg 6 for 15 minutes, then reduce to 350°F (180°C) Reg 4 for a further 15 minutes. Ice the top of the tart while still warm.

Boiled Rice Pudding
Serves 4

This recipe is adapted from one published in The Experienced English Housekeeper, *by Elizabeth Raffald, dedicated to the Hon. Elizabeth Warburton, first edition 1789. The white wine sauce may well convert non-rice pudding fans of all ages.*

4 oz (110 g) pudding rice

5 egg yolks

4 oz (110 g) butter

4 oz (110 g) sugar

1 small nutmeg, grated

grated rind of ½ lemon

8 oz (225 g) currants

Boil the rice in water until soft, and then drain. Beat it in a marble mortar (or mix in a blender) with the egg yolks, butter, sugar, nutmeg and lemon rind. Add the currants and mix well. Put the mixture into a pudding basin and cover with a pudding cloth or foil. Steam for 1 hour. Serve with a white wine sauce (see page 165, Snowdon Pudding recipe).

Curds

1 pt (575 ml) milk
2 tsp plain flour
1 tsp vinegar

Blend the flour to a smooth cream with a little of the milk and add the vinegar. Boil up the rest of the milk and pour when boiling on to the blended flour and vinegar. Stir well all the time. Return to the pan, stir until boiling, and let the curds boil up. Cool in a basin and when cool strain through muslin. When the curd is dry, break it with a fork and use as required. Curds may also be made using fresh milk and rennet, and following the directions on the bottle of rennet. Raw milk which has soured produces a curd, and this may be filtered and used.

Yorkshire Curd Tart
Serves 6

6 oz (175 g) sweet shortcrust pastry (see page 252)
1 oz (25 g) butter, melted
2 oz (50 g) caster sugar
2 eggs, separated
grated rind of 1 lemon
1 oz (25 g) currants or sultanas
8 oz (225 g) curd cheese
pinch ground nutmeg

Roll out the pastry and use to line an 8 in (20 cm) flan ring or flan tin. Heat the oven to 375°F (190°C) Reg 5. Mix together the butter, sugar, egg yolks, lemon rind, fruit and curd cheese. Whisk the egg whites until stiff and fold into the cheese mixture. Spoon the filling into the pastry case and sprinkle with nutmeg. Cook for about 30 minutes or until the filling is set. Reduce the oven temperature to 350°F (180°C) Reg 4 if the pastry browns too quickly. Serve warm or cold.

Yorkshire Cheesecake
Serves 6

Smaller versions of this dish were at one time made in saucers, so that men could put one in their pocket when working all day out in the Dales.

6 oz (175 g) shortcrust pastry (see page 252)
1 oz (25 g) butter, softened
1 tbsp caster sugar
1 tbsp golden syrup
1 oz (25 g) currants
$\frac{1}{2}$ oz (15 g) chopped candied peel
1 large egg, beaten
1 tbsp rum or brandy
8 oz (225 g) curds (see above)

Line an 8 in (20 cm) flan ring with the pastry. Cream the butter with the sugar and syrup. Mix in the currants and peel, together with the beaten egg and rum or brandy. Stir in the curds. Pour into the pastry case (do *not* bake blind first). Cook for 35 minutes in the centre of the oven at 400°F (200°C) Reg 6. Serve cold, cut into wedges.

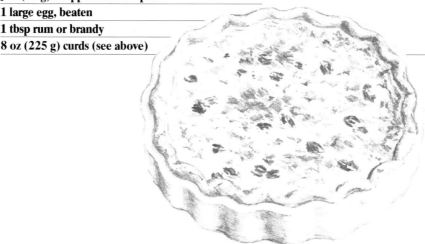

Newcastle Pudding

Serves 4

4 oz (110 g) glacé cherries

5 slices well-buttered bread

2 oz (50 g) sugar

2 eggs

pinch mixed spice

½ pt (275 ml) milk

sweet white sauce to serve (see page 23)

Butter a 1 pt (575 ml) basin. Cut the cherries in half and use to line the bottom and sides of the basin. Fill the basin with the bread slices, cut to fit. Beat together the remaining ingredients and pour over the bread until soaked. Cover with foil and steam for 2 hours. Turn out on to a serving dish and serve with a thin, sweet white sauce.

Stanhope Cream

Serves 4

1 pkt jelly, any flavour

½ pt (275 ml) water

2 oz (50 g) butter

2 oz (50 g) sugar

1 egg, separated

½ pt (275 ml) warm milk

Melt the jelly in the water. Cream the butter and sugar together. Add the egg yolk and milk. Stir in the jelly. Whisk the egg white until stiff and fold into the mixture. Pour into a plain glass serving dish and leave to set. This looks very attractive in a plain glass dish because it separates into 3 layers.

Old Westmorland Sweetbake

Serves 8

8 oz (225 g) shortcrust pastry (see page 252)

2 oz (50 g) butter

12 oz (350 g) mixed dried fruit and peel

2 oz (50 g) soft brown sugar

a little mixed spice

2 tsp lemon juice

1 small sherry glass rum

caster sugar to decorate

Line a deep 7 in (18 cm) sandwich tin with most of the pastry. Melt the butter over a slow heat in a saucepan and stir in the fruit. Add the sugar and stir over a low heat until the sugar is melted (do not overheat). Stir in the rum, spice and lemon juice. Fill the pastry case with the mixture and level the surface. Use the pastry trimmings to make very thin strips and lay these in a trellis pattern over the mixture. Bake at 350°F (180°C) Reg 4 for 30–40 minutes. Dredge with caster sugar. Serve hot or cold with cream if desired.

Wet Nellie or Lord Nelson Cake

Serves 8

This is a Liverpudlian speciality, but not so very different from John Peel Tart.

8 oz (225 g) shortcrust pastry (see page 252)

8 oz (225 g) sponge cake crumbs

4 oz (110 g) raisins

grated rind and juice of 1 lemon

4 tbsp milk

4 oz (110 g) golden syrup

milk and caster sugar to glaze

Use half the pastry to line a 7 in (18 cm) sandwich tin. Put the cake crumbs in a bowl and add the raisins and lemon rind. Bind with the lemon juice, syrup and milk. Turn into the pastry case and cover with the remaining pastry, sealing the edges. Brush with milk and sprinkle with sugar. Bake at 375°F (190°C) Reg 5 for 35 minutes.

Manchester Pudding
Serves 4

*This is a variation on Queen of Puddings: the meringue is here spread on the pudding
without the additional layer of jam and the two are baked together.*

¾ pt (425 ml) milk

1 oz (25 g) butter

grated rind of 1 lemon

3 eggs, separated

3 oz (75 g) caster sugar

3 oz (75 g) breadcrumbs

Put the milk, butter and lemon rind in a saucepan and heat gently to melt the butter. Meanwhile, beat together the egg yolks and 1 oz (25 g) of the sugar. Pour the milk mixture on to the yolks. Stir in the breadcrumbs. Place the mixture in a buttered 2 pt (1.2 l) pie dish. Leave to stand for 15 minutes. Whisk the egg whites until stiff and whisk in the rest of the sugar. Spread the meringue over the pudding and bake at 325°F (160°C) Reg 3 for 40 minutes, reducing the heat to 300°F (150°C) Reg 2 for a further 20 minutes.

Manchester Tart
Serves 4–6

6 oz (175 g) flaky pastry (see page 253)

raspberry or strawberry jam

pared rind of 1 lemon

½ pt (275 ml) milk

2 oz (50 g) fresh breadcrumbs

2 oz (50 g) butter

2 eggs, separated

3 oz (75 g) caster sugar

1 tbsp brandy

caster sugar for dredging

Roll out the dough and use it to line an 8 in (20 cm) pie dish. Spread the bottom with jam. Put the lemon rind and milk in a saucepan and bring to the boil. Remove from the heat and strain over the breadcrumbs. Leave to stand for 5 minutes, then beat in the butter, the egg yolks, 1 oz (25 g) of the sugar and the brandy. Pour into the pastry case. Bake in a preheated oven at 375°F (190°C) Reg 5 for 45 minutes. Whisk the egg whites until stiff. Fold in the remaining sugar. Spread the meringue over the top of the filling and dredge with sugar. Bake for a further 15 minutes or until the meringue is browned. Serve cold with cream.

Cakes, Breads and Biscuits

Yule Bread

Makes a 2 lb (900 g) loaf

*This loaf was the forerunner of today's Christmas Cake, and was enjoyed in farmhouses with
mulled ale and wedges of cheese.*

12 oz (350 g) strong plain flour
4 oz (110 g) butter
4 oz (110 g) sugar
pinch salt
$\frac{1}{2}$ oz (15 g) fresh yeast or $\frac{1}{4}$ oz (7 g) dried yeast
$\frac{1}{4}$ pt (150 ml) milk
1 egg, beaten
6 oz (175 g) currants
4 oz (110 g) sultanas
2 oz (50 g) chopped mixed candied peel
$\frac{1}{2}$ tsp ground cinnamon
$\frac{1}{4}$ tsp ground nutmeg

Sieve the flour into a bowl. Rub in the butter and stir in the sugar, reserving 1 tsp. Add the salt. Mix the fresh yeast with the sugar and add to the lukewarm milk (or sprinkle dried yeast on milk with sugar and leave till frothy). Add to the flour with the egg and work to a soft dough. Cover and leave to prove for 1 hour. Work in the currants, sultanas, peel and spices and knead well. Shape to fit a greased 2 lb (900 g) loaf tin. Cover and leave to prove for 45 minutes. Bake for 20 minutes at 425°F (220°C) Reg 7, then reduce to 375°F (190°C) Reg 5 and continue for 1 hour.

Wilfra Apple Cake

*St Wilfred of Ripon, to whom the cathedral is dedicated, is remembered each year during
'Wilfra Week'. On the first Saturday in August a procession of decorated floats and bands
weaves its way through the narrow streets of Ripon headed by 'St Wilfred' riding a white horse
led by a monk. It used to be the tradition that every household should provide dishes of jam
and lemon curd tarts to be handed to passers-by.*

12 oz (350 g) shortcrust pastry (see page 252)
1 lb (450 g) peeled and thinly sliced cooking apples (peeled weight)
3 oz (75 g) demerara sugar, or 2 tbsp golden syrup
3 oz (75 g) grated Cheddar Cheese
caster sugar and milk to glaze

Line a well-greased Swiss Roll tin with two-thirds of the pastry. Fill with the sliced apple and sprinkle with sugar or golden syrup. Spread grated cheese evenly on top. Cover with the rest of the pastry and seal the edges. Brush the top with milk and sprinkle with caster sugar. Bake at 350°F (180°C) Reg 4 for about 40 minutes. When cold, cut into squares.

Lancashire Cheese Scones

Makes approx 10

8 oz (225 g) self-raising flour
$\frac{1}{4}$ tsp salt
1 tsp dry mustard
1 oz (25 g) margarine or lard
4 oz (110 g) Lancashire Cheese, finely grated or crumbled
$\frac{1}{4}$ pt (150 ml) milk

Heat the oven to 425°F (220°C) Reg 7. Lightly grease a baking tray. Sieve together the flour, salt and mustard. Rub in the fat until the mixture resembles fine breadcrumbs. Reserve 1 tbsp cheese and stir in the remainder. Mix to a soft dough with the milk and knead lightly. Roll out on a floured board to a thickness of $\frac{3}{4}$-1 in (1.5-2.5 cm) and cut into rounds or triangles. Brush the tops with milk and sprinkle with the remaining cheese. Place on the baking sheet. Cook for 15-20 minutes near the top of the oven until golden brown and firm. Serve just cool enough to eat.

Goosnargh Cakes
Makes approx 12

This uniquely flavoured biscuit comes from the village of Goosnargh, a few miles north-east of Preston. There are many stories about its origins, but what probably happened was that an imaginative housewife, wanting a change from shortbread biscuits, came up with this alternative.

6 oz (175 g) plain flour
1 tsp caraway seeds
$\frac{1}{2}$ tsp coriander
4 oz (110 g) butter
1 oz (25 g) caster sugar
extra caster sugar for topping

Lightly grease a baking tray. Sieve the flour into a bowl, add the caraway seeds and coriander, the butter cut into pieces, and the sugar. Rub in the butter and knead well to form a smooth paste. Roll out to a thickness of $\frac{3}{8}$ in (9 mm) and cut into 2 in (5 cm) rounds. Spread 1 tsp caster sugar evenly on top of each biscuit and press in evenly. Place the biscuits on the tray and leave to stand in a cool place for at least 2 hours. Bake at 275°F (140°C) Reg 1 for 30–40 minutes until firm and a deep cream colour – not golden. Cool on a wire rack.

Sly Cake
Makes 12

6 oz (175 g) currants, cleaned
3 oz (75 g) caster sugar
1 oz (25 g) ground almonds
2 oz (50 g) butter
1 tbsp water
8 oz (225 g) sweet shortcrust pastry (see page 252)

Mix together the currants, sugar and ground almonds. Melt the butter and add it to the mixture. Add the water. Roll out the pastry thinly and use to line an oblong tin about 9 × 6 in (23 × 15 cm). Spread the mixture over the pastry and cover with the rest of the pastry. Cook at 400°F (200°C) Reg 6 until nicely browned. Allow to cool, then cut into squares for serving.

Grasmere Gingerbread
Makes approx 18

1lb (450 g) plain flour
2 tsp ground ginger
1 tsp bicarbonate of soda
1 tsp cream of tartar
8 oz (225 g) margarine or butter
8 oz (225 g) soft brown sugar

Sift together the flour, ginger, bicarbonate of soda and cream of tartar. Rub in the fat, then add the sugar and mix well. Grease a 10 × 12 in (25 × 30 cm) flat tin, and press the mixture into it. Bake for about 30 minutes at 300°F (150°C) Reg 2. Allow to cool slightly before cutting into pieces.

Caldbeck Rolled Gingerbread

Makes 12–15

1 lb (450 g) plain flour	Mix all the dry ingredients together. Rub in the lard, add the treacle and the water. Knead to a stiff dough. Place on a flat baking sheet and roll out to a thickness of about $\frac{3}{4}$ in (2 cm). Mark diagonally with a fork. Bake at 325°F (160°C) Reg 3 for about 40 minutes. Cut into 3 in (7.5 cm) squares when cold.
7 oz (220 g) caster sugar	
1 tsp mixed spice	
1 tsp cinnamon	
1 tsp ginger	
1½ tsp bicarbonate of soda	
1 tsp salt	
6 oz (175 g) lard	
2 tbsp treacle	
approx 4 fl oz (110 ml) warm water	

Girdle Cakes

Makes approx 12

Although it is possible to buy girdles (griddles) in ironmongers' shops, they are no longer common household items. A frying pan, lightly greased with lard, may be used instead. So also, surprisingly, may a ceramic hob on a modern electric oven, in which case no grease is required. Make the cakes small enough to fit within the ceramic hob.

8 oz (225 g) plain flour	Sift flour and baking powder into the flour. Rub in the other dry ingredients and mix well. Add sufficient milk to form a soft dough. Knead lightly, roll out $\frac{1}{2}$ in (1 cm) thick, cut into small round cakes approx 7 in (18 cm) in diameter and bake on a hot girdle until golden brown on both sides. Split open and butter whilst hot.
1 tsp baking powder	
2 oz (50 g) lard	
2 oz (50 g) margarine	
1 tbsp sugar	
2 oz (50 g) currants	
4–6 tbsp milk	

Dales Cut-And-Come-Again Cake

Cut-and-come-again cakes are great favourites in Britain, and in fact are unique to these islands. The probable reason for the name is that the cakes dried somewhat while cooking, partly because the sugar caramelized in the hot oven, so it was necessary to leave them to 'come again' or soften.

8 oz (225 g) self-raising flour	Heat the oven to 325°F (160°C) Reg 3. Grease and line a deep 6 in (15 cm) diameter cake tin; brush with melted fat. Sift together the flour and the cocoa. Cream the margarine and the sugar until light and fluffy. Gradually add the eggs to the sugar and margarine, beating after each addition. Stir in the golden syrup, sultanas, currants and lemon juice. Fold in the flour and cocoa. Place the mixture in the tin and smooth the surface. Bake in the centre of the oven for about 1½ hours.
1½ tbsp cocoa	
8 oz (225 g) margarine	
6 oz (175 g) caster sugar	
2 eggs, beaten	
2 tbsp golden syrup	
4 oz (110 g) sultanas	
4 oz (110 g) currants	
1 tbsp lemon juice	

Note:
This cake will keep for a month and retain its moisture.

Yorkshire Parkin
Makes 12-16

The battle over the origins of this favourite cake will go on, I hope, for ever. Parkin is truly a Northern cake, that much is certain; the softer gingerbread belongs to the South (sorry, Grasmere!). Northern cooks favoured oatmeal above flour, and the marriage of oatmeal and thick brown treacle established a long tradition. Whether the oatmeal should be fine, coarse or of the pinhead type is another topic for lively discussion; my feeling about this is, long live the variations!

6 oz (175 g) plain flour

1½ tsp bicarbonate of soda

1 tsp ground ginger

2 oz (50 g) medium oatmeal

3 oz (75 g) brown sugar

3 oz (75 g) margarine

4 oz (110 g) golden syrup

1 egg, beaten

milk

Sift the flour, bicarbonate of soda and ground ginger into a bowl. Mix with oatmeal. Melt the sugar, syrup and margarine in a saucepan and pour over the flour mixture. Add the egg and enough milk to mix to a soft consistency. Pour into a well-greased and lined Yorkshire Pudding tin and cook for approx 1 hour at 325°F (160°C) Reg 3, until firm to the touch. Allow to cool in the tin. When cold, remove from the tin and cut into slices or squares. The eating qualities are improved if the Parkin is kept for two weeks in an airtight container. Put a cut apple in the tin – it absorbs moisture.

Orange and Ginger Parkin

4 oz (110 g) butter

1 lb (450 g) golden syrup or old-fashioned brown, not black, treacle

12 oz (350 g) caster sugar

4 oz (110 g) self-raising flour

pinch salt

1 lb (450 g) fine oatmeal

1½ tsp ground ginger

1 tbsp stem ginger, shredded

2 eggs

milk

crystallized orange (optional)

1 tbsp candied orange peel

3 pieces stem ginger, cut into thinnest shreds

Melt the butter and treacle or syrup in a non-stick pan over a low heat. It should be fully melted, but not very hot. Mix all the dry ingredients together. Mix in the treacle and butter. Beat the eggs and add these. Mix in the shredded ginger and candied peel if used. Mix to a sloppy consistency with milk. Pour into a well-buttered large loaf tin, or 8 in (20 cm) diameter cake tin. Bake at 350°F (180°C) Reg 4 for 1-1¼ hours or until cooked. The Parkin should be left for two weeks or more in an airtight tin to mature – or, as they say up there in Yorkshire and Lancashire, 'until it comes again.'

Lancashire Parkin

Makes 12–16

This recipe has more oatmeal and syrup and less flour in it than Yorkshire Parkin.

8 oz (225 g) oatmeal

3 oz (75 g) plain flour

1 tsp ground ginger

2 oz (50 g) brown sugar

pinch salt

½ tsp (scant) bicarbonate of soda

4 oz (110 g) margarine or lard

8 oz (225 g) golden syrup or syrup and treacle

2½ fl oz (75 ml) milk

Mix the oatmeal, flour, ground ginger, sugar, salt and bicarbonate of soda. Melt the fat and the syrup in a pan and add to the dry ingredients. Stir in the milk to make a soft consistency. Cook in a greased and lined shallow tin for 1¼ hours at 300°F (150°C) Reg 2. Allow to cool in the tin. When cold, cut into squares or slices.

Funeral Biscuits

Makes approx 10

Two kinds of funeral cake/biscuit were common in the North. The first had a spongy texture and was usually made by a local baker and sold in the village shop. The second type was more like a shortbread and this was made by the deceased's family and relations. Both kinds were round in shape and when cold were cut in half, one half being placed on top of the other. Each pair of halves was then wrapped up in a special way in unwaxed white paper, and sealed with black sealing wax. While the mourners were waiting for the cortège to come out of the house, two women dressed in deepest black would go round and distribute the Funeral Cakes and glasses of wine.

8 oz (225 g) plain flour

6 oz (175 g) butter

6 oz (175 g) sugar

1 oz (25 g) currants

1 egg, beaten

Rub the butter into the flour. Add the sugar and currants. Mix to a stiffish dough with the beaten egg. Knead a little and roll out. Cut into circles about the size of a small saucer. Bake at 350°F (180°C) Reg 4 until golden brown.

Fat Rascals

Makes 15–20

Another name given to Fat Rascals was Turf Cakes. These were cooked on Whitby Moors over an open turf or peat fire on a girdle.

8 oz (225 g) plain flour

¼ tsp salt

1 rounded tsp baking powder

2½ oz (65 g) lard

1 oz (25 g) sugar

2½ oz (65 g) currants

4–5 tbsp milk and water

egg yolk, beaten

Sift together the flour, salt and baking powder. Rub in the lard until the mixture is like fine breadcrumbs. Stir in the sugar and currants. Add just enough milk and water to make a soft dough. Roll out on a floured board to 1 in (2.5 cm) thickness. Cut into 2 in (5 cm) rounds and place close together on a greased baking tray. Brush with a little beaten egg yolk. Bake at 425°F (220°C) Reg 7 for 15 minutes. Cool on a wire rack.

Eccles Cakes
Makes 12–16

*Elizabeth Raffald, the doyenne of eighteenth-century English cooks, had a niece in Eccles
who was a pastry cook (she herself lived in Manchester). There is good reason to believe that
the niece was encouraged to make her puff pastry into a superior type of Chorley Cake
(another local delicacy) and so the Eccles Cake was born.*

8 oz (225 g) flaky or puff pastry (see page 253)

2 oz (50 g) melted butter

2 oz (50 g) soft brown sugar

2 oz (50 g) chopped mixed peel

4 oz (110 g) currants

pinch mixed spice

egg white and caster sugar to glaze

Heat the oven to 450°F (230°C) Reg 8. Roll out the pastry to $\frac{1}{8}$ in (3 mm) thick and cut into rounds using a small saucer as a guide. Fold trimmings carefully and re-roll. Mix butter, sugar, peel, currants and spice together and put $\frac{1}{2}$ tbsp of this mixture on the centre of each circle of pastry. Brush the edges of the pastry with egg white and gather the edges together to seal. Turn the cake over and re-shape into a circle. Gently re-roll, keeping the shape, until the filling can be seen. Brush over with egg white and slash the pastry on top in a chequered pattern. Leave the cakes to rest in the refrigerator for 10–15 minutes. Cook at the top of the oven reducing the heat to 425°F (220°C) Reg 7 after the door is shut. Bake until golden and crisp – approx 15 minutes. Place on a cooking rack and sprinkle with caster sugar while still hot.

Date and Nut Loaf

This is a very old recipe, dating from c.1730.

6 oz (175 g) dates, chopped

8 fl oz (220 ml) boiling water

1 tsp bicarbonate of soda

2 oz (50 g) butter

1 oz (25 g) lard

4 oz (110 g) sugar

1 egg, beaten

4 oz (110 g) almonds and walnuts, chopped

8 oz (225 g) plain flour

Cover the dates with the boiling water and leave to cool. Add the bicarbonate of soda. Cream the butter, lard and sugar together, and add the egg, nuts and dates. Stir in the flour. Mix well and put into a well-greased loaf tin. Bake for 1 hour at 400°F (200°C) Reg 6. Served sliced.

Cumberland Plate Cake

Serves 6–8

8 oz (225 g) shortcrust pastry (see page 252)

1 lb (450 g) fresh fruit (rhubarb, gooseberries, plums, blackcurrants or apples)

1–2 heaped tbsp sugar

1 tsp plain flour

caster sugar to decorate

Roll out half the pastry and use to line an 8 or 9 in (20 or 23 cm) ovenproof plate. Arrange the fresh fruit on top of the pastry, and sprinkle it with the sugar and flour (which thickens the juice). Damp the edges of the pastry with water and use the remaining pastry to make the lid. Trim, and press the edges well together. Cut a few slits in the top. Cook at 425°F (220°C) Reg 7 for 20–30 minutes. Dredge with caster sugar while still hot.

Bedale Plum Cake

5 oz (150 g) plain flour

½ tsp baking powder

pinch mixed spice

4 oz (110 g) butter

4 oz (110 g) brown sugar

2 eggs

2 oz (50 g) raisins

2 oz (50 g) currants

1 oz (25 g) candied peel

grated rind and juice of ½ lemon

Grease and line a 6 in (15 cm) cake tin. Sieve the flour, baking powder and spice together. Cream the butter and sugar until light and fluffy. Add the eggs, then add the fruit and flour mixture and the lemon juice. Beat well, place the mixture in the prepared tin and bake at 350°F (180°C) Reg 4 for about 1 hour.

Mint Pasty

Pastry

8 oz (225 g) plain flour

3 oz (75 g) lard

1 tsp salt

3 tbsp cold water (approx)

Filling

2 oz (50 g) butter

2 oz (50 g) sugar

3 oz (75 g) currants

3 tbsp fresh mint, chopped

To make the pastry, sieve flour and salt into a bowl and rub in the fat. Add cold water to mix to a stiff dough. To make the filling, cream the butter and sugar together, add the currants and mint. Roll out the pastry into a large round and place the filling on one half of the pastry. Double over the other half of the pastry, damp the edges and crimp together. Bake at 425°F (220°C) Reg 7 for 15 minutes. Serve hot or cold, cut into wedges.

Singing Hinnies

A North Country housewife was once baking this scone for tea, so the story goes, and on repeatedly being asked by her children if it was ready to eat, her final reply was: 'No, it's just singing, hinnies.' 'Hinnie' is a term of endearment still much used in Northumberland, and the reason for the 'singing' is that the butter and cream melt while baking on the girdle and this sets up a squeaking or singing noise.

8 oz (225 g) plain flour
1 tsp baking powder
½ tsp salt
2 oz (50 g) butter
2 oz (50 g) lard
1 oz (25 g) currants
milk and sour cream

Sift the salt and baking powder with the flour. Rub the fats into the flour, then add the currants and enough milk and sour cream to make a soft dough. Roll out and bake both sides on a hot girdle until pale golden and firm, about 3 minutes each side. Turn with a spatula or a pair of wooden 'hands' to avoid breaking.

Lardy Cake

Bread Dough
½ oz (15 g) fresh yeast (or 1 tsp dried yeast)
¼ pt (150 ml) warm water
1 tsp sugar
8 oz (225 g) strong plain flour
1 tsp salt

Filling
3 oz (75 g) lard
3 oz (75 g) currants or sultanas
3 oz (75 g) sugar
milk and extra sugar to glaze

To make the bread dough, disperse the yeast in a few tsp of the water and mix in the sugar. Leave until frothy in a warm place, then add the flour, salt and the rest of the water to make a dough. Knead well and leave to rise until doubled in size. To make the filling, mix together the lard, fruit and sugar and divide into 3 portions. Roll out the dough into an oblong shape and spread 1 portion of the fruit mixture on two-thirds of the dough. Fold into three by folding over the empty third then fold again and repeat the process twice. Form the dough into a square or oblong. Place in an 8 in (20 cm) square tin, score across the top diagonally both ways, brush with milk and sprinkle with sugar. Bake at 400°F (200°C) Reg 6 for 35–40 minutes. Leave to stand in the tin for a few minutes so that the cake absorbs any free lard. Remove from the tin and when cold, cut into slices or squares.

Yorkshire Oven-Bottom Cake

This cake was traditionally made at the end of the baking day when the loaves were taken out. Before the days of metal trays, the cake was baked directly on the floor of the oven.

4 oz (110 g) white bread dough (see page 251)
1 oz (25 g) lard

Cut the lard into 6 pieces and press into the dough. Fold over and knead the fat into the dough, giving a lumpy appearance. Put on a greased baking sheet and bake for 15 minutes at 425°F (220°C) Reg 7 until golden brown. Wrap in a clean tea towel and place on a cushion (this will keep the 'cake' soft and tender). Cut in irregular pieces, split and spread thickly with butter or jam.

Miscellaneous

Carlins

Carlins are small brown dried pulses that look like chick peas. On Carlin Sunday, which is the Fifth Sunday in Lent, it has long been the custom to serve carlins, particularly in public houses during licensing hours. Although modern supermarkets may not stock them, carlins are available in most grocers' shops in market towns.

8 oz (225 g) carlins

pinch salt

1 oz (25 g) butter

dash rum and soft brown sugar to serve

Soak the carlins overnight in water. Drain, and place in a saucepan of boiling water with a pinch of salt. Boil for about 20 minutes or until cooked, but not overdone. Melt the butter in a saucepan, add the drained carlins and fry for 2–3 minutes. Serve hot with brown sugar and rum sprinkled over them.

Cumberland Rum Butter

This is a North Cumbrian method of making rum butter, which in those parts is usually served at Christenings. It is said that the butter symbolizes the richness of life; the sugar is the sweetness of life; the rum the spirit of life, and the nutmeg the spice of life.

8 oz (225 g) soft light brown sugar

6 oz (175 g) butter

2 tbsp rum

grated nutmeg

Roll the brown sugar between two sheets of greaseproof paper to ensure that there are no lumps. Soften the butter slowly – but do not melt down to an oil. Add the sugar to the butter, and nutmeg to taste. Stir well and add the rum. Stir again until well blended and smooth. Pour into a china bowl and allow to set.

Fig Sue

In farmhouses in the old days this traditional drink was served in blue and white porridge basins.

4 oz (110 g) figs

1 tbsp sugar

1 pt (575 ml) water

2 pt (1.2 l) ale

pinch ground ginger

Stew the figs, ginger and sugar in the water until tender. Rub through a sieve. Warm the ale in a pan and add the fig puree. Stir in well until at boiling point.

Scotland

My first-ever visit to Scotland was during the early days of the war, when as a schoolboy I went with my family to North Berwick. Hardly Scotland, you might say! But I vividly recall that short schoolboy's holiday, not only because I was able to see my eldest brother, an airman in uniform stationed at Drem, but

I actually met and ate my first-ever lobster in a tiny pub in the village of Cramond! I had no notion of how to tackle this complex fishy beastie with an apparent century of legs and arms, wearing bright red armour as hard as steel. There it lay on the plate, alongside which a frilly-capped lady had placed a pair of pliers, or what seemed like pliers, a tiny silver hammer and a very long two-pronged fork. What does a callow West Riding chap do, I thought, somewhat daunted? I watched my father out of the corner of one eye as he dismembered, disconnected, crushed and gently bashed away with that little silver hammer and finally lifted the sweet, sea-scented, succulent meat from each section. And *he* only had one arm – the other having disappeared in the name of textile-progress in an industrial accident at his Yorkshire mill before the First World War!

I must since have devoured many hundreds of these, my favourite sea food, from France to the Far East and west to the coastal towns of New England, where they're *nearly* as good as those Scottish ones.

Another impression of that first visit to Scotland was of Brodie's bakery in the aforementioned grey-stone town of North Berwick. I had been staying *en famille* at The Royal Hotel. I had never stayed in a *real* hotel before. It was at The Royal, where the waiters looked like penguins and the chambermaids were starched stiff like nursing sisters, that I decided I wanted to be an hotelier! My whole life grew from the seeds of change sown in that short weekend. At Brodie's I bought bread which was broken off in sections from long, long loaves with floury tops, a style of loaf unseen by the average Sassenach. Everything in that bakery looked – and was – better than at home: soft, pappy baps, a brown bread more treacly in texture than ours in Yorkshire, and there

were oatcakes like huge wash-leathers. I now had a new standard of flavour for bread which remains with me to this day, surpassing the ubiquitous (and in my opinion over-rated) crusty French affair.

I was not to visit the 'Athens of the North' until after the war, when in the early Fifties I paid my first visit to the now-famous International Music Festival at Edinburgh. The awe-inspiring views and vistas of Edinburgh were a revelation to me, and to this day when seeing a foreign city for the first time a clear picture of this ancient capital will loom in my mind – a yardstick for any fresh competitor. On reflection it was perhaps the symmetry of Edinburgh's New Town that impressed me most – that eighteenth-century square mile of perfection. No-one was more delighted than me when the Georgian House in Charlotte Square first opened its doors to us, the public, giving a very clear picture of domestic life in Edinburgh in the eighteenth century – though without the famous Mrs Fraser's recipes from that era.

I have vivid and happy recollections, while walking down Princes Street, of ladies in musquash coats much loved by the well-to-do of Morningside at that time, sitting bolt upright on little gilt chairs in Jenners' exclusive store, sipping milky coffee and eating shortbread. At last I realized that this national biscuit was enjoyed in its home capital, where each lady had, and has, her own (guarded) recipe, where proportions of butter to flour differed and the argument still raged as to whether ground rice improved the texture, and should they be thick or thin, cut in fingers or fanned out in the 'petticoat tails' much favoured in bygone Scotland. Long may these differences survive and the battle continue to make shortbread by 'the true way'.

I must not dally longer in my favourite city, so over to Glasgow, barely forty short miles away but enormously different. I love Glasgow. It's mighty, it's handsome, it's strong and it's *pink!* Forceful buildings abound in Buchanan, Sauchiehall and Argyle Streets. Great department stores, banks, kirks and colleges – all manifestations of the Victorian wealth of these Clydeside folk. It is perhaps in this vast city that the arts are best appreciated, for the names of Charles Rennie Mackintosh and Greek Thomson and Burrell ring in the ears, and their inventive work is there for all to see. It is also in this city that huge progress has been made, for the Scottish Opera and its brother the Scottish National Orchestra were born and thrive in the exquisitely restored Theatre Royal.

I fear the Scottish reader will by now be saying: 'Hasn't the man been to Scotland proper? Has he no ken of the countryside, the Highlands and Islands, the Lowlands, lochs and burns?' I fear I'm a townie by nature. Oh yes, I've *driven* through much of the beautiful lowlands from Edinburgh over breathtaking hills to the tiny village of Moniaive, then on to the fair city of Ayr and Culzean Castle to feel history within its walls. I've gone down to Dumfries along the Solway Firth to see whether the salmon from its waters tastes better than that of the Tay or the Dee. I couldn't tell!

I've *flown* to Aberdeen, only to find myself enjoying its shops and handsome spired buildings more than the tourist trip to Balmoral! The pleasurable part of that first glimpse of the granite city was to address a thousand Scottish ladies in the spacious Beach Ballroom on some aspect or other of British cookery, and to urge every Scottish cook present to clasp her national recipes close to her heart – the black buns and broses, bannocks, baps and broths, shortbreads, skinks and scones, and to encourage them to develop new and home-based dishes using all that is excellent from the gardens, coasts and rivers of this lovely country. There is so much to go at, from the luxury of the only truly excellent smoked salmon in the world to kippers, Arbroath Smokies, the light and dark-toned marmalades of Dundee, and its famous cake, and the abundant game (furred or feathered) which is on the doorstep of every Scottish kitchen. Exciting recipes abound, though I hazard a guess that a true Scot prefers, as I do, game which is high, and plain roast, uncluttered by 'foreign' sauces.

No, I've never been to the Islands. The Outer Hebrides are waiting, as are the Orkneys and Shetlands, but I have a very clear picture of what to

expect when the journey is eventually made. I'll want to taste Clapshot, White Soup, Bride's Bonn and Orkney Cheese.

Home cooking has changed as much in Scotland as anywhere in the British Isles. There is little difference in the fare offered in Scottish homes from that available elsewhere, but the Scots housewife still reigns supreme in many branches of cookery. Like her counterpart in the Midland counties and the North of England, she is not averse to making an effort, and is embarrassed if her tins, freezer and cupboards are not laden with manifestations of that effort. 'I'll put the kettle on, you'll be wanting your tea,' is the greeting to every visitor.

There is an abundance of fish in Scotland's lochs, rivers and coastal waters. In the beautiful Highlands, cattle are bred for the world's best meat, butter and cheese. There is also still plenty of evidence that the kail-pot, bakestone and griddle are used, and even Meal Monday must be remembered by many as the day when students halfway through term were given leave to replenish their stock of oatmeal (said to be the reason for strong, intelligent Scotsmen!). There is also a modicum of evidence of the Auld Alliance between the Royal households of France and Scotland, when banqueting and feasting was the order of the day, until John Knox poured cold water on this high living. As in the South with the Puritans, rich dishes were condemned even to the point of passing a law in 1581 regulating what folk could eat according to their rank, thus creating a 'have and have-not' situation where the rich still ate in the French manner and the less well-off ate, well, less well!

Happily, the Scottish housewife has not let slip her knowledge of and skill at baking, jam-making and preserving. Certainly, the search in this country for things regional has been a special pleasure, as the following recipes will show, and I suspect it will be a wee while, if ever, before the great rock of Scottish regional cookery is submerged in a sea of pizza and pasta.

Soups

Scotch Broth

Serves 8

This most enduring of recipes produces a soup which is said, moreover, to taste even better on the second day.

2 oz (50 g) dried peas
1½–2 lb (700–900 g) neck of mutton or runner of beef
3½ pt (2 l) water
2 oz (50 g) barley
salt to taste
4 oz (110 g) carrot, cut into small dice
4 oz (110 g) turnip, cut into small dice
4 oz (110 g) leek, cut into small dice
2 oz (50 g) onion, cut into small dice
pepper
chopped parsley to garnish

Soak the dried peas overnight, and discard water. Joint the meat and remove as much fat as possible. Put into cold water and bring slowly to the boil, skimming well. When all the scum has been removed add the washed barley, dried peas and salt, and simmer for 30 minutes. Add the carrot, turnip, leek and onion, add pepper and continue to simmer for 2 hours. Remove the meat, cut some small pieces off the bones and return to the pan. Skim if necessary, adjust seasoning, boil up, add parsley and serve.

Barley Soup

Serves 4

This is a very basic recipe but was typical of the economical food served to country families in the past. I have recently read two books by Anna Blair on the history of the country people in an Ayrshire parish, and this sort of broth is one of the variations on their rather frugal fare.

3 oz (75 g) barley
1 pt (575 ml) water
1 pt (575 ml) milk
½ oz (15 g) butter
salt and pepper
12 spring onions
parsley, chopped

Wash barley and put on with water to boil slowly for 1 hour. Make up quantity if it boils away. Add spring onions and boil for 15 minutes more. Add milk, butter and seasoning, and bring to boil again. Add chopped parsley and serve.

Mussel Soup

Serves 4

Fresh mussels from the sea, plus a touch of oatmeal in the liquor, make a distinctive seafood recipe.

4 pt (2.2 l) mussels
1–2 oz (25–50 g) fine oatmeal
milk as required

To prepare mussels for cooking, scrape each one free of sand and seaweed and wash in several waters, for the fine sand is an awful nuisance with mussels. Finally put them in a colander and let cold water run over them for a few minutes. Place them in a deep pan with a tight-fitting lid and sprinkle a very little salt over them but *no* water. Put the pan (covered) over a gentle heat and leave them for about 10 minutes, shaking every now and then to prevent sticking. When all the shells are open remove from heat and strain the liquor through a fine strainer, measuring the liquor, and making up to 2 pt (1.15 l) if necessary with the milk. Meantime toast 1 tbsp fine oatmeal for every 1 pt (575 ml) of liquor and remove mussels from their shells, trimming off the black beard. Bring the mussel liquor to boil, sprinkle in the toasted oatmeal and simmer for 15 minutes. Add the mussels and cook for a further minute or two. Serve hot. Mussels should never be overcooked or they will go tough.

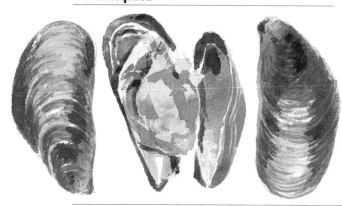

Cock-A-Leekie

Serves 6-8

From the Scotch this is, quite simply, a soup made with chicken and leeks.

1 boiling fowl	
6 prunes	
salt and pepper	
2 leeks, finely sliced	
2 oz (50 g) long grain rice	

Place fowl in saucepan with sufficient water to cover it. Bring to boil and simmer for 1 hour. Add salt and pepper and prunes, and simmer for a further hour. Add the leeks with the rice, and cook for a further 45 minutes. Taste for seasoning. Serve hot sprinkled with chopped parsley.

Note:
Either cut up prunes and return to soup or remove completely if appearance is not liked.

Game Soup

Serves 4-5

Scotland still has a good quantity of game, although the price has risen steeply since this traditional recipe was formulated. However, trimmings or carcases of birds such as pheasant, blackcock, grouse and ptarmigan, as well as the elderly birds which are no good for roasting, can be used; also odd joints from a hare, venison and so on.

2 oz (50 g) butter	
1 onion	
1 carrot	
1 or 2 sticks celery	
1 or 2 carcases of game birds or $2\frac{3}{4}$ pt (1.5 l) game stock	
bay leaf	
6 peppercorns	
1 tsp salt	
1 oz (25 g) butter	
1 oz (25 g) plain flour	
2 tsp redcurrant jelly	
2 tsp lemon juice	
2 tbsp sherry or red wine	

Melt 2 oz (50 g) butter in a saucepan, and toss the onion, carrot and celery. Either brown the game carcases, then add water, or else add the game stock. Add bay leaf, peppercorns and salt, and simmer for 1 hour. Remove carcases. Remove any meat from the bones and either chop finely with stock or blend together in liquidizer. Melt 1 oz (25 g) butter in another saucepan, make a roux with the flour and gradually add the stock. Adjust seasoning, add jelly, lemon juice and sherry.

Hotch Potch

Serves 4-6

This is a traditional thick harvest broth, at its best when made with new and very fresh vegetables.

2 lb (900 g) neck of lamb chops	Put the lamb in a saucepan, add half the salt and pepper and bring to the boil. Remove any scum from the top, cover and simmer for 1 hour. Add the turnips, carrots, onions, beans and half the peas, cover and simmer for 1½ hours. Now add the cauliflower, lettuce, sugar, mint, the rest of the peas and the seasoning. Cover and simmer for approx 30 minutes, by which time both meat and vegetables should be tender. Sprinkle with parsley and serve.
1 tsp salt	
½ tsp pepper	
5 pt (2.8 l) water	
4 small turnips, chopped	
4 medium carrots, chopped	
6 spring onions (whole), chopped	
8 oz (225 g) broad beans	
1 lb (450 g) peas	
1 medium cauliflower, cut small	
1 small lettuce, shredded	
1 tsp sugar	
2 tsp mint, chopped	
1 tbsp parsley, chopped	

Salmon Soup

Serves 6-8

Scottish salmon is of excellent quality and is held in high regard. Good Scots housewives use the head and possibly the tail to make a very special soup.

1 salmon head and a small piece cut off the tail	Simmer all together except sherry and cream for approx 1 hour. Strain off stock, sieve, liquidize or process the vegetables in a little of it and include flesh from the head. Return stock, puree and flaked tail flesh to the rinsed saucepan, bring to the boil and add sherry. Taste for seasoning, carefully add cream and do not allow soup to reboil. Sprinkle with chopped fresh parsley if liked.
8 oz (225 g) sole or plaice bones and trimmings	
1 medium leek, roughly chopped	
2 medium carrots, roughly chopped	
1 medium onion, roughly chopped	
1 stick celery	
3 ripe tomatoes, skinned and de-seeded	
1 sprig thyme	
1 sprig fennel	
½ oz (15 g) sea salt	
12 white peppercorns	
pinch nutmeg	
3 pt (1.8 l) water	
2 fl oz (55 ml) double cream	
1-2 fl oz (28-55 ml) sherry	

Fish

Cullen Skink
Serves 4

This is, literally, a soup (skink) from Cullen, a fishing village on the Moray Firth.

1 finnan haddock	
1 pt (575 ml) water	
1 pt (575 ml) milk	
mashed potatoes	
small piece of butter	
salt and pepper	

Skin the haddock, put in a pan and cover with boiling water. Simmer for about 5 minutes or until fish is cooked. Remove bones, return them to stock and boil for about 30 minutes. Meanwhile flake fish. Strain stock and add to flaked fish and milk. Bring to the boil, and add enough mashed potatoes to make a creamy consistency. Season with pepper and salt. Add butter and serve hot.

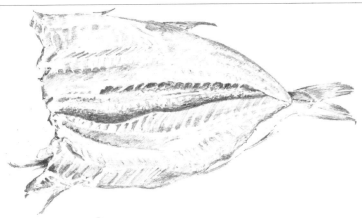

Rizzered Haddies
Serves 4

For this dish it is best to use fair-sized haddocks. If they are too small they get very dry.

4 finnan haddocks	
2 oz (50 g) white or wholemeal flour	
1 tsp salt	
$\frac{1}{4}$ tsp pepper	
butter	

Skin, clean and wipe the fish, and cover them well with seasoned flour. Put on a grid-iron and cook over a clear hot fire (or grill) until a medium brown. They should be served very hot, and melted butter offered with them.

Salmon Mousse
Serves 4–6

8 oz (225 g) cooked salmon or	
4 oz (110 g) smoked salmon	
$\frac{1}{2}$ oz (15 g) gelatine	
4 tbsp fish stock or water	
12 oz (350 g) cottage cheese	
squeeze of lemon juice	
1 tbsp sherry	
2 egg whites	
salt and cayenne pepper	

Remove any bones and skin from fish. Dissolve gelatine in stock or water over a bowl of hot water. Place all ingredients except egg whites in a liquidizer or food processor and run until smooth and well-mixed. Remove to a bowl and fold in firmly-beaten egg whites. Pour into a soufflé dish or individual ones. Allow to set. Garnish with lemon and parsley.

Poached/Baked Salmon

The very simplest ways of cooking salmon are best and the only problem to be avoided is overcooking, for this makes it dry and uninteresting. Frozen salmon must be completely thawed first.

To serve cold

1 cut or whole salmon – allow 4 oz (110 g) raw fish per person

10 peppercorns

1 tbsp salt

mayonnaise (see page 22)

To serve hot

1 portion or whole salmon

butter

hollandaise sauce (see page 22)

Poach either a cut or whole salmon. For a whole fish place in a large pan covered with cold water, add the salt and peppercorns and bring slowly to just under boiling point. Hold at this stage for 10–20 minutes depending on size of fish, and allow to cool slowly in the water. A cut of salmon should be started in tepid water, hold heat for 8–10 minutes and then cool in water. Serve with a good mayonnaise.

Wrap whole or portion of fish in a well-buttered piece of foil and make into a secure parcel. Bake at 300°F (150°C) Reg 2 for 12–15 minutes per pound. Serve hot with hollandaise sauce or plain melted butter. If baked fish is to be served cold, cool in the unopened foil.

Trout Fried in Oatmeal

Serves 1

1 large or 2 small trout per person

coarse oatmeal

salt and pepper

butter

parsley

wedges of lemon

Clean the trout and split them open at the belly, then remove the backbone. Season some coarse oatmeal with salt and pepper, and roll the fish on both sides in it. Heat 2 tbsp butter for each portion of fish in a frying pan and when bubbling, but not brown, fry the fish on both sides until golden. Drain and serve garnished with parsley and wedges of lemon. This recipe is also used for herrings.

Haddock Garnished in Sauce

Serves 4

1 pt (575 ml) fish stock

4 full fillets fresh haddock

3 oz (75 g) shellfish, eg mussels, cockles or prawns

½ oz (15 g) plain flour

½ oz (15 g) butter

2 tsp mushroom ketchup

Poach the fish in stock for 15–20 minutes, then carefully remove to a fireproof dish. Cook the shellfish for 5–7 minutes. Remove and use to garnish fish. Thicken stock with flour and butter kneaded together which should be added in small pieces and whisked until sauce is boiling and thick. Add ketchup to taste and add salt and pepper if necessary. Pour over fish and place in a moderate oven to ensure dish is piping hot.

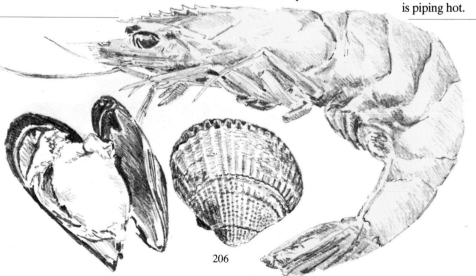

Game Pie
Serves 8-10

Filling

1 hare

1 small grouse or half a pheasant

6 oz (175 g) pork fat (taken from the loin)

2 lb (900 g) venison

$\frac{1}{4}$ pt (150 ml) Jamaica rum

8 fl oz (220 ml) red wine (Burgundy type)

1 tsp ground ginger

1 clove garlic, crushed

1 egg, beaten

salt and freshly milled pepper

1 lb (450 g) extra pork fat

Special crust

$\frac{1}{3}$ pt (185 ml) water

4 oz (110 g) lard

2 oz (50 g) butter

1 lb (450 g) plain white flour

1 oz (25 g) icing sugar

1 tsp salt

1 tsp finely grated orange rind

1 tsp ground mace

Jelly

aspic jelly powder

gelatine crystals

$\frac{3}{4}$ pt (425 ml) boiling water

$\frac{1}{4}$ pt (150 ml) dry sherry

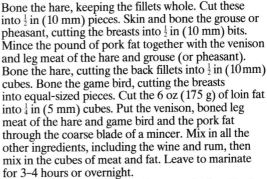

Bone the hare, keeping the fillets whole. Cut these into $\frac{1}{2}$ in (10 mm) pieces. Skin and bone the grouse or pheasant, cutting the breasts into $\frac{1}{2}$ in (10 mm) bits. Mince the pound of pork fat together with the venison and leg meat of the hare and grouse (or pheasant). Bone the hare, cutting the back fillets into $\frac{1}{2}$ in (10 mm) cubes. Bone the game bird, cutting the breasts into equal-sized pieces. Cut the 6 oz (175 g) of loin fat into $\frac{1}{4}$ in (5 mm) cubes. Put the venison, boned leg meat of the hare and game bird and the pork fat through the coarse blade of a mincer. Mix in all the other ingredients, including the wine and rum, then mix in the cubes of meat and fat. Leave to marinate for 3-4 hours or overnight.

To make the pie crust, bring the water, lard and butter to the boil in a pan. In a large bowl sieve the flour, sugar, salt, pepper and mace together (but not the orange rind: add this after sieving). Make a well in the mixture. Pour in all the hot liquid butter and lard mixture. Mix it to a soft dough with a fork and leave to cool a little. Butter a deep loose-bottomed cake tin approx 8-10 in (20-25 cm) in diameter. Put this to chill. Knead the dough lightly on a floured work surface. Cut off one-third and retain for the lid of the pie. Roll the remaining dough into a large circle as big as the base of your tin plus the height of the sides. Fold this dough into four, place in the bottom of the tin and unfold, pressing into place, up and somewhat over the edge of the tin. Spoon the filling into the pastry shell pressing well into the corners. Wet the edges of the pastry. Roll out a lid and fit this, pinching the edges together. Make a hole in the centre and fit a foil funnel to allow the steam to escape. Stand the pie on a tray and bake in a preheated oven at 400°F (200°C) Reg 6 for 1 hour. Lower the temperature to 350°F (180°C) Reg 4 and bake for a further 2 hours. Remove the outside of the cake tin, but not the base. Brush the pie all over with beaten egg and return it to the oven for a further 30 minutes to brown all over. Leave to cool.

When the pie is quite cold, make up 1 pt (575 ml) of commercial aspic jelly following the instructions on the packet, but substituting half the aspic crystals for plain gelatine crystals and using $\frac{3}{4}$ pt (425 ml) boiling water and $\frac{1}{4}$ pt (150 ml) dry sherry for extra flavour. Leave this to cool to the point where it is just beginning to thicken but not gel. Remove the foil funnel from the pie and pour the jelly in through the hole in the lid using a small kitchen funnel. The amount of jelly required will depend on how much the meat has shrunk during cooking. Serve cold.

Game Chips

potatoes	
nut or vegetable oil for frying	
salt	

Waxy potatoes are best for game chips. Peel, wash and slice them as thick as a 50p piece, either using a mandoline or a sharp knife. A food processor can be used but the size of your chips will be reduced somewhat. To make 'basket weave' chips, the potato is cut over the crenellated blade of a mandoline, turning it a half-turn between each cut. Wash the cut potatoes well in cold water, then using nut or vegetable oil fry them in small batches at 325°F (160°C). Drain them on a rack, then fry them again in very hot oil at 375°F (190°C) until crisp and golden brown. Salt them lightly. These can be made days in advance. All you have to do is heat them up in the oven for a minute just before serving.

Butter-fried Breadcrumbs

These are often served with game as an alternative to game chips.

8 slices decrusted white bread	
4 oz (110 g) unsalted butter	

Pick or pluck the bread into minute crumbs. You can use a grater if you like, but the result is different. Melt the butter evenly in a heavy-bottomed skillet. Add the crumbs and, over a low heat, fry them until golden brown. You must stir them and turn them all the time or they will burn at the edges, and you won't get even browning. The crumbs can be heated through in the oven on a shallow baking tray before being transferred to a heated boat for serving. They can also be frozen.

Sassermaet

Serves 6

1 lb (450 g) beef	
8-12 oz (225–350 g) suet	
1 heaped tsp ginger	
1 heaped tsp cinnamon	
1 heaped tsp mixed spice	
salt and pepper	
1 tsp ground cloves	
sugar	
$\frac{1}{4}$ tsp ground nutmeg	

Mince beef and suet finely, then add ginger, cinnamon, mixed spice, pepper and salt to taste, ground cloves, sugar and nutmeg. Mix well together and make into brunies (patties). Fry slowly for 30–45 minutes from a cold pan, adding no other fat.

Potted Hough

Serves 6-8

Hough is the Scottish word for shin of beef.

2 lb (900 g) hough	
1 nap bone	
6 $\frac{1}{4}$ pt (3.5 l) cold water	
seasonings	
spices or herbs (optional)	

Wash meat and bone and place in water. Bring to the boil and skim. Season and add any herbs or spices. Simmer for 4 hours or until very tender. Shred or mince beef and replace in strained liquor. Bring to the boil and pour into wetted moulds. Allow to set in a cool place.

Mince Collops

Serves 4

Collops, like escallops, are slices of meat; here the meat is minced and served with poached eggs on top.

1 lb (450 g) minced steak	
½ pt (275 ml) water	
seasonings	
½ oz (15 g) plain flour	
4 eggs, poached	
sippets of toast	

Heat saucepan and add mince, flour and seasonings. Stir till browned. Add water and simmer gently for 1 hour. Pour on a hot dish and place poached eggs on mince. Garnish with sippets of toast.

Note:
A chopped onion, or a little oatmeal instead of flour, may be added to steak mince when it is being browned.

Roast Grouse

Serves 4

The main problem when roasting game birds is to keep them moist. Some people are not too keen on birds actually shot on the glorious 12th, preferring game to be 'high' or well hung, but it is a matter for individual taste. Hanging helps to break down any possible tough tissues and eliminates the need to over-roast them which makes them dry.

4 grouse

1 onion, quartered

1 tsp ground bay or 4 small pieces fresh bay leaf

4 oz (110 g) softened butter

1 tsp salt

1 tsp ground thyme or large sprig fresh thyme

1 tbsp brandy

4 rashers fat bacon

4 oz (110 g) butter

Gravy

giblets from the grouse

1 tsp plain white flour

1 sherry glass brandy

¾ pt (425 ml) light chicken or game stock (use ½ stock cube)

1 glass red wine

extra butter

Make a paste of the bay, butter, salt, thyme and brandy and rub this all over the birds, leaving about 1 tsp to go inside the birds with a little extra bay and thyme. Wrap a rasher of fat bacon over the breasts, and tie down with linen thread. In an iron skillet, melt a further 4 oz (110 g) butter until foaming and giving off an almond smell. Brown each bird on all sides for 1–2 minutes. Now stand them all the right way up in the skillet and transfer this to the oven, preheated at 475°F (240°C) Reg 9, roasting them for no more than 35 minutes if you like your game bloody, or longer if you prefer things more well done. Transfer the birds when cooked to a warm serving dish to let them 'set'. To make the gravy, put the giblets into the roast pan, sprinkle over 1 tsp plain white flour and stir well in. Allow the flour to take on a good brown colour – almost to burning point. Pour over a sherry glass of brandy and flame it. Pour into skillet a wine glass of claret or other red wine and ½ pt (275 ml) chicken or game stock. Simmer for 45 minutes, and strain. Leave to settle at the side of the stove for 5 minutes when any excess fat will rise to the surface. Skim this off. If the gravy is not of a good rich brown colour, add one or two drops of pure caramel or gravy browning which *is* pure caramel. You should end up with about ⅓ pt (185 ml) of gravy which should be fairly thin and bright. Grouse are served whole and can have the added luxury of being served on top of a heart-shaped crouton (see page 20) spread with a little pâté.

Venison

A marvellously rich and tasty meat now widely available again everywhere. It can be prepared in many ways to suit all preferences.

Marinade

2 parts oil to 1 part wine or vinegar or wine and vinegar mixed

1 onion, thinly sliced

grated lemon rind

pinch herbs

salt and pepper

Place marinade in a dish large enough to hold venison (it should cover bottom of dish). Place venison in marinade and turn frequently. Drain venison but do not wash.

Stewing Simmer neatly cut pieces, which have been dipped in seasoned flour, and brown well for about 4 hours or until tender. A little port wine or redcurrant jelly may be added to the gravy before serving.

Roasting Either roast as for beef, but baste very thoroughly. Cook 25–30 minutes per lb (450 g) plus 25 minutes. Or wrap venison in a well-buttered or oiled piece of foil, or a flour paste, and bake for 25–35 minutes per lb (450 g) plus 30 minutes. During the last 30 minutes open the foil and allow venison to brown. Serve with brown gravy and redcurrant jelly.

Olives Slices may be stuffed and rolled as beef olives. Cook gently until tender.

Pot-roasting In usual way as for beef.

Braised After marinating, braise as for beef until tender.

Curry Venison meat is delicious used in curry.

Haggis

Serves 10–12

The name of this grandiose sausage, wrapped in the belly of a sheep, is thought to derive from the French hacher, *to chop.*

1 stomach bag of sheep

1 pluck, ie liver, heart and lungs

4 oz (110 g) beef suet

12 oz (350 g) medium to coarse oatmeal

2 onions, finely diced

½ oz (15 g) salt

1 tsp freshly ground black pepper

1 pt (575 ml) stock

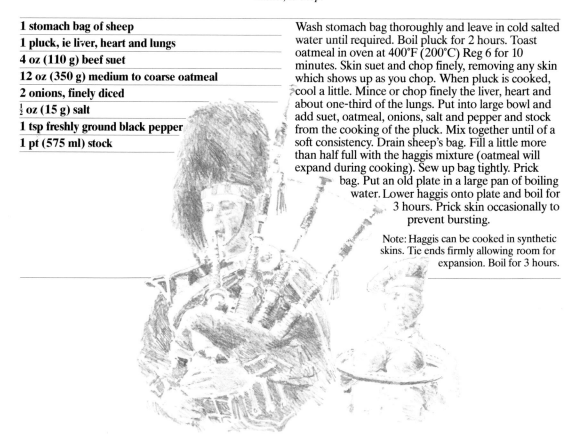

Wash stomach bag thoroughly and leave in cold salted water until required. Boil pluck for 2 hours. Toast oatmeal in oven at 400°F (200°C) Reg 6 for 10 minutes. Skin suet and chop finely, removing any skin which shows up as you chop. When pluck is cooked, cool a little. Mince or chop finely the liver, heart and about one-third of the lungs. Put into large bowl and add suet, oatmeal, onions, salt and pepper and stock from the cooking of the pluck. Mix together until of a soft consistency. Drain sheep's bag. Fill a little more than half full with the haggis mixture (oatmeal will expand during cooking). Sew up bag tightly. Prick bag. Put an old plate in a large pan of boiling water. Lower haggis onto plate and boil for 3 hours. Prick skin occasionally to prevent bursting.

Note: Haggis can be cooked in synthetic skins. Tie ends firmly allowing room for expansion. Boil for 3 hours.

Small Mutton Pies

Serves 4–6

Traditional street-fare, these pasties with a lamb or mutton filling were known in Glasgow at one time as 'Tuppenny Struggles'.

1 lb (450 g) hot water crust pastry (see page 252)
gravy or stock
1 lb (450 g) lean lamb, minced
salt and pepper
pinch nutmeg
1 egg, beaten, or milk

Prepare pastry and set aside one-third for lids in a warm place. Divide remainder into 6 pieces. Roll out to fit tins if available or mould around a jam jar. Moisten meat with gravy or stock and season. Divide equally amongst pastry cases. Cover with remaining pastry, brush with egg or milk and make a hole in centre. Bake at 400°F (200°C) Reg 6 for 45 minutes to 1 hour. Lower heat if overbrowning and lightly cover with greaseproof paper.

Forfar Bridies

Serves 4

These bridies, or pasties, are of the same family as the Small Mutton Pies, above, made with beef instead of mutton.

1 lb (450 g) rump steak or topside
3 oz (75 g) beef suet
2 medium onions, finely chopped
salt and ground black pepper to taste
Pastry
12 oz (350 g) plain flour
3 oz (75 g) margarine
3 oz (75 g) lard
water to mix
salt

Make the pastry first. Rub the fat into the flour, add salt and mix to a very stiff dough with water. Divide into 4 equal-sized pieces and roll out onto a floured board into 4 large ovals. Beat out the steak with a meat bat or rolling pin and cut up roughly into $\frac{1}{2}$ in (10 mm) cubes. Chop the suet finely. Put the meat into a bowl with the suet and onions. Add seasonings and mix well. Divide meat into 4 portions and cover half of each oval with meat leaving a rim for sealing. Wet edges, fold over and seal. Crimp edge and make a hole in the top. Bake on a greased baking sheet for 45 minutes.

Savouries

Aberdeen Toasties
Serves 4

6 oz (175 g) haddock fillets, cooked, skinned and flaked

¼ pt (150 ml) coating cheese sauce (see page 22)

2 egg yolks

salt and pepper

4 slices buttered toast

Put the haddock, sauce, egg yolks, salt and pepper into a saucepan and heat gently, stirring. Pour on to the toast and, if liked, brown under the grill.

Neeps 'n Tatties
Serves 4–6

Neeps are, strictly, turnips – but in some areas this is the word for swedes, which are a comparatively recent vegetable developed, probably, from a hybrid between the turnip and one of the cabbage/cauliflower family of European brassicas. In this recipe, either may be used, though swedes are favoured.

1 lb (450 g) swedes, peeled and diced

8 oz (225 g) potatoes, peeled and diced

salt and pepper

grated nutmeg

1 oz (25 g) butter

chopped parsley to garnish

Cook the swedes and potatoes in boiling salted water until tender. Drain well, then mash very thoroughly. Season well with salt, pepper and nutmeg, then beat in the butter. Serve hot, garnished with parsley.

Clapshot
Serves 4–6

A traditional Orkney dish that may be eaten by itself or combined with meat or fish. It is often served as an accompaniment to Haggis.

1 lb (450 g) potatoes, boiled

1 lb (450 g) turnips, boiled

1 oz (25 g) chives

1 oz (25 g) butter or dripping

salt and pepper

Mash together the potatoes and turnips. Add chives and dripping or butter. Season and serve very hot.

Scots Woodcock
Serves 2

4 slices bread, with crusts removed if desired

½ oz (15 g) butter

8 anchovy fillets

4 egg yolks

½ pt (275 ml) single cream

pinch cayenne pepper and salt

chopped parsley

Toast bread on both sides, spread with butter and sandwich in pairs with well-chopped or pounded anchovies. Keep warm while a custard is made over hot water by beating yolks, cream, cayenne and salt. When thick, pour over toasted sandwiches and sprinkle with chopped parsley. Serve hot.

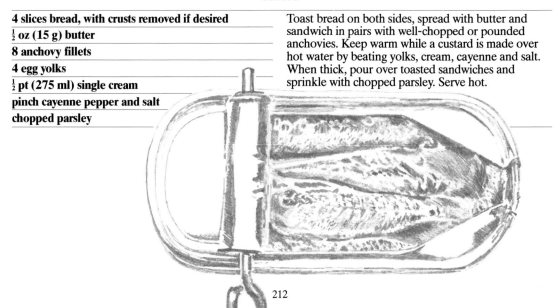

Puddings and Desserts

Urney Pudding

Serves 4

4 oz (110 g) butter

2 oz (50 g) sugar

2 eggs, beaten

4 oz (110 g) plain flour

pinch bicarbonate of soda dissolved in 1–2 tbsp milk

4 oz (110 g) strawberry jam

Cream the butter and sugar, add the beaten eggs and flour alternately and finally mix in the jam and the milk and soda. Turn into a well-greased pudding basin, cover with greaseproof paper or foil and steam for 1½ hours. Serve hot with custard sauce.

Dunesslin Pudding

Serves 4

4 tbsp jam or stewed fruit

2 oz (50 g) plain flour

1 oz (25 g) sugar

1 oz (25 g) butter

½ pt (275 ml) milk

squeeze of lemon juice or a few drops of vanilla essence

2 eggs, well beaten

Put the jam or fruit at the bottom of a 2 pt (1.15 l) pudding dish which has been lightly buttered. Mix the flour and sugar in a thick saucepan over heat, and gradually add the milk, stirring well, then add the butter cut into small pieces. Stir until it boils and becomes thick. Cool slightly, add the lemon juice or vanilla and the well-beaten eggs. Beat until smooth, then pour over the jam or fruit evenly and brown in a moderate oven at 350°F (180°C) Reg 4 for about 20 minutes.

Carrageen Mould

Serves 4

Carrageen is a seaweed found below the high-water mark on the west coast of Scotland. It should be washed, dried and bleached, and can then be kept.

½ oz (15 g) dried carrageen

1 pt (575 ml) milk

rind of 1 lemon or a few drops of vanilla essence

1 oz (25 g) sugar

Place the dried carrageen in a bowl and cover with hot water, then stir well and drain thoroughly. Boil this in the milk with the lemon rind and simmer for about 15 minutes, or until it is soft and thick. Strain into a bowl and add the sugar, stirring well to dissolve it. Pour into a wetted mould and leave to set.

Marmalade Tart

Serves 4

The name comes from marmelo, *the Portuguese word for quince. These, and oranges too, were exported to England as early as the fifteenth century. By association, the name was transferred to the orange-based product of which the Scots became the master-manufacturers.*

4 oz (110 g) shortcrust pastry (see page 252)

2 eggs

3 tbsp milk

1 oz (25 g) sugar

1 oz (25 g) melted butter

2 tbsp marmalade

Line a 7 in (18 cm) ovenproof plate with pastry. Beat eggs and add other ingredients. Pour mixture into lined plate, bake at 400°F (200°C) Reg 6 for 10 minutes, then lower to 325°F (160°C) Reg 3 for a further 20 minutes.

Marmalade Pudding

Serves 3–4

3 oz (75 g) butter or margarine

3 oz (75 g) sugar

4 oz (110 g) marmalade, preferably home-made

2 eggs, separated

3 oz (75g) self-raising flour

pinch salt

Sauce

2 oz (50 g) sugar

$\frac{1}{2}$ pt (275 ml) water

3 oz (75 g) marmalade

Cream butter and sugar. Stir in the marmalade, then add egg yolks and flour mixed with salt. Beat white of eggs until stiff and gently fold into mixture. Put into a greased bowl or mould, cover and steam for $1\frac{1}{2}$ hours. Serve with Marmalade Sauce. To make sauce, boil sugar, water and marmalade together rapidly for 5 minutes until they form a syrup. Serve without straining.

Cranachan

Serves 4

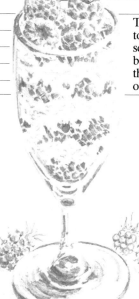

2 oz (50 g) oatmeal

$\frac{1}{2}$ pt (275 ml) double cream

sugar to taste

8 oz (225 g) raspberries

Toast oatmeal lightly. Whip cream softly and sweeten to taste. Fold oatmeal through cream and layer in serving glasses with raspberries. Other soft fruit can be used if preferred and the fruit can be folded through the cream too. Eat soon after mixing in oatmeal for a crunchy, nutty flavour.

Scots Trifle

Serves 6

6 trifle sponges

strawberry or raspberry jam

grated rind of $\frac{1}{2}$ lemon

$\frac{1}{4}$ pt (150 ml) sherry

2 eggs

2 oz (50 g) sugar

18 fl oz (500 ml) milk

$\frac{1}{4}$ pt (150 ml) double cream

glacé cherries, angelica and ratafia biscuits to decorate

Split the sponges and spread thickly with the jam. Sandwich together again and place in a shallow dish. Sprinkle the lemon rind over the sponges. Pour the sherry over and allow the sponges to absorb it. Whisk together the eggs and sugar and scald the milk. Pour this over the egg mixture then return to pan and stir carefully over a very low heat until it thickens. Pour over the sponges and allow to get cold. Whip cream lightly and spread over the top. Decorate with glacé cherries, angelica and ratafia biscuits.

Fairy Pudding
Serves 4

18 fl oz (500 ml) water	Boil together the water, lemon juice, rind and sugar and strain over the slaked cornflour. Return the mixture to the pan, bring to the boil once more and cook for 2–3 minutes. Remove from the heat and allow to cool. Whisk the egg whites until stiff and fold into the cornflour mixture. Pour all into a wetted mould and allow to set. Whisk together the egg yolks, sugar and cornflour until thick and creamy. Scald the milk and pour over the egg mixture, stirring all the time. Rinse out the pan and return all to it. Stir over a low heat until it thickens, then allow to cool. When ready to serve, turn the pudding out on a dish and pour the cooled sauce around it.
rind and juice of 1 lemon	
2 oz (50 g) sugar	
1 oz (25 g) cornflour, slaked with a little cold water	
2 egg whites	
Sauce	
2 egg yolks	
1 tsp cornflour	
1 oz (25 g) sugar	
18 fl oz (500 ml) milk	
vanilla essence to taste	

Drambuie Cream
Serves 6

20 sponge fingers	Stir over heat all the ingredients except port until all are melted well together. Cool for 15 minutes. Add port and strain into the base of a mould with straight sides. When jelly is on the point of setting, place approx 20 sponge fingers into the jelly and leave to set.
¼ pt (150 ml) water	
1 oz (25 g) sugar	
1 tbsp lemon juice	
1 tbsp gelatine	
1 tsp redcurrant jelly	To make the cream, blend sugar, gelatine and well-beaten eggs together, pour on milk and cook over a gentle heat stirring all the time. Do not let it boil, allow to cool but not set. Whip cream, fold in Drambuie and cooled custard, pour into prepared mould. Chill and when set dip base of mould quickly into hot water before turning out.
¼ pt (150 ml) port	
Cream	
¾ pt (425 ml) milk, scalded	
3 oz (75 g) caster sugar	
¾ oz (20 g) gelatine	
2 eggs, beaten	
½ pt (275 ml) double cream	
4 fl oz (110 m) Drambuie	

Atholl Brose

This concoction has been famous since the 1470s and is named after the Duke of Atholl. It is traditionally drunk on St Andrew's Day.

3 oz (75 g) fine oatmeal	Mix the oatmeal and water together in a bowl and allow it to soak for 30 minutes. Strain using a fine sieve, pressing gently with a spoon until the meal is dry. Discard the oatmeal and mix the liquid and honey using a silver spoon. Pour into a 40 fl oz bottle and fill up with whisky. Shake well before using. Serve as a liqueur.
1 pt (575 ml) water	
2 tbsp liquid heather honey	
whisky	A delicious pudding can be made by pouring a good measure of Atholl Brose into a glass. Top it with whipped cream and chill well. Sprinkle top with lightly toasted oatmeal to give a pleasant nutty flavour.

Edinburgh Rock

1 lb (450 g) sugar	Dissolve sugar in water, add tartar and boil to 260°F (130°C). Pour gently on to an oiled slab or tin; put colour and flavour in centre and when cool enough to handle turn in edges and start to pull and fold till firm. Cut into lengths with scissors and leave in a warm place for a day or two until it becomes crumbly.
generous ¼ pt (150 ml) water	
generous pinch cream of tartar	
colours and flavourings	

Hatted Kit

Serves 4

The original recipe of this dish was passed down to the contributor by her mother, who used to take the bowl to the cow and milk the cow directly into the dish, because this put a better 'hat' on the 'kit': nowadays, bottled milk allows the dish to be made anywhere!

1 pt (575 ml) milk	Warm the milk and pour into a dish. Add the rennet and leave to set. Lift the curd into a sieve and press the whey through the sieve until the curd is quite stiff. Sweeten with half the sugar and add a little grated nutmeg. Whip the cream with the remaining sugar and a little more nutmeg, then gently mix with the curd.
2 tsp rennet	
2 tbsp soft brown sugar	
a little grated nutmeg	
½ pt (275 ml) double cream	

Lemon Steamed Pudding

Serves 4–5

5 oz (150 g) breadcrumbs	Mix all the dry ingredients, the suet and the lemon rind in a bowl. Add the eggs and milk, mix well and stir in the lemon juice. Turn into a buttered pudding basin, cover tightly with greaseproof paper and foil and steam for 2½ hours.
4 oz (110 g) plain flour	
3 tsp baking powder	
4 oz (110 g) sugar	
grated rind of 2 lemons	
2 eggs, beaten	
7 fl oz (200 ml) milk	
juice of 1 lemon	

Cakes, Breads and Biscuits
Dundee Cake

2 oz (50 g) almonds	Grease and line an 8 in (20 cm) round tin. Blanch the almonds and chop half of them. Sieve dry ingredients. Cream butter and sugar, add grated rind then eggs one at a time alternating with the flour. Mix in the remaining ingredients including the chopped almonds. Place in the prepared tin, smooth top and arrange the remaining split almonds neatly on top. Bake for approx 3 hours at 325°F (160°C) Reg 3.
11 oz (300 g) flour, 3 oz (75 g) of it self-raising	
pinch salt and mixed spice	
8 oz (225 g) butter	
8 oz (225 g) soft brown sugar	
grated rind of 1 orange and 1 lemon	
4 large eggs	
8 oz (225 g) currants	
8 oz (225 g) sultanas	
6 oz (175 g) raisins	
4 oz (110 g) chopped mixed peel	
4 oz (110 g) chopped cherries	

Note:
If a large fruit cake like this is rested in the fridge for a few hours before baking, this helps to
keep the fruit from sinking.

Oat Biscuits
Makes 20–24

4 oz (110 g) porridge oats	Mix together the oats, flour, sugar, coconut and baking powder. Add the butter and egg and blend well. Roll out the mixture to $\frac{1}{4}$ in (5 mm) thickness and cut into shapes with biscuit cutters. Place on a greased baking sheet and bake in a preheated oven at 350°F (180°C) Reg 4 for 20 minutes. Cool on a wire rack.
2 oz (50 g) plain flour, sifted	
3 oz (75 g) sugar	
2 oz (50 g) desiccated coconut	
1 tsp baking powder	
4 oz (110 g) butter or margarine, melted	
1 egg, beaten	

Oatcakes
Makes 3

5 oz (150 g) oatmeal	Mix dry ingredients, add fat, then sufficient water to make a moderately stiff dough. Roll out as thinly as possible to a large round, divide into 3 farls (wedges). Bake on a hot girdle till corners begin to curl, remove to grill pan and toast until crisp but not brown. Oatcakes may also be baked in the oven at 350°F (180°C) Reg 4 for approx 20 minutes. When rolling out, dust with plenty of oatmeal, use short sharp strokes with the rolling pin, and handle quickly.
1 tbsp melted bacon dripping	
generous pinch salt	
generous pinch bicarbonate of soda	
hot water to mix	

Note:
In Ayrshire the round was traditionally divided into 3 farls before baking on a girdle. If they
are baked in the oven, they can be cut into 3 in (7.5 cm) rounds.

Aberdeen Butteries
Makes 8–10

¾ oz (20 g) fresh yeast
¼ pt (150 ml) tepid milk and water mixed
1 tsp sugar
1 oz (25 g) butter or margarine
9 oz (250 g) strong plain flour
½ tsp salt
2 oz (50 g) butter or margarine, mixed with 2 oz (50 g) lard

Blend yeast with a little of the liquid, add remaining liquid and sugar. Rub 1 oz (25 g) of fat into flour and salt, and mix to a soft elastic dough with yeast and liquid. Knead firmly for about 5 minutes. Replace in bowl, cover and leave in a warm place to double in size. Knock back risen dough by kneading on a floured board. Roll out to a strip ¾ in (2 cm) thick, spread one-third of mixed fats over two-thirds of the dough and fold as for puff pastry (see page 253). Give dough a half turn and repeat rolling and folding twice more, using all the fat. Allow dough to rest in a cool place for a short time. Roll out again and divide into 8–10 pieces. Place on baking sheets, cover and leave approx 20 minutes to rise again. Brush with a little melted butter and bake at 450°F (230°C) Reg 8 for 15–20 minutes until golden brown. Serve warm.

Scotch Baps
Makes 10

1 oz (25 g) fresh yeast
½ pt (300 ml) mixed lukewarm milk and water (approx)
1 lb (450 g) strong plain flour
2 tsp salt
2 oz (50 g) butter or margarine

Cream the yeast with a little of the liquid and leave in a warm place until frothy. Sift the flour and salt into a bowl. Rub in the fat, then make a well in the centre of the mixture. Add the yeast, the remaining liquid and mix to a dough. Turn out and knead for 10 minutes or until smooth, firm and elastic. Shape into a ball and put into an oiled polythene bag. Leave to rise in a warm place until doubled in bulk. Turn the dough out of the bag. Knock back and knead until firm. Divide into small portions about the size of a duck egg and shape into baps. Place on a greased and floured baking sheet. Cover loosely with oiled polythene and leave to rise in a warm place until doubled in size. Bake in a preheated oven at 400°F (200°C) Reg 6 for 15–20 minutes. The finished baps should not be glazed but floury on top.

Shetland Bride's Bonn (or Bun)
Makes 4–6

This bun was baked by the bride's mother and broken over the bride's head after the marriage ceremony. It differs from shortbread mainly in that it is baked on a girdle and contains caraway seeds. The girdle (not griddle) was used a lot in Scotland because even up to the early part of this century many kitchens did not have an oven.

4 oz (110 g) plain flour
2 oz (50 g) butter
1 oz (25 g) caster sugar
½ tsp caraway seeds
a little milk

Rub butter into flour. Add sugar and caraway seeds. Mix to a stiff consistency with milk. Roll out into round shape 2 in (5 cm) thick. Cut into triangles. Bake on a fairly hot girdle for 3 minutes on each side, or in an oven at 350°F (180°C) Reg 4 for 20 minutes.

Petticoat Tails

Makes 9

These are a thin version of shortbread, cut in a special way that recalls the bell-shaped petticoats once so fashionable.

6 oz (175 g) plain flour

3 oz (90 g) butter

2½ oz (65 g) sugar

caraway seeds (optional)

Rub butter into flour and sugar and knead to a firm dough without adding liquid. Roll out to a circle ½ in (1 cm) thick and pinch the edges. Cut a piece from the centre with a round cutter - about 2 in (5 cm) - and cut the rest into 8 pieces. Bake on an oven tray at 325°F (160°C) Reg 3 for 25–30 minutes until golden brown. Dredge with caster sugar and cool on a wire tray. Some cooks like to knead in a few caraway seeds.

Morayshire Gingerbread

8 oz (225 g) butter

4 oz (100 g) sugar

8 oz (225 g) treacle

2 eggs

1 lb (450 g) plain flour

2 tsp ground ginger

2 tsp mixed spice

3 oz (75 g) ground almonds

3 oz (75 g) chopped peel

4 oz (110 g) currants

4 oz (110 g) sultanas

1 tsp bicarbonate of soda

½ pt (275 ml) beer

pinch salt

pinch ground cloves

Cream butter and sugar, add treacle and beat in eggs. Sift together flour, ginger, spice, ground cloves and salt and add ground almonds, peel and fruit. Dissolve baking soda in beer and mix all together. Put in a large greased cake tin and bake at 325°F (160°C) Reg 3 for 2 hours. Cut into slices to serve.

Shortbread

Makes 8–10

4 oz (110 g) butter	Cream butter and sugar. Add flour and rice flour (or cornflour, or semolina). Knead well until smooth. Roll out to a round approx 8 in (20 cm) in diameter. Prick with a fork and pinch edges. Bake at 375°F (190°C) Reg 5 for 10 minutes. Lower to 325°F (160°C) Reg 3 for a further 25–30 minutes. When golden brown, dust with caster sugar and either cut into wedges while hot or allow to cool and break into rough pieces when serving.
2 oz (50 g) caster sugar	
6 oz (150 g) plain flour	
2 oz (50 g) rice flour, or fine semolina, or cornflour	

Scones

These derive from the Dutch Schoonbrot, *a four-cornered cake made as long ago as the sixteenth century.*

Girdle Scones

Makes 4

8 oz (225 g) plain flour	Sieve dry ingredients into a bowl, make a well in the centre, and add sufficient milk to make a light elastic dough. Turn on to a floured board and knead lightly until smooth. Roll out to under $\frac{1}{2}$ in (1 cm) thick, cut into 4 and place on a preheated girdle or thick frying pan. Bake until risen and starting to brown, turn over and continue baking until cooked through. This will take about 8–10 minutes in all. Cool on a wire tray covered with a clean tea towel. If buttermilk is available use only half the quantity of cream of tartar.
$\frac{1}{2}$ tsp bicarbonate of soda	
1 tsp cream of tartar	
pinch salt	
1 tsp sugar (optional)	
$\frac{1}{4}$ pt (150 ml) sweet milk or buttermilk (approx)	

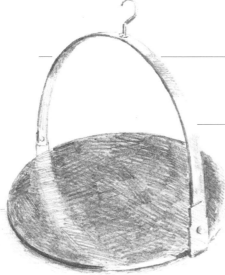

Syrup Scones

Add 2 tsp syrup with milk.

Wholemeal Scones

Substitute half to three-quarters of the flour with wholemeal flour.

Fruit Scones

Add 2 oz (50 g) currants, sultanas or raisins to the dry ingredients.

Treacle Scones

Add $\frac{1}{4}$ tsp each of cinnamon, ginger and mixed spice with the dry ingredients and 1 large tbsp black treacle with the milk. Beware of scones overbrowning for treacle burns easily.

Sour Scones
Makes 8

8 oz (225 g) oatmeal	Soak the oatmeal in the buttermilk for two days. Sift the flour and bicarbonate of soda and add, with a pinch of salt, 1 tsp of caraway seeds. Roll out thinly into two rounds on a floured board and bake both sides on a girdle. Cut each round into 4 scones.
buttermilk	
8 oz (225 g) plain flour	
$\frac{1}{2}$ tsp bicarbonate of soda	
pinch salt	
1 tsp caraway seeds	

Potato Scones
Makes 4

6 oz (175 g) sieved boiled potatoes (still warm)	Mix cream or butter into potato, sieve in half of the flour, mix well with a knife. Knead in sufficient of remaining flour until dough is no longer sticky. Roll out as thinly as possible, cut into four, prick well with a fork and bake quickly on both sides on a hot girdle. Cool in a clean cloth. Too much flour toughens this type of scone.
2 oz (50 g) flour	
1 tsp cream or knob of butter	

Oven Scones
Makes 10-12

8 oz (225 g) plain flour, $\frac{1}{2}$ tsp bicarbonate of soda and 1 tsp cream of tartar or 8 oz (225 g) self-raising flour	Sieve dry ingredients into a bowl, rub in margarine until like fine breadcrumbs. Mix to a light elastic dough, knead on a lightly floured board until smooth. Roll to $\frac{3}{4}$ in (2 cm) thick, and cut into rounds. Bake at 450°F (230°C) Reg 8 for 10-12 minutes. Cool on a wire tray covered with a cloth.
pinch salt	
1 oz (25 g) sugar	
$1\frac{1}{2}$ oz (40 g) margarine	
milk to mix, approx $\frac{1}{4}$ pt (150 ml)	

Note:
A very soft scone is produced if margarine is omitted and $1\frac{1}{2}$ tbsp good cooking oil is substituted and added with the milk.

Pancakes (Dropped Scones)
Makes 18-20

8 oz (225 g) plain flour	Sieve dry ingredients well together to incorporate air. Add egg, softened syrup and sufficient milk to make a thick pouring batter. Drop from the point of a spoon on to a well-heated girdle (greased with a little fat, if necessary – see Note). Turn over pancakes when brown and bake until edges are no longer sticky. Cool on a cloth on a wire tray.
pinch salt	
$\frac{1}{2}$ tsp bicarbonate of soda	
1 tsp cream of tartar	
2 oz (50 g) caster sugar	
1 oz (25 g) syrup	
1 egg	
milk to mix	

Note:
Modern heavy cast aluminium girdles are best left ungreased. The old iron type was always rubbed with a piece of suet.

Clootie Dumpling
Serves 6

3 oz (75 g) breadcrumbs
3 oz (75 g) plain flour
3 oz (75 g) prepared suet
1 tsp cinnamon
$\frac{1}{2}$ tsp ground ginger
$\frac{1}{2}$ tsp baking soda
grating of nutmeg
2 oz (50 g) brown sugar
2 oz (50 g) sultanas
2 oz (50 g) currants
1 tbsp syrup
4 fl oz (125 ml) milk or buttermilk

Mix all ingredients together with milk until a fairly soft consistency. Scald a pudding cloth. Squeeze out water when cooled. Spread out cloth and dredge flour thickly over the cloth. (This puts a skin on dumpling.) Spread cloth in large bowl. Pour mixture on to cloth. Draw corners of cloth evenly together. Tie cloth with string allowing room for dumpling to expand. Put an old plate in a pan of boiling water. Put dumpling on plate. Boil for 2 hours, adding more boiling water as required.

Fife Bannock
Makes 4

6 oz (175 g) plain flour
4 oz (100 g) oatmeal
$\frac{1}{2}$ tsp bicarbonate of soda
1 tsp cream of tartar
$\frac{1}{2}$ tsp salt
$\frac{1}{2}$ tsp caster sugar
1 tbsp butter
milk or sour cream

Mix dry ingredients and rub in butter. Mix to a scone dough with milk. Roll out until $\frac{1}{2}$–$\frac{3}{4}$ in (1–2 cm) thick. Cut into 4. Bake on a fairly hot girdle or in the oven at 400°F (200°C) Reg 6 for 10 minutes.

Selkirk Bannock

8 oz (225 g) plain flour
$\frac{1}{2}$ tsp salt
$\frac{1}{4}$ pt (125 ml) milk
$\frac{1}{2}$ oz (15 g) fresh yeast
2 oz (50 g) lard
2 oz (50 g) sugar
4 oz (110 g) sultanas
1 oz (25 g) chopped peel

Sieve flour and salt. Warm milk and dissolve yeast in a small quantity of it, add 1 tsp sugar to yeast mixture. Melt lard in remaining milk and warm until tepid. Mix flour to a soft elastic dough with liquids using more milk if required. Knead well for about 5 minutes, replace in bowl, cover closely and allow to double in bulk in a warm place. Mix fruit and sugar and knead into risen dough, shape into a round and place on a greased oven sheet. Cover again and leave to rise until puffy – approx 20 minutes. Bake at 400°F (200°C) Reg 6 for 15 minutes, reduce heat to 375°F (190°C) Reg 5 for a further 25 minutes. The bannock should then be golden brown. Brush with 2 tsp caster sugar dissolved in an equal quantity of water to glaze. Cool on a wire tray.

Scottish Crumpets
Makes 10–12

1 egg	
1 oz (25 g) sugar	
$\frac{1}{4}$ pt (150 ml) milk	
4 oz (110 g) plain flour	
pinch salt	
$\frac{1}{2}$ tsp bicarbonate of soda	
small tsp cream of tartar	
2 tbsp milk	

Beat egg with sugar till thick, add $\frac{1}{4}$ pt (150 ml) milk, then sieved flour and salt. Dissolve cream of tartar and bicarbonate of soda in 2 tbsp milk, and stir this quickly into mixture. Pour on to hot girdle in large spoonfuls, cook until brown, turn over and brown second side. Cool in a clean cloth on a wire tray.

Black Bun

This fruit cake is traditionally served at Hogmanay. It improves with keeping and so it is a good idea to make it several weeks beforehand.

Filling

8 oz (225 g) plain flour
4 oz (110 g) sugar
2 tsp ground ginger
2 tsp ground cinnamon
2 tsp ground allspice
1 tsp bicarbonate of soda
1 tsp cream of tartar
14 oz (400 g) currants
14 oz (400 g) large blue raisins
2 oz (50 g) chopped mixed peel
2 oz (50 g) blanched almonds
$\frac{1}{4}$ pt (150 ml) milk (approx)

Pastry

8 oz (225 g) plain flour
4 oz (110 g) butter
1 tsp (5 ml) baking powder
pinch salt
cold water
1 egg, beaten

To make pastry, rub butter into flour and salt and baking powder, and mix to a stiff dough with water. Grease an 8 in (20 cm) round tin or any tin of similar volume. Roll out two-thirds of the pastry thinly and line tin with it. Sieve the dry ingredients together, add fruit and nuts and mix thoroughly with milk. Pack into pastry case. Turn over top edges of pastry, damp edges and cover with remaining pastry, press edges well together. Brush with beaten egg, prick well with a fork and plunge a skewer right down through filling about four times. Bake at 400°F (200°C) Reg 6 for 1 hour. Reduce heat to 325°F (160°C) Reg 3 for a further 2 hours. Protect top with greaseproof paper or foil during baking. If stored well in a cake tin Black Bun will keep for a year.

Northern Ireland

When it comes to city halls, there isn't one in the British Isles to better the design of Sir Brumwell Thomas in Belfast. Every block of Portland stone was imported from the mainland to make this masterly building in Donegal Square whose white towers and magnificent dome have dominated the city since it was opened in 1906. My first impressions of Northern Ireland were of the handsome industrial city of Belfast. Though somewhat battle-scarred, it has many redeeming features, not least of which is its situation, nestling as it does at the foot of the Antrim hills and alongside Belfast Lough.

The City Hall is but one of its jewels. Another, the restored Opera House, ranks equally with those many theatres in mainland Britain which have also recently had facelifts, as does the classical Court House and the Customs House and Head Post Office near the waterside. Another impressive building but a few miles from the city centre is the cream-stoned palace at Stormont. Belfast is a city of wide streets with broad vistas towards the hills which surround it. It is also the city of 'The Pan'! The place held by the frying pan in the Northern Irish lifestyle is unique. Its function is essential and gives rise to many a humorous statement:

'My missus always gives me the pan for breakfast, so she does.' Or: 'They tuk half my sister's stummick away and now she can ate onything. The other day she even had the pan.' Or again, the story of the man – as told by the legendary John Pepper – who arrived from England at the door of his lodgings in County Antrim to be greeted by his new landlady: 'You've come a long way. I suppose you'd like the pan?' But perhaps this one: 'My husband's just dying about the dip' may better help any bewildered reader who hasn't yet realized that 'the pan' is indeed the frying pan where bacon, eggs, sausage, black puddin', potato bread and other goodies are fried daily to fill and warm the bellies of man, woman and child alike in every corner of the Province – and not to be missed, I can assure you.

Also not to be missed are any of the breads offered at table, such as Soda Bread, Wheaten Bread, Potato Bread, and – my all-time favourite – Treacle Bread, which is served split, well buttered with good Irish butter and washed down with tea. Tea – now there's another topic of humour, another

subject on which the folk from Kilkeel to Londonderry hold forth with their delicious musical turn of phrase. 'I like my tea all mil-k,' says one, and another replies: 'I take that little mil-k, you wouldn't know it was tea.'

Before leaving the Belfast area, a visit to the unique Ulster Folk and Transport Museum, hidden in the woods at Cultra, will tell you more about the old days than any book. It will also demonstrate how simple almost to the point of being spartan was country life in that part of the British Isles. The plain griddles and cast-iron cookpots hanging from cranes over peat fires, with the odd ham hanging to smoke in the chimney over an open flat hearth, with no sign of an oven, are positive indications of the people's simple self-sufficiency.

A trip north of Belfast brings you to the world's ninth wonder, the Giant's Causeway – passing the Old Bushmill's distillery on the way, I might add, where a wee dram of Irish whiskey doesn't go amiss. Near to this wonder-of-the-world is the town of Ballycastle, where on the last Monday and Tuesday of August the Lammas Fair is held. Lammas (or Low Mass) has been going on for well over three hundred years, and throughout all this time two traditional delicacies have been provided: Dulse and Yellowman. Yellowman is a delicious-tasting yellow toffee made with good Irish butter, corn syrup and brown sugar. Dulse is a reddish-brown dried seaweed which can be eaten raw or added to fish

or vegetable soups. It can be soaked, then cooked in milk and added to mashed potatoes, thus changing the name to Dulse Champ. Sloke, or sea spinach (laver in England and Wales), also appears on many local tables. And you shouldn't be surprised if a bowl of boiled willicks (winkles) appears with a clutch of pins to pick them from their shells and a bowl of oatmeal in which to dip them. All good simple stuff.

You won't find many exotic foods in Northern Ireland, unless you count the excellent fresh fish such as trout and salmon from the loughs and rivers and oak-smoked salmon with brown bread and butter. Yet they almost always serve a chicken with thin slivers of boiled ham. Perhaps this was once a way of extending the chicken to feed a large family: each complements the other so well it would be a pity if the habit ever disappeared.

One of the best surprises for me happened at the races one day. I was asked if I'd care to partake of a slice of Bookmaker's Sandwich. This extraordinary gargantuan sandwich is not to be missed, should you ever come across one. A pound and a half of grilled fillet steak is actually sandwiched between a whole loaf, which is split and buttered and heavily pressed before being carved to reveal juice-soaked bread slices surrounding succulent steak pieces. Unsurpassable, I'd say!

On the sweeter side of the Northern Irish table are the bracks and breads, with Barm Brack probably taking the lead. This rich yeast bread is well packed with dried fruits and spices and, whilst eaten all the year round, is nevertheless traditional fare at Hallowe'en.

Endless discussion surrounds the different versions of Irish Stew. Known throughout the Western Hemisphere (though I feel few have ever eaten a true one *in situ*, so to speak), Irish Stew was originally made from mutton or goat. This was because lamb was too expensive. Irish sheep were

reared for wool as well as for eating, and no farmer would have sacrificed his lambs to the stove. Some cooks put carrots in their stew, others turnips, or even both. There are even cooks who commit the deadly sin of casting in handfuls of pearl barley. The purists consider that all or any of these spoil the flavour: they insist it should be thick and creamy from the floury potato and onion, and not too liquid or soupy. It does indeed appear that some finely-chopped parsley is the only extra flavour it needs.

There is precious little difference in the traditional foods between Eire and Northern Ireland, which is a natural enough state of affairs when you consider the age of the island as a whole. There is an obvious affinity with the Scots and the North of England through the tradition of baking and the use of oatmeal, and with the Welsh with their use of leeks, onions and seaweed. Bacon and sausage, eggs and cheese form a goodly part of Irish cooking to this day, for many of the people are farmers and there are still many country folk who feel that reliance on home produce should be the rule.

Finally, throughout the land there is a drink, of comparatively recent origin, which has put Ireland on the international map: Irish Coffee. You can 'ate it an' drink it' and its warmth is just typical of what the people are all about.

Soups

Leek and Oatmeal Soup (Brotchán Foltchep)
Serves 4–6

Brotchán is Gaelic for broth. Another traditional broth uses young nettle tops.

6 large leeks	Clean leeks thoroughly taking care to remove all the grit. Cut into chunks approx 1 in (2.5 cm) long. Melt the butter and gently fry the leeks. Add seasoning. When soft add the milk/stock and oat flakes and bring to the boil, and then simmer gently for about 45 minutes in a pan with a tight-fitting lid. Add parsley and re-heat.
2 oz (50 g) butter	
2 pt (1.2 l) stock or milk	
2 oz (50 g) oat flakes	
salt and pepper	
1 tbsp chopped parsley	

Potato Soup
Serves 4

1 large onion	Chop the onion and shred the leeks. Melt the butter in a saucepan, add the vegetables and cook, covered by a tight-fitting lid, for 10–15 minutes. Meanwhile, slice the potatoes thinly and add, together with the seasoning and stock. Bring to the boil and simmer gently for 1½ hours. Sprinkle in the sago and continue cooking for a further 20 minutes or until the sago is clear. Add the milk and break down any large pieces with a wooden spoon. Just before serving, stir in the chopped parsley.
1–2 leeks	
1 oz (25 g) butter or margarine	
2 lb (900 g) potatoes	
salt and pepper	
2 pt (1.2 l) stock or water	
1 tbsp sago	
½ pt (275 ml) milk	
chopped parsley	

Irish Broth
Serves 4

½–1 lb (225–450 g) neck of lamb	Place meat, diced and sliced vegetables, barley, water and seasoning in a pan and bring to the boil. Simmer slowly for about 2 hours until the meat comes away from the bone. Lift meat from the broth and skim. Cut meat from the bone and cut it up finely, return meat and grated carrot to the broth. Simmer for a further 30 minutes. Before serving, sprinkle generously with chopped parsley.
1 oz (25 g) barley	
1 turnip, diced	
1 carrot, diced	
1 leek, sliced	
1 large potato, diced	
1 carrot, grated	
salt and pepper	
1¾ pt (1 l) cold water	
chopped parsley	

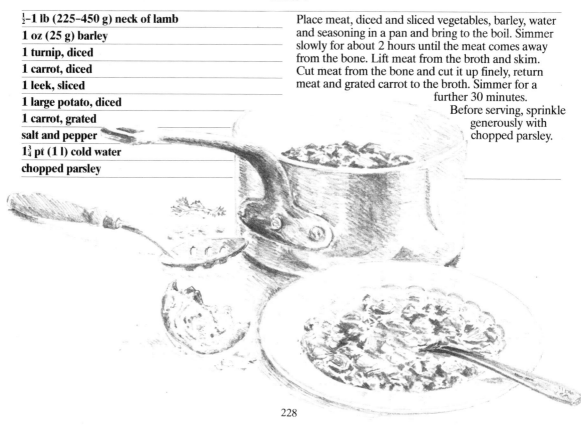

Baked Whiting with Tomato and Mushroom Sauce

1 lb (450 g) whiting fillets
salt and pepper
Sauce
1 tbsp onion, chopped
1 tbsp parsley
1 clove garlic
1 oz (25 g) butter
1 tbsp olive oil
½ pt (275 ml) fish stock
1 × 8 oz (225 g) tin tomatoes
salt and pepper
1 tsp cornflour and 1 tbsp cream
8 oz (225 g) mushrooms
parsley or cress to decorate
black olives to decorate (approx 8)

Fry gently onion, parsley, garlic in oil and butter. Add fish stock and sieved tomatoes, salt and pepper. Boil gently until thick, adding the cornflour and cream, for about 15 minutes. Fry mushrooms quickly and tip over fish which has been baked for 15 minutes in a buttered ovenproof dish at 350°F (180°C) Reg 4. Top with the tomato sauce and decorate well with parsley or cress and black olives. For special occasions white wine with stock may be added. Dill and fennel can be used as flavourings instead of parsley.

Seafood Crumble
Serves 4

1 lb (450 g) haddock
3 eggs, hard-boiled and chopped
4 oz (110 g) prawns
seasoning and parsley
Sauce
1 oz (25 g) plain flour
1 oz (25 g) fat
½ pt (275 ml) milk
Crumble
1½ oz (40 g) butter
3 oz (75 g) plain flour
3 oz (75 g) Cheddar Cheese, grated
salt and pepper

Make up the sauce and fold in fish, eggs, prawns, seasoning and parsley. Pour into an ovenproof dish. To make the crumble, rub the butter into the flour until the mixture resembles fine breadcrumbs, then add cheese, salt and pepper. Cover the mixture with crumble topping. Bake at 350°F (180°C) Reg 4 for 20–30 minutes. Garnish with sprigs of parsley.

Cockelty Pie
Serves 4

4 oz (110 g) cockles
2 oz (50 g) melted butter
½ onion
juice of 1 lemon
salt and pepper
8 oz (225 g) flaky pastry (see page 253)
1 egg, for glazing

Scrub the cockles well, removing all traces of sand and grit. Place in a large pan and cover with lightly salted water. Bring rapidly to the boil, and as soon as the shells open, remove from the heat and allow to cool. Remove cockles from shells. Discard any cockles if the shell has not opened of its own accord. Melt butter in pan, add cockles, onion, lemon juice and seasoning and cook for 5 minutes. Remove from heat and pour into 7 in (18 cm) oval pie-dish. Roll out pastry and put crust on pie and glaze well. Bake at 425°F (220°C) Reg 7 for 30 minutes. Serve hot.

Meat

Irish Stew

Serves 4

Irish stew is a traditional country dish. It has its origin in the cottage, where cooking utensils were scarce and it was convenient to cook the meat, vegetables and potatoes together in the one pot hanging over the turf fire. While mutton is probably the most frequently used meat for an Irish stew, it can also be made with beef, a piece of brisket for instance, or with pork fillet, pork steak or griskin. Pork ribs are also good and are sometimes combined in the stew with a pig's kidney. If mutton is the choice, the most suitable cuts are neck or breast, but for a superior dish shoulder chops are excellent.

1–1½ lb (450–675 g) neck of mutton

salt and pepper

1 onion

2 lb (900 g) potatoes

hot water

1 tbsp parsley, chopped

Cut the neck of mutton into portion pieces and trim away excessive fat. Season well. Slice the onions and potatoes. Arrange the meat in the bottom of a strong pan. Cover with the onions mixed with a proportion of the potatoes and finally add the rest of the potatoes in layers. Season well. Add sufficient water to cover the meat amply. Place the lid on the pan and cook gently for 1½–2 hours or until the meat is tender. Stir or shake the pan occasionally to prevent the stew from sticking. It should not be watery when cooked, for the potatoes should thicken the gravy. Serve on a hot dish, sprinkling generously with chopped parsley. To be at its best, it must be very hot and well seasoned.

Note:
An alternative method is to stew the meat partially before adding the onions and potatoes. In this way they are less liable to be overcooked.

Savouries

Dulse

Dulse is a reddish-brown edible seaweed which has various culinary uses. Try it as a supper dish with oatcakes.

dulse

milk

butter

salt and pepper

Wash the freshly gathered dulse to remove sand. Put it into a saucepan with enough milk to almost cover the dulse. Add the butter, and salt and pepper to taste. Stew until tender, about 3–4 hours.

Champp
Serves 4

Champ, or thump, is an Irish method of serving mashed potatoes. It is a favourite meal for a fast day, and is also a traditional Halloween dish, the custom being to place the first two portions on top of the flat pier at the front gate for the fairies. In old cottages with a clay floor there is sometimes a large 'pot hole' or hollow into which the iron cooking pot is placed while the potatoes are mashed, or beetled, with a long handled masher, or beetle. This was often the work of the man of the house; his wife, meanwhile, added the hot milk.

2 lb (900 g) potatoes

1 lb (450 g) peas, shelled or frozen

salt and pepper

½ pt (275 ml) milk

2 oz (50 g) butter

2 tbsp chopped chives

2 tbsp chopped parsley

Cook and mash potatoes. Cook the peas in the milk with seasoning, and when cooked add to the mashed potatoes and mix well. Stir in the chopped parsley and chives. To serve, divide mixture into 4 and form into a mound on the plate. Make a hollow in the centre and place a lump of butter in the middle of each.
Variations: instead of peas use nettle heads, or scallions (variously, shallots, leeks or onions).

Pratie Oaten
Makes approx 12

Those staples of Irish life, oatmeal and potato, are here combined to make a tasty breakfast dish.

2 lb (900 g) potatoes, mashed

4 oz (110 g) butter, melted

4 oz (110 g) fine oatmeal

salt and pepper

Having mashed the potatoes, work in the oatmeal to form a soft dough that leaves the sides of the pan dry. Add seasoning, and beat in the melted butter. Roll out dough on a floured surface (use oatmeal) to a thickness of 1 in (2.5 cm) and cut into rounds 3 in (7.5 cm) in diameter. Cook on a heated, oiled griddle or heavy-based frying pan. Serve hot with eggs, bacon and sausages.

Colcannon
Serves 4

Ulster's answer to Bubble and Squeak, it is traditionally served at Halloween, when the future is foretold according to who finds the silver coin, thimble, button, ring or horseshoe which have been dropped into the mixture during cooking. The finder of the ring will marry within the year, whereas the finder of the thimble will not marry at all. Likewise, finding the coin means riches, the button…

1 lb (450 g) potatoes

1 small onion, minced

2 fl oz (50 ml) milk

1 oz (25 g) butter

8 oz (225 g) kale or cabbage, cooked

salt and pepper

Boil potatoes in their skins. Cook the minced onion in the milk with salt and pepper. When potatoes are cooked, peel them and press them through a sieve then add to the milk and onion. Stir in the butter and beat well. Serve at once, adding more butter if desired.

Puddings and Desserts

Visitors' Trifle
Serves 8

1 stale sponge cake

4 tbsp raspberry jam

1 glass Irish whiskey

2 glasses sherry

2 egg whites

$\frac{1}{2}$ pt (275 ml) cream

$\frac{1}{2}$ tbsp sugar

2 oz (50 g) almonds, blanched and split

Custard

1 egg

2 egg yolks

1 tbsp sugar

$\frac{3}{4}$ pt (425 ml) milk

Split the sponge cake into 4 layers. Spread the layers generously with the jam and restack. Put them in a glass dish. Mix the whiskey and sherry and pour over the layered cake. Cover with a plate and leave to soak for 1 hour.

To make the custard, beat the egg and egg yolks together with the sugar. Scald the milk and pour over the eggs while beating. Cook the custard in a bowl over a pan of hot water until it thickens to a cream. Pour it over the cake while hot. Leave to get cold. Beat the 2 egg whites to a peak. Whip the cream with $\frac{1}{2}$ tbsp sugar. Fold the whites into the beaten cream and pile over the trifle. Decorate with the blanched and split almonds, which are spiked into the cream.

Carrageen Peppermint Cream
Serves 4–6

Carrageen moss is an edible seaweed that is found all along the coast of the West of Ireland. It is picked by the fishermen and left to bleach in the sun. It is very easy to digest and is thought to be excellent for complaints of the stomach and chest. You can buy it in shops that deal in health foods.

1 handful carrageen moss

$1\frac{1}{2}$ pt (850 ml) milk

pinch salt

2 tbsp sugar

6 drops peppermint oil

green vegetable colouring

Chocolate Sauce

3 oz (75 g) bitter chocolate

4 oz (110 g) sugar

1 tsp instant coffee

$\frac{1}{2}$ pt (275 ml) water

$\frac{1}{4}$ tsp vanilla extract

$1\frac{1}{2}$ tsp cornflour

Soak the carrageen in cold water for 15 minutes until soft. Rinse well. Boil it with the milk and salt until the liquid is thick and creamy. Add the sugar, peppermint oil and colouring. Strain to remove carrageen and discard. Pour liquid into a wetted mould and leave to set.

To make the sauce, put the chocolate, sugar, coffee and water into a saucepan. Boil and stir gently until melted. Simmer for 5 minutes. Add the vanilla and cornflour, blended with a little water. Boil the mixture again to cook the cornflour. Turn out the carrageen cream and add the sauce, either hot or cold.

Cakes, Breads and Biscuits
Irish Bannock

12 oz (350 g) plain flour
1 tsp bicarbonate of soda
1 tsp cream of tartar
1 oz (25 g) caster sugar
4 oz (110 g) sultanas
$\frac{1}{2}$ pt (275 ml) buttermilk or sour milk

Sieve the flour, soda and cream of tartar into a bowl. Stir in the sugar and sultanas. Work in the milk to make a soft mixture. Put into a greased 7 in (18 cm) sponge tin. Put in the mixture and spread lightly to cover the surface. Bake for 30 minutes at 400°F (200°C) Reg 6. Remove from tin and sprinkle surface with a little extra caster sugar. Wrap the bannock in a clean tea cloth so that the surface remains soft. Serve sliced with butter.

Potato Bread or Fadge
Makes 12

Fadge is the Ulster term for this potato cake or bread, popular at breakfast time.

1 lb (450 g) potatoes, mashed
4 oz (110 g) flour
$\frac{1}{2}$ tsp salt
1 oz (25 g) butter or margarine, melted

Place hot mashed potato in a bowl and add flour, salt and melted butter and knead to a soft dough. Allow mixture to cool, then roll out to $\frac{1}{4}$ in (5 mm) thick. Cut out into 3 in (7.5 cm) rounds and bake on a hot, lightly oiled griddle or heavy frying pan and brown on both sides. Spread on a tea towel to cool. May be eaten cold, hot buttered or fried in bacon fat and then served with eggs and bacon or sausages. (If using leftover potatoes, no extra salt is needed.)

Wheaten Bread

4 oz (110 g) plain flour
1 tsp salt
1 tsp baking soda
12 oz (350 g) wheaten or wholemeal flour
1 tsp golden syrup
$1\frac{1}{2}$ oz (40 g) butter
15 fl oz (425 ml) buttermilk

Sieve the plain flour, salt and baking soda, add the wheaten meal or wholemeal, rub in the butter and golden syrup. Mix lightly, adding sufficient buttermilk to give a soft but not sticky dough. Turn on to a surface sprinkled with wheaten or wholemeal flour and form into a round cake approx $1\frac{1}{2}$ in (4 cm) thick. Mark into quarters and place on a floured baking tray. Bake for 30–35 minutes at 450°F (230°C) Reg 8.

Treacle Bread

1 lb (450 g) plain flour
1 tsp salt
1 tsp baking soda
1 tsp ground ginger
1 oz (25 g) caster sugar
2 tbsp treacle
buttermilk

Sieve the dry ingredients. Mix the treacle with 4 tbsp (50 ml) buttermilk and add to the dry ingredients. Add more buttermilk, sufficient to form a soft dough. Turn on to a floured board and shape into a round cake. Mark into quarters. Bake for 30–35 minutes at 450°F (230°C) Reg 8.

Irish Tea Brack

This is an easy-to-make version of the Barm Brack which uses yeast.

12 oz (350 g) mixed dried fruit

10 fl oz (275 ml) boiling black tea

1 egg

1 tsp mixed spice

4 tsp marmalade

8 oz (225 g) caster sugar

14 oz (400 g) self-raising flour

Place mixed fruit in a bowl, cover with hot tea and leave to soak overnight. The next day, add to the tea and fruit the remaining ingredients and mix well. Bake in a greased 7 in (18 cm) square tin at 375°F (190°C) Reg 5 for 1½ hours on middle shelf. Allow to cool in tin. Slice and serve buttered. Store in an airtight tin.

Barm Brack

Barm is the old word for yeast.

1 lb (450 g) risen white bread dough (see page 251)

3 oz (75 g) sugar

3 oz (75 g) lard

3 eggs

2 oz (50 g) stoned raisins

2 oz (50 g) chopped mixed candied peel

Work the sugar and lard into the dough. Add the beaten eggs, a little at a time, and then the raisins and peel. Work together until well mixed. Shape to fit a greased 2 lb (900 g) loaf tin. Cover and leave to prove for 45 minutes. Bake for 30 minutes at 425°F (220°C) Reg 7, then reduce heat and continue baking for 30 minutes at 350°F (180°C) Reg 4. Cool on a wire rack.

Fruit Loaf

The home breadmaking tradition is very strong in Ulster, amongst both farm and town dwellers. This yeast loaf is usually reserved for special occasions.

2 oz (50 g) fresh yeast

10 fl oz (275 ml) warm potato water

8 oz (225 g) caster sugar

4 oz (110 g) butter

2 eggs

5 oz (150 g) warm mashed potato

20 oz (600 g) plain flour

5 oz (150 g) raisins

1 tsp salt

Cream the yeast with the warm potato water. Place all remaining ingredients in a large bowl. Make a well in the centre and pour in yeast liquid. Mix well. Turn out on to a floured surface and knead well for at least 5 minutes. Return to bowl, cover with a clean cloth and, in a warm place, allow dough to rise for 1 hour. Remove from bowl and knead again. Divide mixture in half and place in greased loaf tins 9 × 5 in (23 × 13 cm). Cover and allow to rise again for about 45 minutes. Bake for 1 hour at 350°F (180°C) Reg 4.

Irish Wholemeal Gingerbread

4 oz (110 g) plain white flour

4 oz (110 g) plain wholemeal flour

pinch salt

1 tsp ground mixed spice

3 tsp ground ginger

1½ oz (40 g) demerara sugar

1½ oz (40 g) mixed candied peel, chopped

1½ oz (40 g) sultanas

4 oz (110 g) butter or margarine

4 oz (110 g) golden syrup

4 oz (110 g) black treacle

1 egg

¼ pt (150 ml) milk

1 tsp bicarbonate of soda

1 oz (25 g) split blanched almonds

Stir together white and wholemeal flours, salt, spice, ginger, sugar, peel and sultanas. Heat the fat, syrup and treacle together until the fat has melted. Pour into the dry ingredients and mix well, then beat in the egg. Warm the milk and stir in the soda. Add to the mixture and beat to a smooth batter. Put into a greased and lined 9 × 6 in (23 × 15 cm) tin. Scatter the blanched almonds on top. Bake for 45 minutes at 350°F (180°C) Reg 4 and cool in the tin before turning out. Keep in an air-tight tin for 2 or 3 days before using.

Filling Cakes

Makes 10–12

10 oz (275 g) self-raising flour

2 oz (50 g) caster sugar

1 tsp baking powder

3 oz (75 g) margarine

milk for mixing and glazing

Filling

4 oz (110 g) sultanas

4 oz (110 g) currants

2 oz (50 g) caster sugar

½ tsp ground mixed spice

3 fl oz (75 ml) water

To make the filling, place ingredients in a saucepan and bring slowly to the boil, simmer for 10 minutes and then allow to cool. To make the cakes, mix flour and sugar with baking powder. Rub in the margarine. Mix to a soft but not sticky dough with the milk. Roll out into an oblong about 6 in (15 cm) wide and about ¼ in (5 mm) thick. Spread the filling over to within ¼ in (5 mm) of the edge. Roll up like a Swiss Roll, using a floured knife, and cut into ½ in (1 cm) thick slices.

Place on a greased baking sheet, brush over with a little milk. Bake for 20–25 minutes at 350°F (180°C) Reg 4.

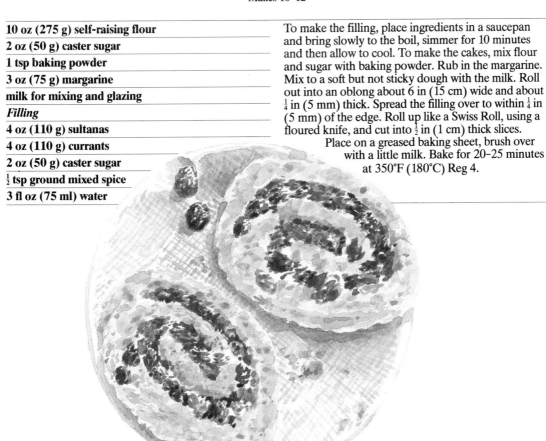

Soda Bread

1 lb (450 g) plain flour
1 tsp salt
1 tsp baking soda
10–15 fl oz (275–425 ml) buttermilk

Sieve the dry ingredients into a bowl. Mix lightly and quickly, adding sufficient buttermilk to give a soft but not sticky dough. Turn on to a well-floured surface and shape into a round cake approx 1½ in (4 cm) thick. Transfer to a greased or floured baking sheet or an 8 in (20 cm) sandwich tin and mark into quarters. Bake at 450°F (230°C) Reg 8 for 30–35 minutes. Soda Bread can also be cooked on a griddle, and for this it should be rolled more thinly than bread for the oven, about ¾ in (2 cm) thick. At the right heat the bread should brown after cooking for 3–4 minutes.

Boxty Bread

Serves 4

Boxty is an Irish word for the ubiquitous potato.

8 oz (225 g) grated raw potatoes
8 oz (225 g) mashed potatoes
8 oz (225 g) plain flour
2 oz (50 g) butter or bacon fat, melted
salt and pepper

Mix all ingredients together. Divide the mixture in two and press each piece out into a flat round about ½ in (1 cm) thick on a greased baking sheet. Mark each round into quarters. Bake for 40 minutes at 300°F (150°C) Reg 2.

Boxty Pancakes

Halloween is a holiday in Ireland celebrated by parties and fireworks. The traditional fare includes roast goose, apple cake or dumpling, nuts and toffee apples. Charms such as a ring or a coin are wrapped in paper, perhaps accompanied by a suitable motto and buried in the apple cake or dumpling (as with Colcannon, above). In some parts of the country, when the potatoes are being lifted, the very large ones - too big for storing - are grated and made into Boxty, either pancakes or bread.

1 lb (450 g) potatoes
4 oz (110 g) self-raising flour
3–4 fl oz (75–110 ml) milk
salt and pepper
2 oz (50 g) butter or margarine

Peel and grate the potatoes, place in a clean tea towel and wring out as much liquid as possible. Sieve the flour and stir in the milk and potatoes. Add seasoning. Heat the butter in a heavy frying pan or use a griddle. Drop about 1 tbsp (15 ml) on to the pan for each pancake. Brown on both sides. Serve hot sprinkled with a little salt.

Miscellaneous

Yellowman

On the last Monday in August a fair is held at Ballycastle. It has been held there for over 350 years, and one of the traditional foods at the fair is Yellowman, a hard brittle toffee.

1 oz (25 g) butter

8 oz (225 g) demerara sugar

1 lb (450 g) tin golden syrup or corn syrup

2 fl oz (50 ml) malt vinegar

1 tsp baking soda

Melt the butter and brush around the saucepan. Add sugar, syrup and vinegar. Stir well until all ingredients are melted, bring to the boil, then boil without stirring until toffee hardens, forming a brittle ball if dropped in cold water. Then add the baking soda, stir well and pour on to a greased baking tray. Turn edges into the centre and pull and stretch the toffee until it is pale golden. Then pour on to a greased baking sheet and cut into squares.

Irish Coffee

Serves 1

2 tsp sugar

1 glass hot, strong black coffee

1 measure Irish whiskey

1 tbsp whipped cream

Heat a stemmed whiskey goblet. Add the sugar and enough of the hot coffee to dissolve the sugar. Stir well. Add the Irish whiskey and fill the glass to within 1 in (2.5 cm) of the brim with more very hot black coffee. Float the cream on top. Do not mix the cream through the coffee. The hot, whiskey-laced coffee is sipped through the velvety cream (the cream will not float unless sugar is used).

Irish Coffee Pudding

Serves 10–12

This recipe is a lot of work, but makes an enjoyable way of 'eating' your whiskey and is recommended for parties.

6 eggs

8 oz (225 g) sugar

8 fl oz (220 ml) water with 1 tbsp instant coffee or 8 fl oz (220 ml) very strong black coffee

1½ oz (40 g) powdered gelatine

3 fl oz (85 ml) Irish whiskey or Irish Mist liqueur

½ pt (275 ml) double cream

8 fl oz (220 ml) double cream, whipped

1 tbsp caster sugar

3 oz (75 g) crushed walnuts

Separate the yolks from the whites of eggs. In a bowl, cream the yolks with the sugar. Blend the instant coffee with the water (or use strong black coffee). Heat it but do not boil. Completely dissolve the gelatine in the hot coffee and add all to the yolks and sugar. Beat well and put the bowl over a pan of boiling water. Continue beating until mixture begins to thicken. Remove from heat and, when the bowl has cooled a little, put over cracked ice and continue to stir. When the mixture is on the point of setting, whip the cream and fold it in. Add the whiskey or liqueur and fold in the well-beaten egg whites. Pour into a 7 in (18 cm) soufflé case that has a collar of strong greaseproof paper tied around it. The paper should come up 3 in (7.5 cm) above the top of the soufflé case. Oil a jam jar or a bottle and press it down into the centre of the pudding. Leave to set. Remove the paper collar by easing around the circumference with a knife dipped in hot water. Remove the jar (or bottle) and fill the centre with 8 fl oz (220 ml) double cream, whipped, and 1 tbsp caster sugar. Decorate the exposed sides of the pudding with crushed walnuts that you press on with the palm of your hand.

The Channel Islands and Isle of Man

It would be right to expect that a trip to the Isle of Man would have revealed half a dozen or so regional dishes still in existence; however, the surrounding influences of Scotland, Ireland, Wales and coastal Lancashire have combined to give the Manx people such a wide variety of dishes that they do not appear to have felt the need to develop many of their own specialities.

This beautiful island, but thirty miles long and even fewer wide, which manages to get into its scenery such a lovely variety of views, has a paucity of regional dishes. It has the soaring spine of hills down the centre of its landscape reaching to the peak of Snaefell, with dramatic cliffs on the one side and sweeping bays on the other, its lacy pattern of roads bordered with unexpected hedgerows of shimmering bright pink wild fuschias, palm trees growing in clutches alongside ancient yews and spatterings of bright yellow gorse amongst blankets of purple heather, making a patchwork of colour to delight the tourist. Yet there are only two foods to delight the tourist industry, which nudges finance and herring fishing for premier place as this tax haven's main source of revenue. Both are excellent. They are the Manx Kipper, delicately smoked over oak chippings as any self-respecting plump herring should be, and Manx Ice Cream, developed for the droves of trippers to the Victorian resort of Douglas on the island's east coast. Ask any true local if they can think of an island dish and I doubt whether they will be able to recall one, other than 'herring and potatoes', which is still served regularly in farmsteads and fishermen's cottages throughout the island; good it is, and wholesome, but not exactly exotic!

That no-one has thought to develop the use of the kipper beyond the simple grilling or boiling of it is perhaps understandable, for the islanders were for centuries a peasant people. What is perhaps more interesting is the lack of local use in the kitchen of their unique 'Queenies', delicious miniature scallops found near the shores of the island. They are a great luxury to a mainlander: not dissimilar to the sweet-fleshed scallops so popular in New England and the Southern States of the USA, Queenies are crying out loud to be marinated, made into a seafood cocktail or 'chowdered', but alas they are bundled off to France, where at least they are appreciated and earn their keep.

Almost Lilliputian in lifestyle, the Isle of Man has the oldest Parliament in the world – the Tynwald – whose millennium was celebrated some few years

ago. It has a legal system very different from ours, but with all its strange and ancient traditions it is a friendly place – in spite of the influx of 'come-overs' and 'when-Is' in search of an escape from mainland Britain's crippling taxation, who have brought to the island that degree of sophistication the inhabitants might well have preferred not to have.

Our other tax havens are another story. I paid my first visit to the Channel Islands only last year, and then only briefly. Like many other mainlanders making a first visit to these Commonwealth islands, I was fascinated to see how they run themselves semi-independently, clinging to our Queen as their figurehead, using our diplomatic services for their international affairs and joining in the Common Market, yet holding on staunchly to their ancient roots and traditions. Governing themselves in an almost doll's house-like way, they hold to their Bailiffs and Bailiwicks, Statesmen, States and Lieutenant Governors, even Government Houses, where flags are flown and centuries-old traditions are played out. Yet the total resident population of the largest of these islands (Jersey) is but a scant 75,000.

Guernsey, Alderney and Sark are all part of the Bailiwick of Guernsey. They claim to be less 'touristy' and certainly operate independently of neighbouring Jersey, with its tall apartment blocks and its more determined efforts to capture the tourist, no matter where he is from.

Nestling as they all do in that right-angle of France well known to geography students as they draw their maps of Europe, it is not surprising that there is a strong French influence well evident to this day on these one-time French islands. Many street and house names are in Old French, and many of the island dishes are known by their traditional French names.

It is in the island homes, not in the tourist hotels and restaurants, that you will find these native dishes and perhaps hear the native *patois* spoken. Perhaps the food owes less to French cooking than to the fact that these ancient islanders (and, as with the Isle of Man, they *are* ancient in lineage) were self-providing farmers and fishermen, catching and growing their own foods. Every farm had its orchard, as they did in far-off Somerset and Devon and nearby Normandy, and many dishes contain apples and pears. Cider is a popular drink, particularly on feast days, and *Sethée d'Nièr Beurre*, or Black Butter Night. *Nièr Beurre* is not what you might at first expect, if you are thinking of the French *Beurre Noir*, to be served traditionally with grilled skate. It is a rich, thick, dark spicy apple preserve made in a huge brass or iron *paîle* half filled with apples, cider and spices and suspended from a ratchet over a wood fire glowing on a farmhouse hearth.

A deal of seafood is enjoyed by the islanders, who net crabs and shrimps, lobsters and mussels and prise ormers from the rocks to pop into casseroles, and *La Soupe d'Andgülle* (Conger Soup) is not to be missed, if you can find it, when in *Jerri* (Jersey to any Brit!) You may even be lucky enough to eat it garnished traditionally (and not unexpectedly on this flower island) with marigold petals!

As I wandered round the twisting streets and steep steps in the attractive town of St Peter Port, I bought and ate a whole Guernsey *Gâche*, warm from the baker's oven. Moist and fruity, it was an experience I will long remember. Somewhat different from our own Sally Lunn or Lardy Cake, which is as near a comparison as I can come up with, for it is a cross between the two, and different too from its elder sister in Jersey, *D' La Gâche dé Cannelle*, in which, as might be expected from the name, cinnamon is prominent and the cake has a crumbly texture.

Alas, the professionals, in a misplaced attempt to attract tourists to these charming islands, are too busy offering *Nouvelle Cuisine* when they ought to be confecting 'new cooking' based on their natural products. Their rich, thick cream alone is an inspiration to me to get out my pans and invent some exotic sauce for the conger, or a dressing for a scintillating salad using tomatoes from the acres of glasshouses. And who could resist a new potato from Jersey bathed in double cream and spiced with a dredge of nutmeg as an accompaniment to a butter-grilled lobster netted locally? In the meantime, I know the recipes in this chapter will wake up the taste buds and start the cooks dreaming.

Ormers

Serves 4

Ormers are a favourite delicacy in the Channel Islands. They are molluscs, about 4–5 in (10–12.5 cm) long and are found on the rocks at low tide. Their shells are rough and grey outside, but have a beautiful iridescent lining.

8 ormers

plain flour

fat for shallow-frying

Remove the ormers from their shells. Soak and scrub the ormers until they are white. Beat with a steak mallet or rolling pin to make them tender. Dry the ormers with a clean cloth, and flour. Heat the fat in a pan and fry the ormers quickly until brown on both sides. Place in a casserole with the juices from the pan made into a sauce with the flour and water. Bring to the boil and simmer until tender – at least 3–4 hours. They are best served plain with plain boiled potatoes. If liked, cubes of belly pork may be substituted for half the ormers, fried with them and included in the casserole. Sliced carrots and onions can be added for the last hour of cooking.

Casseroled Ormers

Serves 4

Ormers are rarer now than they used to be, but there is a scheme in Guernsey to farm them and it is hoped that they will soon be more plentiful.

16 ormers

1 oz (25 g) plain flour

fat for browning

1 slice bacon

sprig parsley

salt

1 pt (575 ml) water

Remove the ormers from the shells, discard the entrails and scrub until the flesh is white and firm. Beat with a mallet or rolling pin to tenderize. Roll the ormers in flour and fry until brown. Place the fish in a casserole with the bacon, parsley and salt to taste. Cover with water and bake at 300°F (150°C) Reg 2 for at least 4 hours until tender. If necessary thicken with 1 tbsp flour mixed in cold water for the last half hour of cooking time.

Razor Fish
Serves 2

The tides around Jersey's shores are among the biggest in the world – at times up to 40 ft (12 m). When these high tides recede they leave exposed a vast expanse of rocks, sand and shallow pools where, at the right time of year, shellfish such as cockles, winkles and razor fish may be gathered. Razor fish, which are much the size and shape of an old-fashioned cut-throat razor, lie buried beneath wet sand, only betraying their presence by a small keyhole-shaped depression in the surface. They may be dug out with a garden fork, probed for with strong wire bent to form a hook, or brought to the surface by putting a pinch of salt in the 'keyhole'. Sometimes this only drives them further into the sand, but as a rule they will shoot up so that 2–3 in (5–7.5 cm) of shell is exposed. This must be grasped quickly before the creature has time to withdraw, and pulled gently until it releases its hold on the sand. Too sharp a pull results in an empty shell.

Ingredients	
12–16 razor fish	Pour enough boiling water over the fish to cover them. This kills them and opens the shells. Remove from shells and rinse very thoroughly many times to remove all traces of sand. Dry with a clean cloth, flour, and shallow-fry in a little hot fat until they begin to 'pop'. Longer cooking will make them tough. Alternatively, they may be stewed until tender or made into soup.
plain flour	
cooking fat for shallow-frying	

Salted Dried Conger

Conger is delicious dried and grilled. The drying is best done by hanging the salted fish on a clothes line in a cool airy place, well out of the reach of dogs and cats. Bluebottles and flies are also attracted to the fish so it must be enclosed in a muslin bag large enough to cover it completely. Purpose-made bags usually have a cane ring at top and bottom to keep the fish from touching the muslin.

Ingredients	
1 conger eel	Take the best part of the conger, wipe clean, dry well, take out the backbone, lay out flat, sprinkle with salt and roll up. Protect from flies, leave for 2 or 3 days (if wanted for immediate use), then dry again with a clean cloth or kitchen paper and sprinkle with pepper and more salt. Hang up in a muslin bag to dry in the air. Dry thoroughly for about 2 or 3 days. To cook, cut off sufficient for a meal and grill. If the conger is to be kept longer, allow 4 or 5 days each for salting and drying.
salt	
pepper	

Baked Stuffed Conger
Serves 4

Ingredients	
4 oz (110 g) breadcrumbs	Make a stuffing using the breadcrumbs, onion, margarine, parsley and seasoning. Bind together with beaten egg. Clean and wash fish, insert stuffing in fish to fill cavity, secure by tying and place in baking pan with fold underneath. Brush with melted fat. Add the water or fish stock and bake for 2 hours at 325°F (160°C) Reg 3.
1 medium onion	
1 oz (25 g) margarine	
parsley	
1 egg	
salt and pepper	
1½ lb (675 g) slice top cut of conger	
melted fat	
½ pt (275 ml) water or fish stock	

Fried Sand Eels

Serves 2

Sand eels are only about 6 in (15 cm) long. They taste delicious either fried, or dried and then grilled.

1 lb (450 g) sand eels	Rinse the fish thoroughly to remove all traces of sand and dry with a clean cloth. Cut from the back of the head just through to the spine and pull the head off. This will also remove the gut. Flour the fish and fry till brown in a little hot fat.
plain flour	
cooking fat for shallow-frying	

Note:

If you catch your own sand eels do not wash them in tap water; rinse in sea water if necessary to remove the sand. Wipe clean and lay in salt for 4 hours. String them through the heads, attach the string to a short stick and hang them in a muslin bag on a clothes line to dry, protecting them from flies etc, as for conger eels (see above). Dry thoroughly if they are to be kept for any length of time before cooking.

Lady Crabs or Velvet Fiddlers

These velvety crabs are dark brown when alive and bright red when cooked. They are good to eat but fiddly to pick.

Cook as for spider crabs, but boil for 10 minutes only.

Spider Crab

Serves 3–4

Spider crabs, in season from May to August, are very popular in Jersey, where they are usually sold alive. They have a much rounder body and longer legs than the edible crab usually sold in England.

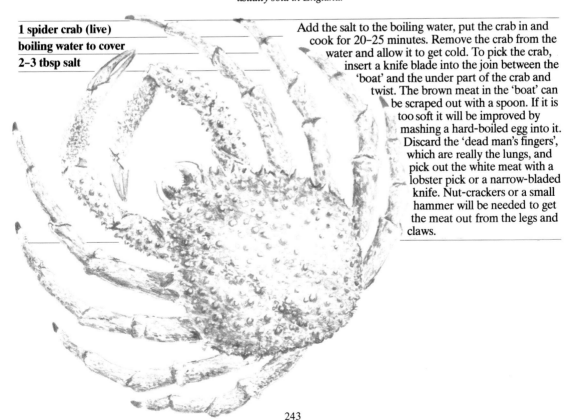

1 spider crab (live)	Add the salt to the boiling water, put the crab in and cook for 20–25 minutes. Remove the crab from the water and allow it to get cold. To pick the crab, insert a knife blade into the join between the 'boat' and the under part of the crab and twist. The brown meat in the 'boat' can be scraped out with a spoon. If it is too soft it will be improved by mashing a hard-boiled egg into it. Discard the 'dead man's fingers', which are really the lungs, and pick out the white meat with a lobster pick or a narrow-bladed knife. Nut-crackers or a small hammer will be needed to get the meat out from the legs and claws.
boiling water to cover	
2–3 tbsp salt	

Meat and Savouries

Panais à la Graisse
Serves 6

2 lb (900 g) shin of beef	Place the beef in a thick stewing pan and cover with water. Bring to the boil and simmer for at least 1 hour. Add the sugar and parsnips and cook until tender, taking care that the bottom of the pan does not burn. Mash the parsnips, and add seasoning to taste.
water to cover shin	
2 lumps sugar	
3 lb (1.4 kg) parsnips, scraped and cut into rounds	
seasoning	

Guernsey Bean Jar
Serves 4–5

This dish was traditionally eaten for Sunday morning breakfast until the 1920s. The 'jars' were taken to the local bakery to be cooked slowly overnight in the cooling ovens, and the children were sent out next morning to bring them home for breakfast.

1 pig's trotter or piece of shin beef	Soak beans overnight, boil until tender, strain off water. Place all ingredients in stone jar or earthenware dish, add 1 pt (575 ml) slightly thickened stock, cover down. Bake well in slow oven at 275°F (140°C) Reg 1 for 4–5 hours.
1 onion	
parsley	
salt and pepper	
1 lb (450 g) small dried haricot beans	
1 pt (575 ml) stock	

Jersey Bean Pot
Serves 6–8

Jersey Bean Pot used to be a favourite, and filling, Sunday breakfast, and on Saturday afternoons crocks full of soaked beans, with a pig's trotter tucked in amongst them, would be left with the baker to be placed in his bread oven after the last batch of bread had been baked. Sunday morning would see a procession of people hurrying homeward carrying steaming crocks of beans. For a cheap and tasty supper dish, try bringing the beans to the boil and then leaving them to simmer all day.

4 oz (110 g) large haricots	Soak the dried beans overnight in a large casserole – they will swell during soaking and again during cooking. Add the pork and trotter and more water if necessary to ensure that they are well covered. Put on the lid and bake at 300°F (150°C) Reg 2 for 7–8 hours. Add the salt when the beans are tender.
4 oz (110 g) small haricots	
4 oz (110 g) butter beans	
4 oz (110 g) broad beans	
water	
8 oz (225 g) belly pork or strip of back fat	
1 pig's trotter	
salt	

Fricot

Fricot is the Jersey equivalent of Bubble and Squeak, but made with green beans rather than cabbage. Very popular eaten with fried bacon or sausages, it was – and is – a dish in its own right, not just a convenient way of using up leftovers.

onions, sliced	Fry the sliced onions gently until tender. Peel the boiled potatoes and slice into the pan. Add the cooked beans and seasoning, and fry gently until lightly browned and hot through, stirring from time to time. The proportions can be varied to taste.
fat for frying	
potatoes, boiled in their skins	
runner or French beans, sliced and cooked	
salt and pepper	

Fliottes

Makes 16

*Just as pancakes are traditionally served on Shrove Tuesday, Fliottes are a Jersey speciality
served on Good Friday; the custom continues in many island homes.*

8 oz (225 g) plain flour
4 oz (110 g) sugar
2 eggs
pinch salt
2 pt (1.2 l) milk, or milk and water
knob butter

Mix together the flour, sugar, eggs and salt, adding sufficient extra milk to make a thick batter. Boil the milk in a large pan, adding the knob of butter. When the milk is boiling, drop in tablespoons of the batter, allowing each Fliotte to float separately. Allow to simmer for some minutes until cooked. Serve hot with some of the milk. A little sugar may be sprinkled on the Fliottes when served.

Bourdelots

Serves 4–6

*These apples baked in pastry are always made with dessert apples which need no sweetening
and keep their shape when cooked.*

1 lb (450 g) shortcrust pastry (see page 252)
6 large sweet apples, peeled and cored

Roll the pastry out on a floured board and cut into rounds large enough to cover each apple completely. Place 1 apple on each round of pastry. Mould the pastry over the apple, tucking the ends into the core hole at the top. Place, folded side down, on a greased baking tray and bake at 350°F (180°C) Reg 4 for about 1 hour. Test with a skewer to make sure the apple is cooked. Serve hot.

Gâche à Pomme

These are traditional Guernsey apple squares.

12 oz (350 g) shortcrust pastry (see page 252)
1½ lb (675 g) cooking apples
2 oz (50 g) caster sugar
3–4 cloves or 1 tsp ground cinnamon

Make a shortcrust pastry. Roll out, and line a shallow baking tin with half the pastry. Into this add thinly sliced peeled cooking apples in layers, sprinkle with sugar and a few cloves or powdered cinnamon. Finally cover with more pastry, sealing the edges. Bake at 400°F (200°C) Reg 6 for 35–40 mins. Cut into squares and serve either hot or cold, with cream.

Vraic Buns

Makes 25–30

The vast expanses left uncovered at low tide are a source, not only of fish, but also of seaweed (known in Jersey as vraic*). This was much prized as a fertilizer, especially for sandy soils, and was also dried and used for fuel. Farmers would cut and gather seaweed from the rocks, and load it on their horse-drawn carts. This had to be done between tides, which take no account of mealtimes, so these large Vraic Buns were baked to stay the pangs of hunger.*

3 lb (1.4 kg) plain flour
salt
8 oz (225 g) butter
1½ pt (850 ml) tepid water
1 oz (25 g) fresh yeast or ½ oz (15 g) dried yeast
9 oz (250 g) sugar
8 oz (225 g) large raisins
3 eggs, beaten
½ nutmeg, grated

Sieve the flour and salt into a bowl. Rub in the butter. Mix the yeast with a little of the tepid water and 1 oz (25 g) of the sugar, make a well in the centre of the flour, then add the yeast mixture and the rest of the water all at once. Blend well into a firm dough and leave to prove until doubled in size. Mix in the remaining sugar, add the raisins, beaten eggs and nutmeg and knead well. Shape into buns and place on a greased baking sheet. Leave to prove for about 20 minutes. Bake at 450°F (230°C) Reg 8 for 20–25 minutes.

Gâche dé Cannelle

This cinnamon crumble cake is delicious eaten warm with a mug of hot freshly brewed coffee.

7 oz (200 g) plain flour
1 oz (25 g) cornflour
2 tsp baking powder
½ tsp salt
4 oz (110 g) light brown sugar
4 oz (110 g) butter
1 egg, beaten
about 5 tbsp milk
Topping
1½ oz (40 g) plain flour
2 oz (50 g) demerara sugar
1 tbsp ground cinnamon
1½ oz (40 g) butter

Sift together the flour, cornflour, baking powder, salt and light brown sugar. Rub in the butter until the mixture resembles fine breadcrumbs. Add the egg and enough milk to make a soft dropping consistency. Turn the mixture into a greased and lined 7½ in (19 cm) deep straight-sided sandwich tin. Prepare the topping, mixing the dry ingredients and rubbing in the butter with a light touch. Place this crumble mixture evenly on top of the cake mixture. Bake at 375°F (190°C) Reg 5 for about 45 minutes. Allow to cool a little in the tin to just set the crumble, then turn out and serve hot or cold.

Guernsey Gâche

1½ lb (675 g) plain flour

salt

1 oz (25 g) fresh yeast or ½ oz (15 g) dried yeast

1 tsp sugar

2–3 fl oz (70 ml) tepid water

8 oz (225 g) butter

1 lb (450 g) sultanas or currants, washed and dried

a little mixed peel

½ pt (275 ml) tepid water (⅓ boiling, ⅔ cold)

Sift the flour and salt into a warm bowl and keep warm. Mix the yeast with the sugar and 2–3 fl oz (70 ml) tepid water. Rub the fat into the flour and add the fruit and peel. Add the ½ pt (275 ml) tepid water and the prepared yeast and knead the mixture until it leaves the sides of the bowl and the hands clean. Put to rise in a warm place for 1½ hours, covered with a cloth or in a polythene bag. Knead slightly and place in a well-greased 9×7½ in (23×19 cm) tin. Bake at 400°F (200°C) Reg 6 for 1 hour. Turn out on to a wire rack to cool.

La Grande Charrue Cake

This cake was made by the farmers' wives and taken to the fields hot for their husbands who were using the 'big plough'. This was a communal horse-drawn plough called la grande charrue, *or* tchérue, *which was taken from farm to farm with all available men coming to help. During breaks in the work, they were refreshed by slices of this cake and cans of hot tea.*

6 oz (175 g) plain flour

2 oz (50 g) sugar

4 oz (110 g) chopped suet

6 oz (175 g) currants

pinch each salt, ginger and nutmeg

1 egg, beaten

milk mixed with hot water

Mix together the flour, sugar, suet, currants, salt and spices. Add the egg and mix with the milk and water to a smooth paste (not too soft). Place in a greased shallow baking tin 7 in (18 cm) square and bake at 325°/350°F (160°/180°C) Reg 3/4 for 1–1½ hours. Serve hot or cold.

Jersey Wonders

Makes about 30

Home-made Jersey Wonders are very popular on the island. They keep well and are a useful stand-by, but to be eaten at their best they should be still warm from cooking. Many of the older Jersey people believed that success in making Wonders depended on the state of the tide, and that if they were cooked when the tide was rising, the fat would also rise and boil over. Nowadays Wonders are cooked and sold hot at many of the fairs and fêtes held during the summer months. They come in various shapes, including butterflies and figures-of-eight.

4 oz (110 g) butter

1 lb (450 g) plain flour

4 oz (110 g) sugar

3 eggs (size 1), beaten

1½ lb (675 g) lard for deep-frying

Rub the butter into the flour until it resembles breadcrumbs, and stir in the sugar. Add the beaten eggs, mix well and knead into a smooth paste. Roll out on to a floured board to ¼ in (5 mm) thickness, using as little flour as possible. Cut with a 2½ in (6 cm) biscuit cutter. Pull gently into an oval shape, cut a slit about 1½ in (4 cm) long down the middle, poke one end through the slit and pull gently to straighten. Heat the lard in a large deep pan, as for chips, until smoking hot and cook the Wonders, a few at a time, until golden brown, turning them so that both sides brown. They will swell in cooking. Lift out with a slatted spoon and drain on a cake cooling rack with a dish underneath to catch the drips. All the Wonders should be rolled and shaped before cooking commences – it is impossible to make and cook at the same time. They will keep for several weeks, and are said to fare better in an earthenware crock.

Buttermilk Cake

Buttermilk was readily obtained on the farms as the farmer's wife churned the fresh milk to make the golden Guernsey butter. Buttermilk can now sometimes be bought from dairies, but if fresh milk is left to turn sour and the cream taken off, the remaining sour milk can be used – thus the Guernsey French name for this cake is Gâche à Lait Sûr or Sour Milk Cake. Another method is to 'sour' the milk by adding 1 tbsp vinegar to ½ pt (275 ml) milk.

1 lb (450 g) plain flour

1 tsp nutmeg

6 oz (175 g) butter or margarine

8 oz (225 g) dark brown sugar

4 eggs, beaten

½ pt (275 ml) buttermilk (approx)

2 tsp bicarbonate of soda

4 oz (110 g) lemon peel, chopped

12 oz (350 g) currants, washed and dried

12 oz (350 g) sultanas or seedless raisins, washed and dried

a little warm water

Sift the flour with the nutmeg and rub in the butter lightly until the mixture is like fine breadcrumbs. Stir in the sugar. Hollow out the centre of the ingredients and pour in the beaten eggs. Mix together. Dissolve the soda in the warm water and gradually add to the mixture, with the buttermilk. Stir in the chopped lemon peel, and currants and sultanas (or raisins). Mix to a dropping consistency. Place the mixture in a greased and lined 8 in (20 cm) square tin, 3 in (7.5 cm) deep. Bake for 3 hours at 325°F (160°C) Reg 3. Turn out on to a wire rack, remove lining paper and allow to cool.

─Miscellaneous─

Black Butter (Nièr Beurre)

Makes 8–9 lb (3.6–4 kg)

Despite its name, Black Butter is neither butter nor black. It is apple pulp cooked with sugar and spices until it is a rich brown preserve. It is a very practical way of using a glut of apples. Black Butter will keep for at least a year.

'Time past', to use a Jersey expression, Black Butter was made on the farms in large quantities, and recipes called for 700 lb (317 kg) of apples and 3 lb (1.3 kg) of spice. Black Butter nights were a social occasion. All day long neighbours and friends would peel and slice the apples while a wood fire was kindled and a huge preserving pan was filled with cider, which was boiled till it was reduced by half. Then some of the sliced apples were added, and as they were reduced by cooking, more were added, and so on. This process continued all night and much of the following day, and the preserve had to be stirred all the time to prevent burning. This was hard work, especially when the preserve thickened towards the end of the cooking time, and the men took turns with the rabot, an implement rather like a hoe with a wooden blade, used for the stirring. Black Butter nights are still held from time to time.

15 lb (7 kg) sweet apples, peeled, cored and sliced

4 pt (2.25 l) cider or water

5 lb (2.25 kg) sour apples, peeled, cored and sliced

2½–3 lb (1.1–1.4 kg) sugar

grated rind and juice of 2 lemons

½ tsp cinnamon

½ tsp nutmeg

½ tsp allspice

Place the peeled, cored and sliced sweet apples in a preserving pan with the cider or water, bring to the boil and simmer gently, stirring occasionally, until they are soft. Add the sour apples and continue cooking, reducing the heat as the mixture thickens. When thick, add the sugar and lemon rind and juice and continue to cook, stirring frequently until very thick and dark. When the preserve is cooked, a wooden spoon drawn across the bottom of the preserving pan will leave a clear track. Unless it is cooked to this stage it will not keep well. Add the spices, remove from the heat and pot in warmed jars, cover and label.

Black Butter takes several hours to cook, but will come to no harm if started one day and continued the next. Much of the cooking can be done in the oven of an Aga or similar cooker. Small quantities can be made on a gas or electric cooker, which must be turned very low as cooking progresses, as this preserve has extraordinary 'spitting' power, and will reach every corner of the kitchen with the slightest encouragement.

Isle of Man
Fish/Seafood

Kippers

Method 1	Lightly fry on both sides until cooked.
Method 2	Place in boiling water in a frying pan with a lid. Simmer for about 10 minutes. This method helps to reduce the smell when the food is cooking.

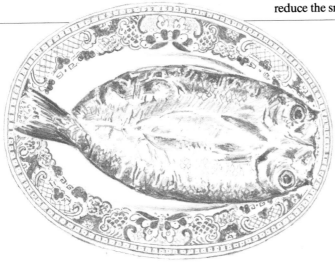

Herring Pie
Serves 4–5

8 oz (225 g) shortcrust pastry (see page 252)	Grease a large ovenproof dish and line with two-thirds of the pastry. Scale, gut and clean the herrings, removing heads, tails and fins. Season the fish with mace, salt and pepper. Put a little butter in the bottom of the pie-dish and then put in the herrings side by side. Place slices of apple over the fish. Lay slices of onion on top of the apple. Put a little butter on top, pour on the water. Cover with the rest of the pastry and bake at 350°F (180°C) Reg 4 for 35–40 minutes.
6 fresh herrings	
½ tsp mace	
salt and pepper	
butter	
3 large cooking apples, pared and thinly sliced	
2 onions, peeled and sliced	
1 fl oz (30 ml) water	

Herring and Potatoes
Serves 4

The traditional drink to accompany this dish is a glass of buttermilk. Many Manx people used to make their own butter, and buttermilk, being a by-product, was widely drunk and used in cooking.

4 salt herrings (soaked overnight)	Cut a small piece off the top and bottom of each potato to allow them to cook more easily. Place the potatoes in a large saucepan and bring to the boil. Do not add salt as the herrings will provide enough. When the potatoes are half-cooked, lay the herrings on top and cook until the potatoes are soft. Lift the herrings carefully out of the pan and keep warm. Drain the potatoes and dry them. Place the potatoes on a serving dish, lay the herrings on top and serve hot with butter. The sliced raw onion can be scattered on top or served as a side dish.
3 lb (1.5 kg) potatoes, scrubbed but not peeled	
butter to serve	
1 onion, peeled and sliced	

249

Potted Herring
Serves 4

This is not a typical 'potted' dish like potted crab (which uses clarified butter to preserve the meat or fish) but a dish traditionally cooked in a large pot or earthenware casserole.

6 fresh herrings 1 tbsp pickling spice vinegar and water in equal proportions 1 or 2 bay leaves seasoning	Take the heads and tails off the herrings, and clean them thoroughly. Bone them and then roll each one up. Place them alongside one another in an ovenproof dish. Sprinkle with pickling spice. Cover with vinegar and water and add the bay leaves and seasoning. Cover with a tightly fitting lid or foil. Bake at 300°F (150°C) Reg 2 for 1–1½ hours. Serve hot or cold.

Manx Queenies
Serves 4

8 scallops ¾ pt (425) milk 1½ (40 g) butter 1½ oz (40 g) plain flour 4 oz (110 g) cheese, grated seasoning browned crumbs	Grease 4 individual fireproof dishes or scallop shells. Cut each scallop into 2 or 3 pieces and simmer in a little of the milk for 10 minutes. Drain, keep the milk and make up to ¾ pt (425 ml). Melt the butter in a non-stick saucepan, add the flour and milk gradually, stirring all the time until it thickens. Add the cheese and seasoning. Divide the scallops into the dishes or shells, pour over the sauce. Sprinkle the tops with a little grated cheese and the browned crumbs. Brown under the grill.

Pudding

Manx Batter Pudding
Serves 4

4 oz (110 g) plain flour pinch salt 2 eggs ½ pt (275 ml) milk 1 oz (25 g) currants	Sieve the flour and salt into a mixing bowl. Make a well in the centre, add the eggs and mix in, slowly adding the milk to make a smooth batter. Beat well and stir in the currants. Pour into a greased pudding basin, cover, and steam for 1–1½ hours. Serve hot.

Breads

Bonnag

This is similar to some Irish soda bread recipes and Welsh soda scones. Bonnag is an old Manx word.

1 lb (450 g) plain flour 1 tsp salt 1 tsp bicarbonate of soda 1 tsp cream of tartar 1 oz (25 g) lard ½ pt (275 ml) buttermilk	Mix the dry ingredients in a bowl. Rub in the lard until the mixture resembles breadcrumbs and add sufficient buttermilk to make a moderately soft dough. Form into rounds, place on greased baking trays and bake at 375°F (190°C) Reg 5 for 40–45 minutes until risen and golden brown. Cool on a wire rack.

Butters, Batter and Dough

Brandy/Lemon Butter

4 oz (110 g) unsalted butter
4 oz (110 g) caster sugar
1 tsp lemon rind, finely grated
1 tbsp boiling water
4 tbsp brandy
1 tsp lemon juice

Cut the butter into 1 in (2.5 cm) cubes and put with the sugar and lemon rind into a basin. Beat until creamy, add the boiling water and continue to beat until every grain of sugar has dissolved. Add the lemon juice and brandy and beat well in. Put into lidded wax cartons and store in the refrigerator until ready for use. Or form into a roll, wrap in foil and freeze. Serve cut into discs.

Rum/Orange Butter

4 oz (110 g) unsalted butter
4 oz (110 g) soft brown sugar
4 tbsp Jamaican rum
1 tbsp orange juice
1 tsp orange rind, grated
$\frac{1}{4}$ tsp cinnamon

Proceed as for Brandy/Lemon Butter, using hot orange juice in place of water.

Clarified Butter

Method 1
Place the butter in a dish or small pan and put in a warm place. You will readily see when it is finished as all the sediment will have dropped to the bottom. Pour off the clear butter and allow to cool before pouring over the filled pots.

Method 2
Put the butter in a small pan, together with some water. Bring the contents to the boil and simmer until all the butter is melted. Leave to set, then take off the cleaned hard butter from the top and pat the underside free of water.

Coating Batter

4 oz (110 g) plain flour
pinch salt
2 eggs
$\frac{1}{2}$ pt (275 ml) milk
1 tbsp oil

Sift the flour and salt into a bowl. Make a well in the centre, add the eggs and a little milk. Mix with a spoon or whisk until smooth, gradually adding all the milk. Add the oil. Leave to stand for 30 minutes. Use the batter to coat the food; fry immediately.

White Bread Dough
Makes 4 × 1 lb (450 g) loaves or 36 rolls

3 lb (1.5 kg) strong plain white flour
1 oz (25 g) salt
1 oz (25 g) lard
1 oz (25 g) fresh yeast or $\frac{1}{2}$ oz (15 g) dried yeast
1 tsp sugar
$1\frac{1}{2}$ pt (900 ml) warm water

Sieve the flour and salt into a bowl and rub in the lard until the mixture resembles fine breadcrumbs. Mix the fresh yeast and sugar and add to the lukewarm water (or sprinkle the dried yeast on the water with the sugar and leave until frothy). Add to the flour and mix to a firm dough. Knead very thoroughly for 10 minutes. Shape into a round ball, put into a greased bowl, cover and leave to prove for 1 hour. Divide the dough into 4 pieces and knead each piece thoroughly. Fold up each piece of dough to fit a greased 1 lb (450 g) loaf tin. Cover and leave to prove again for about 1 hour or until the dough rises just to the top of the tins. Heat the oven to 450°F (230°C) Reg 8. Bake for 30–40 minutes until the loaves shrink slightly from the tins and the crust is a deep golden brown. The baked loaves will sound hollow when tapped on the base. Cool on a wire rack.

Note:
This dough may be made into four plaited loaves or four baps if preferred. If tins are not available, it will also make 36 rolls, each weighing 2 oz (50 g), which will only need 20 minutes' proving and 20 minutes' baking.

Pastry

Shortcrust Pastry

8 oz (225 g) plain flour

pinch salt

2 oz (50 g) hard margarine

2 oz (50 g) lard

2 tbsp cold water

Sieve flour and salt into a bowl. Cut fats into small pieces and add to flour. Rub fat into flour until it resembles fine breadcrumbs. Add sufficient cold water to bind ingredients together. Rest in a cold place. Roll out and use as required.

To spice pastry

Sift in $\frac{1}{2}$ tsp mixed spice per 1 lb (450 g) flour, or a similar quantity of ground cloves or ground cinnamon.

Wholemeal Shortcrust Pastry

8 oz (225 g) wholemeal flour

2 oz (50 g) lard

2 oz (50 g) margarine

$\frac{1}{2}$ tsp salt

4 tbsp water (approx)

Mix the salt into the flour with your fingertips. Rub in the fats until the mixture resembles breadcrumbs. Try to do this lightly. Add the water, cut and stir with a knife until the mixture starts to bind. Gather into a ball with the fingertips and roll out on a board lightly dredged with cornflour.

Note:

This is naturally a rather crumbly pastry because of the large particles in the flour. You may like to start with 85 per cent extraction flour, and see if this suits you better. Alternatively, use half wholemeal flour and half plain white flour.

Rich Shortcrust Pastry

6 oz (175 g) plain flour

3 oz (75 g) butter

1 oz (25 g) lard

$\frac{1}{2}$ tsp salt

1 egg yolk, beaten with 2 tbsp water

Rub fats into flour. Quickly mix into a soft dough. Leave to rest for an hour in a cool place. Roll out and use as required.

Note:

Where a recipe indicates shortcrust pastry, choose either the basic recipe, the Rich Shortcrust, or the Wholemeal Pastry, according to taste.

Sweet Shortcrust Pastry

6 oz (175 g) plain flour

3 oz (75 g) unsalted butter

1 oz (25 g) lard

1 oz (25 g) icing sugar

2 tbsp lemon juice

1 tbsp cold water

1 egg yolk, beaten

Rub fats into flour. Quickly mix into a soft dough. Leave to rest for an hour in a cool place. Roll out and use as required.

Hot Water Crust

$\frac{1}{2}$ tsp salt

$\frac{1}{4}$ tsp icing sugar

ground mace

8 oz (225 g) lard

$\frac{1}{3}$ pt (185 ml) water

1 egg yolk and a little cream or top of milk to glaze

Sieve all the dry ingredients together and put into a large bowl, making a well in the centre. Melt the lard in the water and bring to the boil. Pour all this liquid, at one fell swoop, into the well made in the flour, then quickly and deftly work this into a soft dough using a fork. Do not over-knead this dough or it will become like elastic and your pastry will be tough, albeit easier to manage! The dough should be warm and soft enough to work with, yet not slide down the sides of the mould or tin.

Cheese Pastry

8 oz (250 g) plain flour

4 oz (125 g) margarine

2 oz (75 g) Cheddar Cheese

pinch salt, pepper and dry mustard

cold water

Sieve flour with seasonings into a bowl, cut up margarine and add to flour. Rub fat into flour until it resembles fine breadcrumbs. Grate the cheese finely and add to the other ingredients. Bind ingredients together with cold water. Leave to rest in a cold place. Use as required.

Suet Crust Pastry

Basic Recipe

8 oz (225 g) self-raising flour

3 oz (75 g) fridge-hard butter, grated

2 oz (50 g) suet

1 egg, beaten with a little water

herbs or spices as liked

1 oz (25 g) sugar – for sweet puddings

salt and pepper – for savoury puddings

For a savoury suet crust, add to the basic recipe 1 tsp grated lemon rind, 1 heaped tbsp freshly chopped parsley, salt and freshly milled pepper. Mix with the egg and add the juice of $\frac{1}{2}$ lemon. Add cold water to make up to 6 fl oz (180 ml).

For a spicy suet crust, add $\frac{1}{4}$ tsp ground mace, nutmeg, rosemary or bay leaf. Mix with the egg and make up to 6 fl oz (180 ml) with cold water.

For a sweet suet crust, add 1 oz (25 g) sugar then mix with egg made up to 6 fl oz (180 ml) with cold water. Now proceed as follows. Sieve the flour into a bowl, add the herbs and lemon rind or spices, the salt and pepper or sugar as appropriate. Lightly toss in the suet (and grated butter), and stir loosely with a fork until evenly distributed. Make a well in the centre, add the egg and water mixture and gather into a softish paste with the fork. Turn on to a well-floured work surface and knead into a soft dough. Cut off a good quarter of the dough for the lid. Roll the rest into a large circle and line the basin. This recipe makes enough to line a 2–$2\frac{1}{2}$ pt (1–1.5 l) basin.

Flaky Pastry

8 oz (200 g) plain flour (preferably strong)

3 oz (75 g) hard margarine

3 oz (75 g) lard

water to mix (1 tbsp/oz flour or 150 ml)

$\frac{1}{2}$ tsp salt

Sieve flour and salt into a bowl. Blend the 2 fats together, take one quarter of the fats and rub into the flour. Add water to make a soft dough, and knead lightly. Roll out on a floured surface to an oblong about 15 × 4 in (37.5 × 10 cm). Lightly mark into 3, take another quarter of the fats and dab on to two-thirds of the pastry. Fold the lower one-third over the middle, and the upper one-third over the middle. Turn the pastry a quarter-turn and repeat the process, rolling out, marking and folding until the fats are used up. Roll out once again and fold into 3. Leave to rest in a cold place. Use as required.

Puff Pastry

6 oz (175 g) plain flour

pinch salt

6 oz (175 g) butter

$\frac{1}{4}$ pt (150 ml) iced water (approx)

Sift flour and salt together in a bowl. Rub in a walnut of butter. Add sufficient water to mix to a firm dough. Roll out to an oblong about $\frac{1}{2}$ in (1 cm) thick. The butter should be firm. Put the butter, shaped into an oblong pat, onto the lower half of the dough. Fold the top half down. Press the edges together. Leave to cool for 15–20 minutes. With the sealed ends towards you, roll lightly but firmly away from you into the original oblong. Do not 'push'. Fold the pastry into 3; the bottom third upwards and the top third downwards. Turn the open end towards you. Roll out again to an oblong. Repeat the folding and rolling process twice more. Fold into 3 again and leave to rest before using. Puff pastry is cooked at 425–450°F (220–230°C) Reg 7–8.

Rough Puff Pastry

8 oz (200 g) plain flour (preferably strong)

3 oz (75 g) hard margarine

3 oz (75 g) lard

water to mix (1 tbsp/oz flour or 150 ml)

$\frac{1}{2}$ tsp salt

Sieve flour and salt into a bowl. Blend the two fats together, and place in walnut-sized pieces into the flour. Add the water and mix to a soft dough; knead lightly. Place on a floured surface and roll out into an oblong about 15 × 4 in (37.5 × 10 cm), fold into 3, then a quarter turn and roll out again. Roll and fold the dough 4 times in total. Leave to rest in a cold place. Use as required.

Acknowledgments

The authors wish to thank the following, who contributed recipes for this book:

WI County Federations
Buckinghamshire, Cambridgeshire–Cambridge, Cambridgeshire-Isle of Ely, Cheshire, Cleveland, Cornwall, Cumbria–Cumberland, Cumbria–Westmorland, Derbyshire, Devon, Dorset, Durham, Dyfed–Caerfyrddin, East Kent, East Sussex, Glamorgan, Gloucestershire, Guernsey, Hampshire, Hertfordshire, Isle of Man, Isle of Wight, Jersey, Lancashire, Leicestershire and Rutland, Lincolnshire North, Lincolnshire South, Norfolk, Northamptonshire, Northumberland, North Yorkshire East, Nottinghamshire, Oxfordshire, Powys-Brecknock, Powys-Montgomery, Shropshire, Staffordshire, Somerset, Suffolk East, Warwickshire, West Kent, West Sussex, Wiltshire.

WI members and friends
Anne Aslan, Winifred Barry, Rhiannon Bevan, Bloxham WI, Vera Bonner, Ann Butcher, Mrs Christian, Sheilah Cooke, A. Corkery, Margaret Crowther, M. D. Dickens, Elizabeth Dodd, Mavis Fisher, Mrs Gatley, Mary Greasley (Lackham College of Agriculture), Rosemary Green, Maureen Harris, Rhona Harris, Molly Holden, E. M. Holme, Hovingham WI, Peggy Howey, L. Leedham, Renee Lowe, Jean Manley, Lyn Mann, Ursula Marshall, A. Meddins, Peggy Mills, B. Moore, Isobel Mortimer, Newsham and Aislaby WI, Olive Odell, Sheila Powell, D. Prusiecki, D. M. Richards, Lady Ruddle, Jill Sayers, Mary Scrimgeour, Joan Simpkins, C. Smith, Elizabeth Stirratt, Elsie Taylor, Nancy Totty, Dorothy Tucker, Daisy Walker, Evelyn Walker, Hilda Wooding, Anne Wragg, and many others who supplied information.

Special thanks to the following, who tested, edited and contributed ideas and recipes:
Angela Bending, Laura Brough, Mary Hawke, Pat Hesketh, Peggy Hughes, Sally Lister, Gillian Moorby, Angela Mottram, Mary Norwak, Sheena Sarjeant, Rosemary Wadey, Anne Wallace, Janet Wier.

The authors also acknowledge the following organizations and individuals for their invaluable assistance in finding recipes and historical information for this book:
Kate Easlea (Cooking in Hampshire Past and Present), The English Tourist Board (The Kitchen Manual), the Federation of Women's Institutes of Northern Ireland, the Milk Marketing Board for Northern Ireland, Rosemary Ruddle (Rutland Recipes), the Scottish Tourist Board, the Scottish Women's Rural Institutes, the Wales Gas Board, Kathleen Whitlock (The Compass Cookbook/Radio Bristol, Seven West Country Recipes).